ObjectWindows
Programmer's Guide

VERSION 5.0

Borland®
ObjectWindows®

Borland International, Inc., 100 Borland Way
P.O. Box 660001, Scotts Valley, CA 95067-0001

1E0R0196   WBC1350WW21772
9697989900-9 8 7 6 5 4 3 2 1
D2
ISBN 0-672-30924-6

Table of Contents

Chapter 22
Event handling   217

Chapter 23
Command enabling   227

Chapter 24
ObjectWindows exception handling   237

Chapter 25
Window objects   243

Chapter 26
Menu objects   263

Introduction

ObjectWindows is the Borland C++ application framework for Windows 3.1, Windows 95, Win32s, and Windows NT. ObjectWindows lets you build full-featured Windows applications quickly and easily. ObjectWindows provides the following features:

- Easy creation of OLE 2.0 applications, including containers, servers, and automated applications, using the ObjectComponents Framework
- Doc/View classes for easy data abstraction and display
- Ease of portability between 16- and 32-bit platforms
- Automated message cracking
- Robust exception and error handling
- Allows easy porting to other compilers and environments because it doesn't use proprietary compiler and language extensions
- Encapsulation of Windows GDI objects
- Printer and print preview classes
- Support for Visual Basic controls, including the only available support for using Visual Basic controls in 32-bit environments
- Input validators

How this book is organized

This book is organized into two parts.

Part I, "ObjectWindows Tutorial," contains a tutorial on how to build a basic ObjectWindows application utilizing many of the ObjectWindows library's key features. If you're new to ObjectWindows, or if there are features with which you're not familiar, you should follow the steps in Part I to learn how to program using ObjectWindows.

Part II, "ObjectWindows Programmer's Guide," presents topics in a task-oriented fashion, describing how to use functional groups of ObjectWindows classes to accomplish various tasks.

Typefaces and icons used in this book

The following table shows the special typographic conventions used in this book.

Typeface	Meaning
Monospace	This type represents text that you type or text as it appears onscreen.
Italics	These are used to emphasize and introduce words, and to indicate variable names (identifiers), function names, class names, and structure names.
Bold	This type indicates reserved keywords, format specifiers, and command-line options.
ALLCAPS	This type represents disk directories, file names, and application names. (However, header file names are presented in lowercase to be consistent with how these files are usually written in source code.)
Menu | Choice	This represents menu commands. Rather than use the phrase "choose the Save command from the File menu," Borland manuals use the convention "choose File | Save."

Note This icon indicates material you should take special notice of.

This manual also uses the following icons to indicate sections that pertain to specific operating environments:

 16-bit Windows

 32-bit Windows

ObjectWindows tutorial

This part teaches the fundamentals of programming for Windows using the ObjectWindows application framework. The tutorial is comprised of an application that is developed in 17 progressively more complicated steps, one step per chapter. Each step up in the application represents a step up in the tutorial's lessons. After completing the tutorial, you'll have a full-featured Windows application, with items like menus, dialog boxes, graphical control bar, status bar, MDI windows, and more.

This tutorial assumes that you're familiar with C++ and have some prior Windows programming experience. Before beginning, it might be helpful to read Chapter 19 of this book, which presents a brief, nontechnical overview of the ObjectWindows class hierarchy. This should help you become familiar with the principles behind the structure of the ObjectWindows class library.

For more detailed technical information on any subject discussed in this book, refer to Part II, "ObjectWindows Programmer's Guide,"of this book and the book entitled *ObjectWindows Reference*.

Getting started

Before you begin the tutorial, you should make a copy of the ObjectWindows tutorial files separate from the files in your compiler installation. Use the copied files when working on the tutorial steps. While working on the tutorial, you should try to make the changes in each step on your own. You can then compare the changes you make to the tutorial program.

Tutorial application

The tutorial application that you'll build when following the steps in this book is a line drawing application called Drawing Pad. While this application isn't very fancy, it does demonstrate many important ObjectWindows programming techniques that you'll use all the time in the course of your ObjectWindows development. Each step introduces a small increment in the application's features. You start with the most basic ObjectWindows application and, by the time you're finished with the last step, you'll have created a full-featured Windows application with a tool bar with bitmapped buttons on it, multiple document support, a status bar that displays menu and button hints, and even full OLE 2.0 server support.

Tutorial steps

Each step in the tutorial corresponds to a chapter in this part of the book. Here's a summary of each step in the tutorial:

- **Chapter 1, "Creating a basic application,"** you'll learn how to create the basic ObjectWindows application. This application has no real function except to show that an application *is* running.

- **Chapter 2, "Handing events,"** you'll learn how to use the ObjectWindows event-handling mechanism called response tables.

- **Chapter 3, "Writing in the window,"** you'll learn how to write text into a window by creating a device context object in the window and calling some of the device context object's member functions.

- **Chapter 4, "Drawing in the window,"** you'll learn how to draw a line in a window using more functions of the device context object.

- **Chapter 5, "Changing line thickness,"** you'll learn how change the size of the pen that you use to draw lines in the window. You'll also learn how to use a dialog box to get simple string input from the user.

- **Chapter 6, "Painting the window and adding a menu,"** you'll learn how to take over the window's paint function, along with adding a menu to the window.

- **Chapter 7, "Using common dialog boxes,"** you'll learn how to use some of the Windows common dialog boxes, specifically the File Open dialog box and File Save dialog box. You'll also learn how to check whether your application is ready to close when requested to do so by the user or the system, giving the application a chance to save files or clean up.

- **Chapter 8, "Adding multiple lines,"** you'll learn how to display and paint more than one line in the window using an array container to hold the information about all the lines in the drawing.

- **Chapter 9, "Changing pens,"** you'll learn how to change the pen in the device context to let the user change the line color.

- **Chapter 10, "Adding decorations,"** you'll learn how to add decorations to the application, including a tool bar with bitmapped buttons on it and a status bar that displays hint text for menu items and tool bar buttons.

- **Chapter 11, "Moving to MDI,"** you'll learn how to create a Multiple Document Interface (MDI) application, which lets the user of the application have a number of drawings open at once.

- **Chapter 12, "Using the Doc/View programming model,"** you'll create a Doc/View application. Doc/View provides a programming model that lets you separate the object that actually contains your data (the document) from the object or objects that display your data on-screen (the views). This application is actually a Single Document Interface (SDI) application like Step 10.

- **Chapter 13, "Moving the Doc/View application to MDI,"** you'll combine the lessons of Step 11 and Step 12 to create an MDI Doc/View application.

- **Chapter 14, "Making an OLE container,"** you'll learn to create an OLE 2.0 container from an MDI Doc/View application.

- **Chapter 15, "Making an OLE server,"** you'll learn to create an OLE 2.0 server.

- **Chapter 16, "Making an OLE automation server,"** you'll learn to create an OLE 2.0 automation server.

- **Chapter 17, "Enhancing the linking and embedding capabilities of an OLE server,"** you'll learn how to enhance an OLE 2.0 automation server.

- **Chapter 18, "For further study,"** provides you with some references to help you learn more about ObjectWindows.

Files in the tutorial

The tutorial is composed of a number of different source files:

- The project file is STEPS.IDE. Open this file in the IDE to easily access and build each STEP*XX*.CPP file.

- Each step of the tutorial is contained in a file named STEP*XX*.CPP.

- Later steps in the application use multiple C++ source files. The other files are named STEP*XX*DV.CPP.

- A number of steps have a header file containing class definitions and the like. These header files are named STEP*XX*DV.H.

- A number of steps also have a corresponding resource script file named STEP*XX*.RC.

In each case, *XX* is a number from 01 to 17, indicating which step of the tutorial is in the source file.

1

Creating a basic application

To begin the tutorial, open the file STEP01.CPP, which shows an example of the most basic useful ObjectWindows application. Because of its brevity, the entire file is shown here: You can find the source for Step 1 in the file STEP01.CPP in the directory EXAMPLES\OWL\TUTORIAL.

```
//-------------------------------------------------------------------
// ObjectWindows - (C) Copyright 1991, 1994 by Borland International
// Tutorial application -- step01.cpp
//-------------------------------------------------------------------
#include <owl/applicat.h>
#include <owl/framewin.h>

Class TDrawApp : public TApplication
{
  public:
    TDrawApp() : TApplication() {}

    void InitMainWindow()
    {
        SetMainWindow(new TFrameWindow(0, "Sample ObjectWindows Program"));
    }
};

int
OwlMain(int /* argc */, char* /* argv */ [])
{
  return TDrawApp().Run();
}
```

This simple application includes a number of important features:

- This source file includes two header files, owl\applicat.h and owl\framewin.h. These files are included because the application uses the *TApplication* and

TFrameWindow ObjectWindows classes. Whenever you use an ObjectWindows class you must include the proper header files so your code compiles properly.

- The class *TDrawApp* is derived from the ObjectWindows *TApplication* class. Every ObjectWindows application has a *TApplication* object—or more usually, a *TApplication*-derived object—generically known as the application object. If you try to use a *TApplication* object directly, you'll find that it's difficult to direct the program flow. Overriding *TApplication* gives you access to the workings of the application object and lets you override the necessary functions to make the application work the way you want.

- In addition to an application object, every ObjectWindows application has an *OwlMain* function. The application object is actually created in the *OwlMain* function with a simple declaration. *OwlMain* is the ObjectWindows equivalent of the *WinMain* function in a regular Windows application. You can use *OwlMain* to check command-line arguments, set up global data, and anything else you want taken care of before the application begins execution.

- To start execution of the application, call the application object's *Run* function. The *Run* function first calls the *InitApplication* function, but only if this instance of the application is the first instance (the default *TApplication::InitApplication* function does nothing). After the *InitApplication* function returns, *Run* calls the *InitInstance* function, which initializes each instance of an application. The default *TApplication::InitInstance* calls the function *InitMainWindow*, which initializes the application's main window, then creates and displays the main window.

- *TDrawApp* overrides the *InitMainWindow* function. You can use this function to design the main window however you want it. The *SetMainWindow* function sets the application's main window to a *TFrameWindow* or *TFrameWindow*-derived object passed to the function. In this case, simply create a new *TFrameWindow* with no parent (the first parameter of the *TFrameWindow* is a pointer to the window's parent) and the title "Sample ObjectWindows Program."

This basic application introduces two of the most important concepts in ObjectWindows programming. As simple as it seems, deriving a class from *TApplication* and overriding the *InitMainWindow* function gives you quite a bit of control over application execution. As you'll see in later steps, you can easily craft a large and complex application from this simple beginning.

Where to find more information

Here's a guide to where you can find more information on the topics introduced in this step:

- Application objects, along with their *Init** member functions, are discussed in Chapter 20, "Application and module objects."

- *OwlMain* is discussed in Chapter 20, "Application and module objects."

- *TFrameWindow* is discussed in Chapter 25, "Window objects."

2

Handling events

You can find the source for Step 2 in the file STEP02.CPP in the directory EXAMPLES\
OWL\TUTORIAL. Step 2 introduces response tables, another very important
ObjectWindows feature. Response tables control event and message processing in
ObjectWindows applications, dispatching events on to the proper event-handling
functions. Step 2 also adds these functions.

Adding a window class

Add the response table to the application using a window class called *TDrawWindow*.
TDrawWindow is derived from *TWindow*, and looks like this:

```
class TDrawWindow : public TWindow
{
  public:
    TDrawWindow(TWindow* parent = 0);

  protected:
    // override member function of TWindow
    bool CanClose();

    // message response functions
    void EvLButtonDown(uint, TPoint&);
    void EvRButtonDown(uint, TPoint&);

    DECLARE_RESPONSE_TABLE(TDrawWindow);
};
```

The constructor for this class is fairly simple. It takes a single parameter, a *TWindow* *
that indicates the parent window of the object. The constructor definition looks like this:

```
TDrawWindow::TDrawWindow(TWindow *parent)
{
```

```
        Init(parent, 0, 0);
    }
```

The *Init* function lets you initialize *TDrawWindow*'s base class. In this case, the call isn't very complicated. The only thing that might be required for your purposes is the window's parent, and, as you'll see, even that's taken care of for you.

Adding a response table

The only public member of the *TDrawWindow* class is its constructor. But if the other members are **protected**, how can you access them? The answer lies in the response table definition. Notice the last line of the *TDrawWindow* class definition. This declares the response table; that is, it informs your class that it has a response table, much like a function declaration informs the class that the function exists, but doesn't define the function's activity.

The response table definition sets up your class to handle Windows events and to pass each event on to the proper event-handling function. As a general rule, event-handling functions should be **protected**; this prevents classes and functions outside your own class from calling them. Here is the response table definition for *TDrawWindow*:

```
DEFINE_RESPONSE_TABLE1(TDrawWindow, TWindow)
    EV_WM_LBUTTONDOWN,
    EV_WM_RBUTTONDOWN,
END_RESPONSE_TABLE;
```

You can put the response table anywhere in your source file.

For now, you can keep the response table fairly simple. Here's a description of each part of the table. A response table has four important parts:

• The response table declaration in the class declaration.

• The first line of a response table definition is always the DEFINE_RESPONSE_TABLE*X* macro. The value of *X* depends on your class' inheritance, and is based on the number of immediate base classes your class has. In this case, *TDrawWindow* has only one immediate base class, *TWindow*.

• The last line of a response table definition is always the END_RESPONSE_TABLE macro, which ends the event response table definition.

• Between the DEFINE_RESPONSE_TABLE*X* macro and the END_RESPONSE_TABLE macro are other macros that associate particular events with their handling functions.

The two macros in the middle of the response table, EV_WM_LBUTTONDOWN and EV_WM_RBUTTONDOWN, are response table macros for the standard Windows messages WM_LBUTTONDOWN and WM_RBUTTONDOWN. All standard Windows messages have ObjectWindows-defined response table macros. To find the name of a particular message's macro, preface the message name with EV_. For example, the macro that handles the WM_PAINT message is EV_WM_PAINT, and the macro that handles the WM_LBUTTONDOWN message is EV_WM_LBUTTONDOWN.

These predefined macros pass the message on to functions with predefined names. To determine the function name, substitute *Ev* for WM_, and convert the name to lowercase with capital letters at word boundaries. For example, the WM_PAINT message is passed to a function called *EvPaint*, and the WM_LBUTTONDOWN message is passed to a function called *EvLButtonDown*.

Event-handling functions

As you can see, two of the **protected** functions in *TDrawWindow* are *EvLButtonDown* and *EvRButtonDown*. Because of the macros in the response table, when *TDrawWindow* receives a WM_LBUTTONDOWN or WM_RBUTTONDOWN event, it passes it on to the appropriate function.

The functions that handle the WM_LBUTTONDOWN or WM_RBUTTONDOWN events are very simple. Each function pops up a message box telling you which button you've pressed. The code for these functions should look something like this:

```
void TDrawWindow::EvLButtonDown(uint, TPoint&)
{
  MessageBox("You have pressed the left mouse button",
          "Message Dispatched", MB_OK);
}

void TDrawWindow::EvRButtonDown(uint, TPoint&)
{
  MessageBox("You have pressed the right mouse button",
          "Message Dispatched", MB_OK);
}
```

This illustrates one of the best features of how ObjectWindows handles standard Windows events. The function that handles each event receives what might seem to be fairly arbitrary parameter types (all the macros and their corresponding functions are presented in the *ObjectWindows Reference* in Part 2 of the "ObjectComponents programmer's reference." Actually, these parameter types correspond to the information encoded in the WPARAM and LPARAM variables normally passed along with an event. The event information is automatically "cracked" for you.

The advantages of this approach are two-fold:

- You no longer have to manually extract information from the WPARAM and LPARAM values.

- The predefined functions allow for compile-time type checking, and prevent hard-to-track errors that can be caused by confusing the values encoded in the WPARAM and LPARAM values.

For example, both WM_LBUTTONDOWN and WM_RBUTTONDOWN contain the same type of information in their WPARAM and LPARAM variables:

- WPARAM contains key flags, which specify whether the user has pressed one of a number of virtual keys.

- The low-order word of the LPARAM specifies the cursor's x-coordinate.

- The high-order word of LPARAM specifies the cursor's y-coordinate.

EvLButtonDown and *EvRButtonDown* also have similar signatures. The uint parameter of each function corresponds to the key flags parameter. The values that are normally encoded in the LPARAM are instead stored in a *TPoint* object.

Encapsulated API calls

You might notice that the calls to the *MessageBox* function look a little odd. The Windows API function *MessageBox* takes an HWND for its first parameter. But the *MessageBox* function called here is actually a member function of the *TWindow* class. There are a large number of functions like this: they have the same name as the Windows API function, but their signature is different. The most common differences are the elimination of handle parameters such as HWND and HINSTANCE, replacement of Windows data types with ObjectWindows data types, and so on. In this case, the window class supplies the HWND parameter for you.

Overriding the CanClose function

Another feature of the *TDrawWindow* class is the *CanClose* function. Before an application attempts to shut down a window, it calls the window's *CanClose* function. The window can then abort the shutdown by returning false, or let the shutdown proceed by returning true.

From the point of view of the application, this ensures that you don't shut down a window that is currently being used or that contains unstored data. From the window's point of view, this warns you when the application tries to shut down and provides you with an opportunity to make sure that everything has been cleaned up before closing.

Here is the *CanClose* function from the *TDrawWindow* class:

```
bool TDrawWindow::CanClose()
{
   return MessageBox("Do you want to save?", "Drawing has changed",
                 MB_YESNO | MB_ICONQUESTION) == IDNO;
}
```

For now, this function merely pops up a message box stating that the drawing has changed and asking if the user wants to save the drawing. Because there's no drawing to save, this message is fairly useless right now. But it'll become useful in Step 7, "Using common dialog boxes," when you add the ability to save data to a file.

Using TDrawWindow as the main window

The last thing to do is to actually create an instance of this new *TDrawWindow* class. You might think you can do this by simply substituting *TDrawWindow* for *TFrameWindow* in the *SetMainWindow* call in the *InitMainWindow* function:

```
void InitMainWindow()
{
  SetMainWindow(new TDrawWindow);
}
```

This won't work, for a number of reasons, but primarily because *TDrawWindow* isn't based on *TFrameWindow*. For this code to compile correctly, you'd have to change *TDrawWindow* so that it's based on *TFrameWindow* instead of *TWindow*. Although this is fairly easy to do, it introduces functionality into the *TDrawWindow* class that isn't necessary. As you'll see in later steps, *TDrawWindow* has a unique purpose. Adding frame capability to *TDrawWindow* would reduce its flexibility.

The second approach is to use a *TDrawWindow* object as a client in a *TFrameWindow*. This is fairly easy to do: the third parameter of the *TFrameWindow* constructor that you're already using lets you specify a *TWindow* or *TWindow*-derived object as a client to the frame. The code would look something like this:

```
SetMainWindow(new TFrameWindow(0, "Sample ObjectWindows Program",new TDrawWindow));
```

With this approach, *TFrameWindow* administers the frame window, leaving *TDrawWindow* free to take care of its tasks. This makes for more discreet and modular object design. It also lets you easily change the type of frame window you use, as you'll see in Step 10, "Adding decorations."

Notice that the **new** *TDrawWindow* construction in the *TFrameWindow* constructor doesn't specify a parent for the *TDrawWindow* object. That's because there isn't yet anything to be a parent. The *TFrameWindow* object that will be the parent hasn't been constructed yet. *TFrameWindow* automatically sets the client window's parent to be the *TFrameWindow* once it has been constructed.

Where to find more information

Here's a guide to where you can find more information on the topics introduced in this step:

- Main windows are discussed in Chapter 20, "Application and module objects."

- Interface objects in general, such as windows, dialogs, controls, and so on, are discussed in Chapter 21, "Interface objects."

- Response tables are discussed in Chapter 22, "Event handling."

- Window classes are discussed in Chapter 25, "Window objects."

- Predefined response table macros and their corresponding event-handling functions are listed in the *ObjectWindows Reference* in Part 1, "ObjectWindows programmer's reference."

3

Writing in the window

In Step 3, you'll begin working with the new window that was added to the application in Step 2. Instead of popping up a message box when the mouse buttons are pressed, the event-handling functions will get some real functionality—pressing the left mouse button will cause the coordinates of the point at which the button was clicked to be printed in the window, and pressing the right mouse button will cause the window to be cleared. You can find the source for Step 3 in the file STEP03.CPP in the directory EXAMPLES\OWL\TUTORIAL.

The code for this new functionality is in the *EvLButtonDown* function. The *TPoint* parameter that's passed to the *EvLButtonDown* contains the coordinates at which the mouse button was clicked. You'll need to add a **char** string to the function to hold the text representation of the point. You can then use the *wsprintf* function to format the string. Now you have to set up the window to print the string.

Constructing a device context

To perform any sort of graphical operation in Windows, you must have a device context for the window or area you want to work with. The same holds true in ObjectWindows. ObjectWindows provides a number of classes that make it easy to set up, use, and dispose of a device context. Because *TDrawWindow* works as a client in a frame window, you'll use the *TClientDC* class. *TClientDC* is a device context class that provides access to the client area owned by a window. Like all ObjectWindows device context classes, *TClientDC* is based on the *TDC* class, and is defined in the owl\dc.h header file.

TClientDC has a single constructor that takes an HWND as its only parameter. Because you want a device context for your *TDrawWindow* object, you need the handle for that window. As it happens, the *TWindow* base class provides an HWND conversion operator. This operator is called implicitly whenever you use the window object in places that require an HWND. So the constructor for your *TClientDC* object looks something like this:

```
TClientDC dc(*this);
```

Notice that the **this** pointer is dereferenced. The HWND conversion operator doesn't work with pointers to window objects.

Printing in the device context

Once the device context is set up, you have to actually print the string. The *TDC* class provides several versions of the *TextOut* function. Just like the *MessageBox* function in Step 2, the *TextOut* functions contained in the device context classes looks similar to the Windows API function *TextOut*. The first version of *TextOut* looks exactly the same as the Windows API version, except that the first HDC parameter is omitted:

```
virtual bool TextOut(int x, int y, const char far* str, int count=-1);
```

The HDC parameter is filled by the *TDC* object. The second version of *TextOut* omits the HDC parameter and combines the x- and y-coordinates into a single *TPoint* structure:

```
bool TextOut(const TPoint& p, const char far* str, int count=-1);
```

Because the coordinates are passed into the *EvLButtonDown* function in a *TPoint* object, you can use the second version of *TextOut* to print the coordinates in the window. Your completed *EvLButtonDown* function should look something like this:

```
void TDrawWindow::EvLButtonDown(uint, TPoint& point)
{
  char s[16];
  TClientDC dc(*this);

  wsprintf(s, "(%d,%d)", point.x, point.y);
  dc.TextOut(point, s, strlen(s));
}
```

You need to include the string.h header file to use the *strlen* function.

Clearing the window

TDrawWindow's base class, *TWindow*, provides three different invalidation functions. Two of these, *InvalidateRect* and *InvalidateRgn*, look and function much like their Windows API versions, but omitting the HWND parameters. The third function, *Invalidate*, invalidates the entire client area of the window. *Invalidate* takes a single parameter, a bool indicating whether the invalid area should be erased when it's updated. By default, this parameter is true.

Therefore, to erase the entire client area of *TDrawWindow*, you need only call *Invalidate*, either specifying true or nothing at all for its parameter. To clear the screen when the user presses the right mouse button, you must make this call in the *EvRButtonDown* function. The function would look something like this:

```
void TDrawWindow::EvRButtonDown(uint, TPoint&)
{
  Invalidate();
}
```

Where to find more information

Here's a guide to where you can find more information on the topics introduced in this step:

- Window classes are discussed in Chapter 25.
- Device contexts and the *TDC* classes are discussed in Chapter 32.

4

Drawing in the window

You can find the source for Step 4 in the file STEP04.CPP in the directory EXAMPLES\ OWL\TUTORIAL. In this step, you'll add the ability to draw a line in the window by pressing the left mouse button and dragging. To do this, you'll add two new events, WM_MOUSEMOVE and WM_LBUTTONUP, to the *TDrawWindow* response table, along with functions to handle those events. You'll also add a *TClientDC* * to the class.

Adding new events

To let the user draw on the window, the application must handle a number of events:

- To start drawing the line, you have to look for the user to press the left mouse button. This is already taken care of by handling the WM_LBUTTONDOWN event.

- Once the user has pressed the left button down, you have to look for them to move the mouse. At this point, you're drawing the line. To know when the user is moving the mouse, catch the WM_MOUSEMOVE event.

- You then need to know when the user is finished drawing the line. The user is finished when the left mouse button is released. You can monitor for this by catching the WM_LBUTTONUP event.

You need to add two macros to the window class' response table, EV_WM_MOUSEMOVE and EV_WM_LBUTTONUP. The new response table should look something like this:

```
DEFINE_RESPONSE_TABLE1(TDrawWindow, TWindow)
  EV_WM_LBUTTONDOWN,
  EV_WM_RBUTTONDOWN,
  EV_WM_MOUSEMOVE,
  EV_WM_LBUTTONUP,
END_RESPONSE_TABLE;
```

You also need to add the *EvLButtonUp* and *EvMouseMove* functions to the *TDrawWindow* class.

Adding a TClientDC pointer

The scheme used in Step 3 to draw a line isn't very robust:

- In Step 3, you created a *TClientDC* object in the *EvLButtonDown* function that was automatically destroyed when the function returned. But now you need a valid device context across three different functions, *EvLButtonDown*, *EvMouseMove*, and *EvLButtonUp*.

- You can catch the WM_MOUSEMOVE event and draw from the current point to the point passed into the *EvMouseMove* handling function. But WM_MOUSEMOVE events are sent out whenever the mouse is moved. You only want to draw a line when the mouse is moved with the left button pressed down.

You can take care of both of these problems rather easily by adding a new **protected** data member to *TDrawWindow*. This data member is a *TDC* * called *DragDC*. It works this way:

- When the left mouse button is pressed, the *EvLButtonDown* function is called. This function creates a new *TClientDC* and assigns it to *DragDC*. It then sets the current point in *DragDC* to the point at which the mouse was clicked. The code for this function should look something like this:

```
void
TDrawWindow::EvLButtonDown(uint, TPoint& point)
{
  Invalidate();
  if (!DragDC) {
    SetCapture();
    DragDC = new TClientDC(*this);
    DragDC->MoveTo(point);
  }
}
```

- When the left mouse button is released, the *EvLButtonUp* function is called. If *DragDC* is valid (that is, if it represents a valid device context), *EvLButtonUp* deletes it, setting it to 0. The code for this function should look something like this:

```
void
TDrawWindow::EvLButtonUp(uint, TPoint&)
{
  if (DragDC) {
    ReleaseCapture();
    delete DragDC;
    DragDC = 0;
  }
}
```

- When the mouse is moved, the *EvMouseMove* function is called. This function checks whether the left mouse button is pressed by checking *DragDC*. If *DragDC* is 0, either the mouse button has not been pressed at all or it has been pressed and released. Either way, the user is not drawing, and the function returns. If *DragDC* is valid, meaning that the left mouse button is currently pressed down, the function draws a line from the current point to the new point using the *TWindow::LineTo* function.

```
void
TDrawWindow::EvMouseMove(uint, TPoint& point)
{
  if (DragDC)
    DragDC->LineTo(point);
}
```

Initializing DragDC

You must make sure that *DragDC* is set to 0 when you construct the *TDrawWindow* object:

```
TDrawWindow::TDrawWindow(TWindow *parent)
{
  Init(parent, 0, 0);
  DragDC = 0;
}
```

Cleaning up after DragDC

Because *DragDC* is a pointer to a *TClientDC* object, and not an actual *TClientDC* object, it isn't automatically destroyed when the *TDrawWindow* object is destroyed. You need to add a destructor to *TDrawWindow* to properly clean up. The only thing required is to call **delete** on *DragDC*. *TDrawWindow* should now look something like this:

```
class TDrawWindow : public TWindow
{
  public:
    TDrawWindow(TWindow *parent = 0);
~TDrawWindow() {delete DragDC;}

  protected:
    TDC *DragDC;

    // Override member function of TWindow
    bool CanClose();

    // Message response functions
    void EvLButtonDown(uint, TPoint&);
    void EvRButtonDown(uint, TPoint&);
    void EvMouseMove(uint, TPoint&);
    void EvLButtonUp(uint, TPoint&);

    DECLARE_RESPONSE_TABLE(TDrawWindow);
};
```

Note that, because the tutorial application has now become somewhat useful, the name of the main window has been changed from "Sample ObjectWindows Program" to "Drawing Pad":

```
SetMainWindow(new TFrameWindow(0, "Drawing Pad", new TDrawWindow));
```

Where to find more information

Here's a guide to where you can find more information on the topics introduced in this step:

- Event handling is discussed in Chapter 22.
- Device contexts and the *TDC* classes are discussed in Chapter 30.
- Predefined response table macros and their corresponding event-handling functions are listed in the *ObjectWindows Reference* in Part 1.

Chapter

5

Changing line thickness

You can find the source for Step 5 in the files STEP05.CPP and STEP05.RC in the directory EXAMPLES\OWL\TUTORIAL. In this step, you'll make the drawing capability in the application a little more robust. This step adds the ability to change the thickness of the line. To support this, you can add to the *TDrawWindow* class a *TPen ** drawing object and an **int** to hold the pen width.

Adding a pen

Add the pen to the window class by adding two **protected** members, *Pen* (a *TPen **) and *PenSize* (an **int**). The most important changes that result from adding a pen to the window class are implemented in the *EvLButtonDown* and *EvRButtonDown* functions.

Initializing the pen

The *Pen* object and *PenSize* must be created and initialized before the user has an opportunity to draw with the pen. The best place to do this is in the constructor:

```
TDrawWindow::TDrawWindow(TWindow *parent)
{
  Init(parent, 0, 0);
  DragDC = 0;

  PenSize = 1;
  Pen = new TPen(TColor::Black, PenSize);
}
```

The *TColor::Black* object in the *TPen* constructor is an **enum** defined in the owl\color.h header file. This makes the pen black. You'll learn more about this parameter of the *TPen* constructor later on in Step 9.

Selecting the pen into DragDC

To use the new pen object to draw a line, the pen has to be selected into the device context. The device-context classes have a function called *SelectObject*. This function is similar to the API function *SelectObject*, except that the ObjectWindows version doesn't require a handle to the device context.

You can use *SelectObject* to select a variety of objects into a device context, including brushes, fonts, palettes, and pens. You need to call *SelectObject* before you begin to draw. Add the call in the *EvLButtonDown* function immediately after you create the device context:

```
void
TDrawWindow::EvLButtonDown(uint, TPoint& point)
{
  Invalidate();

  if (!DragDC) {
    SetCapture();
    DragDC = new TClientDC(*this);
    DragDC->SelectObject(*Pen);
    DragDC->MoveTo(point);
  }
}
```

Notice that **Pen** is dereferenced in the *SelectObject* call. This is because the *SelectObject* function takes a *TPen* & for its parameter, and *Pen* is a *TPen* *. Dereferencing the pointer makes *Pen* comply with *SelectObject*'s type requirements.

Changing the pen size

Having the ability to change the pen size in the application is of little use unless the user has access to that ability. To provide that access, you can change the meaning of pressing the right mouse button. Instead of clearing the screen, it now indicates that the user wants to change the width of the drawing pen. Therefore the process of changing the pen size goes into the *EvRButtonDown* function.

Once the user has indicated that he or she wants to change the pen width by pressing the right mouse button, you need to find some way to let the user enter the new pen width. For this, you can pop up a *TInputDialog*, in which the user can input the pen size.

Constructing an input dialog box

The *TInputDialog* constructor looks like this:

```
TInputDialog(TWindow* parent,
             const char far* title,
             const char far* prompt,
             char far* buffer,
             int bufferSize,
             TModule* module = 0);
```

where:

- *parent* is a pointer to the parent window of the dialog box. In this case, the parent is the *TDrawWindow* window. You can simply pass it in using the **this** pointer.

- *title* and *prompt* are the messages displayed to the user when the dialog box is opened. In this case, *title* (which is placed in the title bar of the dialog box) is "Line Thickness," and *prompt* (which is placed right above the input box) is "Input a new thickness:".

- *buffer* is a string. This string can be initialized before using the *TInputDialog*. If *buffer* contains a valid string, it is displayed in the *TInputDialog* as the default response. In this case, initialize *buffer* using the current pen size contained in *PenSize*.

- *bufferSize* is the size of *buffer* in bytes. The easiest way to do this is to use either a **#define** that is used to allocate storage for *buffer* or to use **sizeof**(*buffer*).

- *module* isn't used in this example.

To use *TInputDialog*, you must make sure its resources and resource identifiers are included in your source files and resource script files. These are contained in the file INCLUDE\OWL\INPUTDIA.RC. You should include INPUTDIA.RC in your resource script files and your C++ source files.

Executing an input dialog box

Once you've constructed a *TInputDialog* object, you can either call the *TDialog::Execute* function to execute the dialog box modally or the *TDialog::Create* function to execute the dialog box modelessly. Because there's no need to execute the dialog box modelessly, you can use the *Execute* function.

The *Execute* function for *TInputDialog* can return two important values, IDOK and IDCANCEL. The value that is returned depends on which button the user presses. If the user presses the OK button, *Execute* returns IDOK. If the user presses the Cancel button, *Execute* returns IDCANCEL. So when you execute the input dialog box, you need to make sure that the return value is IDOK before changing the pen size. If it's not, then leave the pen size the same as it is.

If the call to *Execute* does return IDOK, the new value for *PenSize* is in the string passed in for the dialog's buffer. Before this can be used as a pen size, it must be converted to an **int**. Then you should make sure that the value you get from the buffer is a valid pen width. Finally, once you're sure that the input from the user is acceptable, you can change the pen size. *TDrawWindow* now has a function called *SetPenSize* that you can use to change the pen size. The reason for doing it this way, instead of directly modifying the pen, is explained in the next section.

The *EvRButtonDown* function should now look something like this:

```
void
TDrawWindow::EvRButtonDown(uint, TPoint&)
{
  char inputText[6];

  wsprintf(inputText, "%d", PenSize);
```

```
            if ((TInputDialog(this, "Line Thickness",
                              "Input a new thickness:",
                              inputText,
                              sizeof(inputText))).Execute() == IDOK) {
        int  newPenSize = atoi(inputText);

        if (newPenSize < 0)
          newPenSize = 1;

        SetPenSize(newPenSize);
      }
    }
```

Calling SetPenSize

To change the pen size, use the *SetPenSize* function. Although the *EvRButtonDown* function is a member of *TDrawWindow*, and as such has full access to the **protected** data members *Pen* and *PenSize*, it is better to establish a public access function to make the actual changes to the data. This becomes more important later, when the pen is modified more often.

For *TDrawWindow*, you have the **public** *SetPenSize* function. The *SetPenSize* function takes one parameter, an **int** that contains the new width for the pen. After opening the input dialog box, processing the input, and checking the validity of the result, all you need to do is call *SetPenSize*.

SetPenSize is a fairly simple function. To resize the pen, you must first delete the existing pen object. Then set *PenSize* to the new size. Finally construct a new pen object with the new pen size. The function should look something like this:

```
void
TDrawWindow::SetPenSize(int newSize)
{
  delete Pen;
  PenSize = newSize;
  Pen = new TPen(TColor(0,0,0), PenSize);
}
```

Cleaning up after Pen

Because *Pen* is a pointer to a *TPen* object, and not an actual *TPen* object, it isn't automatically destroyed when the *TDrawWindow* object is destroyed. You need to explicitly destroy *Pen* in the *TDrawWindow* destructor to properly clean up. The only thing required is to call **delete** on *Pen*. *TDrawWindow* should now look something like this:

```
class TDrawWindow : public TWindow
{
  public:
    TDrawWindow(TWindow *parent = 0);
    ~TDrawWindow() {delete DragDC; delete Pen;}
```

```
    void SetPenSize(int newSize);

protected:
    TDC *DragDC;
    int PenSize;
    TPen *Pen;

    // Override member function of TWindow
    bool CanClose();

    // Message response functions
    void EvLButtonDown(uint, TPoint&);
    void EvRButtonDown(uint, TPoint&);
    void EvMouseMove(uint, TPoint&);
    void EvLButtonUp(uint, TPoint&);

    DECLARE_RESPONSE_TABLE(TDrawWindow);
};
```

Where to find more information

Here's a guide to where you can find more information on the topics introduced in this step:

- The *TInputDialog* class and dialogs in general are discussed in Chapter 27.
- Device contexts and the *TDC* classes are discussed in Chapter 32.
- The *TPen* class is also discussed in Chapter 32.

6

Painting the window and adding a menu

There are a few flaws with the application from Step 5. The biggest problem is that the drawing window doesn't know how to paint itself. To see this for yourself, try drawing a line in the window, minimizing the application, then restoring it. The line you drew is gone. You can find the source for Step 6 in the files STEP06.CPP and STEP06.RC in the directory EXAMPLES\OWL\TUTORIAL.

Another problem is that the only way the user can access the application is with the mouse. The user can either press the left button to draw a line or the right button to change the pen size.

In Step 6, you'll make it possible for the application to remember the contexts of the window and redraw it. You'll also add some menus to increase the number of ways the user can access the application.

Repainting the window

There are two problems that must be dealt with when you're trying to paint the window:

- There must be a way to remember what was displayed in the window.
- There must be a way to redraw the window.

Storing the drawing

In the earlier steps of the tutorial application, the line in the window was drawn as the user moved the mouse while holding the left mouse button. This approach is fine for drawing the line but doesn't store the points in the line for later use.

Because the line is composed of a number of points in the window, you can store each point in the ObjectWindows *TPoint* class. And because each line is composed of multiple points, you need an array of *TPoint* objects to store a line. Instead of attempting to allocate, manage, and update an array of *TPoint* objects from scratch, the tutorial application uses the Borland container class *TArray* to define a data type called *TPoints*. It also uses the Borland container class *TArrayIterator* to define an iterator called *TPointsIterator*. The definitions of these two types look like this:

```
typedef TArray<TPoint> TPoints;
typedef TArrayIterator<TPoint> TPointsIterator;
```

The *TDrawWindow* class adds a *TPoints* object in which it can store the points in the line. It actually uses a *TPoints* *, a **protected** member called *Line*, which is set to point to a *TPoints* array created in the constructor. The constructor now looks something like this:

```
TDrawWindow::TDrawWindow(TWindow *parent)
{
  Init(parent, 0, 0);
  DragDC = 0;
  PenSize = 1;
  Pen = new TPen(TColor::Black, PenSize);
  Line = new TPoints(10, 0, 10);
}
```

TPoints

The Borland C++ container class library and the *TArray* and *TArrayIterator* classes are explained in detail in the *Borland C++ Programmer's Guide* in Chapter 15, "Using the C++ container classes." For now, here's a simple explanation of how the *TPoints* and *TPointsIterator* container classes are used in the tutorial application. To use the *TArray* and *TArrayIterator* classes, you must include the header file classlib\arrays.h.

The *TArray* constructor takes three parameters, all **int**s:

- The first parameter represents the upper boundary of the array; that is, how high the array count can go.

- The second parameter represents the lower boundary of the array; that is, the number at which the array count begins. This parameter defaults to 0, matching the C and C++ convention of starting arrays at member 0.

- The third parameter represents the array delta. The array delta is the number of members that are added when the array grows too large to contain all the members of the array.

Here's the statement that allocates the initial array of points in the *TDrawWindow* constructor:

```
Line = new TPoints(10, 0, 10);
```

The array of points is created with room for ten members, beginning at 0. Once ten objects are stored in the array, attempting to add another object adds room for ten new members to the array. This lets you start with a small conservative array size, but also alleviates one of the main problems normally associated with static arrays, which is running out of room and having to reallocate and expand the array.

Once you've created an array, you need to be able to manipulate it. The *TArray* class (and, by extension, the *TPoints* class) provides a number of functions to add members, delete members, clear the array, and the like. The tutorial application uses only a small number of the functions provided. Here's a short description of each function:

- The *Add* function adds a member to the array. It takes a single parameter, a reference to an object of the array type. For example, adding a *TPoint* object to a *TPoints* array would look something like this:

```
// Construct a TPoints array (an array of TPoint objects)
TPoints Points(10, 0, 10);

// Construct a TPoint object
TPoint p(3,4);

// Add the TPoint object p to the array
Points.Add(p);
```

- The *Flush* function clears all the members of an array and resets the number of array members back to the initial array size. It takes no parameters. To clear the array in the previous sample code, the function call would look something like this:

```
// Clear all members in the Points array

Points.Flush();
```

- The *GetItemsInContainer* function returns the total number of items in the container. Note that this number indicates the number of actual objects added to the container, not the space available. For example, even though the container may have enough room for 30 objects, it might only contain 23 objects. In this case, *GetItemsInContainer* would return 23.

TPointsIterator

Iterators—in this case the *TPointsIterator* type—let you move through the array, accessing a single member of the array at a time. An iterator constructor takes a single parameter, a reference to a *TArray* of objects (the type of objects in the array is set up by the definition of the iterator). Here's what an iterator looks like when it's set up using the *Line* member of the *TDrawWindow* class:

```
TPointsIterator i(*Line);
```

Note that *Line* is dereferenced because the iterator constructor takes a *TPoints* **&** for its parameter, and *Line* is a *TPoints* *. Dereferencing the pointer makes *Line* comply with the iterator constructor type requirements.

Once you've created an iterator, you can use it to access each object in the array, one at a time, starting with the first member. In the tutorial application, the iterator isn't used very much and you won't learn much about the possibilities of an iterator from it. But the tutorial does use two properties of iterators that require a note of explanation:

- You can move through the objects in the array using the **++** operator on the iterator. This returns a reference to the current object and increments the iterator to the next object in the array. The order in which it performs these two actions depends on whether you use the **++** operator as a prefix or postfix operator. Using it as a prefix operator (for example, **++***i*) increments the iterator to the next object, then returns a reference to that object. Using it as a postfix operator (for example, *i***++**) returns a reference to the current object, then increments the iterator to the next object.

When you attempt to increment the iterator past the last member of the array, the iterator is set to 0. You can use this as a test in any Boolean conditional. For example:

```
TPointsIterator i(*Line);
while(i)
   i++;
```

- You can also access the current object with the *Current* function. Calling the current function returns a reference to the current object. You can then perform operations on the object as if it were a regular instance of the object. For example, you can test a point accessed by an iterator against the value of another point:

```
TPointsIterator i(*Line);
TPoint tmp(5, 6);
if (i.Current() == tmp)
   return true;
else
   return false;
```

Using the array classes

Once the *Line* array is created in the *TDrawWindow* constructor, it is accessed in four main places:

- The *EvLButtonDown* function. The array is flushed at the beginning of the function before the screen is invalidated. The beginning point of the line is then inserted towards the end of the function. The *EvLButtonDown* function should look something like this:

```
void
TDrawWindow::EvLButtonDown(uint, TPoint& point)
{
  Line->Flush();
  Invalidate();
  if (!DragDC) {
    SetCapture();
    DragDC = new TClientDC(*this);
    DragDC->SelectObject(*Pen);
    DragDC->MoveTo(point);
    Line->Add(point);
  }
}
```

- The *EvMouseMove* function. Each point in the line is added to the array as the user draws in the window. The *EvMouseMove* function should look something like this:

```
void
TDrawWindow::EvMouseMove(uint, TPoint& point)
{
  if (DragDC) {
    DragDC->LineTo(point);
    Line->Add(point);
  }
}
```

- The *Paint* function. This function is described in the next section.

- The *CmFileNew* function. This function is described on page 36.

Paint function

In standard C Windows programs, if you need to repaint a window manually, you catch the WM_PAINT messages and do whatever you need to do to repaint the screen. This might lead you to think that the proper way to repaint the window in the *TDrawWindow* class is to add the EV_WM_PAINT macro to the class' response table and set up a function called *EvPaint*.

You can do this if you want. However, a better way is to override the *TWindow* function *Paint*. *TDrawWindow*'s base class *TWindow* actually does quite a bit of work in its *EvPaint* function. It sets up the *BeginPaint* and *EndPaint* calls, creates a device context for the window, and so on.

Paint is a **virtual** member of the *TWindow* class. *TWindow*'s *EvPaint* calls it in the middle of its processing. The default *Paint* function doesn't do anything. You can use it to provide the special processing required to draw a line from a *TPoints* array.

Here is the signature of the *Paint* function. This is added to the *TDrawWindow* class:

```
void Paint(TDC&, bool, TRect&);
```

where:

- The first parameter is the device context set up by the calling function. This is the device context you should use when working.

- If the second parameter is true, you are supposed to clear the device context before painting the window. If it's false, you are supposed to paint over what is already contained in the window.

- The third parameter indicates the invalid area of the device context that needs to be repainted.

In the current case, you always want to clear the window. You can also assume that the entire area of the drawing needs to be repainted. The *Paint* function implements this basic algorithm:

1 Create an iterator to go through the points in the line.

2 Select the pen into the device context passed into the *Paint* function.

3 If this is the first point in the array, set the current point to the coordinates contained in the current array member.

4 While there are still points left in the array, draw lines from the current point to the point contained in the current array member.

The *TDrawWindow::Paint* function now looks something like this:

```
void
TDrawWindow::Paint(TDC& dc, bool, TRect&)
{
  bool first = true;
  TPointsIterator i(*Line);

  dc.SelectObject(*Pen);

  while (i) {
    TPoint p = i++;

    if (!first)
      dc.LineTo(p);
    else {
      dc.MoveTo(p);
      first = false;
    }
  }
}
```

Menu commands

There are a number of steps you need to perform to add a menu choice and its corresponding event handler to your application:

1 Define the event identifier for the menu choice. By convention, this identifier is all capital letters, and begins with CM_. For example, the identifier for the File Open menu choice is CM_FILEOPEN.

2 Add the appropriate menu resource to your resource file.

3 Add an event-handling function for the menu choice to your class. The ObjectWindows 2.5 convention is to name this function the same name as the event identifier, except omitting the underscore and using initial capital letters and lowercase letters for the rest. For example, the function that handles the CM_FILEOPEN event is named *CmFileOpen*.

4 Add an EV_COMMAND macro to your class' response table, associating the event identifier with the event-handling function. This macro takes two parameters; the first is the event identifier and the second is the name of the event-handling function. For example, the response table entry for the File Open menu choice looks like this:

```
EV_COMMAND(CM_FILEOPEN, CmFileOpen),
```

5 The EV_COMMAND macro requires the signature of the event-handling function to take no parameters and return **void**. So the signature of the event-handling function for the File Open menu choice looks like this:

```
void CmFileOpen();
```

Adding event identifiers

You need to add identifiers for each of these menu choices. Here's the definition of the event identifiers:

```
#define CM_FILENEW      201
#define CM_FILEOPEN     202
#define CM_FILESAVE     203
#define CM_FILESAVEAS   204
#define CM_ABOUT        205
```

These identifiers are contained in the file STEP06.RC. The ObjectWindows style places the definitions of identifiers in the resource script file, instead of a header file. This cuts down on the number of source files required for a project, and also makes it easier to maintain the consistency of identifier values between the resources and the application source code.

The actual resource definitions in the resource file are contained in a block contained in an **#ifndef/#endif** block, like so:

```
#ifdef RC_INVOKED
   // Resource definitions here.
   ⋮
#endif
```

RC_INVOKED is defined by all resource compilers, but not by C++ compilers. The resource information is never seen during C++ compilation. Identifier definitions should be placed outside this **#ifndef/#endif** block, usually at the beginning of the file.

Adding menu resources

For now, you want to add five menu choices to the application:

- File | New
- File | Open
- File | Save
- File | Save As
- Help | About

Each of these menu choices needs to associated with the correct event identifier; that is, the File Open menu choice should send the CM_FILEOPEN event.

The menu resource is attached to the application in the *InitMainWindow* function. You need to call the main window's *AssignMenu* function. To get the main window, you can call the *GetMainWindow* function. The *InitMainWindow* function should look like this:

```
void InitMainWindow()
{
```

```
SetMainWindow(new TFrameWindow(0, "Drawing Pad", new TDrawWindow));
GetMainWindow()->AssignMenu("COMMANDS");
}
```

Adding response table entries

Each event identifier needs to be associated with its corresponding handler. To do this, add the following lines to the response table:

```
EV_COMMAND(CM_FILENEW, CmFileNew),
EV_COMMAND(CM_FILEOPEN, CmFileOpen),
EV_COMMAND(CM_FILESAVE, CmFileSave),
EV_COMMAND(CM_FILESAVEAS, CmFileSaveAs),
EV_COMMAND(CM_ABOUT, CmAbout),
```

Adding event handlers

Now you need to add a function to handle each of the events you've just added to the response table. Because these functions will eventually grow rather large, you should declare them in the class declaration and define them outside the class declaration.

The declarations of these function should look something like this:

```
void CmFileNew();
void CmFileOpen();
void CmFileSave();
void CmFileSaveAs();
void CmAbout();
```

Implementing the event handlers

The last step in implementing the event handlers is defining the functions. For now, leave the implementation of these functions to a bare minimum. Most of them can just pop up a message box saying that the function has not yet been implemented. The functions that are set up this way are *CmFileOpen*, *CmFileSave*, *CmFileSaveAs*, and *CmAbout*. Here's how these functions look:

```
void
TDrawWindow::CmFileOpen()
{
  MessageBox("Feature not implemented", "File Open", MB_OK);
}
```

The only function that's implemented in this step is the *CmFileNew* function. That's because it's very easy to set up. All that needs to be done is to clear the array of points and erase the window. The *CmFileNew* function looks like this:

```
void
TDrawWindow::CmFileNew()
{
  Line->Flush();
  Invalidate();
}
```

Where to find more information

Here's a guide to where you can find more information on the topics introduced in this step:

- Event handling is discussed in Chapter 22.
- Window classes are discussed in Chapter 25.
- Menus and menu objects are explained in Chapter 26.
- The Borland C++ container class library and the *TArray* and *TArrayIterator* classes are explained in Chapter 15 of the *Borland C++ Programmer's Guide*.

7

Using common dialog boxes

In this step, you'll implement the event-handling functions you added in Step 6. The *CmFileOpen* function, the *CmFileSave* function, and the *CmFileSaveAs* function use the ObjectWindows classes *TFileOpenDialog* and *TFileSaveDialog*. These classes encapsulate the Windows Open and Save common dialog boxes to prompt the user for file names. You can find the source for Step 7 in the files STEP07.CPP and STEP07.RC in the directory EXAMPLES\OWL\TUTORIAL.

You'll make the *CanClose* function check whether the drawing in the window has changed before the drawing is discarded. If the drawing has changed, the user is given a chance to either save the file, continue without saving the file, or abort the close operation entirely.

Also, to implement the *CmFileOpen* function, the *CmFileSave* function, and the *CmFileSaveAs* function, you need to add two more **protected** functions, *OpenFile* and *SaveFile*, to the window class. These functions are discussed a little later in this step.

Changes to TDrawWindow

To implement the menu commands, add some new data members to the *TDrawWindow* class: *FileData*, *IsDirty*, and *IsNewFile*.

FileData

The *FileData* member is a pointer to a *TOpenSaveDialog::TData* object. The *TOpenSaveDialog* class is the direct base class of both the *TFileOpenDialog* class and the *TFileSaveDialog* class. Both of these classes use the *TOpenSaveDialog::TData* class to contain information about the current file or file operation, such as the file name, the initial directory to search, file name filters, and so on.

FileData is initialized in the *TDrawWindow* constructor to a **new**ed *TOpenSaveDialog::TData* object. Because *FileData* is a pointer to an object, a **delete** statement must be added to the *TDrawWindow* destructor to ensure that the object is removed from memory when the application terminates.

IsDirty

The *IsDirty* flag indicates whether the current drawing is "dirty," that is, whether the drawing has been saved since it was last modified by the user. If the drawing hasn't been modified, or if the user hasn't drawn anything on an empty window, *IsDirty* is set to false. Otherwise, it is set to true. *IsDirty* is set to false in the *TDrawWindow* constructor because the drawing hasn't been modified yet.

Outside of the constructor, the *IsDirty* flag is set in a number of functions:

- In the *EvLButtonDown* function, *IsDirty* is set to true to reflect the change made to the drawing.

- In the *CmFileNew* function, *IsDirty* is set to false when the window is cleared.

- In the *OpenFile* and *SaveFile* functions, *IsDirty* is set to false to reflect that the drawing hasn't been modified since last saved or loaded.

IsNewFile

The *IsNewFile* flag indicates whether the file has a name. A file has a name if it was loaded from an existing file or has been saved to disk to some file name. If the file has a name (that is, if it's been saved previously or was loaded from an existing file), the *IsNewFile* flag is set to false. *IsNewFile* is set to true in the *TDrawWindow* constructor because the drawing hasn't yet been saved with a name.

Outside the constructor, the *IsNewFile* flag is set in a number of functions:

- In the *CmFileNew* function, *IsNewFile* is set to true when the window is cleared.

- In the *OpenFile* and *SaveFile* functions, *IsNewFile* is set to false to reflect that the drawing has been saved to disk.

Improving CanClose

The *CanClose* function that you've been using since Step 2 of this tutorial has a couple of flaws. First, whenever it's called, it prompts the user to save the drawing. This isn't necessary if the drawing hasn't been changed since it was loaded, saved, or the window was cleared. Second, a simple yes or no answer to this question isn't sufficient. For example, if the user didn't intend to close the window, the desired response is to cancel the whole operation.

Checking the *IsDirty* flag tells the *CanClose* function whether it's even necessary to prompt the user for approval of the closing operation. If the drawing isn't dirty, there's no need to ask whether it's OK to close. The user can simply reload the file.

If the file is dirty, then the *CanClose* function pops up a message box. Using the MB_YESNOCANCEL flag in the message box call gives the user three possible choices instead of two:

- Choosing Cancel means the user wants to abort the entire close operation. In this case, when *MessageBox* returns IDCANCEL, the *CanClose* function returns false, signaling to the calling function that it's *not* all right to proceed.

- Choosing Yes means that the user wants to save the file before proceeding. When *MessageBox* returns IDYES, the *CanClose* function calls the *CmFileSave* function (*CmFileSave* is explained later in this section). After calling *CmFileSave*, *CanClose* returns true, signaling to the calling function that it's all right to proceed.

- Choosing No means that the user doesn't want to save the file before proceeding. In this case, *CanClose* takes no further action and returns true.

The code for the new *CanClose* function looks something like this:

```
bool
TDrawWindow::CanClose()
{
  if (IsDirty)
    switch(MessageBox("Do you want to save?", "Drawing has changed",
                      MB_YESNOCANCEL | MB_ICONQUESTION)) {
      case IDCANCEL:
        // Choosing Cancel means to abort the close -- return false.
        return false;
      case IDYES:
        // Choosing Yes means to save the drawing.
        CmFileSave();
    }
  return true;
}
```

Note that the *CmFileNew* function is modified in this step to take advantage of the new *CanClose* function.

CmFileSave function

The *CmFileSave* function is relatively simple. It checks whether the drawing is new by testing *IsNewFile*. If *IsNewFile* is true, *CmFileSave* calls *CmFileSaveAs*, which prompts the user for a file in which to save the drawing. Otherwise, it calls *SaveFile*, which does the actual work of saving the drawing.

The *CmFileSave* function should look something like this:

```
void
TDrawWindow::CmFileSave()
{
  if (IsNewFile)
    CmFileSaveAs();
```

```
    else
        SaveFile();
}
```

CmFileOpen function

The *CmFileOpen* function is also fairly simple. It first checks *CanClose* to make sure it's OK to close the current drawing and open a new file. If the *CanClose* function returns false, *CmFileOpen* aborts.

After ensuring that it's OK to proceed, *CmFileOpen* creates a *TFileOpenDialog* object. The *TFileOpenDialog* constructor can take up to five parameters, but for this application you need to use only two. The last three parameters all have default values. The two parameters you need to provide are a pointer to the parent window and a reference to a *TOpenSaveDialog::TData* object. In this case, the pointer to the parent window is the **this** pointer. The *TOpenSaveDialog::TData* object is provided by *FileData*.

Once the dialog box object is constructed, it is executed by calling the *TFileOpenDialog::Execute* function. There are only two possible return values for the *TFileOpenDialog*, IDOK and IDCANCEL. The value that is returned depends on whether the user presses the OK or Cancel button in the File Open dialog box.

If the return value is IDOK, *CmFileOpen* then calls the *OpenFile* function, which does the actual work of opening the file. The *Execute* function also stores the name of the file the user selected into the *FileName* member of *FileData*. If the return value is not IDOK (that is, if the return value is IDCANCEL), no further action is taken and the function returns.

The *CmFileOpen* function should look something like this:

```
void
TDrawWindow::CmFileOpen()
{
    if (CanClose())
        if (TFileOpenDialog(this, *FileData).Execute() == IDOK)
            OpenFile();
}
```

CmFileSaveAs function

The *CmFileSaveAs* function can be used in two ways: to save a new drawing under a new name and to save an existing drawing under a name different from its present name.

To determine which of these the user is doing, *CmFileSaveAs* first checks the *IsNewFile* flag. If the file is new, *CmFileSaveAs* copies a null string into the *FileName* member of *FileData*. If the file is not new, *FileName* is left as it is.

The distinction between these two is quite important. If *FileName* contains a null string, the default name in the File Name box of the File Open dialog box is set to the name filter found in the *FileData* object, in this case, *.pts. But if *FileName* already contains a name, that name plus its directory path is inserted in the File Name box.

Once this has been done, *TFileSaveDialog* is created and executed. This works exactly the same as *TFileOpenDialog* does in the *CmFileOpen* function. If the *Execute* function returns IDOK, *CmFileSaveAs* then calls the *SaveFile* function.

The *CmFileSaveAs* function should look something like this:

```
void
TDrawWindow::CmFileSaveAs()
{
  if (IsNewFile)
    strcpy(FileData->FileName, "");

  if ((new TFileSaveDialog(this, *FileData))->Execute() == IDOK)
    SaveFile();
}
```

Opening and saving drawings

The *CmFileOpen*, *CmFileSave*, and *CmFileSaveAs* functions only provide the interface to let the user open and save drawings. The actual work of opening and saving files is done by the *OpenFile* and *SaveFile* functions. This section describes how these functions perform these actions, but it doesn't provide technical explanations of the entire functions.

OpenFile function

The *OpenFile* function opens the file named in the *FileName* member of the *FileData* object as an *ifstream*, one of the standard C++ iostreams. If the file can't be opened for some reason, *OpenFile* pops up a message box informing the user that it couldn't open the file and then returns.

Once the file is successfully opened, the *Line* array is flushed. *OpenFile* then reads in the number of points saved in the file, which is the first data item stored in the file. It then sets up a **for** loop that reads each point into a temporary *TPoint* object. That object is then added to the *Line* array.

Once all the points have been read in, *OpenFile* calls *Invalidate*. This invalidates the window region, causing a WM_PAINT message to be sent and the new drawing to be painted in the window.

Lastly, *OpenFile* sets *IsDirty* and *IsNewFile* both to false. The *OpenFile* function should look something like this:

```
void
TDrawWindow::OpenFile()
{
  ifstream is(FileData->FileName);

  if (!is)
    MessageBox("Unable to open file", "File Error", MB_OK | MB_ICONEXCLAMATION);
  else {
    Line->Flush();
    unsigned numPoints;
```

```
    is >> numPoints;
    while (numPoints--) {
      TPoint  point;
      is >> point;
      Line->Add(point);
    }
  }

  IsNewFile = IsDirty = false;
  Invalidate();
}
```

SaveFile function

The *SaveFile* function opens the file named in the *FileName* member of *FileData* as an *ofstream*, one of the standard C++ iostreams. If the file can't be opened for some reason, *SaveFile* pops up a message box informing the user that it couldn't open the file and then returns.

Once the file has been opened, the function *Line–>GetItemsInContainer* is called. The result is inserted into the file. This number is read in by the *OpenFile* function to determine how many points are stored in the file.

After that, *SaveFile* sets up an iterator called *i* from *Line*. This iterator goes through all the points contained in the *Line* array. Each point is then inserted into the stream until there are no points left.

Lastly, *IsNewFile* and *IsDirty* are set to false. Here is how the *SaveFile* function should look:

```
void
TDrawWindow::SaveFile()
{
  ofstream os(FileData->FileName);

  if (!os)
    MessageBox("Unable to open file", "File Error",
               MB_OK | MB_ICONEXCLAMATION);
  else {
    os << Line->GetItemsInContainer();
    TPointsIterator i(*Line);
    while (i)
      os << i++;
    IsNewFile = IsDirty = false;
  }
}
```

CmAbout function

The *CmAbout* function demonstrates how easy it is to use custom dialog boxes in ObjectWindows. This function contains only one line of code. It uses the *TDialog* class and the IDD_ABOUT dialog box resource to pop up an information dialog box.

TDialog can take up to three parameters:

- The first parameter is a pointer to the dialog box's parent window. Just as with the *TFileOpenDialog* and *TFileSaveDialog* constructors, you can use the **this** pointer, setting the parent window to the *TDrawWindow* object.

- The second parameter is a reference to a *TResId* object. This should be the resource identifier of the dialog box resource.

Note   Usually you don't actually pass in a *TResId* reference. Instead you pass a resource identifier number or string, just as you would for a dialog box created using regular Windows API calls. Conversion operators in the *TResId* class resolve the parameter into the proper type.

- The third parameter, a *TModule **, usually uses its default value.

Once the dialog box object is constructed, all that needs to be done is to call the *Execute* function. Once the user closes the dialog box and execution is complete, *CmAbout* returns. The temporary *TDialog* object goes out of scope and disappears.

The code for *CmAbout* should look like this:

```
void
TDrawWindow::CmAbout()
{
    TDialog(this, IDD_ABOUT).Execute();
}
```

Where to find more information

Here's a guide to where you can find more information on the topics introduced in this step:

- The *CanClose* function is discussed in Chapter 20.

- Dialog boxes, including the *TFileOpenDialog* and the *TFileOpenDialog* classes, are discussed in Chapter 27.

8

Adding multiple lines

You can find the source for Step 8 in the files STEP08.CPP and STEP08.RC in the directory EXAMPLES\OWL\TUTORIAL. Step 8 makes a great leap in terms of usefulness. In this step, you'll add a new class, *TLine*, that is derived from the *TPoints* array you've been using to contain the points in a line. You'll then define another array class, *TLines*, that contains an array of *TLine* objects, enabling us to have multiple lines in the window. You'll add streaming operators to make it a little easier to save drawings. Lastly, you'll develop the *Paint* function further to handle drawings with multiple lines.

TLine class

The *TLine* class is derived from the public base class *TPoints*. This gives *TLine* all the functionality that you've been using with the *Line* member of the *TDrawWindow* class. This includes the *Add*, *Flush*, and *GetItemsInContainer* functions that you've been using. In addition, you can continue to use *TPointsIterator* with the *TLine* class in the same way you used it with *TPoints*.

But because you're creating your own class now, you can also add any additional functionality you need. For example, you should add a data member to contain the size of the pen for each line. Then, to hide the data, add accessor functions to manipulate the data.

In *TLine*, the pen size is contained in a **protected int** called *PenSize*. *PenSize* is accessed by one of two functions, both called *QueryPen*. Both versions of *QueryPen* return an **int**, which contains the value of *PenSize*. Here's the difference between the two functions:

• The first *QueryPen* function takes no parameters. This function returns the pen size.

• The second *QueryPen* function takes a single parameter, an **int**. This function sets *PenSize* to the value passed in, then returns the new value of *PenSize*. You can use the return value to check whether *QueryPen* actually set the pen to the value you passed to it. This version of *QueryPen* checks the value of the parameter to make sure that it's a legal value for the pen size.

TLine also contains a definition for the == operator. This operator checks to see if the two objects are actually the same object. If so, the operator returns true. Defining an array using the *TArray* class (which you'll do later when defining *TLines*) requires that the object used in *TArray* have the == operator defined.

Lastly you should declare two operators, << and >>, to be **friend**s of the *TLine* class. When these operators are implemented later in this section, they'll provide easy access to stream operations for the *SaveFile* and *OpenFile* functions.

Here is the declaration of the *TLine* class:

```
class TLine : public TPoints
{
  public:
    TLine(int penSize = 1) : TPoints(10, 0, 10) { PenSize = penSize; }

    int QueryPen() const { return PenSize; }
    int QueryPen(int penSize);

    // The == operator must be defined for the container class,
    // even if unused
    bool operator ==(const TLine& other) const
      { return &other == this; }
    friend ostream& operator <<(ostream& os, const TLine& line);
    friend istream& operator >>(istream& is, TLine& line);

  protected:
    int PenSize;
};
```

TLines array

Once you've defined the *TLine* class, you can define the *TLines* array and the *TLinesIterator* array. These containers work the same way as the *TPoints* and *TPointsIterator* container classes that you defined earlier. The only difference is that, instead of containing an array of *TPoint* objects like *TPoints*, *TLines* contains an array of *TLine* objects.

Here are the definitions of *TLines* and *TLinesIterator*:

```
typedef TArray<TLine> TLines;
typedef TArrayIterator<TLine> TLinesIterator;
```

Insertion and extraction of TLine objects

Most objects that need to be saved to and retrieved from files on a regular basis are set up to use the insertion and extraction operators << and >>. By declaring these operators as friends of *TLine*, you need to define the operators to handle the particular type of data encapsulated in *TLine*.

Having these operators defined gives you the ability to place an entire *TLine* object into a file with a single line of code. You'll see how this is used when you make the changes to the *OpenFile* and *SaveFile* functions.

Insertion operator <<

In essence, the insertion operator takes on the functionality of the *SaveFile* function used in Step 7. It doesn't have to open a file (that's handled by whatever function uses the operator) and it has an extra piece of data to insert (*PenSize*). Other than that, it's not much different. Compare the definition of this function with the *SaveFile* function from Step 7. Notice the use of *TPointsIterator* with the *TLine* object:

```
ostream& operator <<(ostream& os, const TLine& line)
{
  // Write the number of points in the line
  os << line.GetItemsInContainer() << '

  // Write the pen size
  os << ' ' << line.PenSize;

  // Get an iterator for the array of points
  TPointsIterator j(line);

  // While the iterator is valid (i.e. it hasn't run out of points)
  while(j)
    // Write the point from the iterator and increment the array.
    os << j++;

  os << '

  // return the stream object
  return os;
}
```

Extraction operator >>

Much like the insertion operator, the extraction operator takes on the functionality of the *OpenFile* function in Step 7. It doesn't have to open a file itself and it has an extra piece of data to extract. Other than that, it's implemented similarly to the *OpenFile* function:

```
istream& operator >>(istream& is, TLine& line)
{
  unsigned numPoints;

  is >> numPoints;

  is >> line.PenSize;

  while (numPoints--) {
    TPoint point;
    is >> point;
```

```
        line.Add(point);
    }
    // return the stream object
    return is;
}
```

Extending TDrawWindow

There are a number of changes required in *TDrawWindow* to accommodate the new *TLine* class. First there are a number of changes in data members:

- *PenSize* is removed. Each individual line now contains its pen size.

- The *Line* data member is changed from a *TPoints* * to a *TLine* *. The *Line* object holds the points in the line currently being drawn.

- The *Lines* data member, a *TLines* *, is added. The *Lines* object contains all the *TLine* objects.

There are also a number of functions that are modified or added:

- The *SetPenSize* function is made **protected** because changes to the pen size should be made to the *TLine* class. *SetPenSize* should now be used only by the *TDrawWindow* class internally. *SetPenSize* also sets the pen size for the current line by calling that line's *QueryPen* function.

- The *GetPenSize* function is added. This function implements the *TInputDialog* that was handled in *EvRButtonDown*. This is because two functions now use this same dialog box, *EvRButtonDown* and *CmPenSize*.

- The *EvRButtonDown* function now calls *GetPenSize* to open the input dialog box.

- The *CmPenSize* function handles the CM_PENSIZE event. This event comes from a new menu choice, Pen Size, on a new menu, Tools. This function is added to give the user another way to change the pen size.

- The *OpenFile* and *SaveFile* functions are modified to store an array of *TLine* objects instead of an array of *TPoint* objects. By using the insertion and extraction operators, these functions change very little from their prior forms.

In addition, the *Paint* function is changed quite a bit, as described in the following section.

Paint function

The *Paint* function must now perform two iterations instead one. Instead of iterating through a single array of points, *Paint* must now iterate through an array of lines. For each line, it must set the pen width and then iterate through the points that compose the line.

Paint does this by first creating an iterator from *Lines*. This iterator goes through the array of lines. For each line, *Paint* queries the pen size of the current line. It sets the window's *Pen* to this size and selects this pen into the device context. It then creates an iterator for the current line and increments the line array iterator.

The next part of *Paint* looks like the *Paint* function from Step 7. That's because it does basically the same thing as that function—it takes the array of points and draws the line in the window.

Here is the code for the new *Paint* function:

```
void
TDrawWindow::Paint(TDC& dc, bool, TRect&)
{
  // Iterates through the array of line objects.
  TLinesIterator i(*Lines);

  while (i) {
    // Set pen for the dc to current line's pen.
    TPen pen(TColor::Black, i.Current().QueryPen());
    dc.SelectObject(pen);

    // Iterates through the points in the line i.
    TPointsIterator j(i++);
    bool first = true;

    while (j) {
      TPoint p = j++;

      if (!first)
        dc.LineTo(p);
      else {
        dc.MoveTo(p);
        first = false;
      }
    }
  }
}
```

Where to find more information

Here's a guide to where you can find more information on the topics introduced in this step:

- Window classes are discussed in Chapter 25.

- The Borland C++ container class library and the *TArray* and *TArrayIterator* classes are explained in the *Borland C++ Programmer's Guide* in Chapter 15, "Using the Borland C++ container classes."

9

Changing pens

You can find the source for Step 9 in the files STEP09.CPP and STEP09.RC in the directory EXAMPLES\OWL\TUTORIAL. In Step 9, you'll add a *TColor* member to the *TLine* class, letting the user draw with lines of different widths *and* different colors. To change the color of the line, you'll add the *CmPenColor* function. This function handles the CM_PENCOLOR menu command. *CmPenColor* uses the *TChooseColorDialog* class to let the user change colors. It also adds some helper functions to deal with changes to the width and color and give external classes access to information about the line.

Along with adding color to the pen, Step 9 adds functionality to the streaming operators to deal with the new attributes of the *TLine* class. It also adds a *Draw* function to the *TLine* class to make the class more self-sufficient and to make the *Paint* function simpler.

Changes to the TLine class

A number of changes to the *TLine* class declaration are required to accommodate the new functionality:

- There is a new **protected** data member, *Color* (a *TColor* object). *Color* and *PenSize* make up the attributes necessary to construct a *TPen* object.

- The constructor signature has changed from

  ```
  TLine(int penSize = 1);
  ```

  to

  ```
  TLine(const TColor &color = (TColor) 0, int penSize = 1);
  ```

  The constructor itself changes to set *PenSize* to the constructor's second parameter and to create a new *TPen* object and assign it to *Pen*. If no parameters are specified and the first parameter takes on its default value, *TColor::Black* is used as the pen color.

- The two *QueryPen* functions are abandoned in favor of three new functions: *QueryPenSize*, which returns the pen size as an **int**; *QueryColor*, which returns the pen color as a *TColor*; and *QueryPen*, which returns the pen as a *TPen*.

- Instead of using the query functions to set the pen attributes, there are two new functions called *SetPen*. One takes a single **int** parameter and the other takes a *TColor* **&** and two **int**s. The pen query and set functions are discussed in the next section.

- A *Draw* function is added so that the *TLine* class dictates how it is drawn. This function is **virtual** so that it can be easily overridden in a derived class.

Here's how the new *TLine* class declaration should look:

```
class TLine : public TPoints {
  public:
  // Constructor to allow construction from a color and a pen size.
  // Also serves as default constructor.
  TLine(const TColor &color = TColor(0), int penSize = 1)
  : TPoints(10, 0, 10), PenSize(penSize), Color(color) {}

  // Functions to modify and query pen attributes.
  int QueryPenSize() { return PenSize; }
  TColor& QueryColor() { return Color; }
  void SetPen(TColor &newColor, int penSize = 0);
  void SetPen(int penSize);

  // TLine draws itself. Returns true if everything went OK.
  virtual bool Draw(TDC &) const;

  // The == operator must be defined for the container class,
  // even if unused
  bool operator ==(const TLine& other) const
    { return &other == this; }
    friend ostream& operator <<(ostream& os, const TLine& line);
    friend istream& operator >>(istream& is, TLine& line);

  protected:
    int PenSize;
    TColor Color;
};
```

Pen access functions

In Step 8, the *QueryPen* function could be used both to access the current size of the pen and to set the size of the pen. The new *TLine* query functions—*QueryPenSize* and *QueryColor*—can't be used to modify the pen attributes. These functions only return pen attributes.

To set pen attributes, there are two new functions called *SetPen*. The first *SetPen* sets just the pen size. The other *SetPen* can be used to set the color, size, and style of the pen. But by letting the second and third parameters take on their default values, you can use the second constructor to set just the color. Here's the code for these functions:

```
void
TLine::SetPen(int penSize)
{
  if (penSize < 1)
    PenSize = 1;
  else
    PenSize = penSize;
}

void
TLine::SetPen(TColor &newColor, int penSize)
{
  // If penSize isn't the default (0), set PenSize to the new size.
  if (penSize)
    PenSize = penSize;

  Color = newColor;
}
```

Draw function

The *Draw* function draws the line in the window, taking that functionality from the window's *Paint* function. This functionality is moved because the *TLine* object can now dictate how it gets painted onscreen. Take a look at the code for the *Draw* function below and compare this to the *Paint* function from Step 8. From a certain point, the two bits of code are nearly identical:

```
bool
TLine::Draw(TDC &dc) const
{
  // Set pen for the dc to the values for this line
  TPen pen(Color, PenSize);
  dc.SelectObject(pen);

  // Iterates through the points in the line i.
  TPointsIterator j(*this);
  bool first = true;

  while (j) {
    TPoint p = j++;

    if (!first)
      dc.LineTo(p);
    else {
      dc.MoveTo(p);
      first = false;
    }
  }
  dc.RestorePen();
  return true;
}
```

After putting all this code into the *TLine* class, the *TDrawWindow::Paint* function is greatly simplified:

```
void
TDrawWindow::Paint(TDC& dc, bool, TRect&)
{
  // Iterates through the array of line objects.
  TLinesIterator i(*Lines);

  while (i)
    i++.Draw(dc);
}
```

Insertion and extraction operators

There also some changes to the insertion and extraction operators that are necessary to handle the revised *TLine* class.

- The insertion operator is modified to write out the *PenSize* and *Color* member. It then writes out the points just as it did before.

- The extraction operator reads in the data and uses the *PenSize* and *Color* data in the *SetPen* function. Each point is read in from the file and added to the object.

Changes to the TDrawWindow class

There are a few fairly minor changes to the *TDrawWindow* class to accommodate the revised *TLine* class:

- The *Pen* data member is constructed from the size and color of the current line.

- The *SetPenSize* function is removed. The function *GetPenSize* opens a *TInputDialog* for the user to enter a new pen size in. *GetPenSize* then calls the function *Line->SetPen* to actually set the pen size.

- The *CmPenColor* function is added to handle the CM_PENCOLOR event. This event is sent from the new Tools menu choice Pen Color.

CmPenColor function

The *CmPenColor* function opens a *TChooseColorDialog* for the user to select a color from. Like *TFileOpenDialog* and *TFileSaveDialog*, *TChooseColorDialog* is an encapsulation of one of the Windows common dialog boxes.

Also like *TFileOpenDialog* and *TFileSaveDialog*, the *TChooseColorDialog* constructor can take up to five parameters, but in this case you need only two. The last three all have default values. The two parameters you need to provide are a pointer to the parent window and a reference to a *TChooseColorDialog::TData* object. In this case, the pointer to the parent window is simply the **this** pointer. The *TChooseColorDialog::TData* object is provided by *colors*.

Setting the *Color* member of *colors* to a particular color makes that color (or its closest equivalent displayed in the dialog box) the default color in the dialog box. By setting *Color* to the color of the current pen, you ensure that the Color dialog box reflects the current state of the application.

Setting the *CustColors* member of the *colors* object to some array of *TColor* objects sets those colors in the Custom Colors section of the Color dialog box. You can use whatever colors you want for the *CustColors* array. The values that are used in the tutorial produce a range of monochrome colors that goes from black to white.

Creating and executing a *TChooseColorDialog* works exactly the same as for a *TFileOpenDialog* or *TFileSaveDialog*. Although the Color dialog box has an extra button (the Define Custom Colors button), that button is handled by the Windows part of the common dialog box. Therefore there are only two possible results for the *Execute* function, IDOK and IDCANCEL. If the user selects Cancel, you ignore any changes from the dialog box.

On the other hand, if the user selects OK, you need to change the pen color to the new color chosen by the user. The *TChooseColorDialog* places the color chosen by the user into the *Color* member of the *colors* object. *Color* is a *TColor*, which fits nicely into the *SetPen* function of a *TLine* object.

Here's the code for the *CmPenColor* function:

```
void
TDrawWindow::CmPenColor()
{
  TChooseColorDialog::TData colors;
  static TColor custColors[16] =
  {
    0x010101L, 0x101010L, 0x202020L, 0x303030L,
    0x404040L, 0x505050L, 0x606060L, 0x707070L,
    0x808080L, 0x909090L, 0xA0A0A0L, 0xB0B0B0L,
    0xC0C0C0L, 0xD0D0D0L, 0xE0E0E0L, 0xF0F0F0L
  };

  colors.Flags = CC_RGBINIT;
  colors.Color = TColor(Line->QueryColor());
  colors.CustColors = custColors;
  if (TChooseColorDialog(this, colors).Execute() == IDOK)
    Line->SetPen(colors.Color);
}
```

Where to find more information

Here's a guide to where you can find more information on the topics introduced in this step:

- The *TPen* and *TColor* classes are discussed in Chapter 33.

- Dialog boxes, including the *TChooseColorDialog* class, are discussed in Chapter 27.

10

Adding decorations

The only changes in Step 10 are in the *InitMainWindow* function. But these changes let you make your application more attractive and easier and more intuitive to use. In this step, you'll add a control bar with bitmap button gadgets and a status bar that displays the current menu choice. You can find the source for Step 10 in the files STEP10.CPP and STEP10.RC in the directory EXAMPLES\OWL\TUTORIAL.

There are four main changes in this step:

- Changing the main window from a *TFrameWindow* to a *TDecoratedFrame*.

- Creating a status bar and inserting it into the decorated frame window.

- Creating a control bar, along with its button gadgets, and inserting it into the decorated frame.

- Adding resources, such as a string table (which provides descriptions of each of the available menu choices) and bitmaps for the button gadgets.

Changing the main window

Changing from a *TFrameWindow* to a *TDecoratedFrame* is quite easy. Because *TDecoratedFrame* is based on *TFrameWindow*, a decorated frame can be used just about anywhere that a regular frame window is used. In this case, just create a *TDecoratedFrame* and pass it as the parameter to the *SetMainWindow* function.

Even the constructors of the *TFrameWindow* and *TDecoratedFrame* are alike. The only difference is the fourth parameter, which wasn't being used anyway. The fourth parameter for *TFrameWindow* is a **bool** that tells the frame window whether it should shrink to the size of its client window.

The fourth parameter for *TDecoratedFrame* is also a **bool**. This parameter indicates whether the decorated frame should track menu selections. Menu tracking displays a text description of the currently selected menu choice or button in a message bar or status bar. If you specify **true** for this parameter, you *must* supply a message or status bar for the window. If you don't, your application will crash the first time it tries to send a message to the message or status bar.

If you're using a status bar, you must include the resources for it in your resource file. These resources are contained in the file STATUSBA.RC in the INCLUDE\OWL directory.

The only other difference is that the decorated frame requires some preparation, such as adding decorations like the control bar and status bar, before it can become the main window. So instead of constructing and setting the window in one step, you must construct the window, prepare it, then set it as the main window.

Creating the status bar

Status bars are created using the *TStatusBar* class. *TStatusBar* is based on the *TMessageBar* class, which is itself based on *TGadgetWindow*. Both message bars and status bars display text messages. But status bars have more options than message bars. For example, you can have multiple text gadgets, styled borders, and mode indicators (such as Insert or Overwrite mode) in a status bar.

The *TStatusBar* constructor takes five parameters, although you only use the first two. The rest of the parameters take on their default values:

- The first parameter is a pointer to the status bar's parent window. In this case, use *frame*, which is the pointer to the decorated frame window constructed earlier.

- The second parameter is a *TGadget::TBorderstyle* **enum**. It can be one of *None*, *Plain*, *Raised*, *Recessed*, or *Embossed*. This parameter determines the style of the status bar. This parameter defaults to *Recessed*.

- The third parameter is a *TModeIndicator* **enum**. It determines the keyboard modes that the status bar should show. These indicators can be one or more of *ExtendSelection*, *CapsLock*, *NumLock*, *ScrollLock*, *Overtype*, and *RecordingMacro*. This parameter defaults to 0, meaning to indicate no keyboard modes.

- The fourth parameter is a *TFont* *. This contains the font that should be used in the status bar. This defaults to *TGadgetWindowFont*.

- The fifth parameter is a *TModule* *. It defaults to 0.

Here is the status bar constructor:

```
TStatusBar* sb = new TStatusBar(frame, TGadget::Recessed);
```

Once the status bar is created, it is ready to be inserted into the decorated frame. This is described on page 63.

Creating the control bar

Creating the control bar is more involved than creating the status bar. You first construct the actual *TControlBar* object. Then you create the gadgets that make up the controls on the bar and insert them into the control bar.

Constructing TControlBar

The *TControlBar* constructor takes four parameters, although you need to use only the first parameter here. The rest of the parameters take on their default values:

- The first parameter is a pointer to the parent window. As with the status bar, use *frame* here to make the decorated frame the control bar's parent.

- The second parameter is a *TTileDirection* **enum**. A *TTileDirection* **enum** can have two values, *Horizontal* and *Vertical*. This tells the control bar which way to tile its controls. This parameter defaults to *Horizontal*.

- The third parameter is a *TFont **. This contains the font that should be used in the status bar. This defaults to *TGadgetWindowFont*.

- The fourth parameter is a *TModule **. It defaults to 0.

Here is the control bar constructor:

```
TControlBar *cb = new TControlBar(frame);
```

Building button gadgets

Button gadgets are used as control bar buttons. They associate a bitmap button with an event identifier. When the user presses a button gadget, it sends that event identifier. You can set this up so that pressing a button on the control is just like making a choice from a menu. In this section, you'll see how to set up buttons to replicate each of your current menu choices.

Button gadgets are created using the *TButtonGadget* class. The *TButtonGadget* constructor takes six parameters, of which you need to use only the first three:

- The first parameter is a reference to a *TResId* object (see the note on page 43 regarding the *TResId* class). This should be the resource identifier of the bitmap you want on the button. There are no real restrictions on the size of the bitmap you can use in a button gadget. There are, however, practical considerations: the control bar height is based on the size of the objects contained in the control bar. If your bitmap is excessively large, the control bar will be also.

- The second parameter is the gadget identifier for this button gadget. Usually the gadget identifier, event identifier, and bitmap resource identifier are the same. For example, the button gadget for the File | New command uses a bitmap resource called CM_FILEOPEN, has the gadget identifier CM_FILEOPEN, and posts the event CM_FILEOPEN.

  The bitmap is given the same identifier in the resource file as the event identifier. This makes it a little easier on you when working with the code. This is *not* a rule, however, and you can name the bitmap and event identifier whatever you like. The only stipulation is that the event identifier must be defined and have some sort of processing enabled and the resource identifier must be valid.

  You should also notice that there are a number of entries in the application's string resource table that have the same IDs as the gadgets and events. When a string exists with the same identifier as a button gadget, that string is displayed in the status bar when the gadget is pressed.

- The third parameter is a *TType* **enum**. This indicates what type of button this is. There are three possible button types, *Command*, *Exclusive*, and *NonExclusive*. In this application, all the buttons are command buttons. This parameter defaults to *Command*.

- The fourth parameter is a **bool** indicating whether the button is enabled. By default this parameter is **false**.

- The fifth parameter is a *TState* **enum**. This parameter indicates the initial state of the button, and can be *Up*, *Down*, or *Indeterminate*. This parameter defaults to *Up*.

- The sixth parameter is a **bool** that indicates the repeat state of the button. If the repeat state is **true**, the button repeats when it is pressed and held. By default, this parameter is **false**.

Separator gadgets

There is another type of gadget commonly used when constructing control bars, called a separator gadget. Normally gadgets in a control bar are right next to each other. A separator gadget provides a little bit of space between two gadgets. This lets you separate gadgets into groups, place them in predetermined spots on the control bar, and so on.

Separator gadgets are contained in the *TSeparatorGadget* class. This is a simple class that takes a single **int** parameter. By default the value of this parameter is 6. This parameter indicates the number of pixels of space the separator gadget should take up.

Inserting gadgets into the control bar

Once your gadgets are constructed, you need to insert them into the control bar. The control bar can take gadgets because it is derived from the class *TGadgetWindow*. *TGadgetWindow* provides the basic functionality that lets you use gadgets in a window. *TControlBar* refines that functionality, producing a control bar.

You can insert gadgets into the control bar using the *Insert* function. This version of the *Insert* function is inherited by *TControlBar* from *TGadgetWindow* (later you'll use another version of this function contained in *TDecoratedFrame*). This function takes three parameters, although you need to use only the first parameter in the tutorial application:

- The first parameter is a reference to a *TGadget* or *TGadget*-derived object.

- The second parameter is a *TPlacement* **enum**, which can have a value of *Before* or *After*. This parameter indicates whether the gadget should be placed before or after the gadget's sibling. The default value is *After*. This parameter has no effect if there is no sibling specified.

- The gadget's sibling is specified by the third parameter, which is a *TGadget**. The sibling should have already been inserted into the control bar. This parameter defaults to 0.

In the tutorial application, constructing the gadgets and inserting them into the control bar is accomplished in a single step. Here is the code where the gadgets are inserted into the control bar:

```
cb->Insert(*new TButtonGadget(CM_FILENEW, CM_FILENEW,
        TButtonGadget::Command));
cb->Insert(*new TButtonGadget(CM_FILEOPEN, CM_FILEOPEN,
        TButtonGadget::Command));
cb->Insert(*new TButtonGadget(CM_FILESAVE, CM_FILESAVE,
        TButtonGadget::Command));
cb->Insert(*new TButtonGadget(CM_FILESAVEAS, CM_FILESAVEAS,
        TButtonGadget::Command));
cb->Insert(*new TSeparatorGadget);
cb->Insert(*new TButtonGadget(CM_PENSIZE, CM_PENSIZE,
        TButtonGadget::Command));
cb->Insert(*new TSeparatorGadget);
cb->Insert(*new TButtonGadget(CM_ABOUT, CM_ABOUT,
        TButtonGadget::Command));
```

Notice that the button gadgets replicate the menu commands you already have. This provides an easy way for the user to access frequently used menu commands. Of course, you aren't restricted to using gadgets in a control bar as substitutes or shortcuts for menu commands. Using the *TType* parameter, you can set up gadgets on a control bar to work like radio buttons (by using *Exclusive* with a group of gadgets), check boxes (using *NonExclusive*), and so on.

Inserting objects into a decorated frame

Now that you've constructed the decorations for your *TDecoratedFrame* window, all you need to do is insert the decorations into the window and make the window the main window.

Inserting decorations into a decorated frame is similar to inserting gadgets into a control bar. The *TDecoratedFrame::Insert* function takes two parameters:

- The first is a reference to a *TWindow* or *TWindow*-derived object. This *TWindow* object is the decoration. In this case, the *TWindow*-derived objects are the *TStatusBar* object and the *TControlBar* object.

- The second parameter is a *TLocation* **enum**. This parameter can have one of four values, *Top*, *Bottom*, *Left*, or *Right*. This indicates where in the decorated frame the gadget is to be placed.

Here is the code for inserting the decorations into the decorated frame:

```
// Insert the status bar and control bar into the frame
frame->Insert(*sb, TDecoratedFrame::Bottom);
frame->Insert(*cb, TDecoratedFrame::Top);
```

Once you've inserted the decorations into the frame, the last thing you have to do is set the main window to *frame* and set up the menu:

```
// Set the main window and its menu
SetMainWindow(frame);
GetMainWindow()->AssignMenu("COMMANDS");
```

Where to find more information

Here's a guide to where you can find more information on the topics introduced in this step:

- Decorated frame windows are discussed in Chapter 25.
- Gadgets are discussed in Chapter 30.
- Status bars and control bars are discussed in both Chapter 25 and Chapter 30.

11

Moving to MDI

This chapter describes how to convert the application created in Step 10 to use the Multiple Document Interface, or MDI for short. The application in Step 10 is what is known as a Single Document Interface, or SDI, application. That means the application can support and display only a single document at a time.

In the sense that it's used here, document doesn't have the same meaning you might be used to. Instead of a paper document or a word-processing document, a document refers to any set of data that your application displays and manipulates. In the case of the tutorial application, documents are the drawing files that the application creates. Converting the application to use MDI adds the ability to support multiple drawings open at the same time in multiple child windows. Figure 11.1 shows the difference between the SDI version of the Drawing Pad application and the MDI version that you'll produce in this step.

Figure 11.1   SDI versus MDI Drawing Pad application

SDI version

MDI version

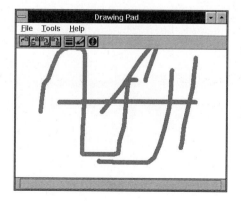
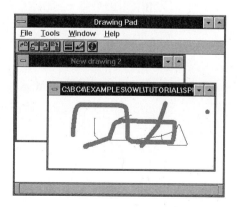

Understanding the MDI model

An MDI application functions a little differently from an SDI application. In Step 10, the Drawing Pad application displayed a single drawing in a window. The window that actually displayed the drawing was a client of the frame window. The frame window managed general application tasks, such as menu handling, resizing, painting menus and control bars, and so on. The client window managed tasks specific to the application, such as handling mouse movements and button clicks in the client area, painting the lines in the drawing, responding to application-specific events, and so on.

In comparison, MDI applications divide tasks up three ways instead of two:

- The frame window functions much as it does in the SDI application, handling basic application functionality.

- The client window handles tasks related to creating, managing, and closing MDI child windows, along with any related functions. For example, the client window might manage the File | Open command since, in order to open an MDI child window, you usually need something to display in it.

- MDI child windows display the data in an MDI application and give the user the ability to manipulate and control the data. These windows handle application-specific tasks, much like the client window did in Step 10.

In this step, you'll take the example from Step 10 and restructure it to support MDI functionality. It's not as complicated as it may seem; most of the new classes you'll construct can be taken straight from the existing *TDrawWindow* class!

Adding the MDI header files

There are a number of new header files you need to include to add MDI capability to your application. This section describes the header files that need to be changed or added. It also describes the classes that are defined in each header file.

Changing the resource script file

You need to change the include statement for the STEP10.RC resource script file to include the STEP11.RC resource script file. There are only two changes you need to make to STEP11.RC:

1 Include the resource header file owl\mdi.rh.

2 Add a pop-up menu called Window between the Tools menu and the Help menu. This menu should have four items, described in Table 11.1.

The functions that handle these events are described later on page 75.

Table 11.1   MDI Window menu items and identifiers

Menu item text	Command identifier
Cascade	CM_CASCADECHILDREN
Tile	CM_TILECHILDREN
Arrange Icons	CM_ARRANGEICONS
Close All	CM_CLOSECHILDREN

Replacing the frame window header file

In the place of owl\decframe.h, you need to include owl\decmdifr.h. This header file contains the definition of the *TDecoratedMDIFrame* class, which is derived from *TMDIFrame* and *TDecoratedFrame*. *TMDIFrame*, defined in the owl\mdi.h header file, adds the support for containing an MDI client window to the support already provided by *TFrameWindow* for command processing and keyboard navigation. As shown in the previous step of the tutorial, *TDecoratedFrame* provides the ability to support decorations such as control bars and status bars. Since the tutorial application already supports decorations from the previous step, you can use the decorated version of the MDI frame window to keep this functionality.

Adding the MDI client and child header files

You need to add the owl\mdi.h and owl\mdichild.h header files. owl\mdi.h contains the definition of the *TMDIFrame* and *TMDIClient* classes. *TMDIClient* provides the functionality necessary for managing MDI child windows. MDI child windows are the windows that the user of your application actually works with and that display the data contained in each document. *TMDIClient* provides the ability to

- Close all of the open MDI child windows

- Find the active MDI child window

- Initialize a new MDI child object

- Create a new MDI child window

- Arrange and manage MDI child windows, including arranging icons for minimized child windows and cascading or tiling open child windows

owl\mdichild.h contains the definition of the *TMDIChild* class, which is derived from *TWindow*. *TMDIChild* overrides a number of *TWindow*'s functions to provide the ability to function as an MDI child.

You usually derive new classes from both *TMDIClient* and *TMDIChild* to provide the specific functionality required by your application. Creating new classes from *TMDIClient* and *TMDIChild* to support the Drawing Pad application is discussed later in this step.

Changing the frame window

The first step in moving the drawing application to MDI is to change the frame window. MDI applications use specialized MDI frame windows. As discussed earlier, ObjectWindows provides two MDI frame window classes, *TMDIFrame* and *TDecoratedMDIFrame*. Because we're using the *TDecoratedMDIFrame* class for the frame window, discussion of the *TMDIFrame* class is left for Chapter 25.

Here's the constructor for *TDecoratedMDIFrame*:

```
TDecoratedMDIFrame(const char far* title,
                   TResId menuResId,
                   TMDIClient& clientWnd = *new TMDIClient,
                   bool trackMenuSelection = false,
                   TModule* module = 0);
```

where:

- *title* is the caption for the frame window.

- *menuResId* is the resource identifier for the frame window's main menu.

- *clientWnd* is the MDI client window for the frame window.

- *trackMenuSelection* indicates whether this frame should track menu selections. This is the same thing as menu tracking for the *TDecoratedFrame* you constructed in the last step.

- *module* is a pointer to a program module. *module* is used to initialize the *TWindow* base object.

Besides adding the owl\decmdifr.h header file, two other changes are required to use a *TDecoratedMDIFrame* in the tutorial application. The first is changing the line in the *TDrawApp::InitMainWindow* function where the frame window is created:

```
TDecoratedMDIFrame *frame = new TDecoratedMDIFrame("Drawing Pad",
                                      TResId("COMMANDS"),
                                      *new TDrawMDIClient,
                                      true);
```

As before, the frame window caption is Drawing Pad. The frame window is initialized with the COMMANDS menu resource. The client window is a new *TDrawMDIClient*, which is a *TMDIClient*-derived class that you'll define a little bit later in this step. The final parameter indicates that menu tracking should be on for this window. The *module* parameter is left to its default value of 0.

The second change is removing the *AssignMenu* call at the end of the *InitMainWindow* function of Step 10. This call is no longer necessary because the menu resource is set up by the second parameter of the *TDecoratedMDIFrame* constructor.

Your *InitMainWindow* function should now look something like this:

```
void
TDrawApp::InitMainWindow()
{
  // Create a decorated MDI frame
  TDecoratedMDIFrame *frame = new TDecoratedMDIFrame("Drawing Pad",
                                                     TResId("COMMANDS"),
                                                     *new TDrawMDIClient,
                                                     true);

  // Construct a status bar
  TStatusBar* sb = new TStatusBar(frame, TGadget::Recessed);

  // Construct a control bar
  TControlBar *cb = new TControlBar(frame);
  cb->Insert(*new TButtonGadget(CM_FILENEW, CM_FILENEW, TButtonGadget::Command));
  cb->Insert(*new TButtonGadget(CM_FILEOPEN, CM_FILEOPEN, TButtonGadget::Command));
  cb->Insert(*new TButtonGadget(CM_FILESAVE, CM_FILESAVE, TButtonGadget::Command));
  cb->Insert(*new TButtonGadget(CM_FILESAVEAS, CM_FILESAVEAS, TButtonGadget::Command));
  cb->Insert(*new TSeparatorGadget);
  cb->Insert(*new TButtonGadget(CM_PENSIZE, CM_PENSIZE, TButtonGadget::Command));
  cb->Insert(*new TButtonGadget(CM_PENCOLOR, CM_PENCOLOR, TButtonGadget::Command));
  cb->Insert(*new TSeparatorGadget);
  cb->Insert(*new TButtonGadget(CM_ABOUT, CM_ABOUT, TButtonGadget::Command));

  // Insert the status bar and control bar into the frame
  frame->Insert(*sb, TDecoratedFrame::Bottom);
  frame->Insert(*cb, TDecoratedFrame::Top);

  // Set the main window and its menu
  SetMainWindow(frame);
}
```

These are the only changes necessary to the *TDrawApp* class to support MDI functionality.

Creating the MDI window classes

The functionality contained in the *TDrawWindow* class in the previous step needs to be divided up into two classes in the MDI model. The reason for this is that there are two windows that handle messages and user input:

- MDI client windows are created during the construction of the MDI frame class. This window is open as long as the frame window is still open (in this case, for the life of the application). This window handles the CM_FILEOPEN, CM_FILENEW, and CM_ABOUT commands.

  When the application is first started up, or when there are no drawings open, the only commands that make sense are opening drawing files, creating new drawings, and opening the About... dialog box. Other commands available in the tutorial application, such as saving drawings, changing the pen size or color, and so on, apply to a particular drawing, which must already be open and displayed in a child window.

- MDI child windows are created by the MDI client window in response to CM_FILENEW or CM_FILEOPEN commands handled by the client window. In the tutorial application, MDI child windows handle the events handled by *TDrawWindow* in Step 10 that aren't handled by *TDrawMDIClient*:

  - WM_LBUTTONDOWN
  - WM_RBUTTONDOWN
  - WM_MOUSEMOVE
  - WM_LBUTTONUP
  - CM_FILESAVE
  - CM_FILESAVEAS
  - CM_PENSIZE
  - CM_PENCOLOR

  Note that each of these commands pertains to a specific drawing or window; that is, each event only makes sense in the context of an open drawing contained in a child window. For example, in order for the user of the application to save a drawing, there must already be a drawing open. Contrast this to the events handled by the MDI client window, which either open a new child window containing a new or existing drawing or are independent of a drawing altogether.

The next sections discuss how to create the MDI client and child window classes for the tutorial application.

Creating the MDI child window class

You need to create a class declaration for the *TDrawMDIChild* class, along with defining the functions for the class. You can reuse most of the class declaration for *TDrawWindow* from Step 10, along with most of the functions with only a few changes.

Declaring the TDrawMDIChild class

The class declaration for *TDrawMDIChild* is very similar to the declaration of the *TDrawWindow* class from Step10. Here are the changes you need to make:

1 Change all occurrences of *TDrawWindow* to *TDrawMDIChild*. This includes the name of the destructor, which otherwise doesn't change.

2 Remove the *CmFileNew*, *CmFileOpen*, and *CmAbout* functions from the class declaration.

3 The constructor for *TMDIChild* requires a *TMDIClient* reference in place of *TDrawWindow*'s *TWindow **. This parameter indicates the parent of the MDI child window. In this case, you want to add a *TDrawMDIClient* reference to the constructor and pass this to the *TMDIChild* constructor. In addition, you should add a **const char*** for the MDI child window's caption.

4 In the response table, remove the entries for handling the CM_FILENEW, CM_FILEOPEN, and CM_ABOUT events.

Your class declaration should look something like this:

```
class TDrawMDIChild : public TMDIChild {
  public:
    TDrawMDIChild(TDrawMDIClient& parent, const char* title = 0);
   ~TDrawMDIChild() { delete DragDC; delete Line; delete Lines; delete FileData; }

  protected:
    TDC *DragDC;
    TPen *Pen;
    TLines *Lines;
    TLine *Line; // To hold a single line at a time that later gets
                 // stuck in Lines
    TOpenSaveDialog::TData
             *FileData;
    bool IsDirty, IsNewFile;

    void GetPenSize(); // GetPenSize always calls Line->SetPen().

    // Override member function of TWindow
    bool CanClose();

    // Message response functions
    void EvLButtonDown(uint, TPoint&);
    void EvRButtonDown(uint, TPoint&);
    void EvMouseMove(uint, TPoint&);
    void EvLButtonUp(uint, TPoint&);
    void Paint(TDC&, bool, TRect&);
    void CmFileSave();
    void CmFileSaveAs();
    void CmPenSize();
    void CmPenColor();
    void SaveFile();
    void OpenFile();

    DECLARE_RESPONSE_TABLE(TDrawMDIChild);
};

DEFINE_RESPONSE_TABLE1(TDrawMDIChild, TWindow)
    EV_WM_LBUTTONDOWN,
    EV_WM_RBUTTONDOWN,
    EV_WM_MOUSEMOVE,
    EV_WM_LBUTTONUP,
```

```
    EV_COMMAND(CM_FILESAVE, CmFileSave),
    EV_COMMAND(CM_FILESAVEAS, CmFileSaveAs),
    EV_COMMAND(CM_PENSIZE, CmPenSize),
    EV_COMMAND(CM_PENCOLOR, CmPenColor),
END_RESPONSE_TABLE;
```

Creating the TDrawMDIChild functions

Just about all of the functions in *TDrawMDIChild* can be carried over from the
TDrawWindow class. The only thing you need to do is change the class identifier in the
function declarations from *TDrawWindow* to *TDrawMDIChild*. For example, the
declaration for the *EvLButtonDown* function changes from this:

```
void
TDrawWindow::EvLButtonDown(uint, TPoint& point)
{
   ⋮
}
```

to this:

```
void
TDrawMDIChild::EvLButtonDown(uint, TPoint& point)
{
   ⋮
}
```

Change the class identifiers for the following functions:

GetPenSize	*CanClose*
EvLButtonDown	*EvRButtonDown*
EvMouseMove	*EvLButtonUp*
Paint	*CmFileSave*
CmFileSaveAs	*CmPenSize*
CmPenColor	*SaveFile*
OpenFile	

There is one minor change you need to make to the *CmFileSaveAs* function. Because the
name of the drawing usually changes when the user calls the File | Save As command,
you need to set the caption of the window to the file name. To do this, use the *SetCaption*
function. This function takes a **char***, which in this case should be the *FileName* member
of the *FileData* object. The *CmFileSaveAs* function should now look like this:

```
void
TDrawMDIChild::CmFileSaveAs()
{
  if (IsNewFile)
    strcpy(FileData->FileName, "");
  if ((TFileSaveDialog(this, *FileData)).Execute() == IDOK)
    SaveFile();
  SetCaption(FileData->FileName);
}
```

Creating the TDrawMDIChild constructor

The main difference between *TDrawMDIChild* and the *TDrawWindow* class, other than the fact that *TDrawMDIChild* has three fewer functions than *TDrawWindow*, is in the constructor.

Initializing data members

Like *TDrawWindow*, *TDrawMDIChild* contains the device context object that displays the drawing and manages the arrays that contain the line drawing information. It also contains the *IsDirty* flag, setting it to false when the drawing is first created or opened and setting it to true when the drawing is modified. So the variables that contain the data for these functions—*DragDC*, *Line*, *Lines*, and *IsDirty*—need to be initialized in the *TDrawMDIChild* constructor. This looks just the same as their initialization in the *TDrawWindow* class.

```
DragDC = 0;
Lines = new TLines(5, 0, 5);
Line = new TLine(TColor::Black, 1);
IsDirty = false;
```

There are some notable changes from *TDrawWindow*'s constructor here, however. First, the *Init* function is no longer called. *TMDIChild* does not provide an *Init* function. Instead, you should just call the base class constructor in the *TDrawMDIChild* initialization list, like so:

```
TDrawMDIChild::TDrawMDIChild(TDrawMDIClient& parent, const char* title)
  : TMDIChild(parent, title)
{
  ⋮
}
```

Initializing file information data members

You can no longer simply initialize the *IsNewFile* variable to true, assuming that you are creating a new drawing whenever you create a window. In earlier steps this was a valid assumption: when the window was created, it hadn't opened a file yet, but was available to be drawn in. The *IsNewFile* flag was only set to false once a drawing had either been saved to a file or an existing drawing had been opened from a file into a window that had already been created.

In this case, the MDI client parent window will handle the file creation and opening operations. It then creates a child window to contain the new or existing drawing. The child window has to find out from the parent whether this is a new drawing or an existing drawing opened from a file.

For the same reason, the MDI child window does not necessarily create the *TOpenSaveDialog::TData* referenced by the *FileData* member. The *TDrawMDIClient* class has a function (or will have, when you get around to creating it) called *GetFileData*. This function takes no parameters and returns a pointer to a *TOpenSaveDialog::TData* object. If the MDI client window is creating the child window in response to a CM_FILEOPEN event, it creates a new *TOpenSaveDialog::TData* object containing the information about the file to be opened. *GetFileData* returns a pointer to that object. But if the client window is creating the child window in response to a CM_FILENEW event, *TDrawMDIClient* doesn't create a *TOpenSaveDialog::TData* object and *GetFileData* returns 0.

So the MDI child can find out whether this is a new drawing or not by testing the return value of *GetFileData*. If *GetFileData* returns a valid object, then it should assign the pointer to this object to its *FileData* member and set *IsNewFile* to false. It can then call the *OpenFile* function to load the drawing just as it did before. If *GetFileData* doesn't return a valid object (that is, it returns 0), the MDI child should set *IsNewFile* to true and create a new *TOpenSaveDialog::TData* object. The file name in the new object is set in the *CmFileSaveAs* function, just as it was in previous steps.

The constructor for *TDrawMDIChild* should look something like this:

```
TDrawMDIChild::TDrawMDIChild(TDrawMDIClient& parent, const char* title)
  : TMDIChild(parent, title)
{
  DragDC = 0;
  Lines = new TLines(5, 0, 5);
  Line = new TLine(TColor::Black, 1);
  IsDirty = false;

  // If the parent returns a valid FileData member, this is an open operation
  // Copy the parent's FileData member, since that'll go away
  if(FileData = parent.GetFileData()) {
    // Not a new file
    IsNewFile = false;
    OpenFile();
  }
  // But if the parent returns 0, this is a new operation
  else {
    // This is a new file
    IsNewFile = true;
    // Create a new FileData member
    FileData = new TOpenSaveDialog::TData(OFN_HIDEREADONLY|OFN_FILEMUSTEXIST,
      "Point Files (*.PTS)|*.pts|", 0, "", "PTS");
  }
}
```

Note that, in the case of an open operation, the child assigns the pointer returned by *GetFileData* to its *FileData* member. Once this is done, the child takes over responsibility for the *TOpenSaveDialog::TData* object, including responsibility for cleaning it up. Since this is already done in the destructor, you don't have to do anything else.

Creating the MDI client window class

The *TDrawMDIClient* class manages the multiple child windows open on its client area and all the attendant functionality, such as creating new children, closing windows either singly or all at one time, tiling or cascading the windows, and arranging the icons of minimized children. *TDrawMDIClient* inherits a great deal of this functionality from the *TMDIClient* class.

TMDIClient functionality
It is important to understand the *TMDIClient* class, for the main reason that it is going to do a lot of work for you. *TMDIClient* is virtually derived from the *TWindow* class.

TMDIClient overrides two of *TWindow*'s virtual functions, *PreProcessMsg* and *Create*, to provide specific keyboard and menu handling functionality required by the client window. *TMDIClient* also handles a number of events, which are described in Table 11.2.

Table 11.2   Events handled by TMDIClient

Event	Response function	Purpose
CM_CREATECHILD	CmCreateChild	Creates a new MDI child window
CM_TILECHILDREN	CmTileChildren	Tiles all non-minimized MDI child windows vertically
CM_TILECHILDRENHORIZ	CmTileChildrenHoriz	Tiles all non-minimized MDI child windows horizontally
CM_CASCADECHILDREN	CmCascadeChildren	Cascades all non-minimized MDI child windows
CM_ARRANGEICONS	CmArrangeIcons	Arranges the icons of all minimized MDI child windows
CM_CLOSECHILDREN	CmCloseChildren	Closes all open MDI child windows

The Drawing Pad application actually only provides menu items for four of these— CM_TILECHILDREN, CM_CASCADECHILDREN, CM_ARRANGEICONS, and CM_CLOSECHILDREN.

These response functions are simply wrappers for other *TMDIClient* functions that actually perform the work necessary. Each response function calls a function with the same name without the *Cm* prefix, so that *CmCreateChild* calls the *CreateChild* function. The only exception is *CmTileChildrenHoriz*, which calls the *TileChildren* function with the MDITILE_HORIZONTAL parameter.

Another function provided by *TMDIClient* is the *GetActiveMDIChild* function, which returns a pointer to the active MDI child window. Note that there can only be one active MDI child window at any time, but there is always one active MDI child window, even if all the MDI child windows are minimized.

There is one other function to discuss, *InitChild*. This is the only function in *TMDIClient* that you need to override in *TDrawMDIClient*. *InitChild* and overriding it to work with *TDrawMDIClient* are discussed on page 77.

Data members in TDrawMDIClient

TDrawMDIClient requires a couple of new data members. These should both be declared private.

The first is *NewChildNum*. The only function of this variable is to keep track of the number of new drawings created by the *CmFileNew* function. This number is used for the window caption of all new drawings. It is initialized to 0 in the *TDrawMDIClient* constructor.

The second is *FileData*, a pointer to a *TOpenSaveDialog::TData* object, just like the *FileData* member of *TDrawMDIChild*. *FileData* is used to hold the file information when a user opens an existing file. It is set to 0 in the constructor. *FileData* is also set to 0 once the MDI child window has been opened. As shown on page 73, the object returned by *GetFileData* is assigned to the *FileData* member of *TDrawMDIChild*. The object returned by *GetFileData* is actually the object (or lack thereof in the case of a new file) pointed to by *TDrawMDIClient*'s *FileData* member.

Adding response functions

In addition to the events handled by *TMDIClient*, *TDrawMDIClient* also handles the events formerly handled by *TDrawWindow* and not handled by *TDrawMDIChild*— CM_FILENEW, CM_FILEOPEN, and CM_ABOUT. The *CmAbout* response function is mostly unchanged from the *TDrawWindow* version, other than changing the class specifier. On the other hand, the *CmFileNew* and *CmFileOpen* functions must be substantially changed.

CmFileNew

The *CmFileNew* function is actually simplified from its *TDrawWindow* version. It no longer has to deal with flushing the line arrays, invalidating the window, and setting flags. Instead it sets *FileData* to 0 so that the MDI child object can tell that it is displaying a new drawing, increments *NewChildNum*, then calls *CreateChild*. *CreateChild* is the function that actually creates and displays the new MDI child window. It is discussed in more detail in the discussion of the *InitChild* function on page 77.

The *CmFileNew* function should now look something like this:

```
void
TDrawMDIClient::CmFileNew()
{
  FileData = 0;
  NewChildNum++;
  CreateChild();
}
```

CmFileOpen

There are a number of differences between the *TDrawWindow* version of *CmFileOpen* and the *TDrawMDIClient* version.

- The *TDrawMDIClient* version no longer needs to call the *CanClose* function, because no windows need to be closed to open a new window.

- The *TDrawMDIClient* needs to create a new *TOpenSaveDialog::TData* object to use with the *TFileOpenDialog* object.

- If the call to *TFileOpenDialog.Execute* returns ID_OK, the *TDrawMDIClient* version calls *CreateChild* instead of *OpenFile*.

- Once the *CreateChild* call returns, you need to set *FileData* to 0. Although it may seem like you should delete the *FileData* object before discarding the pointer to it, the object is actually taken over by the MDI child object, which deletes the object when the MDI child is destroyed.

Your *CmFileOpen* function should look something like this:

```
void
TDrawMDIClient::CmFileOpen()
{
  // Create FileData.
```

```
FileData = new TOpenSaveDialog::TData(OFN_HIDEREADONLY|OFN_FILEMUSTEXIST,
                          "Point Files (*.PTS)|*.pts|", 0,
                          "", "PTS");
// As long as the file open operation goes OK...
if ((TFileOpenDialog(this, *FileData)).Execute() == IDOK)
  // Create the child window.
  CreateChild();
// FileData is no longer needed.
FileData = 0;
}
```

GetFileData

The only new function required for *TDrawMDIClient* is *GetFileData*. This function is
called by *TDrawMDIChild* in its constructor. This function should take no parameters
and return a pointer to a *TOpenSaveDialog::TData* object. Its function is to return a
pointer to the object pointed to by *TDrawMDIClient*'s *FileData* member. If *FileData*
references a valid object (that is, during a file open operation), *GetFileData* should return
FileData. If *FileData* doesn't reference a valid object (that is, during a file new operation),
GetFileData should return 0.

The actual function definition is very simple and can be inlined by defining the function
inside the class declaration. Your *GetFileData* function should look something like this:

```
TOpenSaveDialog::TData *GetFileData() { return FileData ? FileData : 0; }
```

Overriding InitChild

The only *TMDIClient* function that *TDrawMDIChild* overrides is the *InitChild* function.
InitChild takes no parameters and returns a pointer to a *TMDIChild* object. The
CreateChild function calls *InitChild* before creating a new MDI child window. It is in
InitChild that you create the *TMDIChild* or *TMDIChild*-derived object for the MDI child
window. This is the only function of *TMDIClient* that you'll override when you create
the *TDrawMDIClient* class.

The *InitChild* function for *TDrawMDIClient* is fairly straightforward. If *FileData* is 0, you
should create a character array to contain a default window title. This can be initialized
using the value of *NewChildNum* so that each new drawing has a different title.

Then you should create a *TMDIChild** and create a new *TDrawMDIChild* object. The
constructor for *TDrawMDIChild* takes two parameters, a reference to a *TDrawMDIClient*
object for its parent window and a **const char*** containing the MDI child window's
caption. In this case, the first parameter should be the dereferenced **this** pointer. The
second parameter should be either the *FileName* member of the *FileData* object, if
FileData references a valid object, or the character array you created earlier if it doesn't.

Once the MDI child object has been created, you need to call the *SetIcon* function for the object. *SetIcon* associates an icon resource with the function's object. This icon is displayed in the client area when the child window is minimized. You can set the icon to the icon provided for the tutorial application called IDI_TUTORIAL.

The last step of the function is to return the *TMDIChild* pointer. Your *InitChild* function should look something like this:

```
TMDIChild*
TDrawMDIClient::InitChild()
{
  char title[15];
  if(!FileData)
    wsprintf(title, "New drawing %d", NewChildNum);
  TMDIChild* child = new TDrawMDIChild(*this, FileData ? FileData->FileName : title);
  child->SetIcon(GetApplication(), TResId("IDI_TUTORIAL"));
  return child;
}
```

Where to find more information

MDI frame, client, and child windows are described in Chapter 25.

Chapter

12

Using the Doc/View programming model

Step 12 introduces the Doc/View model of programming, which is based on the principle of separating data from the interface for that data. Essentially, the data is encapsulated in a document object, which is derived from the *TDocument* class, and displayed on the screen and manipulated by the user through a view object, which is derived from the *TView* class.

The Doc/View model permits a greater degree of flexibility in how you present data than does a model that links data encapsulation and user interface into a single class. Using the Doc/View model, you can define a document class to contain any type of data, such as a simple text file, a database file, or in this tutorial, a line drawing. You can then create a number of different view classes, each of which displays the same data in a different manner or lets the user interact with that data in a different way.

For Step 12, however, you'll simply convert the application from its current model to the Doc/View model. Step 12 uses the SDI model so that you can more easily see the changes necessary for converting to Doc/View without being distracted by the extra code added in Step 11 to support MDI functionality. (You'll create an MDI Doc/View application in Step 13.) But even though the code for Step 12 will look very different from the code from Step 10, the running application for Step 12 will look nearly identical to that of Step 10. You can find the source for Step 12 in the files STEP12.CPP, STEP12.RC, STEP12DV.CPP, and STEP12DV.RC in the directory EXAMPLES\OWL\TUTORIAL.

Organizing the application source

The source for Step 12 is divided into four source files:

• STEP12.CPP contains the application object and its member definitions. It also contains the *OwlMain* function.

- STEP12.RC contains identifiers for events controlled by the application object, the resources for the frame window and its decorations, the About dialog box, and the application menu.

- STEP12DV.CPP contains the *TLine* class, the document class *TDrawDocument*, the view class *TDrawView*, and the associated member function definitions for each of these classes.

- STEP12DV.RC contains identifiers for events controlled by the view object and the resources for the view.

You should divide your Doc/View code this way to distinguish the document and its supporting view from the application code. The application code provides the support framework for the document and view classes, but doesn't contribute directly to the functionality of the Doc/View model. This also demonstrates good design practice for code reusability.

Doc/View model

The Doc/View model is based on three ObjectWindows classes:

- The *TDocument* class encapsulates and controls access to a set of data. A document object handles user access to that data through input from associated view objects. A document object can be associated with numerous views at the same time (for the sake of simplicity in this example, the document object is associated with only a single view object).

- The *TView* class provides an interface between a document object and the user interface. A view object controls how data from a document object is displayed on the screen. A view object can be associated with only a single document object at any one time.

- The *TDocManager* class coordinates the associations between a document object and its view objects. The document manager provides a default File menu and default handling for each of the choices on the File menu. It also maintains a list of document templates, each of which specifies a relationship between a document class and a view class.

The *TDocument* and *TView* classes provide the abstract functionality for document and view objects. You must provide the specific functionality for your own document and view classes. You must also explicitly create the document manager and attach it to the application object. You must also provide the document templates for the document manager. These steps are described in the following sections.

TDrawDocument class

The *TDrawDocument* class is derived from the ObjectWindows class *TFileDocument*, which is in turn derived from the *TDocument* class. *TDocument* provides a number of input and output functions. These **virtual** functions return dummy values and have no real functionality. *TFileDocument* provides the basic functionality required to access a data file in the form of a stream.

TDrawDocument uses the functionality contained in *TFileDocument* to access line data stored in a file. It uses a *TLines* array to contain the lines, the same as in earlier steps. The array is referenced through a pointer called *Lines*.

Creating and destroying TDrawDocument

TDrawDocument's constructor takes a single parameter, a *TDocument* *, that is a pointer to the parent document. A document can be a parent of a number of other documents, treating the data contained in those documents as if it were part of the parent. The constructor passes the parent pointer on to *TFileDocument*. The constructor also initializes the *Lines* data member to 0.

The destructor for *TDrawDocument* deletes the *TLines* object pointed to by *Lines*.

Storing line data

The document class you're going to create controls access to the data contained in a drawing. But you still need some way to store the data. You've already created the *TLine* class and the *TLines* array in previous steps. Luckily, this code can be recycled. The line data for each document is stored in a *TLines* array, and accessed by the document through a **protected** *TLines* * data member called *Lines*.

The *TPoints* and *TLines* arrays, their iterators, and the *TLine* class are now defined in the STEP12DV.CPP file. In the Doc/View model, these classes are an integral part of the document class you're about to build. The code for these classes doesn't change at all from Step 10.

Implementing TDocument virtual functions

TDrawDocument needs to implement a few of the **virtual** functions inherited from *TDocument*. These functions provide streaming and the ability to commit changes to the document or to discard all changes made to the document since the last save.

Opening and closing a drawing

Although *TFileDocument* provides the basic functionality required for stream input and output, it doesn't know how to read the data for a line. To provide this ability, you need to override the *Open* and *Close* functions.

Here's the signature of the *Open* function:

```
bool Open(int mode, const char far* path=0);
```

where:

- *mode* is the file open mode. In this case, you can ignore the mode parameter; the file is opened the same way each time, with the *ofRead* flag.

- *path* contains the document path. If a path is specified, the document's current path is changed to that path. If no path is specified (that is, *path* takes its default value), the path is left as it is. The path is used by the document when creating the document's streams.

The *Open* function is similar to the *OpenFile* function used in earlier steps in the tutorial. There are differences, though:

- The *Open* function creates the *TLines* array for the document object. In earlier steps, this was done in the *TDrawWindow* constructor, because *TDrawWindow* was responsible for containing all the *TLine* objects. Now the document is responsible for containing all the *TLine* objects, so it needs to create storage space for the data before it reads it in.

- If *path* is passed in, *Open* sets the document path to *path* with the *SetDocPath* function.

- *Open* checks whether the document has a path. If the document doesn't have a path, it is a new document, in which case there's no need to read in data from a file. If the document has a path, *Open* calls the *InStream* function. This function is defined in *TFileDocument* and returns a *TInStream* *.

  TInStream is the standard input stream class used by Doc/View classes. *TInStream* is derived from *TStream* and *istream*. *TStream* is an abstract base class that lets documents access standard streams. *TInStream* is essentially a standard *istream* adapted for use with the Doc/View model. There's also a corresponding *TOutStream* class, derived from *TStream* and *ostream*. You'll use *TOutStream* when you create the *Commit* function.

- After the input stream has been created, the data is read in and placed in the *TLines* array pointed to by *Lines*. When all the data is read in, the input stream is deleted.

- *Open* then calls the *SetDirty* function, passing false as the function parameter. The *SetDirty* function, and its equivalent access function *isDirty*, are the equivalent of the *IsDirty* flag in earlier steps of the tutorial. A document is considered to be dirty if it contains any changes to its data that have not been saved or committed.

- The last thing the *Open* function needs to do is return. If the document was successfully opened, *Open* returns true.

Here's how the code for your *Open* function might look:

```
bool
TDrawDocument::Open(int /*mode*/, const char far* path)
{
  Lines = new TLines(5, 0, 5);
  if (path)
    SetDocPath(path);
  if (GetDocPath()) {
    TInStream* is = InStream(ofRead);
    if (!is)
      return false;

    unsigned numLines;
    char fileinfo[100];
```

```
  *is >> numLines;
  is->getline(fileinfo, sizeof(fileinfo));
  while (numLines-) {
    TLine line;
    *is >> line;
    Lines->Add(line);
  }
  delete is;
}
SetDirty(false);
NotifyViews(vnRevert, false);
return true;
}
```

Closing the drawing is less complicated. The *Close* function discards the document's data and cleans up. In this case, it deletes the *TLines* array referenced by the *Lines* data member and returns true. Here's how the code for your *Close* function should look:

```
bool TDrawDocument::Close()
{
  delete Lines;
  Lines = 0;
  return true;
}
```

Lines is set to 0, both in the constructor and after closing the document, so that you can easily tell whether the document is open. If the document is open, *Lines* points to a *TLines* array, and is therefore not 0. But setting *Lines* to 0 makes it easy to check whether the document is open. The *IsOpen* function lets you check this from outside the document object:

```
bool IsOpen() { return Lines != 0; }
```

Saving and discarding changes

TDocument provides two functions for saving and discarding changes to a document:

- The *Commit* function commits changes made in the document's associated views by incorporating the changes into the document, then saving the data to persistent storage. *Commit* takes a single parameter, a *bool*. If this parameter is false, *Commit* saves the data only if the document is dirty. If the parameter is true, *Commit* does a complete write of the data. The default for this parameter is false.

- The *Revert* function discards any changes in the document's views, then forces the views to load the data contained in the document and display it. *Revert* takes a single parameter, a *bool*. If this parameter is true, the view clears its window and does not reload the data from the document. The default for this parameter is false.

For *TDrawDocument*, the document is updated as each line is drawn in the view window. The only function of *Commit* for the *TDrawDocument* class is to save the data to a file.

Commit checks to see if the document is dirty. If not, and if the force parameter is false, *Commit* returns true, indicating that the operation was successful.

If the document is dirty, or if the force parameter is true, *Commit* saves the data. The procedure to save the data is similar to the *SaveFile* function in previous steps, but, as with the *Open* function, there are a few differences.

Commit calls the *OutStream* function to open an output stream. This function is defined in *TFileDocument* and returns a *TOutStream **. *Commit* then writes the data to the output stream. The procedure for this is almost exactly identical to that used in the old *SaveFile* function.

After writing the data to the output stream, *Commit* turns the *IsDirty* flag off by calling *SetDirty* with a false parameter. It then returns true, indicating that the operation was successful.

Here's how the code for your *Commit* function might look:

```
bool
TDrawDocument::Commit(bool force)
{
  if (!IsDirty() && !force)
    return true;

  TOutStream* os = OutStream(ofWrite);
  if (!os)
    return false;

  // Write the number of lines in the figure
  *os << Lines->GetItemsInContainer();

  // Append a description using a resource string
  *os << ' ' << string(*GetDocManager().GetApplication(),IDS_FILEINFO) << '

  // Get an iterator for the array of lines
  TLinesIterator i(*Lines);

  // While the iterator is valid (i.e. you haven't run out of lines)
  while (i) {
    // Copy the current line from the iterator and increment the array.
    *os << i++;
  }
  delete os;

  SetDirty(false);
  return true;
}
```

There's only one thing in the *Commit* function that you haven't seen before:

```
// Append a description using a resource string
*os << ' ' << string(*GetDocManager().GetApplication(), IDS_FILEINFO) << '
```

This uses a special constructor for the ANSI *string* class:

```
string(HINSTANCE instance, uint id, int len = 255);
```

This constructor lets you get a string resource from any Windows application. You specify the application by passing an HINSTANCE as the first parameter of the *string* constructor. In this case, you can get the current application's instance through the document manager. The *GetDocManager* function returns a pointer to the document's document manager. In turn, the *GetApplication* function returns a pointer to the application that contains the document manager. This is converted implicitly into an HINSTANCE by a conversion operator in the *TModule* class. The second parameter of the *string* constructor is the resource identifier of a string defined in STEP12DV.RC. This string contains version information that can be used to identify the application that created the document.

The *Revert* function takes a single parameter, a bool indicating whether the document's views need to refresh their display from the document's data. *Revert* calls the *TFileDocument* version of the *Revert* function, which in turn calls the *TDocument* version of *Revert*. The base class function calls the *NotifyViews* function with the **vnRevert** event. The second parameter of the *NotifyViews* function is set to the parameter passed to the *TDrawDocument::Revert* function. *TFileDocument::Revert* sets *IsDirty* to false and returns. If *TFileDocument::Revert* returns false, the *TDrawDocument* should also return false.

If *TFileDocument::Revert* returns true, the *TDrawDocument* function should check the parameter passed to *Revert*. If it is false (that is, if the view needs to be refreshed), *Revert* calls the *Open* function to open the document file, reload the data, and display it.

Here's how the code for your *Revert* function might look:

```
bool
TDrawDocument::Revert(bool clear)
{
  if (!TFileDocument::Revert(clear))
    return false;
  if (!clear)
    Open(0);
  return true;
}
```

Accessing the document's data

There are two main ways to access data in *TDrawDocument*: adding a line (such as a new line when the user draws in a view) and getting a reference to a line in the document (such as getting a reference to each line when repainting the window). You can add two functions, *AddLine* and *GetLine*, to take care of each of these actions.

The *AddLine* function adds a new line to the document's *TLines* array. The line is passed to the *AddLines* function as a *TLine* **&**. After adding the line to the array, *AddLine* sets the *IsDirty* flag to true by calling *SetDirty*. It then returns the index number of the line it just added. Here's how the code for your *AddLines* function might look:

```
int
TDrawDocument::AddLine(TLine& line)
{
  int index = Lines->GetItemsInContainer();
  Lines->Add(line);
```

```
        SetDirty(true);
        return index;
    }
```

The *GetLine* function takes an **int** parameter. This **int** is the index of the desired line. *GetLine* should first check to see if the document is open. If not, it can try to open the document. If the document isn't open and *GetLine* can't open it, it returns 0, meaning that it couldn't find a valid document from which to get the line.

Once you know the document is valid, you should also check to make sure that the index isn't too high. Compare the index to the return value from the *GetItemsInContainer* function. As long as the index is less, you can return a pointer to the *TLine* object. Here's how the code for your *GetLine* function might look:

```
TLine*
TDrawDocument::GetLine(int index)
{
    if (!IsOpen() && !Open(ofRead | ofWrite))
        return 0;
    return index < Lines->GetItemsInContainer() ? &(*Lines)[index] : 0;
}
```

TDrawView class

The *TDrawView* class is derived from the ObjectWindows *TWindowView* class, which is in turn derived from the *TView* and *TWindow* classes. *TView* doesn't have any inherent windowing capabilities; a *TView*-derived class gets these capabilities by either adding a window member or pointer or by mixing in a window class with a view class.

TWindowView takes the latter approach, mixing *TWindow* and *TView* to provide a single class with both basic windowing and viewing capabilities. By deriving from this general-purpose class, *TDrawView* needs to add only the functionality required to work with the *TDrawDocument* class.

The *TDrawView* is similar to the *TDrawWindow* class used in previous steps. In fact, you'll see that a lot of the functions from *TDrawWindow* are brought directly to *TDrawView* with little or no modifications.

TDrawView data members

The *TDrawView* class has a number of **protected** data members.

```
TDC *DragDC;
TPen *Pen;
TLine *Line;
TDragDocument *DrawDoc;
```

Three of these should look familiar to you. *DragDC*, *Pen*, and *Line* perform the same function in *TDrawView* as they did in *TDrawWindow*.

Although a document can exist with no associated views, the opposite isn't true. A view must be associated with an existing document. *TDrawView* is attached to its document when it is constructed. It keeps track of its document through a *TDrawDocument* * called *DrawDoc*. The base class *TView* has a *TDocument* * member called *Doc* that serves the same basic purpose. In fact, during base class construction, *Doc* is set to point at the *TDrawDocument* object passed to the *TDrawView* constructor. *DrawDoc* is added to force proper type compliance when the document pointer is accessed.

Creating the TDrawView class

The *TDrawView* constructor takes two parameters, a *TDrawDocument* **&** (a reference to the view's associated document) and a *TWindow* * (a pointer to the parent window). The parent window defaults to 0 if no value is supplied. The constructor passes its two parameters to the *TWindowView* constructor, and initializes the *DrawDoc* member to point at the document passed as the first parameter.

The constructor also sets *DragDC* to 0 and initializes *Line* with a new *TLine* object.

The last thing the constructor does is set up the view's menu. You can use the *TMenuDescr* class to set up a menu descriptor from a menu resource. Here's the *TMenuDescr* constructor:

```
TMenuDescr(TResId id);
```

where *id* is the resource identifier of the menu resource.

The *TMenuDescr* constructor takes the menu resource and divides it up into six groups. It determines which group a particular menu in the resource goes into by the presence of separators in the menu resource. The only separators that actually divide the resource into groups are at the pop-up level; that is, the separators aren't contained in a menu, but they're at the level of menu items that appear on the menu bar. For example, the following code shows a small snippet of a menu resource:

```
COMMANDS MENU
{
  // Always starts with the File group
  POPUP "&File"
  {
    MENUITEM "&Open", CM_FILEOPEN
    MENUITEM "&Save", CM_FILESAVE
  }
  MENUITEM SEPARATOR
    // Edit group
  MENUITEM SEPARATOR
    // Container group
  MENUITEM SEPARATOR
  // This one is in the Object group
  POPUP "&Objects"
  {
    MENUITEM "&Copy object", CM_OBJECTCOPY
    MENUITEM "Cu&t object", CM_OBJECTCUT
  }

  // No more items, meaning the Window group and Help group are also empty
}
```

A menu descriptor would separate this resource into groups like this: the File menu would be placed in the first group, called the File group. The second group (Edit group) and the third group (Container group) are empty, because there are no pop-up menus between the separators that delimit those groups. The Tools menu is in the Object group. Because there are no menu resources after the Tools menu, the last two groups, the Object group and Help group, are also empty.

Although the groups have particular names, these names just represent a common name for the menu group. The menu represented by each group does not necessarily have that name. The document manager provides a default File menu, but the other menu names can be set in the menu resource.

In this case, the view supplies a menu resource called IDM_DRAWVIEW, which is contained in the file STEP12DV.RC. This menu is called Tools, which has the same choices on it as the Tools menu in earlier steps: Pen Size and Pen Color. To insert the Tools menu as the second menu on the menu bar when the view is created or activated, the menu resource is set up to place the Tools menu in the second group, the Edit group, so that the menu resource looks something like this:

```
IDM_DRAWVIEW MENU
{
  // Edit Group
  MENUITEM SEPARATOR
  POPUP "&Tools"
  {
    MENUITEM "Pen &Size",   CM_PENSIZE
    MENUITEM "Pen &Color",  CM_PENCOLOR
  }
}
```

You can install the menu descriptor as the view menu using the *TView* function *SetViewMenu* function, which takes a single parameter, a *TMenuDescr* *. *SetViewMenu* sets the menu descriptor as the view's menu. When the view is created, this menu is merged with the application menu.

Here's how the call to set up the view menu should look:

```
SetViewMenu(new TMenuDescr(IDM_DRAWVIEW));
```

The destructor for the view deletes the device context referenced by *DragDC* and the *TLine* object referenced by *Line*.

Naming the class

Every view class should define the function *StaticName*, which takes no parameters and returns a **static const char far** *. This function should return the name of the view class. Here's how the *StaticName* function might look:

```
static const char far* StaticName() {return "Draw View";}
```

Protected functions

TDrawView has a couple of **protected** access functions to provide functionality for the class.

The *GetPenSize* function is identical to the *TDrawWindow* function *GetPenSize*. This function opens a *TInputDialog*, gets a new pen size from the user, and changes the pen size for the window and calls the *SetPen* function of the current line.

The *Paint* function is a little different from the *Paint* function in the *TDrawWindow* class, but it does basically the same thing. Instead of using an iterator to go through the lines in an array, *TDrawView::Paint* calls the *GetLine* function of the view's associated document. The return from *GetLine* is assigned to a **const** *TLine ** called *line*. If *line* is not 0 (that is, if *GetLine* returned a valid line), *Paint* then calls the line's *Draw* function. Remember that the *TLine* class is unchanged from Step 10. The line draws itself in the window.

Here's how the code for the *Paint* function might look:

```
void
TDrawView::Paint(TDC& dc, bool, TRect&)
{
  // Iterates through the array of line objects.
  int i = 0;
  const TLine* line;
  while ((line = DrawDoc->GetLine(i++)) != 0)
    line->Draw(dc);
}
```

Event handling in TDrawView

The *TDrawView* class handles many of the events that were previously handled by the *TDrawWindow* class. Most of the other events that *TDrawWindow* handled that aren't handled by *TDrawView* are handled by the application object and the document manager; this is discussed later in Step 12.

In addition, *TDrawView* handles two new messages: VN_COMMIT and VN_REVERT. These view notification messages are sent by the view's document when the document's *Commit* and *Revert* functions are called.

Here's the response table definition for *TDrawView*:

```
DEFINE_RESPONSE_TABLE1(TDrawView, TWindowView)
  EV_WM_LBUTTONDOWN,
  EV_WM_RBUTTONDOWN,
  EV_WM_MOUSEMOVE,
  EV_WM_LBUTTONUP,
  EV_COMMAND(CM_PENSIZE, CmPenSize),
  EV_COMMAND(CM_PENCOLOR, CmPenColor),
  EV_VN_COMMIT,
  EV_VN_REVERT,
END_RESPONSE_TABLE;
```

The following functions are nearly the same in *TDrawView* as the corresponding functions in *TDrawWindow*. Any modifications to the functions are noted in the right column of the table:

Function	TDrawView version
EvLButtonDown	Does not set *IsDirty*. This is taken care of in *EvLButtonUp*.
EvRButtonDown	No change.
EvMouseMove	No change.
EvLButtonUp	Checks to see if the mouse was moved after the left button press. If so, calls the document's *AddLine* function to add the point.
CmPenSize	No change.
CmPenColor	No change.

The *VnCommit* function always returns true. In a more complex application, this function would add any cached data to the document, but in this application, the data is added to the document as each line is drawn.

The *VnRevert* function invalidates the display area, clearing it and repainting the drawing in the window. It then returns true.

Defining document templates

Once you've created a document class and an accompanying view class, you have to associate them so they can function together. An association between a document class and a view class is known as a document template class. The document template class is used by the document manager to determine what view class should be opened to display a document.

You can create a document template class using the macro DEFINE_DOC_TEMPLATE_CLASS, which takes three parameters. The first parameter is the name of the document class, the second is the name of the view class, and the third is the name of the document template class. The macro to create a template class for the *TDrawDocument* and *TDrawView* classes would look like this:

```
DEFINE_DOC_TEMPLATE_CLASS(TDrawDocument, TDrawView, DrawTemplate);
```

Once you've created a document template class, you need to create a document registration table. Document registration tables contain information about a particular Doc/View template class instance, such as what the template class does, the default file extension, and so on. A document registration table is actually an object of type *TRegList*, although you don't have to worry about what the object actually looks; you'll very rarely need to directly access a document registration table object.

Start creating a document registration table by declaring the BEGIN_REGISTRATION macro. This macro takes a single parameter, the name of the document registration class, which is used as the name of the *TRegList* object.

The next lines in your document registration table create entries in the document registration table. For a Doc/View template, you need to enter four items into this table:

- A description of the Doc/View template

- The default file extension when saving a file
- A filter string that is used to filter file names in the current directory
- Document creation flags

For the first three of these, you specify them using the REGDATA macro:

```
REGDATA(key, value)
```

key indicates what the *value* string pertains to. There are three different keys you need for creating a document registration table:

- *description* indicates *value* is the template description
- *extension* indicates *value* is the default file extension
- *docfilter* indicates *value* is the file-name filter
- The other macro you need to use to create a document registration table is the REGDOCFLAGS macro. This macro takes a single parameter, one or more document creation flags; if you specify more than one, the flags should be ORed together. For now, you can get by using two flags, *dtAutoDelete* and *dtHidden*. These flags are described in the *ObjectWindows Reference Guide* and Chapter 28.

A typical document registration table looks something like this:

```
BEGIN_REGISTRATION(DrawReg)
  REGDATA(description, "Point Files (*.PTS)")
  REGDATA(extension, ".PTS")
  REGDATA(docfilter, "*.pts")
  REGDOCFLAGS(dtAutoDelete | dtHidden)
END_REGISTRATION
```

Once you've created a document registration table, all you need to do is create an instance of the class. The class type is the name of the document template class. You also should give the instance a meaningful name. The constructor for any document template class looks like this:

```
TplName name(TRegList& reglist);
```

where:

- *TplName* is the class name you specified when defining the template class.
- *name* is whatever name you want to give this instance.
- *reglist* is the name of the registration table you created; it's the same name you passed as the parameter to the BEGIN_REGISTRATION macro.

Here's how the template instance for *TDrawDocument* and *TDrawView* classes might look:

```
DrawTemplate drawTpl(DrawReg);
```

Supporting Doc/View in the application

STEP12.CPP contains the code for the application object and the definition of the main window. The application object provides a framework for the Doc/View classes defined in STEP12DV.CPP. This section discusses the changes to the *TDrawApp* class that are required to support the new Doc/View classes. The *OwlMain* function remains unchanged.

InitMainWindow function

The *InitMainWindow* function requires some minor changes to support the Doc/View model:

- The *TDecoratedFrame* constructor takes a 0 in place of the *TDrawWindow* constructor for the frame's client window. The client window is set in the *EvNewView* function.

- The *AssignMenu* call is changed to a *SetMenuDescr* call. The *SetMenuDescr* function, which is inherited from *TFrameWindow*, takes a *TMenuDescr* as its only parameter. The *TMenuDescr* object should be built using the COMMANDS menu resource. This call looks something like this:

```
GetMainWindow()->SetMenuDescr(TMenuDescr("COMMANDS"));
```

- A call to *SetDocManager* is added. This function sets the *DocManager* member of the *TApplication* class. It takes a single parameter, a *TDocManager **.

- The *TDocManager* constructor takes a single parameter, which consists of one or more flags ORed together. The only flag that is required is either *dmSDI* or *dmMDI*. These flags set the document manager to supervise a single-document interface (*dmSDI*) or a multiple-document interface (*dmMDI*) application.

In this case, you're creating an SDI application, so you should specify the *dmSDI* flag. In addition, you should specify the *dmMenu* flag, which instructs the document manager to provide its default menu.

The call to the *SetDocManager* function should look like this:

```
SetDocManager(new TDocManager(dmSDI | dmMenu));
```

InitInstance function

The *InitInstance* function is overridden because there are a couple of function calls that need to be made *after* the main window has been created. *InitInstance* should first call the *TApplication* version of *InitInstance*. That function calls the *InitMainWindow* function, which constructs the main window object, then creates the main window.

After the base class *InitInstance* function has been called, you need to call the main window's *DragAcceptFiles* function, specifying the true parameter. This enables the main window to accept files that are dropped in the window. Drag and drop functionality is handled through the application's response table, as discussed in the next section.

To enable the user to begin drawing in the window as soon as the application starts up, you also need to call the *CmFileNew* function of the document manager. This creates a new untitled document and view in the main window.

The *InitInstance* function should look something like this:

```
void
TDrawApp::InitInstance()
{
  TApplication::InitInstance();
  GetMainWindow()->DragAcceptFiles(true);
  GetDocManager()->CmFileNew();
}
```

Adding functions to TDrawApp

The *TDrawApp* class adds a number of new functions. It overrides the *TApplication* version of *InitInstance*. It adds a response table and takes the *CmAbout* function from the *TDrawWindow* class. It adds drag and drop capability by adding the EV_WM_DROPFILES macro to the response table and adding the *EvDropFiles* function to handle the event. It also handles a new event, WM_OWLVIEW, that indicates a view request message. Two functions handle this message. *EvNewView* handles a WM_OWLVIEW message with the *dnCreate* parameter. *EvCloseView* handles a WM_OWLVIEW message with the *dnClose* parameter.

Here's the new declaration of the *TDrawApp* class, along with its response table definition:

```
class TDrawApp : public TApplication
{
  public:
    TDrawApp() : TApplication() {}

  protected:
    // Override methods of TApplication
    void InitInstance();
    void InitMainWindow();

    // Event handlers
    void EvNewView   (TView& view);
    void EvCloseView(TView& view);
    void EvDropFiles(TDropInfo dropInfo);
    void CmAbout();
  DECLARE_RESPONSE_TABLE(TDrawApp);
};

DEFINE_RESPONSE_TABLE1(TDrawApp, TApplication)
  EV_OWLVIEW(dnCreate, EvNewView),
  EV_OWLVIEW(dnClose,  EvCloseView),
  EV_WM_DROPFILES,
  EV_COMMAND(CM_ABOUT, CmAbout),
END_RESPONSE_TABLE;
```

CmAbout function

The *CmAbout* function is nearly identical to the *TDrawWindow* version. The only difference is that the *CmAbout* function is no longer contained in its parent window class. Instead of using the **this** pointer as its parent, it substitutes a call to *GetMainWindow* function. The function should now look like this:

```
void
TDrawApp::CmAbout()
{
   TDialog(GetMainWindow(), IDD_ABOUT).Execute();
}
```

EvDropFiles function

The *EvDropFiles* function handles the WM_DROPFILES event. This function gets one parameter, a *TDropInfo* object. The *TDropInfo* object contains functions to find the number of files dropped, the names of the files, where the files were dropped, and so on.

Because this is an SDI application, if the number of files is greater than one, you need to warn the user that only one file can be dropped into the application at a time. To find the number of files dropped in, you can call the *TDropInfo* function *DragQueryFileCount*, which takes no parameters and returns the number of files dropped. If the file count is greater than one, pop up a message box to warn the user.

Now you need to get the name of the file dropped in. You can find the length of the file path string using the *TDropInfo* function *DragQueryFileNameLen*, which takes a single parameter, the index of the file about which you're inquiring. Because you know there's only one file, this parameter should be a 0. This function returns the length of the file path.

Allocate a string of the necessary length, then call the *TDropInfo* function *DragQueryFile*. This function takes three parameters. The first is the index of the file. Again, this parameter should be a 0. The second parameter is a **char ***, the file path. The third parameter is the length of the file path. This function fills in the file path in the **char** array from the second parameter.

Once you've got the file name, you need to get the proper template for the file type. To do this, call the document manager's *MatchTemplate* function. This function searches the document manager's list of document templates and returns a pointer to the first document template with a pattern that matches the dropped file. This pointer is a *TDocTemplate **. If the document manager can't find a matching template, it returns 0.

Once you've located a template, you can call the template's *CreateDoc* function with the file path as the parameter to the function. This creates a new document and its corresponding view, and opens the file into the document.

Once the file has been opened, you must make sure to call the *DragFinish* function. This function releases the memory that Windows allocates during drag and drop operations.

Here's how the *EvDropFiles* function should look:

```
void
TDrawApp::EvDropFiles(TDropInfo dropInfo)
{
  if (dropInfo.DragQueryFileCount() != 1)
    ::MessageBox(0,"Can only drop 1 file in SDI mode","Drag/Drop Error",MB_OK);
  else {
    int fileLength = dropInfo.DragQueryFileNameLen(0)+1;
    char* filePath = new char [fileLength];
    dropInfo.DragQueryFile(0, filePath, fileLength);
    TDocTemplate* tpl = GetDocManager()->MatchTemplate(filePath);
    if (tpl)
      tpl->CreateDoc(filePath);
    delete filePath;
  }
  dropInfo.DragFinish();
}
```

EvNewView function

The WM_OWLVIEW event informs the application when a view-related event has happened. All functions that handle WM_OWLVIEW events return **void** and take a single parameter, a *TView* &. When the event's parameter is *dnCreate*, this indicates that a new view object has been created and requires the application to set up the view's window.

In this case, you need to set the view's window as the client of the main window. There are two functions you need to call to do this: *GetWindow* and *SetClientWindow*.

The *GetWindow* function is member of the view class. It takes no parameters and returns a *TWindow* *. This points to the view's window.

Once you have a pointer to the view's window, you can set that window as the client window with the main window's *SetClientWindow* function, which takes a single parameter, a *TWindow* *, and sets that window object as the client window. This function returns a *TWindow* *. This return value is a pointer to the old client window, if there was one.

Before continuing, you should check that the new client window was successfully created. *TView* provides the *IsOK* function, which returns false if the window wasn't created successfully. If *IsOK* returns false, you should call *SetClientWindow* again, passing a 0 as the window pointer, and return from the function.

If the window was created successfully, you need to check the view's menu with the *GetViewMenu* function. If the view has a menu, use the *MergeMenu* function of the main window to merge the view's menu with the window's menu.

The code for *EvNewView* should look like this:

```
void
TDrawApp::EvNewView(TView& view)
{
  GetMainWindow()->SetClientWindow(view.GetWindow());
  if (!view.IsOK())
```

```
        GetMainWindow()->SetClientWindow(0);
    else if (view.GetViewMenu())
      GetMainWindow()->MergeMenu(*view.GetViewMenu());
  }
```

EvCloseView function

If the parameter for the WM_OWLVIEW event is *dnClose*, this indicates that a view has been closed. This is handled by the *EvCloseView* parameter. Like the *EvNewView* function, the *EvCloseView* function returns **void** and takes a *TView* & parameter.

To close a view, you need to remove the view's window as the client of the main window. To do this, call the main window's *SetClientWindow* function, passing a 0 as the window pointer. You can then restore the menu of the frame window to its former state using the *RestoreMenu* function of the main window.

When the *EvNewView* function creates a new view, the caption of the frame window is set to the file path of the document. You need to reset the main window's caption using the *SetCaption* function.

Here's the code for the *EvCloseView* function:

```
void
TDrawApp::EvCloseView(TView& /*view*/)
{
  GetMainWindow()>SetClientWindow(0);
  GetMainWindow()->RestoreMenu();
  GetMainWindow()->SetCaption("Drawing Pad");
}
```

Where to find more information

Here's a guide to where you can find more information on the topics introduced in this step:

- The *InitMainWindow* and *InitInstance* functions are discussed in Chapter 20.
- Menu and menu descriptor objects are described in Chapter 26.
- The Doc/View classes are discussed in Chapter 28.
- The drag and drop functions are discussed in the *ObjectWindows Reference*.

13

Moving the DOC/View application to MDI

The Doc/View model is much more useful when it is used in a multiple-document interface (MDI) application. The ability to have multiple child windows in a frame lets you open more than one view for a document. You can find the source for Step 13 in the files STEP13.CPP, STEP13.RC, STEP13DV.CPP, and STEP13DV.RC in the directory EXAMPLES\OWL\TUTORIAL.

In Step 13, you'll add MDI capability to the application. This requires new functionality in the *TDrawDocument* and *TDrawView* classes. In addition, you'll add new features such as the ability to delete or modify an existing line and the ability to undo changes. You'll also create a new view class called *TDrawListView* to take advantage of the ability to display multiple views. *TDrawListView* shows an alternate view of the drawing stored in *TDrawDocument*, displaying it as a list of line information.

Supporting MDI in the application

STEP13.CPP contains the code for the application object and the definition of the main window. The application object provides a framework for the Doc/View classes defined in STEP13DV.CPP. This section discusses the changes to the *TDrawApp* class that are required to provide MDI support for your Doc/View application. The *OwlMain* function remains unchanged.

Changing to a decorated MDI frame

To support an MDI application, you need to change the *TDecoratedFrame* you've been using to a *TDecoratedMDIFrame*. Then, inside the decorated MDI frame, you need to create an MDI client window with the class *TMDIClient*. To easily locate the client window later, add a *TMDIClient ** to your *TDrawApp* class. Call the pointer *Client*. This client window contains the MDI child windows that display the various views.

The constructor for *TDecoratedMDIFrame* is described on page 66. The parameters for the constructor in this case are different from the parameters used in creating the decorated MDI frame used in Step 11.

- There's no menu resource for this window. Instead, you'll construct a *TMenuDescr*, just as you did for Step 12.

- You need to create the client window explicitly so that you can assign it to the *Client* data member. Unlike Step 11, where you used a custom client window class derived from *TMDIClient*, in this step you can use a *TMDIClient* object directly. The functionality that was added to the *TDrawMDIClient* class, such as opening files, creating new drawings, and so on, is now handled by the document manager. Thus, *TMDIClient* is sufficient to handle the chore of managing the MDI child windows.

- Lastly, you should turn menu tracking on.

The window constructor should look like this:

```
TDecoratedMDIFrame* frame = new TDecoratedMDIFrame("Drawing Pad", 0,
                                    *(Client = new TMDIClient)true);
```

Changing the hint mode

You might have noticed in Step 12 that the hint text for control bar buttons didn't appear until you actually press the button. You can change the hint mode so that the text shows up when you just run the mouse over the top of the button.

To make this happen, call the control bar's *SetHintMode* function with the *TGadgetWindow::EnterHints* parameter:

```
cb->SetHintMode(TGadgetWindow::EnterHints);
```

This causes hints to be displayed when the cursor is over a button, even if the button isn't pressed. You can reset the hint mode by calling *SetHintMode* with the *TGadgetWindow::PressHints* parameter. You can also turn off menu tracking altogether by calling *SetHintMode* with the *TGadgetWindow::NoHints* parameter.

Setting the main window's menu

You need to change the *SetMenuDescr* call a little. The COMMANDS menu resource has been expanded to provide placeholder menus for the document manager's and views' menu descriptors. Also, the decorated MDI frame provides window management functions, such as cascading or tiling child windows, arranging the icons of minimized child windows, and so on.

The call to the *SetMenuDescr* function should now look like this:

```
GetMainWindow()->SetMenuDescr(TMenuDescr("COMMANDS"));
```

Setting the document manager

You also need to change how you create the document manager in an MDI application. The only change you need to make in this case is to change the *dmSDI* flag to *dmMDI*. You need to keep the *dmMenu* flag:

```
SetDocManager(new TDocManager(dmMDI | dmMenu));
```

InitInstance function

You need to make one change to the *InitInstance* function: remove the call to *CmFileNew*. This makes the frame open with no untitled documents. In the SDI application, opening the frame with an untitled document was OK. If the user opened a file, the untitled document was replaced by the new document. But in an MDI application, if the user opens an existing document, the untitled document remains open, requiring the user to close it before it'll go away.

Opening a new view

When you open a new view, you must provide a window for the view. In Step 12, *EvNewView* used the same client window again and again for every document and view. In an MDI application, you can open numerous windows in the *EvNewView* function. Each window you open inside the client area should be a *TMDIChild*. You can place your view inside the *TMDIChild* object by calling the view's *GetWindow* function for the child's client window.

Once you've created the *TMDIChild* object, you need to set its menu descriptor, but only if the view has a menu descriptor itself. After setting the menu descriptor, call the MDI child's *Create* function.

The *EvNewView* function should now look something like this:

```
void
TDrawApp::EvNewView(TView& view)
{
  TMDIChild* child = new TMDIChild(*Client, 0, view.GetWindow());
  if (view.GetViewMenu())
    child->SetMenuDescr(*view.GetViewMenu());
  child->Create();
}
```

Modifying drag and drop

In the SDI version of the tutorial application, you had to check to make sure the user didn't drop more than one file into the application area. But in MDI, if the user drops in more than one file, you can open them all, with each document in a separate window. Here's how to implement the ability to open multiple files dropped into your application:

1 Find the number of files dropped into the application. Use the *DragQueryFileCount* function. Use a **for** loop to iterate through the files.

2 For each file, get the length of its path and allocate a **char** array with enough room. Call the *DragQueryFile* function with the file's index (which you can track using the loop counter), the **char** array, and the length of the path.

3 Once you've got the file name, you can call the document manager's *MatchTemplate* function to get the proper template for the file type. This is done the same way as in Step 12; see page 92.

4 Once you've located a template, call the template's *CreateDoc* function with the file path as the parameter to the function. This creates a new document and its corresponding view, and opens the file into the document.

5 Once all the files have been opened, call the *DragFinish* function. This function releases the memory that Windows allocates during drag and drop operations.

Here's how the new *EvDropFiles* function should look:

```
void
TDrawApp::EvDropFiles(TDropInfo dropInfo)
{
  int fileCount = dropInfo.DragQueryFileCount();
    for (int index = 0; index < fileCount; index++) {
      int fileLength = dropInfo.DragQueryFileNameLen(index)+1;
      char* filePath = new char [fileLength];
      dropInfo.DragQueryFile(index, filePath, fileLength);
      TDocTemplate* tpl = GetDocManager()->MatchTemplate(filePath);
      if (tpl)
        tpl->CreateDoc(filePath);
      delete filePath;
    }
    dropInfo.DragFinish();
}
```

Closing a view

In Step 12, when you wanted to close a view, you had to remove the view as a client window, restore the main window's menu, and reset the main window's caption. You no longer need to do any of this, because these tasks are handled by the MDI window classes. Here's how your *EvCloseView* function should look:

```
void
TDrawApp::EvCloseView(TView& /*view*/)
{  // nothing needs to be done here for MDI
}
```

Changes to TDrawDocument and TDrawView

You need to make the following changes in the *TDrawDocument* and *TDrawView* classes. These changes include defining new events, adding new event-handling functions, adding document property functions, and more.

Defining new events

First you need to define three new events to support the new features in the *TDrawDocument* and *TDrawView* classes. These view notification events are *vnDrawAppend*, *vnDrawDelete*, and *vnDrawModify*. These events should be **const int**s, and defined as offsets from the predefined value *vnCustomBase*. Using *vnCustomBase* ensures that your new events don't overlap any ObjectWindows events.

Next, use the NOTIFY_SIG macro to specify the signature of the event-handling function. The NOTIFY_SIG macro takes two parameters, the event name (such as *vnDrawAppend* or *vnDrawDelete*) and the parameter type to be passed to the event-handling function. The size of the parameter type can be no larger than a **long**; if the object being passed is larger than a **long**, you must pass it by pointer. In this case, the parameter is just an **unsigned int** to pass the index of the affected line to the event-handling function. The return value of the event-handling function is always **void**.

Lastly, you need to define the response table macro for each of these events. By convention, the macro name uses the event name, in all uppercase letters, preceded by EV_VN_. Use the **#define** macro to define the macro name. To define the macro itself, use the VN_DEFINE macro. Here's the syntax for the VN_DEFINE macro:

```
VN_DEFINE(eventName, functionName, paramSize)
```

where:

- *eventName* is the event name.

- *functionName* is the name of the event-handling function.

- *paramSize* is the size of the parameter passed to the event-handling function; this can have four different values:
  - void
  - int (size of an int parameter depends on the platform)
  - long (32-bit integer or far pointer)
  - pointer (size of a pointer parameter depends on the memory model)

You should specify the value that most closely corresponds to the event-handling function's parameter type.

The full definition of the new events should look something like this:

```
const int vnDrawAppend = vnCustomBase+0;
const int vnDrawDelete = vnCustomBase+1;
const int vnDrawModify = vnCustomBase+2;

NOTIFY_SIG(vnDrawAppend, unsigned int)
NOTIFY_SIG(vnDrawDelete, unsigned int)
NOTIFY_SIG(vnDrawModify, unsigned int)

#define EV_VN_DRAWAPPEND VN_DEFINE(vnDrawAppend, VnAppend, int)
#define EV_VN_DRAWDELETE VN_DEFINE(vnDrawDelete, VnDelete, int)
#define EV_VN_DRAWMODIFY VN_DEFINE(vnDrawModify, VnModify, int)
```

Changes to TDrawDocument

TDrawDocument adds some new **protected** data members:

- *UndoLine* is a *TLine **. It is used to store a line after the original in the *Lines* array is modified or deleted.

- *UndoState* is an **int**. It indicates the nature of the last user operation, so that an undo can be performed by reversing the operation. It can have one of four values:
  - *UndoNone* indicates that no operations have been performed to undo.
  - *UndoDelete* indicates that a line was deleted from the document.
  - *UndoAppend* indicates that a new line was added to the document.
  - *UndoModify* indicates that a line in the document was modified.

- *UndoIndex* is an **int**. It contains the index of the last modified line, so that the modification can be undone.

- *FileInfo* is a *string*. It contains information about the file. This string is equivalent to the file information stored in the *TDrawDocument::Commit* function of Step 12.

The *TDrawDocument* constructor should be modified to initialize *UndoLine* to 0 and *UndoState* to *UndoNone*. The *TDrawDocument* destructor is modified to delete *UndoLine*.

You need to modify the *Open* function slightly to read the file information string from the document file and use it to initialize the *FileInfo* member. If the document doesn't have a valid document path, initialize *FileInfo* using the string resource IDS_FILEINFO.

Modify the *AddLine* function to notify any other views when a line has been added to the drawing. You can use the *NotifyViews* function with the *vnDrawAppend* event. The second parameter to the *NotifyViews* call should be the new line's array index. You also need to set *UndoState* to *UndoAppend*. The *AddLine* function should now look like this:

```
int
TDrawDocument::AddLine(TLine& line)
{
  int index = Lines->GetItemsInContainer();
  Lines->Add(line);
  SetDirty(true);
  NotifyViews(vnDrawAppend, index);
  UndoState = UndoAppend;
  return index;
}
```

Property functions

Every document has a list of properties. Each property has an associated value, defined as an **enum**, by which it is identified. The list of **enum**s for a derived document object should always end with the value *NextProperty*. The list of **enum**s for a derived document object should always start with the value *PrevProperty*, which should be set to the *NextProperty* member of the base class, minus 1.

Each property also has a text string describing the property contained in an array called *PropNames* and an **int** containing implementation-defined flags in an array called

PropFlags. The property's **enum** value can be used in an array index to locate the property string or flag for a particular property.

TDrawDocument adds two new properties to its document properties list: *LineCount* and *Description*. The **enum** definition should look like this:

```
enum {
  PrevProperty = TFileDocument::NextProperty-1,
  LineCount,
  Description,
  NextProperty,
};
```

By redefining *PrevProperty* and *NextProperty*, any class that's derived from your document class can create new properties without overwriting the properties you've defined.

TDrawDocument also adds an array of **static char** strings. This array contains two strings, each containing a text description of one of the new properties. The array definition should look like this:

```
static char* PropNames[] = {
  "Line Count",
  "Description",
};
```

Lastly, *TDrawDocument* adds an array of **ints** called *PropFlags*, which contains the same number of array elements as *PropNames*. Each array element contains one or more document property flags ORed together, and corresponds to the property in *PropNames* with the same array index. The *PropFlags* array definition should look like this:

```
static int PropFlags[] = {
  pfGetBinary|pfGetText, // LineCount
  pfGetText,             // Description
};
```

TDrawDocument overrides a number of the *TDocument* property functions to provide access to the new properties. You can find the total number of properties for the *TDrawDocument* class by calling the *PropertyCount* function. *PropertyCount* returns the value of the property **enum** *NextProperty*, minus 1.

You can find the text name of any document property using the *PropertyName* function. *PropertyName* returns a **char ***, a string containing the property name. It takes a single **int** parameter, which indicates the index of the parameter for which you want the name. If the index is less than or equal to the **enum** *PrevProperty*, you can call the *TFileDocument* function *PropertyName*. This returns the name of a property defined in *TFileDocument* or its base class *TDocument*. If the index is greater than or equal to *NextProperty*, you should return 0; *NextProperty* marks the last property in the document class. If the index has the same or greater value than *NextProperty*, the index is too high to be valid. As long as the index is greater than *PrevProperty* but less than *NextProperty*, you should return the string from the *PropNames* array corresponding to the index. The code for this function should look like this:

```
const char*
TDrawDocument::PropertyName(int index)
```

```
  {
    if (index <= PrevProperty)
      return TFileDocument::PropertyName(index);
    else if (index < NextProperty)
      return PropNames[index-PrevProperty-1];
    else
      return 0;
  }
```

The *FindProperty* function is essentially the opposite of the *PropertyName* function. *FindProperty* takes a single parameter, a **const char** *. It tries to match the string passed in with the name of each document property. If it successfully matches the string with a property name, it returns an **int** containing the index of the property. The code for this function should look like this:

```
int
TDrawDocument::FindProperty(const char far* name)
{
  for (int i=0; i < NextProperty-PrevProperty-1; i++)
    if (strcmp(PropNames[i], name) == 0)
      return i+PrevProperty+1;
  return 0;
}
```

The *PropertyFlags* function takes a single **int** parameter, which indicates the index of the parameter for which you want the property flags. These flags are returned as an **int**. If the index is less than or equal to the **enum** *PrevProperty*, you can call the *TFileDocument* function *PropertyName*. This returns the name of a property defined in *TFileDocument* or its base class *TDocument*. If the index is greater than or equal to *NextProperty*, you should return 0; *NextProperty* marks the last property in the document class. If the index has the same or greater value than *NextProperty*, the index is too high to be valid. As long as the index is greater than *PrevProperty* but less than *NextProperty*, you should return the member of the *PropFlags* array corresponding to the index. The code for this function should look like this:

```
int
TDrawDocument::PropertyFlags(int index)
{
  if (index <= PrevProperty)
    return TFileDocument::PropertyFlags(index);
  else if (index < NextProperty)
    return PropFlags[index-PrevProperty-1];
  else
    return 0;
}
```

The last property function is the *GetProperty* function, which takes three parameters. The first parameter is an **int**, the index of the property you want. The second parameter is a **void** *. This should be a block of memory that is used to hold the property information. The third parameter is an **int** and indicates the size in bytes of the block of memory.

There are three possibilities the *GetProperty* function should handle:

- The *LineCount* property can be requested in two forms, text or binary. To get the *LineCount* property in binary form, call the *GetProperty* function with the third parameter set to 0. If you do this, the second parameter should point to a data object of the proper type to contain the property data. To get the *LineCount* property as text, call the *GetProperty* function with the second parameter pointing to a valid block of memory and the third parameter set to the size of that block.

- The *Description* property can be requested in text form only. Just copy the *FileInfo* string into the destination array passed in as the second parameter.

- If the property requested is neither *LineCount* nor *Description*, call the *TFileDocument* version of *GetProperty*.

The code for the *GetProperty* function should look like this:

```
int
TDrawDocument::GetProperty(int prop, void far* dest, int textlen)
{
  switch(prop)
  {
    case LineCount:
    {
      int count = Lines->GetItemsInContainer();
      if (!textlen) {
        *(int far*)dest = count;
        return sizeof(int);
      }
      return wsprintf((char far*)dest, "%d", count);
    }
    case Description:
      char* temp = new char[textlen]; // need local copy for medium model
      int len = FileInfo.copy(temp, textlen);
      strcpy((char far*)dest, temp);
      return len;
  }
  return TFileDocument::GetProperty(prop, dest, textlen);
}
```

New functions in TDrawDocument

Step 13 adds a number of new functions to *TDrawDocument*. These functions let you modify the document object by deleting lines, modifying lines, clearing the document, and undoing changes.

The first new function is *DeleteLine*. As its name implies, the purpose of this function is to delete a line from the document. *DeleteLine* takes a single **int** parameter, which gives the array index of the line to be deleted.

1 *Delete* should check that the index passed in to it is valid. You can check this by calling the *GetLine* function and passing the index to *GetLine*. If the index is valid, *GetLine* returns a pointer to a line object. Otherwise, it returns 0.

2   Once you have determined the index is valid, you should set *UndoLine* to the line to be deleted and set *UndoState* to *UndoDelete*. This saves the old line in case the user requests an undo of the deletion.

3   You should then detach the line from the document using the container class *Detach* function. This function takes a single **int** parameter, the array index of the line to be deleted.

4   Turn the *IsDirty* flag on by calling the *SetDirty* function.

5   Lastly, notify the views that the document has changed by calling the *NotifyViews* function. Pass the *vnDrawDelete* event as the first parameter of the *NotifyViews* call and the array index of the line as the second parameter.

The code for the *DeleteLine* function should look like this:

```
void
TDrawDocument::DeleteLine(unsigned int index)
{
  const TLine* oldLine = GetLine(index);
  if (!oldLine)
    return;
  delete UndoLine;
  UndoLine = new TLine(*oldLine);
  Lines->Detach(index);
  SetDirty(true);
  NotifyViews(vnDrawDelete, index);
  UndoState = UndoDelete;
}
```

The *ModifyLine* function takes two parameters, a *TLine* **&** and an **int**. The **int** is the array index of the line to be modified. The affected line is replaced by the *TLine* **&**.

1   As with the *DeleteLine* function, you need to set up the undo data members before replacing the line. Copy the line to be replaced to *UndoLine* and set *UndoState* to *UndoModify*. You also need to set *UndoIndex* to the index of the affected line.

2   Set the line to the *TLine* object passed into the function.

3   Turn the *IsDirty* flag on by calling the *SetDirty* function.

4   Lastly, notify the views that the document has changed by calling the *NotifyViews* function. Pass the *vnDrawModify* event as the first parameter of the *NotifyViews* call and the array index of the line as the second parameter.

The code for this function should look like this:

```
void
TDrawDocument::ModifyLine(TLine& line, unsigned int index)
{
  delete UndoLine;
  UndoLine = new TLine((*Lines)[index]);
  SetDirty(true);
  (*Lines)[index] = line;
  NotifyViews(vnDrawModify, index);
  UndoState = UndoModify;
  UndoIndex = index;
}
```

The *Clear* function is fairly straightforward. It flushes the *TLines* array referenced by *Lines*, then forces the views to update by calling *NotifyViews* with the *vnRevert* parameter. When the views are updated, there's no data in the document, causing the views to clear their windows. The function should look something like this:

```
void
TDrawDocument::Clear()
{
  Lines->Flush();
  NotifyViews(vnRevert, true);
}
```

The *Undo* function has three different types of operations to undo: append, delete, and modify. It determines which type of operation it needs to undo by the value of the *UndoState* variable:

- If *UndoState* is *UndoAppend*, *Undo* needs to delete the last line in the array.

- If *UndoState* is *UndoDelete*, *Undo* needs to add the line referenced by *UndoLine* to the array.

- If *UndoState* is *UndoModify*, *Undo* needs to restore the line referenced by *UndoLine* to the array to the position in the array indicated by *UndoIndex*.

Here's how the code for the *Undo* function should look:

```
void
TDrawDocument::Undo()
{
  switch (UndoState) {
    case UndoAppend:
      DeleteLine(Lines->GetItemsInContainer()-1);
      return;
    case UndoDelete:
      AddLine(*UndoLine);
      delete UndoLine;
      UndoLine = 0;
      return;
    case UndoModify:
      TLine* temp = UndoLine;
      UndoLine = 0;
      ModifyLine(*temp, UndoIndex);
      delete temp;
  }
}
```

Each operation uses one of these new modification functions. That way, each undo operation can itself be undone.

Changes to TDrawView

TDrawView modifies a number of its functions, including deleting the *GetPenSize* function. This function should be moved to the *TLine* class, so that the pen size is set in the line itself. You can call the *TLine::GetPenSize* function from the *CmPenSize* function.

The same thing should be done with the *CmPenColor* function; move the functionality of this function to the *TLine::GetPenColor* function. You can call the *TLine::GetPenColor* function from the *CmPenColor* function.

To accommodate the new editing functionality in the *TDrawDocument* and *TDrawView* classes, you need to add menu choices for Undo and Clear. These choices should post the events CM_CLEAR and CM_UNDO. The menu requires a change in the menu resource to group the menus properly. The call should look like this:

```
SetViewMenu(new TMenuDescr(IDM_DRAWVIEW));
```

You can redefine the right button behavior by changing the *EvRButtonDown* function (there are now two other ways to change the pen size, the Tools | Pen Size menu command and the Pen Size control bar button). You can use the right mouse button as a shortcut for an undo operation. The *EvRButtonDown* function should look like this:

```
void
TDrawView::EvRButtonDown(uint, TPoint&)
{
   CmUndo();
}
```

New functions in TDrawView

Step 13 adds a number of new functions to *TDrawDocument*. These functions implement an interface to access the new functionality in *TDrawDocument*.

You need to override the *TView* **virtual** function *GetViewName*. The document manager calls this function to determine the type of view. This function should return a **const char** * referencing a string containing the view name. This function should look like this:

```
const char far* GetViewName() { return StaticName(); }
```

After adding the new menu items Clear and Undo to the Edit menu, you need to handle the events CM_CLEAR and CM_UNDO. Add the following lines to your response table:

```
EV_COMMAND(CM_CLEAR, CmClear),
EV_COMMAND(CM_UNDO, CmUndo),
```

You also need functions to handle the CM_CLEAR and CM_UNDO events. If the view receives a CM_CLEAR message, all it needs to do is to call the document's *Clear* function:

```
void
TDrawView::CmClear()
{
   DrawDoc->Clear();
}
```

If the view receives a CM_UNDO message, all it needs to do is to call the document's *Undo* function:

```
void
TDrawView::CmUndo()
{
```

```
    DrawDoc->Undo();
}
```

The other new events the view has to handle are the view notification events, *vnDrawAppend*, *vnDrawDelete*, and *vnDrawModify*. You should add the response table macros for these events to the view's response table:

```
DEFINE_RESPONSE_TABLE1(TDrawView, TWindowView)
  EV_VN_DRAWAPPEND,
  EV_VN_DRAWDELETE,
  EV_VN_DRAWMODIFY,
END_RESPONSE_TABLE;
```

The event-handling functions for these macros are *VnAppend*, *VnDelete*, and *VnModify*. All three of these functions return a bool and take a single parameter, an **int** indicating which line in the document is affected by the event.

The *VnAppend* function gets notification that a line was appended to the document. It then draws the new line in the view's window. It should create a device context, get the line from the document, call the line's *Draw* function with the device context object as the parameter, then return true. The code for this function looks like this:

```
bool
TDrawView::VnAppend(unsigned int index)
{
  TClientDC dc(*this);
  const TLine* line = DrawDoc->GetLine(index);
  line->Draw(dc);
  return true;
}
```

The *VnModify* function forces a repaint of the entire window. It might seem more efficient to just redraw the affected line, but you would need to paint over the old line, repaint the new line, and restore any lines that might have crossed or overlapped the affected line. It is actually more efficient to invalidate and repaint the entire window. So the code for the *VnModify* function should look like this:

```
bool
TDrawView::VnModify(unsigned int /*index*/)
{
  Invalidate();  // force full repaint
  return true;
}
```

The *VnDelete* function also forces a repaint of the entire window. This function faces the same problem as *VnModify*; simply erasing the line will probably affect other lines. The code for the *VnDelete* function should look like this:

```
bool
TDrawView::VnDelete(unsigned int /*index*/)
{
  Invalidate();  // force full repaint
  return true;
}
```

TDrawListView

The purpose of the *TDrawListView* class is to display the data contained in a *TDrawDocument* object as a list of lines. Each line will display the color values for the line, the pen size for the line, and the number of points that make up the line. *TDrawListView* will let the user modify a line by changing the pen size or color. The user can also delete a line.

TDrawListView is derived from *TView* and *TListBox*. *TView* gives *TDrawListView* the standard view capabilities. *TListBox* provides the ability to display the information in the document object in a list.

Creating the TDrawListView class

The *TDrawListView* constructor takes two parameters, a *TDrawDocument* & (a reference to the view's associated document) and a *TWindow* * (a pointer to the parent window). The parent window defaults to 0 if no value is supplied. The constructor passes the first parameter to the *TView* constructor and initializes the *DrawDoc* member to point at the document passed as the first parameter.

TDrawListView has two data members, one **protected** *TDrawDocument* * called *DrawDoc* and one **public int** called *CurIndex*. *DrawDoc* serves the same purpose in *TDrawListView* as it did in *TDrawView*, namely to reference the view's associated document object. *CurIndex* contains the array index of the currently selected line in the list box.

The *TDrawListView* constructor also calls the *TListBox* constructor. The first parameter of the *TListBox* constructor is passed the parent window parameter of the *TDrawListView* constructor. The second parameter of the *TListBox* constructor is a call to the *TView* function *GetNextViewId*. This function returns a **static unsigned** that is used as the list box identifier. The view identifier is set in the *TView* constructor. The coordinates and dimensions of the list box are all set to 0; the dimensions are filled in when the *TDrawListView* is set as a client in an MDI child window.

The constructor also sets some window attributes, including the *Attr.Style* attribute, which has the WS_BORDER and LBS_SORT attributes turned off, and the *Attr.AccelTable* attribute, which is set to the IDA_DRAWLISTVIEW accelerator resource defined in STEP13DV.RC.

The constructor also sets up the menu descriptor for *TDrawListView*. Because *TDrawListView* has a different function from *TDrawView*, it requires a different menu. Compare the menu resource for *TDrawView* and the menu resource for *TDrawListView*.

Here's the code for the *TDrawListView* constructor:

```
TDrawListView::TDrawListView(TDrawDocument& doc,TWindow *parent)
  : TView(doc), TListBox(parent, GetNextViewId(), 0,0,0,0), DrawDoc(&doc)
{
  Attr.Style &= ~(WS_BORDER | LBS_SORT);
  Attr.AccelTable = IDA_DRAWLISTVIEW;
  SetViewMenu(new TMenuDescr(IDM_DRAWLISTVIEW));
}
```

TDrawListView has no dynamically allocated data members. The destructor therefore does nothing.

Naming the class

Like the *TDrawView* class, *TDrawListView* should define the function *StaticName* to return the name of the view class. Here's how the *StaticName* function might look:

```
static const char far* StaticName() {return "DrawList View";}
```

Overriding TView and TWindow virtual functions

The document manager calls the view function *GetViewName* to determine the type of view. You need to override this function, which is declared **virtual** function in *TView*. This function should return a **const char** * referencing a string containing the view name. This function should look like this:

```
const char far* GetViewName() { return StaticName(); }
```

The document manager calls the view function *GetWindow* to get the window associated with a view. You need to override this function also, which is declared **virtual** function in *TView*. It should return a *TWindow* * referencing the view's window. This function should look like this:

```
TWindow* GetWindow() { return (TWindow*) this; }
```

You also need to supply a version of the *CanClose* function. This function should call the *TListBox* version of *CanClose* and also call the document's *CanClose* function. This function should look like this:

```
bool CanClose() {return TListBox::CanClose() && Doc->CanClose();}
```

You also need to provide a version of the *Create* function. You can call the *TListBox* version of *Create* to actually create the window. But you also need to load the data from the document into the *TDrawListView* object. To do this, call the *LoadData* function. You'll define the *LoadData* function in the next section of this step. The *Create* function should look something like this:

```
bool
TDrawListView::Create()
{
  TListBox::Create();
  LoadData();
  return true;
}
```

Loading and formatting data

You need to provide functions to load data from the document object to the view document and to format the data for display in the list box. These functions should be **protected** so that only the view can call them.

The first function is *LoadData*. To load data into the list box, you need to first clear the list of any items that might already be in it. For this, you can call the *ClearList* function, which is from the *TListBox* base class. After that, get lines from the document and format each line until the document runs out of lines. You can tell when there are no more lines in the document; the *GetLine* function returns 0. Lastly, set the current selection index to 0 using the *SetSelIndex* function. This causes the first line in the list box to be selected. The code for the *LoadData* function looks something like this:

```
void
TDrawListView::LoadData()
{
  ClearList();
  int i = 0;
  const TLine* line;
  while ((line = DrawDoc->GetLine(i)) != 0)
    FormatData(line, i++);
  SetSelIndex(0);
}
```

The *FormatData* function takes two parameters. The first parameter is a **const** *TLine* * that references the line to modified or added to the list box. The second parameter contains the index of the line to modified.

The code for *FormatData* should look something like this:

```
void
TDrawListView::FormatData(const TLine* line, int unsigned index)
{
  char buf[80];
  TColor color(line->QueryColor());
  wsprintf(buf, "Color = R%d G%d B%d, Size = %d, Points = %d",
           color.Red(), color.Green(), color.Blue(),
           line->QueryPenSize(), line->GetItemsInContainer());

  DeleteString(index);
  InsertString(buf, index);
  SetSelIndex(index);
}
```

Event handling in TDrawListView

Here's the response table for *TDrawListView*:

```
DEFINE_RESPONSE_TABLE1(TDrawListView, TListBox)
  EV_COMMAND(CM_PENSIZE, CmPenSize),
  EV_COMMAND(CM_PENCOLOR, CmPenColor),
  EV_COMMAND(CM_CLEAR, CmClear),
  EV_COMMAND(CM_UNDO, CmUndo),
  EV_COMMAND(CM_DELETE, CmDelete),
  EV_VN_ISWINDOW,
  EV_VN_COMMIT,
  EV_VN_REVERT,
  EV_VN_DRAWAPPEND,
  EV_VN_DRAWDELETE,
```

```
EV_VN_DRAWMODIFY,
END_RESPONSE_TABLE;
```

This response table is similar to *TDrawView*'s response table in some ways. The two views share some events, such as the CM_PENSIZE and CM_PENCOLOR events and the *vnDrawAppend* and *vnDrawModify* view notification events.

But each view also handles events that the other view doesn't. This is because each view has different capabilities. For example, the *TDrawView* class handles a number of mouse events, whereas *TDrawListView* handles none. That's because it makes no sense in the context of a list box to handle the mouse events; those events are used when drawing a line in the *TDrawView* window.

TDrawListView handles the CM_DELETE event, whereas *TDrawView* doesn't. This is because, in the *TDrawView* window, there's no way for the user to indicate which line should be deleted. But in the list box, it's easy: just delete the line that's currently selected in the list box.

TDrawListView also handles the *vnIsWindow* event. The *vnIsWindow* message is a predefined ObjectWindows event, which asks the view if its window is the same as the window passed with the event.

The *CmPenSize* function is more complicated in the *TDrawListView* class than in the *TDrawView* class. This is because the *TDrawListView* class doesn't maintain a pointer to the current line the way *TDrawView* does. Instead, you have to get the index of the line that's currently selected in the list box and get that line from the document. Then, because the *GetLine* function returns a pointer to a **const** object, you have to make a copy of the line, modify the copy, then call the document's *ModifyLine* function. Here's how the code for this function should look:

```
void
TDrawListView::CmPenSize()
{
  int index = GetSelIndex();
  const TLine* line = DrawDoc->GetLine(index);
  if (line) {
    TLine* newline = new TLine(*line);
    if (newline->GetPenSize())
      DrawDoc->ModifyLine(*newline, index);
    delete newline;
  }
}
```

The interesting aspect of this function comes in the *ModifyLine* call. When the user changes the pen size using this function, the pen size in the view isn't changed at this time. But when the document changes the line in the *ModifyLine* call, it posts a *vnDrawModify* event to all of its views:

```
NotifyViews(vnDrawModify, index);
```

This notifies all the views associated with the document that a line has changed. All views then call their *VnModify* function and update their displays from the document. This way, any change made in one view is automatically reflected in other open views.

The same holds true for any other functions that modify the document's data, such as *CmPenColor*, *CmDelete*, *CmUndo*, and so on.

The *CmPenColor* function looks nearly same as the *CmPenSize* function, except that, instead of calling the line's *GetPenSize* function, it calls *GetPenColor*:

```
void
TDrawListView::CmPenColor()
{
  int index = GetSelIndex();
  const TLine* line = DrawDoc->GetLine(index);
  if (line) {
    TLine* newline = new TLine(*line);
    if (newline->GetPenColor())
      DrawDoc->ModifyLine(*newline, index);
    delete newline;
  }
}
```

The CM_DELETE event indicates that the user wants to delete the line that is currently selected in the list box. The view needs to call the document's *DeleteLine* function, passing it the index of the currently selected line. This function should look like this:

```
void
TDrawListView::CmDelete()
{
  DrawDoc->DeleteLine(GetSelIndex());
}
```

You also need functions to handle the CM_CLEAR and CM_UNDO events for *TDrawListView*. If the user chooses the Clear menu command, the view receives a CM_CLEAR message. All it needs to do is call the document's *Clear* function:

```
void
TDrawListView::CmClear() {
  DrawDoc->Clear();
}
```

If the user chooses the Clear menu command, the view receives a CM_UNDO message. All it needs to do is call the document's *Undo* function:

```
void
TDrawListView::CmUndo()
{
  DrawDoc->Undo();
}
```

These functions are identical to the *TDrawView* versions of the same functions. That's because these operation rely on *TDrawDocument* to actually make the changes to the data.

Like the *TDrawView* class, *TDrawListView*'s *VnCommit* function always returns true. In a more complex application, this function would add any cached data to the document, but in this application, the data is added to the document as each line is drawn.

The *VnRevert* function calls the *LoadData* function to revert the list box display to the data contained in the document:

```
bool
TDrawListView::VnRevert(bool /*clear*/)
{
  LoadData();
  return true;
}
```

The *VnAppend* function gets a single **unsigned int** parameter, which gives the index number of the appended line. You need to get the new line from the document by calling the document's *GetLine* function. Call the *FormatData* function with the line and the line index passed into the function. After formatting the line, set the selection index to the new line and return. The function should look like this:

```
bool
TDrawListView::VnAppend(unsigned int index)
{
  const TLine* line = DrawDoc->GetLine(index);
  FormatData(line, index);
  SetSelIndex(index);
  return true;
}
```

The *VnDelete* function takes a single **int** parameter, the index of the line to be deleted. To remove the line from the list box, call the *TListBox* function *DeleteString*:

```
bool
TDrawListView::VnDelete(unsigned int index)
{
  DeleteString(index);
  HandleMessage(WM_KEYDOWN,VK_DOWN); // force selection
  return true;
}
```

The call to *HandleMessage* ensures that there is an active selection in the list box after the currently selected string is deleted.

The *VnModify* function takes a single **int** parameter, the index of the line to be modified. You need to get the line from the document using the *GetLine* function. Call *FormatData* with the line and its index:

```
bool
TDrawListView::VnModify(unsigned int index)
{
  const TLine* line = DrawDoc->GetLine(index);
  FormatData(line, index);
  return true;
}
```

Where to find more information

Here's a guide to where you can find more information on the topics introduced in this step:

- The MDI window classes are discussed in Chapter 25, "Window objects."
- Menu descriptors are discussed in Chapter 26, "Menu objects."
- The Doc/View model and classes are discussed in Chapter 28, "Doc/View objects."
- *TListBox* is discussed in Chapter 29, "Control objects."

14

Making an OLE container

The next step in the ObjectWindows tutorial shows you how to make an OLE 2 container from the Drawing Pad application. Object Linking and Embedding (OLE) is an extension to Windows that lets the user seamlessly combine several applications into a single workspace. An OLE container application can host server objects, providing additional workspace where the user of your application can expand your application with the capabilities provided by OLE-server-enabled application.

The code for the example used in this chapter is contained in the files STEP14.CPP, STEP14DV.CPP, STEP14.RC, and STEP14DV.RC in the EXAMPLES/OWL/TUTORIAL directory where your compiler is installed.

How OLE works

Two different types of application are necessary for basic OLE operations:

- A *container* can have other applications or objects embedded within it, presenting the data from the embedded object as part of the container's own data set.

- A *server* can be embedded within a container application and can be used to manipulate the data that the server displays in the container's work space.

What is a container?

In this step of the tutorial, you'll make your Doc/View Drawing Pad application into an OLE container. Making Drawing Pad into an OLE container has some important ramifications: the application is no longer limited to displaying a set of lines, but can also display any kind of data that can be presented by any server users embed within their drawings. Although line drawing capability is still in the application and producing line drawings is still the main function of the application, users can now spice up their drawings with bitmaps, spreadsheet charts, even sound files.

Although you can do many of the same tasks by using the Clipboard to transfer data, it's easier to use OLE. Using the Clipboard, your application has to be able to accept the type of data stored there. This means if you want to accept bitmaps in the Drawing Pad application, you have to build the functionality required to accept and display bitmaps. This in no way prepares the application to accept spreadsheet charts, database tables, or or data in other graphic formats. To include another type of data requires implementing more functionality to interpret and display that data.

Using OLE, your application can display any type of data that is supported by an available OLE server. As far as your application is concerned, a bitmap looks exactly like a spreadsheet chart, a database table, or any other kind of object; that is, they all look like OLE server objects.

Also, using the Clipboard, you can build the ability to display a bitmap into your application. But modifying the bitmap after it's been pasted in requires more functionality to be built into your application.

Using OLE, the embedded server handles its embedded data whenever the user wants to modify or change it. The type of data used in the server is of no consequence to the container.

Implementing OLE in ObjectWindows: ObjectComponents

There is a price to pay for the advantages OLE provides for your application: programming an OLE implementation has historically been very messy and time consuming. You needed to modify your code to conform to OLE specifications. Even more than this, OLE doesn't follow the event-based paradigm that Windows applications were previoiusly based on. Instead it implements a new interface-based paradigm, requiring an understanding of standard OLE interfaces, reference counting, and other OLE specifications.

ObjectWindows implements OLE through the ObjectComponents Framework. You can use ObjectComponents to make your application an OLE container or server with only minor modifications to your code. You can use ObjectComponents with the following application types:

- Doc/View ObjectWindows applications
- Non-Doc/View ObjectWindows applications
- Non-ObjectWindows C++ applications

The fewest modifications are required for Doc/View ObjectWindows applications, which is shown in this chapter. Implementing OLE with ObjectComponents in non-Doc/View ObjectWindows applications and non-ObjectWindows C++ applications is described in the *Borland C++ Programmer's Guide* in Part 5, "ObjectComponents Programmer's Guide."

The following steps are required to convert your Doc/View ObjectWindows application to an OLE container application:

- Include the proper header files.
- Register your application and Doc/View objects in the system registration database.
- Create a *TOcApp* object and associating it with your application object.

- Change your frame window class to an OLE-aware frame window class.
- Change your document and view classes's base class to OLE-enabled classes.

The ObjectComponents objects used in this chapter are explained as you add them to the Drawing Pad application. The ObjectComponents Framework is described in detail in Part 5 of the *Borland C++ Programmer's Guide* and in the *ObjectWindows Reference* in Part 2, "ObjectComponents Programmer's Reference."

Adding OLE class header files

You need to add new headers to your files to use the ObjectComponents classes. ObjectComponents adds OLE capabilities by adding deriving new OLE-enabled classes from existing classes.

To add new headers to your files so you can use ObjectComponents classes:

1 In STEP14.CPP, instead of using *TDecoratedMDIFrame*, you'll use *TOleMDIFrame*, which is an OLE-enabled decorated MDI frame. All OLE frame windows, whether they're MDI or SDI, must be able to handle decorations, since many embedded OLE servers provide their own tool bars. The *TOleMDIFrame* class is declared in the owl/olemdifr.h header file.

Your list of include statements in STEP14.CPP should now look something like this:

```
#include <owl/applicat.h>
#include <owl/dialog.h>
#include <owl/controlb.h>
#include <owl/buttonga.h>
#include <owl/statusba.h>
#include <owl/docmanag.h>
#include <owl/olemdifr.h>
#include <stdlib.h>
#include <string.h>
#include "step14.rc"
```

2 In STEP14DV.CPP, you need to include OLE-enabled document and view classes. These classes, *TOleDocument* and *TOleView*, provide standard Doc/View functionality along with the ability to support OLE. They're declared in the header files owl/oledoc.h and owl/oleview.h. Your list of include statements in STEP14DV.CPP should now look something like this:

```
#include <owl/chooseco.h>
#include <owl/dc.h>
#include <owl/docmanag.h>
#include <owl/gdiobjec.h>
#include <owl/inputdia.h>
#include <owl/listbox.h>
#include <owl/oledoc.h>
#include <owl/oleview.h>
#include <classlib/arrays.h>
#include "step14dv.rc"
```

Registering the application for OLE

For OLE to keep track of the applications running on a particular system, any application that wants to use OLE must register in the system-wide OLE registration database. You need to provide a unique identifier number and a description of the application. You also need to create objects that let your application communicate with OLE.

ObjectComponents simplifies the process of registering your application through a set of registration macros. These macros create an object of type *TRegList*, known as a registration table, which contains the information required by the OLE registration database. The macros are the same ones you use when creating a Doc/View template, but you use more of the capabilities available in the *TRegList* class. You can review how to create a table using these macros by seeing page 88.

Once you've created a registration table, you need to pass it to a connector object. A connector object provides the channel through which a Doc/View application communicates with ObjectComponents and, by extension, with OLE. The registration table is passed to an object of type *TOcApp* (ObjectComponents connector objects all begin with *TOc*).

Later, you'll modify the declaration of your *TDrawApp* class to be derived from both *TApplication* and *TOcModule*. Your application object initilizes the *TOcApp* connector object during the application object's construction. The connector object is then accessed through a pointer contained in the *TOcModule* class.

Creating the registration table

You use the REGDATA macro to create a container application's registration table. This is the same macro you used earlier to register your default document extension and file name filter. For your purposes now, you need the following key values:

Table 14.1   Key values and meanings

Key value	Meaning
clsid	String representation of a 16-byte number called a globally unique ID or GUID. This number must be unique to the application. It is used to distinguish your application from every other application on the system. This value is for internal system use only.
description	Application description for the system user to see. This string appears in the OLE registration list.

Your registration table should look something like this:

```
REGISTRATION_FORMAT_BUFFER(100)

BEGIN_REGISTRATION(AppReg)
  REGDATA(clsid, "{383882A1-8ABC-101B-A23B-CE4E85D07ED2}")
  REGDATA(description,"OWL Drawing Pad 2.0")
END_REGISTRATION
```

Note   You must select a unique GUID for your application. There are a number of ways to get a unique identifier for your application. Generating a GUID and describing your application is presented in detail in Chapter 37. For this tutorial, you can use the GUIDs provided in the tutorial examples. Do not use these same numbers when you create other applications.

Other macros can go into your registration table. Those for creating *AppReg* are the bare minimum for a container application object. You'll get to see a more complicated table when you create the registration table for your document class.

Also, because *AppReg* is created in the global name space of your application, it's safer and more informative to refer to it inside your classes and functions using the global scoping qualifier. So instead of:

```
void
MyClass::MyFunc()
{
   OtherFunc(AppReg);
}
```

you would write:

```
void
MyClass::MyFunc()
{
   OtherFunc(::AppReg);
}
```

Creating a class factory

A class factory is pretty much what it sounds like—it's an object that can make more objects. It is used in OLE to provide objects for linking and embedding. When an application wants to embed your application's objects in itself, it's the class factory that actually produces the embedded object.

ObjectWindows makes it easy to create a class factory with the *TOleDocViewFactory* template. All you need to do is create an instance of the template with the application class you want to produce as the template type. In this case, you want to produce instances of *TDrawApp* with your factory. Creating the template would look like this:

```
TOleDocViewFactory<TDrawApp>();
```

You need to pass an instance of this template as the second parameter of the *TOcRegistrar* constructor. You can see how this looks in the sample *OwlMain* below. The objects themselves are created in the factory using the same Doc/View templates used by your application when it's run as a stand-alone application.

TOleDocViewFactory is the class factory template for Doc/View ObjectWindows applications. There are other class factory templates for different types of applications. These are discussed in Chapter 36 and in the *ObjectWindows Reference*.

Creating a registrar object

The registration table contains information about your application object for the system. The registrar object, which is of type *TOcRegistrar*, takes the registration table and registers the application with the OLE registration database. It also parses the application command line looking for OLE-related options.

To create a registrar object:

1 Create a global static pointer to a *TOcRegistrar* object. You can do this using the *TPointer* template, defined in the osl\geometry.h header file (this file is already included by a number of the ObjectWindows header files, so you don't need to include it again). This should look something like this:

```
static TPointer<TOcRegistrar> Registrar;
```

Using *TPointer* instead of a simple pointer, such as *TOcRegistrar* Registrar*, provides automatic deletion when the object referred to is destroyed or goes out of scope. The full range of operations available with regular pointers is available in *TPointer*, while some of the traditional dangers of using pointers are eliminated.

2 Create the actual registrar object. The *TOcRegistrar* constructor takes four parameters:

- A reference to a registration table object
- A pointer to a callback function of type *TComponentCreate*
- A string containing the application's command line
- An instance handle indicating the application instance the registrar is for; this parameter defaults to *_hInstance*, the current application instance

For these parameters, you can pass the following arguments when constructing the registrar object.

- For the first parameter, pass your registration table object.
- For the second parameter, pass in your class factory.
- For the third parameter, pass the application's command line. You can get the command line by calling *TApplication*'s *GetCmdLine* function.
- You don't need to specify the fourth parameter, an instance handle; just let that parameter take its default value.

For example,

```
::Registrar = new TOcRegistrar(AppReg, TOleDocViewFactory<TDrawApp>(),
                               TApplication::GetCmdLine());
```

3 Call the *Run* function. However, instead of calling the application object's *Run* function (which you couldn't do at this point if you wanted to, since you haven't created an application object), call the registrar object's *Run* function. *TOcRegistrar* provides a *Run* function that is called just like *TApplication*'s *Run* function. However, any ObjectWindows OLE application should call the registrar object's *Run* function. This function performs some checks and actions required for your OLE application.

Your *OwlMain* function should now look something like this:

```
int
OwlMain(int /*argc*/, char* /*argv*/ [])
{
    ::Registrar = new TOcRegistrar(AppReg, TOleDocViewFactory<TDrawApp>(),
                                   TApplication::GetCmdLine());
    return ::Registrar->Run();
}
```

Creating an application dictionary

The application dictionary is an object that helps coordinate associations between processes or tasks and *TApplication* pointers. Before diving into OLE, this was relatively simple: a *TApplication* object was pretty much synonymous with a process. With OLE, the environment becomes confused: there can be multiple tasks and processes in a single application, with a container application, a number of embedded servers, possibly more servers embedded within those servers—the neighborhood's gotten a little more crowded.

To deal with this, ObjectWindows provides application dictionaries with the *TAppDictionary* class. The best thing about *TAppDictionary* is that, in order to use it for our purposes here, you don't have to know a whole lot about it. ObjectWindows also provides a macro, DEFINE_APP_DICTIONARY, that creates and initializes an application dictionary object for you.

DEFINE_APP_DICTIONARY takes a single parameter, the name of the object you want to create. You should place this near the beginning of your source file in the global name space. You must at least place it before *TDrawApp*'s constructor, since that's where you'll use it.

Your application dictionary definition should look something like this:

```
DEFINE_APP_DICTIONARY(AppDictionary);
```

Changes to TDrawApp

You need change the *TDrawApp* class to support ObjectComponents. These changes are fairly standard when you're creating a Doc/View application in an OLE container.

- Changing the class declaration
- Changing the class functionality, including
  - Creating an OLE MDI frame
  - Setting the OLE MDI frame's application connector
  - Adding a tool bar identifier

Changing the class declaration

You need to make the following changes to the declaration of the *TDrawApp* class:

1 Derive *TDrawApp* from both *TApplication* and the *TOcModule* class. *TOcModule* provides the interface your application object uses to communicate with OLE through the ObjectComponents Framework. Both *TApplication* and *TOcModule* should be public bases.

2 Change the constructor so that you pass the *TApplication* constructor a single parameter. You should initialize the name of the application object with the value of *description* from *AppReg*. To make this easier, the *TRegList* class overloads the square bracket operators ([]) to return the string associated with the key value passed

between the brackets. So to get the string associated with the *description* key, call
`AppReg["description"]`.

Your *TDrawApp* declaration should now resemble the following code:

```
class TDrawApp : public TApplication, public TOcModule
{
  public:
    TDrawApp() : TApplication(::AppReg["description"]) {}

  protected:
    TMDIClient* Client;

    // Override methods of TApplication
    void InitInstance();
    void InitMainWindow();

    // Event handlers
    void EvNewView(TView& view);
    void EvCloseView(TView& view);
    void EvDropFiles(TDropInfo dropInfo);
    void CmAbout();

  DECLARE_RESPONSE_TABLE(TDrawApp);
};
```

Changing the class functionality

You need to change the main window to a *TOleMDIFrame* object and properly initialize it as follows:

- Creating an OLE MDI frame
- Setting the OLE MDI frame's application connector
- Adding a tool bar identifier

Creating an OLE MDI frame

Next, you need to change your *InitMainWindow* function by changing your frame window object from a decorated MDI frame to an *OLE-aware* decorated MDI frame (note that all OLE-aware ObjectWindows frame window classes are decorated). The window class to use for this is *TOleMDIFrame*. *TOleMDIFrame* is based on *TMDIFrame*, which provides MDI support, and *TOleFrame*, which provides the ability to work with ObjectComponents. Here's the constructor for *TOleMDIFrame*:

```
TOleMDIFrame(const char far* title,
             TResId menuResId,
             TMDIClient& clientWnd = *new TMDIClient,
             bool trackMenuSelection = false,
             TModule* module = 0);
```

The parameters to the *TOleMDIFrame* constructor are the same as those for *TDecoratedMDIFrame*. This makes the conversion simple: all you need to do is change the name of the class when you create the frame window object.

Setting the OLE MDI frame's application connector

In order for the OLE MDI frame to be able to handle embedded OLE objects, it needs to know how to communicate with the ObjectComponents mechanism. This is accessed through the *TOcApp* object associated with the application object. The frame window must be explicitly associated with this object.

To do this, *TOleMDIFrame* provides a function (inherited from *TOleFrame*) called *SetOcApp*. *SetOcApp* returns **void** and takes a pointer to a *TOcApp* object. For the parameter to *SetOcApp*, you can just pass *OcApp*.

Adding a tool bar identifier

OLE servers often provide their own tool bar to replace yours while the server is functioning. The mechanics of this are handled by ObjectComponents, but to put the server's tool bar in place of yours, ObjectWindows must be able to find your tool bar.

ObjectWindows tries to locate your tool bar by searching through the list of child windows owned by the OLE MDI frame window and checking each window's identifier. Up until now, your tool bar hasn't actually had an identifier, which would cause ObjectWindows to not find the tool bar. In order for ObjectWindows to identify the container's tool bar, the container must use the IDW_TOOLBAR as its window ID (the *Id* member of the tool bar's *Attr* member object).

Your *InitMainWindow* function should now look something like this:

```
void
TDrawApp::InitMainWindow()
{
  // Construct OLE-enabled MDI frame
  TOleMDIFrame* frame;
  frame = new TOleMDIFrame(GetName(), 0, *(Client = new TMDIClient), true);

  // Set the frame's OcApp to OcApp
  frame->SetOcApp(OcApp);

  // Construct a status bar
  TStatusBar* sb = new TStatusBar(frame, TGadget::Recessed);

  // Construct a control bar
  TControlBar* cb = new TControlBar(frame);
  cb->Insert(*new TButtonGadget(CM_FILENEW, CM_FILENEW, TButtonGadget::Command));
  cb->Insert(*new TButtonGadget(CM_FILEOPEN, CM_FILEOPEN, TButtonGadget::Command));
  cb->Insert(*new TButtonGadget(CM_FILESAVE, CM_FILESAVE, TButtonGadget::Command));
  cb->Insert(*new TButtonGadget(CM_FILESAVEAS, CM_FILESAVEAS, TButtonGadget::Command));
  cb->Insert(*new TSeparatorGadget);
  cb->Insert(*new TButtonGadget(CM_PENSIZE, CM_PENSIZE, TButtonGadget::Command));
  cb->Insert(*new TButtonGadget(CM_PENCOLOR, CM_PENCOLOR, TButtonGadget::Command));
  cb->Insert(*new TSeparatorGadget);
```

```
cb->Insert(*new TButtonGadget(CM_ABOUT, CM_ABOUT, TButtonGadget::Command));
cb->SetHintMode(TGadgetWindow::EnterHints);

// Set the control bar's id.  Required for OLE tool bar merging
cb->Attr.Id = IDW_TOOLBAR;

// Insert the status bar and control bar into the frame
frame->Insert(*sb, TDecoratedFrame::Bottom);
frame->Insert(*cb, TDecoratedFrame::Top);

// Set the main window and its menu
SetMainWindow(frame);
GetMainWindow()->SetMenuDescr(TMenuDescr("MDI_COMMANDS",1,1,0,0,1,1));

// Install the document manager
SetDocManager(new TDocManager(dmMDI | dmMenu));
}
```

Changes to the Doc/View classes

There are a number of changes you need to make to your *TDrawDocument* and *TDrawView* classes to support OLE containers. For your document class, you need to

1 Add more information to the registration table for creating *TDrawDocument* document templates.

2 Change the base class to *TOleDocument*.

3 Modify the constructor .

4 Add two new functions, *GetLine* and *IsOpen*.

5 Modify the file access functions to store and load OLE objects.

For your view class, you need to

1 Change the base class to *TOleView*.

2 Remove the *DragDC* member.

3 Modify the constructor and destructor to remove statements with *DragDC*.

4 Modify the *Paint* function to call the base class *Paint* function.

5 Modify the mouse action commands to check when the user selects an embedded OLE object.

Changing document registration

The registration table you created on page 88 contains information necessary for the creation of a basic document template. This functions fine when the only thing using the document template is the document manager. But the way that ObjectComponents uses the Doc/View classes requires some more information:

- An identifier string. For this identifier, you want to use the REGDATA macro with the *progid* key value. This is a three part identifier. Each part of the identifier should be a text description, with each part separated by a period. There should be no whitespace or non-alphabetic character in this string other than the period delimiters.

  - The first part of the identifier should be descriptive of the overall application. For example, in the sample code, the first part of the identifier is DrawPad.

  - The second part should describe the part of the application contained in the module associated with the registration table. For the application registration table in the sample code, this part of the identifier is Application. For the document registration table, it's Document.

  - The third part should be a number. In the sample code, this number is 1. If your application supports multiple document types, use a different number for each document type.

  Note that this isn't meant for the users of your application to see. It's entered in the system's OLE registration database and should be unique for every application.

- A description of the document class. For this, you want to use the REGDATA macro with the *description* key value. This value is intended for the users of your application to see; this is the string that appears in the OLE registration database when someone is inserting an object into their container.

- A list of the types of data the container application can pass on to the Clipboard. To register Clipboard formats, use the REGFORMAT macro. This macro takes five parameters:

  - Format priority. The lower the value, the higher the priority. 0 indicates that the format is the highest priority format. When the user tries to paste data into your application, the Clipboard tries to paste it in as the highest priority format that is consistent with the format of the data in the Clipboard.

  - Data format.

  - Presentation aspect used to display data (for example, a bitmap could be displayed as a bitmap, as formatted information about the bitmap such as its dimensions and number of colors, as a hex dump, and so on) or an object might be presented in iconic form.

  - How the data is transferred when not otherwise specified (for example, when data is transferred by a drag-and-drop transaction, the server might prefer to pass the data to the container by means of a temporary file).

  - Whether the document can provide as well as receive this type of data.

  Every OLE application *must* specify that it can handle the *ocrEmbedSource* and *ocrMetafilePict* formats. By default, ObjectComponents always registers *ocrLinkSource*. You'll usually want to register *ocrLinkSource* yourself, though, so that you can set its priority lower. In addition, you can register *ocrBitmap* and *ocrDIB*. Note these formats indicate the type of data your application can pass to the Clipboard, not the type of data your application can accept. Pasting this data to the Clipboard is handled by ObjectComponents. The exact meaning of each of these values is described in the *ObjectWindows Reference*.

The following registration table shows how your registration table should look. The values for the REGFORMAT macro are described in the *ObjectWindows Reference*.

```
BEGIN_REGISTRATION(DocReg)
  REGDATA(progid, "DrawContainer")
  REGDATA(description,"OWL Drawing Pad 2.0 Document")
  REGDATA(extension, "PTS")
  REGDATA(docfilter, "*.pts")
  REGDOCFLAGS(dtAutoOpen | dtAutoDelete | dtUpdateDir | dtCreatePrompt |
    dtRegisterExt)
  REGFORMAT(0, ocrEmbedSource, ocrContent, ocrIStorage, ocrGet)
  REGFORMAT(1, ocrMetafilePict, ocrContent, ocrMfPict, ocrGet)
  REGFORMAT(2, ocrBitmap, ocrContent, ocrGDI|ocrStaticMed, ocrGet)
  REGFORMAT(3, ocrDib, ocrContent, ocrHGlobal|ocrStaticMed, ocrGet)
  REGFORMAT(4, ocrLinkSource, ocrContent, ocrIStream, ocrGet)
END_REGISTRATION
```

Changing TDrawDocument to handle embedded OLE objects

You need to make a few changes to *TDrawDocument* to support embedded OLE objects. These changes mainly affect reading and writing documents that contain OLE objects. The changes are fairly simple; most of the capabilities required to handle embedded OLE objects are handled in the new base class *TOleDocument*. Here's a summary of the changes required.

1 Change *TDrawDocument*'s base class to *TOleDocument*.

2 Modify *TDrawDocument*'s constructor to improve performance.

3 Remove the *IsOpen* function.

4 Add some function calls to the *Commit* and *Open* functions; these function calls read and write OLE objects embedded in the document.

Changing TDrawDocument's base class to TOleDocument

To get your document class ready to work in an ObjectComponents environment, you need to change the base class from *TFileDocument* to *TOleDocument*. *TOleDocument* is based on the *TStorageDocument* class, which is in turn based on *TDocument*. *TStorageDocument* provides the ability to manage and store compound documents. Compound documents provide a way to combine multiple objects into a single disk file, without having to worry about where each of the individual objects are stored or how they are written out or read in. On top of *TStorageDocument*'s capabilities, *TOleDocument* adds the ability to interface with an OLE object, control and display the OLE object, and read and write the object to and from storage.

To change your base class from *TFileDocument* to *TOleDocument*, you first need to change all references from *TFileDocument* to *TOleDocument*. This is fairly simple, since all that needs to change is the actual name; all the function signatures, including the base class constructor's, are the same.

Constructing and destroying TDrawDocument

The only change you need to make to the constructor for *TDrawDocument* (other than changing the base class to *TOleDocument*) basically serves to enhance the performance of the Drawing Pad application, and is not connected to its OLE functionality.

1 Remove the *Lines* member from the constructor's initialization list.

2 Initialize *Lines* in the constructor body, with an initial size of 100, lower boundary of 0, and a delta of 5.

Your constructor should now look something like this:

```
TDrawDocument(TDocument* parent) :
TOleDocument(parent), UndoLine(0), UndoState(UndoNone)
{
    Lines = new TLines(100, 0, 5);
}
```

You don't need to make any changes to the destructor.

Removing the IsOpen function

You need to remove the *IsOpen* function from the *TDrawDocument* class. This function is made obsolete by the change you made to the constructor, since the function tests the validity of the *Lines* member, and *Lines* now always points to a valid object.

TStorageDocument provides an *IsOpen* function that tests whether the document object has a valid *IStorage* member. *IStorage* is an OLE 2 construct that manages compound file storage and retrieval. A compound file is a basically a file that contains references to objects in a number of other locations. To the user, the compound file appears to be a single document. In reality, the different elements of the file are stored in various areas determined by the system and managed through the *IStorage* object. By constructing an OLE container, you're venturing into supporting compound documents in your application. However, since the support is provided through the OLE-enabled ObjectComponents classes, you don't need to worry about managing the compound documents yourself.

Along with removing the *IsOpen* function declaration and definition from *TDrawDocument*, you need to eliminate any references to the *IsOpen* function. This function is called only once, in the *GetLine* function. In this case, you can simply remove the entire statement that contains the call to *IsOpen*. This statement checks the validity of the document's *TLine* object referenced by the *Lines* data member, but the change you made to the constructor, which ensures that each document object is always associated with a valid *TLine* object, makes the check unnecessary. Your *GetLine* function should now look something like this:

```
TLine*
TDrawDocument::GetLine(uint index)
{
    return index < Lines->GetItemsInContainer() ? &(*Lines)[index] : 0;
}
```

The *TDrawDocument* class declaration should now look something like this:

```
class _DOCVIEWCLASS TDrawDocument : public TOleDocument
{
  public:
    enum {
      PrevProperty = TFileDocument::NextProperty-1,
      LineCount,
      Description,
      NextProperty,
    };
    enum {
      UndoNone,
      UndoDelete,
      UndoAppend,
      UndoModify
    };
    TDrawDocument(TDocument* parent = 0);
    ~TDrawDocument() { delete Lines; delete UndoLine; }

    // implement virtual methods of TDocument
    bool Open(int mode, const char far* path=0);
    bool Close();
    bool Commit(bool force = false);
    bool Revert(bool clear = false);

    int FindProperty(const char far* name);   // return index
    int PropertyFlags(int index);
    const char far* PropertyName(int index);
    int PropertyCount() {return NextProperty - 1;}
    int GetProperty(int index, void far* dest, int textlen=0);

    // data access functions
    TLine* GetLine(uint index);
    int AddLine(TLine& line);
    void DeleteLine(uint index);
    void ModifyLine(TLine& line, uint index);
    void Clear();
    void Undo();

  protected:
    TLines* Lines;
    TLine* UndoLine;
    int UndoState;
    int UndoIndex;
    string FileInfo;
};
```

Reading and writing embedded OLE objects

The last change you need to make to your document class provides the ability to save and load OLE objects embedded in a document. This is contained in two functions provided by *TOleDocument*. The functions are named *Open* and *Commit*. As you can probably guess, *Open* reads in the OLE objects contained in the document and *Commit* writes them out, that is, it commits the changes to disk.

To add these changes to your document class:

1 Add the call to *TOleDocument::Commit* in the *Commit* function right before you create the *TOutStream* object by calling the *OutStream* function.

2 Add the call to the *TOleDocument::Open* function in *TDrawDocument*'s *Open* function right before you create the *TInStream* object by calling the *InStream* function.

3 At the end of the procedure, call *TOleDocument::CommitTransactedStorage* to make your changes permanent. By default, *TOleDocument* uses the transacted mode (*ofTransacted*) to buffer changes in temporary storages until they are committed permanently.

That's all you need to do read and store OLE objects in your document! Your *Commit* function should now look something like this:

```
bool TDrawDocument::Commit(bool force)
{
  TOleDocument::Commit(force);

  TOutStream* os = OutStream(ofWrite);

  if (!os)
    return false;

  // Write the number of lines in the figure
  *os << Lines->GetItemsInContainer();

  // Append a description using a resource string
  *os << ' ' << FileInfo << '\n';

  // Get an iterator for the array of lines
  TLinesIterator i(*Lines);

  // While the iterator is valid (i.e. we haven't run out of lines)
  while (i)
    // Copy the current line from the iterator and increment the array.
    *os << i++;

  delete os;

  // Commit the storage if it was opened in transacted mode
  TOleDocument::CommitTransactedStorage();
  SetDirty(false);
  return true;
}
```

Your *Read* function should look something like this:

```
bool TDrawDocument::Open(int mode, const char far* path)
{
  char fileinfo[100];
```

```
TOleDocument::Open(mode, path);
if (GetDocPath()) {
  TInStream* is = (TInStream*)InStream(ofRead);

  if (!is)
    return false;

  unsigned numLines;
  *is >> numLines;
  is->getline(fileinfo, sizeof(fileinfo));

  while (numLines--) {
    TLine line;
    *is >> line;
    Lines->Add(line);
  }

  delete is;

  FileInfo = fileinfo;
} else {
  FileInfo = string(*::Module,IDS_FILEINFO);
}
SetDirty(false);
UndoState = UndoNone;
return true;
}
```

Changing TDrawView to handle embedded OLE objects

You need to make a few changes to *TDrawView* to support embedded OLE objects. These changes mainly affect handling OLE objects through the mouse, including dragging the objects and activating the object's server. The changes are fairly simple; most of the capabilities required to handle embedded OLE objects are handled in the new base class *TOleView*. Here's a summary of the changes required.

1 Change the base class of *TDrawView* to *TOleView*.

2 Remove the *DragDC* member; *TOleView* supplies a *TDC* pointer called *DragDC*.

3 Modify the constructor and destructor to remove initialization and deletion of *DragDC*.

4 Remove the *EvRButtonDown* function.

5 Modify the *Paint* function to call *TOleView::Paint* to force embedded objects to paint themselves.

6 Modify the mouse action functions to deal with user interaction with embedded OLE objects.

7 Modify the class declaration to reflect changes in the view class.

Modifying the TDrawView declaration

Here's the class declaration for *TDrawView*. The modifications to it will be explained in the following sections.

```
class _DOCVIEWCLASS TDrawView : public TOleView
{
  public:
    TDrawView(TDrawDocument& doc, TWindow* parent = 0);
   ~TDrawView() {delete Line;}
    static const char far* StaticName() {return "Draw View";}
    const char far* GetViewName() {return StaticName();}

  protected:
    TDrawDocument* DrawDoc;   // same as Doc member, but cast to derived
      class TPen* Pen;
    TLine* Line;              // To hold a single line sent or received
      from document

    // Message response functions
    void EvLButtonDown(uint, TPoint&);
    void EvMouseMove(uint, TPoint&);
    void EvLButtonUp(uint, TPoint&);
    void Paint(TDC&, bool, TRect&);
    void CmPenSize();
    void CmPenColor();
    void CmClear();
    void CmUndo();

    // Document notifications
    bool VnCommit(bool force);
    bool VnRevert(bool clear);
    bool VnAppend(uint index);
    bool VnDelete(uint index);
    bool VnModify(uint index);

  DECLARE_RESPONSE_TABLE(TDrawView);
};
```

Here's the response table for *TDrawView*.

```
DEFINE_RESPONSE_TABLE1(TDrawView, TOleView)
  EV_WM_LBUTTONDOWN,
  EV_WM_MOUSEMOVE,
  EV_WM_LBUTTONUP,
  EV_COMMAND(CM_PENSIZE, CmPenSize),
  EV_COMMAND(CM_PENCOLOR, CmPenColor),
  EV_COMMAND(CM_EDITCLEAR, CmClear),
  EV_COMMAND(CM_EDITUNDO, CmUndo),
  EV_VN_COMMIT,
  EV_VN_REVERT,
  EV_VN_DRAWAPPEND,
  EV_VN_DRAWDELETE,
  EV_VN_DRAWMODIFY,
END_RESPONSE_TABLE;
```

Changing TDrawView's base class to TOleView

To get your view class ready to work in an ObjectComponents environment, you need to change the base class from *TWindowView* to *TOleView*. *TOleView* is itself based on the *TWindowView* class. *TOleView* provides the ability required to manipulate and move OLE objects and activate an object's server.

To change your base class from *TWindowView* to *TOleView*, you first need to change all references from *TWindowView* to *TOleView*. This is fairly simple, since all that needs to change is the actual name; all the function signatures, including the base class constructor's, are the same.

Removing DragDC

This change is relatively straightforward. *TOleView* provides a pointer to a *TDC* called *DragDC*, obviating the need for this member in the *TDrawView* class. You'll also need to remove a lot of the actions you previously took with *DragDC*. Many of these, such as creating a device context object when the left mouse button is clicked, is taken care of by *TOleView*. These changes are discussed in the next section.

Constructing and destroying TDrawView

The only change you need to make to the *TDrawView* constructor is to remove the initialization of the *DragDC* member. Although *DragDC* was removed from the *TDrawView* class declaration, it is still a class member; it is provided by *TOleView*. But *TOleView* also handles initializing *DragDC*, since *TOleView* needs to check for OLE actions that the user might have taken.

Note that the *TOleView* constructor signature is the same as that of *TWindowView*, meaning all you have to do is change the name and nothing else. Here's how your *TDrawView* constructor should look.

```
TDrawView::TDrawView(TDrawDocument& doc, TWindow* parent) :
  TOleView(doc, parent), DrawDoc(&doc)
{
  Line = new TLine(TColor::Black, 1);
  SetViewMenu(new TMenuDescr(IDM_DRAWVIEW));
}
```

By the same token, the only modification needed to the destructor for *TDrawView* is to remove the statement deleting *DragDC*.

```
~TDrawView()
{
  delete Line;
}
```

Modifying the Paint function

You need to modify the *Paint* function to call *TOleView::Paint*. *TOleView::Paint* finds each linked or embedded object in the document (if there are any) and instructs each one to paint itself. Once this has been done, you can go on and paint the screen just as you did in Step 13. Your new *Paint* function should look something like this:

```
void
TDrawView::Paint(TDC& dc, bool erase, TRect&rect)
```

```
{
  TOleView::Paint(dc, erase, rect);

  // Iterates through the array of line objects.
  int j = 0;
  TLine* line;
  while ((line = const_cast<TLine *>(DrawDoc->GetLine(j++))) != 0)
    line->Draw(dc);
}
```

Selecting OLE objects

The next changes you need to make involve the functions dealing with mouse actions, namely *EvLButtonDown*, *EvMouseMove*, and *EvLButtonUp*. The changes you need to make in these functions involve checking whether the user's mouse actions involve an OLE object and what drawing mode is set. This is mostly handled by *TOleView*; for the most part, all you have to do is call the base class versions of the functions. The changes for each function are discussed in the following sections.

Modifying EvLButtonDown

You don't need to change the basic workings of the *EvLButtonDown* function as it exists in Step 13. What you do need to do is add a couple of extra steps to take into account OLE objects that might be in the view.

1 The first thing you need to do is let the *TOleView* base class determine whether the user selected an OLE object. Do this by calling *TOleView::EvLButtonDown*. This function deactivates any currently selected OLE object, creates a new *TOleDC* object (*TOleDC* is derived from the *TClientDC* class you used in previous steps, adding the ability to handle embedded OLE objects), and checks to see if another OLE object was selected.

2 To check whether the user wants to and is able to draw in the view, you need to check two things: whether a valid device context was created in the call to *TOleView::EvLButtonDown* and whether an OLE object was selected. You can check the validity of the device context simply by testing *DragDC*. You can find out whether an OLE object was selected by calling the *SelectEmbedded* function. *SelectEmbedded* returns **true** if an object was selected and **false** otherwise. If both these conditions weren't met, *EvLButtonDown* can just return.

3 Assuming there is a valid device context and no OLE object was selected, you can go ahead and begin the drawing operation the same as you did in Step 13. The only change you need to make is removing the initialization of *DragDC*, since it's already set to a valid device context object.

Your *EvLButtonDown* function should look something like this:

```
void TDrawView::EvLButtonDown(uint modKeys, TPoint& point)
{
  TOleView::EvLButtonDown(modKeys, point);

  if (DragDC && !SelectEmbedded()) {
    SetCapture();
    Pen = new TPen(Line->QueryColor(), Line->QueryPenSize());
```

```
      DragDC->SelectObject(*Pen);
      DragDC->MoveTo(point);
      Line->Add(point);
   }
}
```

Modifying EvMouseMove

The changes needed to *EvMouseMove* are similar to those required by *EvLButtonDown*.

1 Call the base class version of *EvMouseMove*.

2 Check whether the device context is valid and whether an OLE object was selected.

3 Continue the drawing operation the same way you did in Step 13.

Your *EvMouseMove* function should look something like this:

```
void TDrawView::EvMouseMove(uint modKeys, TPoint& point)
{
  TOleView::EvMouseMove(modKeys, point);

  if (DragDC && !SelectEmbedded()) {
    DragDC->LineTo(point);
    Line->Add(point);
  }
}
```

Modifying EvLButtonUp

With *EvLButtonUp*, you need to do the same things as you did in *EvLButtonDown* and *EvMouseMove*, but with a bit of a twist. In this case, call the base class version of the function last instead of first. *TOleView::EvLButtonUp* performs a number of cleanup operations, including deleting the device context object pointed to by *DragDC*.

1 Check whether the device context is valid and whether an OLE object was selected.

2 Perform the same operations as *EvLButtonUp* in Step 13, except for deleting and zeroing out *DragDC*.

3 Call *TOleView::EvLButtonUp*.

Your *EvLButtonUp* function should look something like this:

```
void TDrawView::EvLButtonUp(uint modKeys, TPoint& point)
{
  if (DragDC && !SelectEmbedded()) {
    ReleaseCapture();
    if (Line->GetItemsInContainer() > 1) {
      DrawDoc->AddLine(*Line);
    }
    Line->Flush();
    delete Pen;
  }

  TOleView::EvLButtonUp(modKeys, point);
}
```

Where to find more information

Here's a guide to where you can find more information on the topics introduced in this step:

- OLE and ObjectComponents containers are discussed in Chapter 36.

- The ObjectComponents classes in general are discussed in more detail in Part 5 of the *Borland C++ Programmer's Guide*.

15

Making an OLE server

Supporting OLE servers by being a OLE container is a big step ahead in flexibility for your applications. It expands the functionality of your application into just about any area you can think of. But one thing is missing: if you can make your application an OLE server, your application can be used to extend the functionality of other applications.

For example, suppose you're developing database forms and you want to add some of your line drawings to make the database forms more attractive. Without OLE, including line drawings in the database form is rather cumbersome, requiring you somehow to capture the drawing and paste it into the form. Then, once it's in the form, you have no way to modify it besides going back to Drawing Pad, editing it, then pasting it back into the form.

If the database is an OLE container, and you've made Drawing Pad an OLE server, you can easily drop line drawings into your database forms. The embedded OLE server lets you modify the line drawing without having to leave your database application.

This chapter describes how to take your Doc/View Drawing Pad application from Step 14 and make it an OLE server. The code for this example can be found in the files STEP15.CPP, STEP15DV.CPP, STEP15.H, STEP15DV.H, STEP15.RC, and STEP15DV.RC in the EXAMPLES/OWL/TUTORIAL directory of your compiler installation.

Note   After making the changes in this step, the Drawing Pad application will be a server-only application; that is, it will no longer support containing embedded OLE objects. This is to demonstrate the unique server functionality added to the application. Changes that remove the container support will be noted. If you want to combine container and server support in a single application, you need only to skip those steps that remove container support.

Converting your application object

There are a few changes you need to make in your application object to become an OLE server.

1 Change the header files.

2 Change the application's registration table.

3 Change the base class constructor to register some more information, including the application dictionary.

4 Hide the window if the application was invoked as a server.

5 Add module identifier parameters to a number of object constructors.

6 Change how you create new views.

7 Change how you find the About dialog box's parent window.

8 Change the *OwlMain* function to check for action options.

Changing the header files

You only need to make two changes to the list of header files in STEP15.CPP.

1 Add the owl\oleview.h header file; the *TOleView* class needs to be used when you create new views

2 Change from including STEP14.RC to STEP15.RC

Changing the application's registration table

You basically need to change your entire application registration table from Step 14. However, only one of these changes is directly related to making the application an OLE server. You need to change the values associated with the *clsid* and *description* keys. Because the end result is an application that is different from Step 14, all of these values should change.

Your new registration table should look something like this:

```
BEGIN_REGISTRATION(AppReg)
  REGDATA(clsid, "{5E4BD320-8ABC-101B-A23B-CE4E85D07ED2}")
  REGDATA(description,"OWL Drawing Pad Server")
END_REGISTRATION
```

Note Remember, don't try to duplicate the GUID or program identifier in your other applications! Preventing such duplication is why these values were changed from Step 14 to Step 15!

Changing the application constructor

For OLE servers, you need to change *TDrawApp*'s base class constructor to take the application dictionary object as a parameter. For a container application, you didn't need to do this. The reason is that a container is always be created as an executable application as opposed to a DLL. When you don't specify an application dictionary in *TApplication*'s constructor, it uses the global application dictionary *::OwlAppDictionary*. This works fine for an executable: since it has its own instance, it's entered in the global application dictionary. But DLLs don't have their own instance.

TApplication provides a couple more parameters to its constructor than you've been using. The first is the name of the application, which you used in the last step to set the application name.

The second is a pointer to a reference to a *TModule* object (that is, *TModule**&). *TApplication*'s constructor sets this pointer to point at the new application object. In this case, you want to pass in the global module object *::Module*. *::Module* is used by ObjectWindows and ObjectComponents to identify the current module. Note that *::Module* is the default value for this parameter.

The last parameter is a pointer to a *TAppDictionary* object. Use a pointer to the *TAppDictionary* object you created using the DEFINE_APP_DICTIONARY macro for this parameter.

Now your constructor should look something like this:

```
TDrawApp() : TApplication(::AppReg["description"], ::Module, &::AppDictionary) {}
```

Hiding a server's main window

Under regular circumstances, when your application is started, it does some setup and initialization, then creates a main window for the user to work in. That's fine when someone is using your application as their primary workplace. But when your application is being used as an OLE server, it's *not* the primary workplace; the main window has already been created by another application. In this case, you need to set your main window to be hidden.

The best place to do this is in *InitMainWindow*, before your window object has been created. To find out whether the application is an embedded server and to hide the main window if so:

1 Call the *IsOptionSet* function of the *TOcRegistrar* object, passing *TOcCmdLine::Embedding* as the function's argument. You can get a reference to the application's registrar object by calling the *GetRegistrar* function. *IsOptionSet* checks to see if the application's command line contained the option passed to it as a parameter. When an application is created as an embedded server, the *-Embedding* option is specified on the command line. Therefore, if the application was created as an embedded server, *IsOptionSet* returns **true** when passed *TOcCmLine::Embedding*. You'll see more of these options later.

2 If *IsOptionSet* returns **true**, the application is being invoked as an embedded server, so set *nCmdShow* to SW_HIDE. This causes the main window to be hidden when it's created and activation to be passed to the window from which the server was invoked.

Identifying the module

When you constructed the *TApplication* base class, you had to add in a couple of new parameters to make sure the object could find itself in complicated OLE environment. You need to do the same basic thing for a number of other objects in your application. In the case of these objects, though, you just need to direct them to the application object, which then handles all the transactions between your application and whatever's outside of the application.

- The MDI client window takes a single parameter, a module pointer.
- The OLE MDI frame takes a *TModule* pointer as a parameter after its menu-tracking parameter (which is the last parameter you used in Step 14).
- The document manager takes a *TApplication* pointer after its flags parameter.

Use *TDrawApp*'s **this** pointer for each of these parameters.

Your *InitMainWindow* function should look something like this:

```
void
TDrawApp::InitMainWindow()
{
  if (GetRegistrar().IsOptionSet(TOcCmdLine::Embedding))
    nCmdShow = SW_HIDE;

  TOleMDIFrame* frame;
  frame = new TOleMDIFrame(GetName(), 0, *(Client = new TMDIClient(this)),
                                      true, this);

  frame->SetOcApp(OcApp);

  // Construct a status bar
  TStatusBar* sb = new TStatusBar(frame, TGadget::Recessed);

  // Construct a control bar
  TControlBar* cb = new TControlBar(frame);
  cb->Insert(*new TButtonGadget(CM_FILENEW, CM_FILENEW,
                                TButtonGadget::Command));
  cb->Insert(*new TButtonGadget(CM_FILEOPEN, CM_FILEOPEN,
                                TButtonGadget::Command));
  cb->Insert(*new TButtonGadget(CM_FILESAVE, CM_FILESAVE,
                                TButtonGadget::Command));
  cb->Insert(*new TButtonGadget(CM_FILESAVEAS, CM_FILESAVEAS,
                                TButtonGadget::Command));
  cb->Insert(*new TSeparatorGadget);
  cb->Insert(*new TButtonGadget(CM_PENSIZE, CM_PENSIZE,
                                TButtonGadget::Command));
  cb->Insert(*new TButtonGadget(CM_PENCOLOR, CM_PENCOLOR, TButtonGadget::Command));
  cb->Insert(*new TSeparatorGadget);
  cb->Insert(*new TButtonGadget(CM_ABOUT, CM_ABOUT, TButtonGadget::Command));
  cb->SetHintMode(TGadgetWindow::EnterHints);
  cb->Attr.Id = IDW_TOOLBAR;
  // Insert the status bar and control bar into the frame
  frame->Insert(*sb, TDecoratedFrame::Bottom);
  frame->Insert(*cb, TDecoratedFrame::Top);
```

```
// Set the main window and its menu
SetMainWindow(frame);
GetMainWindow()->SetMenuDescr(TMenuDescr(IDM_MDICMNDS));

// Install the document manager
SetDocManager(new TDocManager(dmMDI | dmMenu, this));
}
```

Creating new views

When creating a new view window in an OLE server application, you need to be careful about setting the view's parent. In the case where your application is being run as a stand-alone program, you don't have to change anything. The code in *EvNewView* that you used in the last few steps is just fine.

Things become complicated when the server is embedded in a container application. You need to determine one basic thing: is your view using space inside one of the container's windows? You can determine this by answering two questions:

- Is the application being used as an embedded server? If the answer to this question is no (that is, your application is being run on its own), then you can skip the next question: you know your application isn't occupying space in the container's window, because there is no container.

- Has the application been opened for editing? The user can access your embedded server in one of two ways: either in-place editing, where your server's workspace sits inside the workspace of the container, or open editing, where your server opens up for editing, looking pretty much the same as it does when opened on its own. If the user has opened your server for editing then the server is *not* sharing space in the container's window. Only if the user is using your server for in-place editing do you have to worry about sharing space with the container.

The reason you need to determine this has to do with setting the parent window of the view. When the server is being used as an in-place server, you must set the parent window of the view properly. ObjectComponents provides an object known as a view bucket to make this easier. Once you've set your view's parent to the view bucket, ObjectComponents takes care of setting the view's parent when the view is activated, deactivated, moved around, and so on. To set the view's parent, follow this procedure:

1 Downcast the *TView* parameter of the *EvNewView* function to a *TOleView*. Take the address of the object by prefixing it with an ampersand (&) and assign it to a *TOleView* pointer using the TYPESAFE_DOWNCAST macro.

2 Check whether the view is an embedded server by calling the view's associated document's *IsEmbedded* function. The view itself doesn't know if it's embedded. You can find the view's associated document by calling the view's *GetDocument* function. If the document's not embedded, you can stop checking here and just go to the code you used in the last few steps.

3 Check whether the view is activated for open editing. You can check this by calling the *IsOpenEditing* function of the view's remote view. You can get a pointer to the remote view by calling *GetOcRemView*. If *IsOpenEditing* returns **true**, you can stop checking here and go to the code you used in the last few steps.

4 Once you've determined that the application is being used as a server for in-place editing, you can work on setting up the view's parent. Follow this procedure:

   1 Find the window associated with the view. You can get a *TWindow* pointer to this window using the view's *GetWindow* function.

   2 You need to find the remote view bucket associated with the server. To do this, call the *GetMainWindow* function and downcast the return value to a *TOleFrame* pointer. *TOleFrame* provides a function called *GetRemViewBucket*. This function returns a *TWindow* pointer that references the remote view bucket.

   3 Once you've found the remote view bucket, call the view's *SetParent* function with the bucket's *TWindow* pointer as the parameter.

   4 Call the view's *Create* function.

Note that you haven't really set the view's parent as you normally think of it. But the remote view bucket lets you set this once and then lets ObjectComponents take care of the work of keeping track of the active parent window.

The code for this function should look something like this:

```
void
TDrawApp::EvNewView(TView& view)
{
  TOleView* ov = TYPESAFE_DOWNCAST(&view, TOleView);
  if (view.GetDocument().IsEmbedded() && !ov->GetOcRemView()->IsOpenEditing()) {
    TWindow* vw = view.GetWindow();
    vw->SetParent(TYPESAFE_DOWNCAST(GetMainWindow(), TOleFrame)->GetRemViewBucket());
    vw->Create();
  } else {
    TMDIChild* child = new TMDIChild(*Client, 0);
    if (view.GetViewMenu())
      child->SetMenuDescr(*view.GetViewMenu());
    child->Create();
    child->SetClientWindow(view.GetWindow());
  }
}
```

Changing the About dialog box's parent window

In previous versions of the tutorial application, when you created the About dialog box, you simply called the *GetMainWindow* function to find the dialog box's parent window. This is no longer adequate, however, since you don't know if your main window is actually the main window that the application user sees. If your application is embedded in another application, you've already determined in the *TDrawApp* constructor that you're not displaying your main window.

To find the window with focus or other appropriate view window on the desktop (which functions as the dialog's parent), you can call the *GetCommandTarget* function. This function is provided by *TFrameWindow* and returns a handle to the current active window. Note that calling this function works whether or not the application is running as an embedded server or as a stand-alone application, since it returns the command focus window. When the tutorial application is an embedded server, it returns a handle to the focus window of the client application. When the tutorial application is running on its own, it returns a handle to itself.

Note that you still need to call *GetMainWindow* to get a pointer to the tutorial application's main window. You then call the *GetCommandTarget* function of that window object. You also need to create a temporary *TWindow* to pass *GetCommandTarget*'s return value to the *TDialog* constructor. Your modified *CmAbout* function should look something like this:

```
void
TDrawApp::CmAbout()
{
   TDialog(&TWindow(GetMainWindow()->GetCommandTarget()), IDD_ABOUT).Execute();
}
```

Modifying OwlMain

There's only one new thing you need to take care of before running an OLE server application. You need to check the command line to see if one of the standard action options was specified.

There are a couple of standard ObjectComponents command-line options that may be specified for your server application. The presence of one of these "action" options signals that, instead of executing normally, your application should perform a particular action, then exit. For an OLE server application, the action options you need to check for are:

- The *–RegServer* option tells your application to completely register itself in the OLE registration database.

- The *–UnregServer* option tells your application to "unregister" itself, that is, remove its entry in the OLE registration database.

The good thing about these options is that ObjectComponents automatically performs these actions for you when you create the registrar object. The only thing you need to do is check in the *OwlMain* function whether one of these options was set. If so, you can return immediately. If none of the action options was specified, you can go on to the next step.

You can check for these options using the *IsOptionSet* function that you used in the *InitMainWindow* function to check for the *–Embedding* flag. For these options, you should check for the *TOcCmdLine::AnyRegOptions* flag. This flag checks to see if any of the options relevant to your application was set. *IsOptionSet* returns **true** if any of the options was set.

If one of the flags was set, you can return 0 from *OwlMain*. When one of these action options is set, ObjectComponents performs some registration task. Once that task is done, the application is complete. Your application never performs a registration task then executes as normal.

Your *OwlMain* function should look something like this:

```
int
OwlMain(int /*argc*/, char* /*argv*/ [])
{
  Registrar = new TOcRegistrar(AppReg, TOleFactory<TDrawApp>(),
                               TApplication::GetCmdLine());

  if (Registrar->IsOptionSet(TOcCmdLine::RegServer | TOcCmdLine::UnregServer))
    return 0;

  return Registrar->Run();
}
```

Changes to your Doc/View classes

There are a number of changes you need to make to your Doc/View classes to support OLE server functionality:

- Change your header files

- Modify the document registration table to provide extra information needed by an OLE server

- Make some changes to the view notification functions *VnRevert*, *VnAppend*, *VnModify*, and *VnDelete* functions

- Add some new members to *TDrawView*, including a *TControlBar* pointer and some new functions

- Remove calls from the mouse action functions and the *Paint* function

Changing header files

You need to change your list of header files to include a few new header files, along with changing to including the resource script file for Step 15. The new files you need to include are owl/controlb.h and owl/buttonga.h. Your include statements should look something like this:

```
#include <owl/dc.h>
#include <owl/inputdia.h>
#include <owl/chooseco.h>
#include <owl/gdiobjec.h>
#include <owl/docmanag.h>
#include <owl/listbox.h>
#include <owl/controlb.h>
#include <owl/buttonga.h>
#include <owl/olemdifr.h>
#include <owl/oledoc.h>
#include <owl/oleview.h>
#include <classlib/arrays.h>
#include "step15dv.rc"
```

Changing the document registration table

You need to make some fairly extensive changes to your document registration table to support being an OLE server. The parts that don't change are discussed in this section.

Defining the registration table isn't different from before. This basically involves using the BEGIN_REGISTRATION and END_REGISTRATION macros. As before, your table begins with the BEGIN_REGISTRATION macro, which takes the name of the registration as its only parameter. The END_REGISTRATION macro closes out the table definition.

The two REGDATA macros that set the *extension* and *docfilter* table entries remain the same. The REGDOCFLAGS macro also doesn't change.

The parts of the registration table that you need to change are discussed in the next sections.

Program identifier and description

Step 14's program identifier (the value associated with the *progid* key) and its description (the value associated with the *description* key) described the application as a "Draw Container" and "OWL Drawing Pad Container," respectively. These values need to be changed to reflect the application being a server.

Making the application insertable

ObjectComponents provides a special key value called *insertable*. You can register *insertable* using the REGDATA macro. The value associated with the *insertable* key is irrelevant; it's never used, so usually you'll just want to set an empty string for the value.

The presence of the *insertable* key indicates to ObjectComponents that the application is insertable, that is, the application can be embedded into other applications. All ObjectComponents servers must specify the *insertable* key in their registration table!

Setting the server's menu items

When the user activates a server embedded in a container by clicking on the server's view, the container sets a menu item (usually on its Edit menu) that the user can use to access the server. This menu goes to a pop-up menu that provides a number of "verbs"—menu choices that let the user work with the server application and manipulate the data in it.

So there are two things you need to set up for this:

- You need to set up the menu name that the container uses to represent your application on the container's Edit menu. You can do this with the REGDATA macro, using the *menuname* key and the text you want to appear on the menu as the key's value. You want to be considerate of the container application when choosing this name. Use a name that you would normally use in a menu; that is, it should be descriptive of your application but not so long that it forces the menu to be quite large to accommodate the string. In this case, you could use the application name "Drawing Pad."

- You can specify up to twenty verbs for your server application. Specify the verbs for your server application using the REGDATA macro. The key values you use to set up verbs follow the format *verbn*, where n is a number from 0 to 19. The value you associate with each verb is the text that appears on the pop-up menu. Note that you can specify a keyboard shortcut for each verb by preceding the shortcut letter with an ampersand (&). For example, if you specify Edit as a verb, and you want the user to be able to press E to activate that, you specify the string "&Edit" for the value.

  Note that the first verb in the verb list, that is, the value associated with the *verb0* key is the default verb for your server. Thus if the user double-clicks on your embedded server, the server acts just the same as if the user had selected the *verb0* value from the server's menu.

ObjectComponents servers are set up to automatically handle two verbs.

- The Edit verb indicates that the user wants to manipulate the data handled by the server in place in the container. That means that the user works with the data right in the remote view area in the container's window.

- The Open verb indicates that the user wants to open the server application to manipulate the data. In this case, the application opens up as if the user had run the application by itself. The main difference between using the server this way and running the server as a stand-alone application is that the server writes to a document file provided by the container; the container's compound document storage handles the details of saving the data to disk.

Specifying Clipboard formats

For the server application, you can trim down the number of Clipboard formats available. You really only need to provide two formats.

- *ocrEmbedSource* indicates that the server can be copied to the Clipboard as an embeddable source. If someone tries to paste an embeddable source from the Clipboard, they get a copy of the embedded server object in their application.

- *ocrMetafilePict* indicates that the server can be copied to the Clipboard as a metafile representation.

As before, the actual copying operation is handled by ObjectComponents. Note that these are the only formats necessary to support an ObjectComponents server; the other formats provided by the container application are removed. To support dual container/server functionality, you should leave these formats in.

Your finished document registration table should look something like this:

```
BEGIN_REGISTRATION(DocReg)
  REGDATA(progid, "DrawServer")
  REGDATA(menuname, "Drawing Pad")
  REGDATA(description, "OWL Drawing Pad Server")
  REGDATA(extension, "PTS")
  REGDATA(docfilter, "*.pts")
  REGDOCFLAGS(dtAutoOpen | dtAutoDelete | dtUpdateDir | dtCreatePrompt |
              dtRegisterExt
  REGDATA(insertable, "")
```

```
   REGDATA(verb0,  "&Edit")
   REGDATA(verb1,  "&Open")
   REGFORMAT(0, ocrEmbedSource, ocrContent, ocrIStorage, ocrGet)
   REGFORMAT(1, ocrMetafilePict, ocrContent, ocrMfPict, ocrGet)
END_REGISTRATION
```

Changing the view notification functions

You need to make a change to a number of the view notification functions to support proper painting of the server's remote view. The functions you need to change are *VnRevert*, *VnAppend*, *VnModify*, and *VnDelete*. Each of these view notifications indicates that the drawing has been modified in some way and the display needs to be updated.

To force the container to update the view and reflect the changes in the view's appearance, you need to call the *InvalidatePart* function. This function is provided by *TDrawView*'s base class *TOleView*. This function tells the container window that the area inside the embedded server's remote view is invalid and needs repainting. *InvalidatePart* takes a single parameter, a *TOcInvalidate* **enum**. A *TOcValidate* can be one of two values.

- *invData* indicates the data in an embedded object has changed and should be updated in the container.

- *invView* indicates the appearance of an object has changed and should be updated in the container.

In this case, each of these view notification events indicates that the appearance of the drawing has changed, whether it was by discarding changes, appending a new line, modifying one of the current lines, or deleting a line. So when you do call the *InvalidatePart* function, you should call it with the *invView* argument. The *invData* argument is used when the container has a link to data in the server, but the container actually takes care of displaying the data.

You should first call the *Invalidate* function of the view when applicable (each of these functions already calls *Invalidate*, except for *VnAppend*, which doesn't need to), then call the *InvalidatePart* function. Here's how your modified view notification functions should look:

```
bool
TDrawView::VnRevert(bool /*clear*/)
{
  Invalidate();  // force full repaint
  InvalidatePart(invView);
  return true;
}

bool
TDrawView::VnAppend(uint)
{
  InvalidatePart(invView);
  return true;
}

bool
```

```
TDrawView::VnModify(uint /*index*/)
{
  Invalidate();  // force full repaint
  InvalidatePart(invView);
  return true;
}

bool
TDrawView::VnDelete(uint /*index*/)
{
  Invalidate();  // force full repaint
  InvalidatePart(invView);
  return true;
}
```

Adding new members to TDrawView

You need to add some new members to your *TDrawView* class. These members are

- A *TControlBar* pointer
- Two new event handlers for cutting and copying
- Two new event handlers for ObjectComponents events

Adding a control bar

When your application is activated as an embedded server, the container often lets the application provide a tool bar to access its functionality. This tool bar should be different from the regular application tool bar and provides button gadgets only to access the unique functions of your application and not those things handled by containers, that is, the object's editing and viewing commands. For example, opening a file is handled by any adequate container application, so it's not a unique ability of the Drawing Pad application. On the other hand, no container knows how to change Drawing Pad's pen color.

Since the commands supported by this tool bar are a subset of the commands supported by the application's tool bar, you can't simply use that tool bar. Instead you need to provide one for each embedded server view. To support this, just add a *TControlBar* pointer as a protected data member. You should initialize this member to 0 in *TDrawView*'s constructor. The tool bar itself is constructed in one of the new ObjectComponents event handlers. You can see this on page 152.

Cutting and copying data

Your server will often receive requests to cut or copy data to the Clipboard. You need to provide functions to handle these requests.

Cutting

Cutting data is copying information from the drawing, placing that information in the Clipboard, then removing the information from the drawing. This is a fairly common way to exchange data. However, in the context of the Drawing Pad application, this behavior is undefined: what does it mean to cut lines from a window?

But since this is a very common (almost mandatory) function in an OLE server, you should provide at least a place holder for it. You can declare and define a function called *CmEditCut* to do this. This function is called when *TDrawView* receives the CM_EDITCUT event, which you also need to add (it's in the STEP15DV.RC file in the sample code). So follow this procedure:

1 Add the CM_EDITCUT macro to your application.

2 Add the *CmEditCut* function to the *TDrawView* class declaration.

3 Add an EV_COMMAND macro to the response table to call *CmEditCut* when the CM_EDITCUT event is received.

4 Define *CmEditCut* to have no functionality.

Copying

To copy, you can call a member function of one of the classes provided by ObjectComponents. This class is called *TOcRemView* and provides a remote view object for a server document. A remote view handles the view of your server application from the container application. *TOcRemView* provides a function called *Copy*, which copies the document's data to the Clipboard. You get the *TOcRemView* object to work with by calling the *GetOcRemView* function, which is provided by *TOleView*.

1 Add the CM_EDITCOPY macro to your application.

2 Add the *CmEditCopy* function to the *TDrawView* class declaration.

3 Add an EV_COMMAND macro to the response table to call *CmEditCopy* when the CM_EDITCOPY event is received.

4 Define *CmEditCopy* to call *GetOcRemView* and call the *Copy* function of the *TOcRemView* object.

Handling ObjectComponents events

There are a couple of ObjectComponents events that you need to handle.

- OC_VIEWPARTSIZE indicates a request from the container to find out the size of your object's view, that is, the size of the "window" within the container's window in which the user sees your embedded application.

- OC_VIEWSHOWTOOLS indicates a request from the container for a tool bar from the server application.

Reporting server view size

For formatting reasons, a container often needs to find out the size of an embedded server's view. The container signals that it needs this information by sending an ObjectComponents message to the view. The view then needs to calculate the size of the server view and get that information back to the container.

To add this functionality, follow these steps:

1 The container lets the server know that it needs the size of the view by sending the OC_VIEWPARTSIZE, a standard ObjectComponents event. ObjectWindows provides a response table macro for this and other standard ObjectComponents

event. The ObjectComponents event macros are defined in the header file owl/ocfevent.h, which is automatically included. These macros add EV_ to the beginning of the ObjectComponents event name, so that in this case the macro would be EV_OC_VIEWPARTSIZE. Add this macro to your view's response table. Like other standard message macros, it has no parameters and calls a predefined function name when the event is received.

2 Add a function to your *TDrawView* class declaration to handle this event. The function called through the predefined response table macro is *EvOcViewPartSize*. This function returns **bool** and takes a pointer to a *TRect*.

3 Define the *EvOcViewPartSize* function. To do this, create a device context object (in the sample code here, we've used a *TClientDC*). You should place the size of the view in the *TRect* object passed into *EvOcViewPartSize* by pointer. In the Drawing Pad application, the size of the view is limited to 2 inches on the screen. This is an arbitrary measurement; you can also calculate the area necessary to display the information in the document and pass that back. For simplicity, though, it's easiest to pass back an absolute measurement. In this case, set the *top* and *left* members of the *TRect* to 0. You can then get the number of pixels in the size of the view by calling the *GetDeviceCaps* function of the device context object with the LOGPIXELSX parameter to get the width and the LOGPIXELSY parameter to get the height. This actually returns the number of pixels in an inch on the screen. Multiply this result by two in each case and assign the width to the *right* member of the *TRect* object and the height to the *bottom* member.

The completed function should look something like this:

```
bool
TDrawView::EvOcViewPartSize(TRect far* size)
{
  TClientDC dc(*this);

  // a 2" x 2" extent for server
  size->top    = size->left = 0;
  size->right  = dc.GetDeviceCaps(LOGPIXELSX) * 2;
  size->bottom = dc.GetDeviceCaps(LOGPIXELSY) * 2;
  return true;
}
```

Setting up the view's tool bar
The OC_VIEWSHOWTOOLS event indicates that the container in which your server is embedded wants to either show or hide your server's tool bar.

1 Add the OC_VIEWSHOWTOOLS macro to your view's response table.

2 Add a function to your *TDrawView* class declaration to handle this event. The function called through the predefined response table macro is *EvOcViewShowTools*. This function returns **bool** and takes reference to a *TOcToolBarInfo* object. *TOcToolBarInfo* is a simple structure; it only has a couple of members that we're concerned with here.

   • The first is the *Show* member, a **bool**. If *Show* is **true**, the container wants to display your tool bar. If *Show* is **false**, the container wants to hide your tool bar.

- The second is *HTopTB*, an HWND. You pass back the tool bar to the container through this member.

3 If the container wants to hide the tool bar (that is, *Show* is **false**), you need to destroy the tool bar window, delete the tool bar object, and set your *TControlBar* pointer to 0. Before doing this, though, you should check to make sure that the *TControlBar* pointer references a valid object!

4 If the container wants to show the tool bar, you should first check to see that the *TControlBar* pointer doesn't already point to a valid object. If so, you can skip Step 5 and go on to Step 6.

5 The most complicated thing about constructing a tool bar in these circumstances is finding the parent window. This takes a few steps, since you need to find your main window, and then, through the main window, which is an OLE frame window, you need to find the remote view bucket the application is using in the container's window.

    1 The first step is to find the application object. This is the easiest way to find the main window, since the application object provides a function to get a pointer to the main window. To find the application object, call the *GetApplication* function. This returns a *TApplication* pointer to the application object.

    2 Once you've found the application object, you can get a *TFrameWindow* pointer to the main window by calling the *GetMainWindow* function of the application object.

    3 Now that you've found the main window, you need to cast it to a *TOleFrame* window to be able to find the remote view bucket window. Although the main window is already a *TOleFrame* object, *GetMainWindow* returns it as a *TFrameWindow*. Since you are downcasting (that is, casting from a base object to a class derived from that base), you need to be careful. It is quite possible to try to cast an object of one type to an object of another type. If both of these types are derived from the same base class, this can cause serious trouble.

    For example, suppose you have a function that takes a *TWindow* pointer as its only parameter. When the function is called, you assume that the *TWindow* value you received in the function actually referenced a *TControl* object (since *TControl* is derived from *TWindow*, you can safely pass a *TControl* object as a *TWindow* object). But *TControl* and *TFrameWindow* are both derived from *TWindow*. What if the object passed in was actually a *TFrameWindow* object? Serious havoc could ensue.

    ObjectWindows provides a macro called TYPESAFE_DOWNCAST that downcasts objects that are typed as a base class to objects of a derived type. If the downcast isn't typesafe (that is, the object isn't what you're actually trying to downcast to, such as trying to cast a *TFrameWindow* to a *TControl*), the macro returns 0. Otherwise the macro makes the cast for you and returns the appropriate value.

    TYPESAFE_DOWNCAST takes two parameters. The first is the object you want to cast and the second is the type you want to cast the object to.

    4 Once you've found the application's main window and cast it appropriately, you need to call the *GetRemViewBucket* function. This function returns a *TWindow* pointer that references the remote view bucket window. This is quite important:

with the tool bar parented properly, it's easy for the container to switch tool bars automatically among any of the servers that might be embedded in the container.

5 Once you've got a pointer to the remote view bucket window, construct a *TControlBar* object like normal, passing the view pointer as the parent. When the tool bar object is constructed, you can insert button gadgets to control the application. For now, it's sufficient to just add the CM_PENSIZE and CM_PENCOLOR buttons.

6 Once you have a valid tool bar object, create the tool bar itself by calling the object's *Create* function.

7 Once the tool bar is created, cast it to an HWND and assign it to the *TOcToolBarInfo*'s *HTopTB* member. You could instead assign it to one of *TOcToolBarInfo*'s other members to place it somewhere besides the top of the container's window.

8 Assuming everything went alright during this process, return **true**. This lets the container know that everything went alright and it can display the tool bar.

Here's how your *EvOcViewShowTools* function should look:

```
bool
TDrawView::EvOcViewShowTools(TOcToolBarInfo far& tbi)
{
  // Construct & create a control bar for show, destroy our bar for hide
  if (tbi.Show) {
    if (!ToolBar) {
      TOleFrame* frame = TYPESAFE_DOWNCAST(GetApplication()GetMainWindow(),
                                    TOleFrame;
      ToolBar = new TControlBar(frame->GetRemViewBucket());
      ToolBarInsert(*new TButtonGadget(CM_PENSIZE, CM_PENSIZE,
                  TButtonGadget::Command));
      ToolBar->Insert(*new TButtonGadget(CM_PENCOLOR, CM_PENCOLOR,
                  TButtonGadget::Command));
    }
    ToolBar->Create();
    tbi.HTopTB = (HWND)*ToolBar;
  } else {
    if (ToolBar) {
      ToolBar->Destroy();
      delete ToolBar;
      ToolBar = 0;
    }
  }
  return true;
}
```

Removing calls from the Paint and mouse action functions

TDrawView's *Paint* function and its mouse action functions *EvLButtonDown*, *EvLButtonUp*, and *EvMouseMove* all make calls that are necessary to support container functionality. You should remove these calls for your application to function as a server-only application.

- The *Paint* function calls *TOleView::Paint* so that any embedded objects are called and told to paint themselves. Since a server-only application has no embedded objects, this call is no longer necessary.

- *EvLButtonDown*, *EvLButtonUp*, and *EvMouseMove* call the *SelectEmbedded* function to determine whether the user clicked on—and thereby selected—an embedded object. As with Paint, since there are no embedded objects in a server-only application, this call is no longer necessary.

16

Making an OLE automation server

An OLE automation server exposes functionality to other applications in the form of properties and methods. A *property* is analogous to a C++ data member; a *method* is analogous to a C++ member function. An application that uses the properties and methods of an OLE automation server is called an *OLE automation controller*.

In this step, you'll expose some of the functionality of the drawing application, making it possible for OLE automation controllers to open new drawing documents, set pen attributes, and add lines.

It's a relatively simple task to turn a regular OLE server into an OLE automation server. You just make small changes to the application, document, and view classes.

Changing the application class

To change the application class, follow these steps.

1 Include the automation and Step 16 header files.

2 Add the /automation command-line switch to the application registration table.

3 Declare and implement member functions that can be exposed as properties and methods.

4 Expose member functions as properties and methods.

Including the automation and Step 16 header files

Take the #include listing from the STEP15.CPP file and make the following changes:

1 Add the ocf/automacr.h header file.

2 Add the Step 16 resource (.RC), source (.CPP), and header (.H) files.

3 Remove the Step 15 header files.

Note In Step 16, the header file (STEP16.H) is separate from the source file (STEP16.CPP) for the application class.

Add the /automation command-line switch to the application registration table

An OLE automation server must register itself with the /automation command-line switch. Therefore, you must add the /automation switch to the application registration table using the *cmdline* keyword.

For the drawing application, you should also modify the description so it says "..Automation Server" instead of "...Server."

Your new registration table should look something like this:

```
BEGIN_REGISTRATION(AppReg)
  REGDATA(clsid, "{5E4BD320-8ABC-101B-A23B-CE4E85D07ED2}")
  REGDATA(description,"OWL Drawing Pad Automation Server")
  REGDATA(cmdline, "/automation")
END_REGISTRATION
```

Note Remember, never use a GUID or program identifier that another application uses.

Declaring and implementing member functions that can be exposed as properties and methods

Although you can expose the data members of the application class directly, you may want to implement one member function (for read-only or write-only properties) or two member functions (for read/write properties) that handle the tasks of getting and setting values. In this way, you can validate the data being transferred, preventing possible errors.

In addition, for each member function that has parameters with one or more complex data types, you should create a new member function that has parameters with only basic data types. The new function should perform the necessary conversions between data types and then call the original function. By exposing member functions that take only basic data types, you make it easier for an automation controller to use them.

Finally, most OLE automation servers expose a set of standard properties and methods, including the following:

- *Visible* (read/write property)
- *Name* (read-only property)
- *FullName* (read-only property)
- *NewDocument* (method)
- *OpenDocument* (method)
- *Quit* (method)

You should declare and implement member functions for each of the standard properties and methods.

For example, the STEP16.H file contains declarations for the standard properties and methods in the private section of the *TDrawApp* class:

```
void SetShow(bool visible); // Sets the Visible property value.
bool GetShow();             // Gets the Visible property value.
TDrawDocument* OpenDoc;     // Opens or creates a document.
```

Note You don't need to declare or implement a member function for the *Quit* method since these tasks are handled automatically by ObjectComponents if you use the EXPOSE_QUIT macro, as shown in the next section.

The STEP16.CPP file contains the implementations of these functions:

```
// Get the Visible property value.
TDrawApp::SetShow(bool visible)
{
  TFrameWindow* frame = GetMainWindow();
  if (frame && frame->IsWindow()) {
    unsigned flags = visible ? SWP_NOACTIVATE|SWP_NOSIZE|SWP_NOMOVE|
      SWP_SHOWWINDOW : SWP_NOACTIVATE|SWP_NOSIZE|SWP_NOMOVE|SWP_NOZORDER|
      SWP_HIDEWINDOW;
    frame->SetWindowPos(HWND_TOP, 0,0,0,0, flags);
}

// Set the Visible property value.
bool TDrawApp::GetShow()
{
  TFrameWindow* frame = GetMainWindow();
  return (frame && frame->IsWindow() && frame->IsWindowVisible());
}

// Get the Fullname property value.
const char far* TDrawApp::GctPath()
{
  static char buf[_MAX_PATH];
  GetModuleFileName(buf, sizeof(buf)-1);
  return buf;
}

// Open or create a document.
extern TDocTemplate drawTpl;
TDrawDocument* TDrawApp::OpenDoc(const char far* name)
{
  long flags = name ? 0 : dtNewDoc;
  TDocManager* docManager = GetDocManager();
  if (!docManager)
  return 0;
 HWND hWnd = ::GetFocus();
 TDocument* doc = GetDocManager()->CreateDoc(&drawTpl, name, 0, flags);
 ::SetFocus(hWnd);
 return dynamic_cast<TDrawDocument*>(doc);
}
```

Exposing properties and methods to other applications

You expose properties and methods by declaring and defining them.

Declaring properties and methods

To declare properties and methods for the application class, add the DECLARE_AUTOAGGREGATE macro to the end of the application class declaration.

The STEP16.H file contains declarations of the properties and methods for the application class of the drawing application:

```
DECLARE_AUTOAGGREGATE(TDrarwApp)
  AUTOPROP    (Visible, GetShow, SetShow, TBool)
  AUTOFUNC0   (NewDoc, OpenDoc, TAutoObject<TDrawDocument>,)
  AUTOFUNC1   (OpenDoc, OpenDoc, TAutoObject<TDrawDocument>, TAutoString,)
  AUTOPROPRO (AppName, GetName, TAutoString,)
  AUTOPROPRO (FullName, GetPath, TAutoString,)
```

Defining properties and methods

To define properties and methods, use the DEFINE_AUTOAGGREGATE macro.

The STEP16.CPP file contains definitions of the properties and methods for the application class of the drawing application:

```
DEFINE_AUTOAGGREGATE(TDrawApp, OcApp->Aggregate)
  EXPOSE_PROPRW(Visible, TAutoBool,      "Visible",      "Main window shown", 0)
  EXPOSE_METHOD(NewDoc,  TDrawDocument, "NewDocument",  "Create new document", 0)
  EXPOSE_METHOD(OpenDoc  TDrawDocument, "OpenDocument", "Open existing document", 0)
    REQUIRED_ARG(          TAutoString,  "Name")
  EXPOSE_PROPRO(AppName, TAutoString,   "Name",         "Application name", 0)
  EXPOSE_PROPRO(FullName,TAutoString,   "FullName",    "Complete path to application", 0)
  EXPOSE_APPLICATION(TDrawApp,          "Application",  "Application object", 0)
  EXPOSE_QUIT(                          "Quit",         "Shutdown application", 0)
END_AUTOAGGREGATE(TDrawApp,tfAppObject|tfCanCreate,"TDrawApp","Application class", 0)
```

For more information about declaring and defining properties and methods, see the online Help entries for DECLARE_AUTOAGGREGATE and DEFINE_AUTOAGGREGATE.

Changing the document class

The changes you make to the document class are very similar to the changes you make to the application class:

1 Include the automation and Step 16 header files.

2 Update the document registration table.

3 Declare and implement member functions that can be exposed as properties and methods.

4 Update the constructor and destructor of the document class.

5 Expose member functions as properties and methods.

Including the automation and Step 16 header files

Take the `#include` listing from the STEP15DV.CPP file and make the following changes:

1 Add the OCF/AUTOMACR.H header file.

2 Add the Step 16 resource (.RC), source (.CPP), and header (.H) files.

3 Remove the Step 15 header files.

Note In Step 16, the header file (STEP16DV.H) is separate from the source file (STEP16DV.CPP) for the document class.

Update the document registration table

To update the document registration table, change the description to "...Automation Server..." from ..."Server..."

Declaring and implementing member functions that can be exposed as properties and methods

Although you can expose the data members of the document class directly, you may want to implement one member function (for read-only or write-only properties) or two member functions (for read/write properties) that handle the tasks of getting and setting values. In this way, you can validate the data being transferred, preventing errors.

In addition, for each member function that has parameters with one or more complex data types, you should create a new member function that has parameters with only basic data types. The new function should perform the necessary conversions between data types and then call the original function. By exposing member functions that take only basic data types, you make it easier for an automation controller to use them.

When you create new member functions, you may find that you need new data members as well.

For example, the STEP16DV.H file contains the declarations and implementations of eight new member functions of the document class:

```
long GetPenColor() // PenColor property.
{
 return AutoPenColor;
}
```

```
void SetPenColor(long color) // PenColor property.
{
 AutoPenColor = color;
 AutoLine->SetPen(TColor(color));
}

short GetPenSize() // PenSize property.
{
 return AutoPenSize;
}

void SetPenSize(short penSize) // PenSize property.
{
 AutoPenSize = penSize;
 AutoLine->SetPen(penSize);
}

void AddPoint(short x, short y) // AddPoint method.
{
 AutoLine->Add(TPoint(x,y));
}

void AddLine()
{
 AddLine(*AutoLine);
      ClearLine();
}

void ClearLine() // ClearLine method.
{
 delete AutoLine;
 AutoLine = new TLine(AutoPenColor, AutoPenSize);
}
```

In addition, the STEP16DV.H file contains the declarations of three new data members
of the document class:

```
TLine*   AutoLine;
long     AutoPenColor;
short    AutoPenSize;
```

Updating the constructor and destructor of the document class

When you create new data members and member functions of the document class, you
may need to update the document class constructor and destructor.

For example, the STEP16DV.H file contains new lines of code in the constructor and
destructor that initialize and destroy the new data members:

```
TDrawDocument::TDrawDocument(TDocument* parent)
   : TOleDocument(parent), UndoLine(0), UndoState(UndoNone)
{
   Lines        = new TLines(100, 0, 5);
```

```
  AutoPenSize   = 1;
  AutoPenColor  = RGB(0, 0, 0);
  AutoLine      = new TLine(AutoPenColor, AutoPenSize);
}

TDrawDocument::~TDrawDocument()
{
  delete AutoLine;
  delete Lines;
  delete UndoLine;
}
```

Exposing properties and methods to other applications

You expose properties and methods by declaring and defining them.

Declaring properties and methods

To declare properties and methods for the document class, add the
DECLARE_AUTOCLASS macro to the end of the document class declaration.

The STEP16DV.H file contains declarations of the properties and methods for the
document class of the drawing application:

```
DECLARE_AUTOCLASS(TDrawDocument)
  AUTOPROP(PenSize,    GetPenSize,   SetPenSize,  short, )
  AUTOPROP(PenColor,   GetPenColor,  SetPenColor, long, )
  AUTOFUNC2V(AddPoint, AddPoint,     short,       short, )
  AUTOFUNC0V(AddLine,  AddLine, )
  AUTOFUNC0V(ClearLine,ClearLine, )
```

To define properties and methods for the document class, use the
DEFINE_AUTOCLASS macro.

Defining properties and methods

The STEP16.CPP file contains definitions of the properties and methods for the
document class of the drawing application:

```
DEFINE_AUTOCLASS(TDrawDocument)
  EXPOSE_PROPRW(PenSize,     TAutoShort, "PenSize",    "Current pen size", 0)
  EXPOSE_PROPRW(PenColor,    TAutoLong,  "PenColor",   "Current pen color", 0)
  EXPOSE_METHOD(AddPoint,    TAutoVoid,  "AddPoint",   "Add a point to the
                                                       current line", 0)
    REQUIRED_ARG(            TAutoShort, "X")
    REQUIRED_ARG(            TAutoShort, "Y")
  EXPOSE_METHOD(AddLine,     TAutoVoid,  "AddLine",    "Add current line into
                                                       drawing", 0)
  EXPOSE_METHOD(ClearLine,   TAutoVoid,  "ClearLine",  "Erases current line", 0)
  EXPOSE_APPLICATION(        TDrawApp,   "Application","Application object", 0)
END_AUTOCLASS(TDrawDocument, tfNormal,   "TDrawDoc",   "Draw document class", 0)
```

For more information about declaring and defining properties and methods, see the
online Help entries for DECLARE_AUTOCLASS and DEFINE_AUTOCLASS.

17

Enhancing the linking and embedding capabilities of an OLE container / server

In this step, you'll learn how to enhance an OLE container/server so that you can link and embed parts of a document instead of a whole document. Specifically, you'll enhance the drawing application so that you can link and embed individual lines. And along the way, you'll implement functions that select, cut, and copy a line.

Changing the line class

The first step to enhancing the linking and embedding capabilities of the drawing application is to make changes to the *TLine* class:

1 Add new data members for storing the rectangular boundaries of a line and whether or not the line is selected.

2 Update the constructor so the new data members are initialized.

3 Add new member functions that draw a rectangle around a line, invalidate a selection, update a boundary, and change the position of a line.

Adding new data members

A line must keep track of its boundary and whether or not it is selected:

```
TRect Bound;    // Stores the rectangular boundary of the line.
bool Selected; // Stores whether or not the line is selected.
```

Updating the constructor

The Bound and Selected data members should be initialized in the *TLine* constructor:

```
TLine(const TColor& color = TColor(0), int penSize = 1) : TPoints(10,0,10),
    PenSize(penSize), Color(color), Bound(0,0,0,0), Selected(false)
```

By default, the line has no boundary and is not selected.

Adding new member functions

The following sections show the member functions you must add to the *TLine* class.

DrawSelection

When a line is selected, it must draw a rectangle around itself:

```
TLine::DrawSelection(TDC& dc)
{
    TUIHandle(Bound, TUIHandle::DashFramed).Paint(dc);
}
```

For information about the TUIHandle function, search the OWL.HLP file for TUIHandle.

UpdateBound

When a line moves, it must update its boundary, which is stored in the Bound data member:

```
void
TLine::UpdateBound()
{
  // Iterates through the points in the line i.
  TPointsIterator j(*this);
  if (!j)
    return;
  TPoint p = j++;
  Bound.Set(p.x, p.y, 0, 0);

  while (j) {
  p = j++;
  if ((p.x - PenSize) < Bound.left)
    Bound.left = (p.x - PenSize);
  if ((p.x + PenSize) > Bound.right)
    Bound.right = (p.x + PenSize);
  if ((p.y - PenSize) < Bound.top)
    Bound.top = (p.y - PenSize);
  if ((p.y + PenSize) > Bound.bottom)
    Bound.bottom = (p.y + PenSize);
  }
  Bound.right  += 1;
  Bound.bottom += 1;
}
```

UpdatePosition

A line must be able to change its position when a new origin is specified:

```
void
TLine::UpdatePosition(TPoint& newPos)
{
  for (TPointsIterator i(*this); i; i++) {
    TPoint* pt = (TPoint *)&i.Current();
    pt->x += newPos.x;
    pt->y += newPos.y;
  }

  Bound.Offset(newPos.x, newPos.y);
}
```

Invalidate

A line must notify views when it has changed:

```
void
TLine::Invalidate(TDrawView& view)
{
  TOleClientDC dc(view);

  TRect rUpdate(GetBound());
  rUpdate.Inflate(1, 1);
  dc.LPtoDP((TPoint *)&rUpdate, 2);
  TUIHandle handle(rUpdate, TUIHandle::Framed);
  rUpdate = handle.GetBoundingRect();

  view.GetDocument().NotifyViews(vnInvalidate, (long)&rUpdate, 0);
}
```

Changing the document class

You must change the *TOleDocument* class so that it can save and open individual lines.

Saving individual lines

When a document is saved, it calls the *CommitSelection* function of each linked or embedded line it contains. (The document also calls the *Commit* function of each linked or embedded document, as shown in Step 16.)

Here is the *CommitSelection* function:

```
bool
TDrawDocument::CommitSelection(TOleWindow& oleWin, void* userData)
{
  TOleDocument::CommitSelection(oleWin, userData);

  TDrawView* drawView = TYPESAFE_DOWNCAST(&oleWin, TDrawView);
  TOutStream* os = OutStream(ofWrite);
```

```
if (!os || !drawView)
  return false;

// Make the line usable in a container by adjusting its origin
//
TLine* line = (TLine*)userData;
int i = line? 1 : 0;
TPoint newPos(Margin, Margin);
if (line) {
  newPos -= line->GetBound().TopLeft();
  line->UpdatePosition(newPos);
}

// Write the number of lines in the figure
*os << i;

// Append a description using a resource string
*os << ' ' << FileInfo << '\n';

// Copy the current line from the iterator and increment the array.
if (line)
  *os << *line;

delete os;

// restore line
//
if (line)
  line->UpdatePosition(-newPos);

//
// Commit the storage if it was opened in transacted mode
// TOleDocument::CommitTransactedStorage();

return true;
}
```

Opening individual lines

When a document is opened, it calls the *OpenSelection* function of each linked or embedded line it contains. (The document also calls the *Open* function for each linked or embedded document it contains.)

Here is the *OpenSelection* function:

```
bool
TDrawDocument::OpenSelection(int mode, const char far* path, TPoint far* where)
{
  char fileinfo[100];
  TOleDocument::Open(mode, path);   // normally path should be null
```

```
//if (GetDocPath()) {
TInStream* is = (TInStream*)InStream(ofRead);
if (!is)
return false;

unsigned numLines;
*is >> numLines;
is->getline(fileinfo, sizeof(fileinfo));
while (numLines--) {
  TLine line;
  *is >> line;
  if (where) {
    TPoint newPos(where->x, where->y);
    newPos -= line.GetBound().TopLeft();
    line.UpdatePosition(newPos);
  }
  line.UpdateBound();
  Lines->Add(line);
}

delete is;

if (GetDocPath()) {
  FileInfo = fileinfo;
else {
  FileInfo = string(*::Module,IDS_FILEINFO);
}
SetDirty(false);
UndoState = UndoNone;
return true;
}
```

Updating line boundaries when a document is opened

When a linked or embedded document is opened, the boundaries of the lines it contains
must be updated:

```
TDrawDocument::Open(int mode, const char far* path)
{
⋮
while (numLines--) {
  TLine line;
  *is >> line;
  line.UpdateBound();
  ines->Add(line);
}
⋮
}
```

Changing the view class

Next you must change the *TOleView* class:

1 Add new data members for storing the currently selected line and the current mode (normal or selection).

2 Name the Clipboard format.

3 Add the Pen, Select, Cut, and Copy commands.

4 Implement the *Select* function.

5 Implement the *PaintLink* function.

6 Implement or enhance the OLE message handlers.

Adding new data members

To store the currently selected line and current mode (Pen or Selection), declare the following data members of the view class, as shown in the STEP17DV.H file:

```
TLine* Selected;
enum DRAWTOOL {
  DrawSelect = 0,
  DrawPen,
};
DRAWTOOL Tool;
```

Then initialize the data members in the view class constructor, as shown in the STEP17DV.CPP file:

```
TDrawView::TDrawView(TDrawDocument& doc, TWindow* parent) :
  TOleView(doc, parent), DrawDoc(&doc)
{
  Selected = 0;
  Tool = DrawPen;
  ⋮
}
```

Naming the Clipboard format

Since the drawing application will be able to copy selections to the Clipboard, you need to name the Clipboard format. The format name appears in the Paste Link dialog box and is used in the *EvOcClipData* event handler, which is shown later.

You can specify the name of the Clipboard format in the constructor for the view object, as shown in STEP17DV.CPP:

```
TDrawView::TDrawView(TDrawDocument& doc, TWindow* parent) :
  TOleView(doc, parent), DrawDoc(&doc)
{
  ?
  OcApp->AddUserFormatName("DrawPad Native Data",
    "Owl DrawPad native data", DrawPadFormat);
}
```

Adding the Select, Cut, Copy, and Pen commands

In order for a document part to be linked or embedded, it must be selected, cut or copied from a server, and then pasted into a container. So in order for the drawing application to provide lines for linking and embedding, it must have Select, Cut, and Copy commands. These commands typically appear on the Edit menu and as buttons on the toolbar.

Note The Cut and Copy commands were not added in the previous steps of the tutorial because OWL handles the commands automatically for linked and embedded objects. However, in order to work with document parts, you must add the commands manually.

In addition, in order to return to normal mode from the selection mode, you need a Pen command. (When an application is in normal mode, you can perform normal actions, but you can't select document parts. When an application is in selection mode, you can select document parts, but you can't perform normal actions. For example, in the drawing application, the Pen and Select commands allow you to switch between drawing and selecting lines.)

To add the Select, Cut, Copy, and Pen commands,

1 Include the commands in the Edit menu section of the resource (.RC) file.

2 Add the buttons to the toolbar bitmap section of the resource file.

3 Add the commands and their corresponding enablers to the response table for the view class.

4 Insert the new buttons on the Toolbar by enhancing the *TDrawView::EvOcViewShowTools* function.

5 Declare and implement member functions of the view class that correspond to the commands. For the implementations of the member functions for each command, see the STEP17DV.CPP source file.

Implementing the Select function

By implementing the *Select* function, you control how a view responds to left-mouse clicks. (*Select* is a virtual member function of the *TOleWindow* class, from which the view class is derived.)

This is the new *Select* function for the view class, as shown in STEP17DV.CPP:

```
bool
TDrawView::Select(uint modKeys, TPoint& point)
{
  if (Tool != DrawSelect)
  return false;

  // Clicked in lines?
  TLine *line = HitTest(point);
  SetLineSelection(line);
```

```
if (Selected) { // there is a selection
  ⋮
}
else
// Select OLE object, if any
return TOleView::Select(modKeys, point);
}
```

The *Select* function calls the *HitTest* function to determine whether or not the mouse cursor falls within a line boundary. If so, the *SetLineSelection* function is called to store the selected line in the Line data member of the view class. Otherwise, the *TOleView::Select* function is called, which automatically handles the selecting of OLE objects.

To see the implementations of the *HitTest* and *SetLineSelection* functions, see the STEP17DV.CPP file.

Implementing the PaintLink function

When a document wants to draw a linked object, it calls the *PaintLink* function, which is implemented in the step17DV.CPP FILE:

```
bool
TDrawView::PaintLink(TDC& dc, bool erase, TRect& rect, TString& moniker)
{
  TLine* line = 0;
  //Draw the whole document if linking to the whole doc
  //
  if (strcmp(moniker, OleStr(DocContent)) == 0) {
    Paint(dc, erase, rect);
    return true;
}

  // Find the selection with the corresponding moniker
  //
  line = DrawDoc->GetLine(moniker);

  if (!line)
    return false;

  TPoint newPos(Margin, Margin);
  newPos -= rect.TopLeft();
  line->UpdatePosition(newPos);
  line->Draw(dc);
  line->UpdatePosition(-newPos);
  return true;
}
```

Implementing or enhancing OLE message handlers

Next you must implement or enhance the OLE message handlers, as shown in the next sections.

EvOcViewClipData

Implement this event handler to save the selected line to storage when the user copies it and to retrieve a selected line from storage when the user pastes it:

```
bool
TDrawView::EvOcViewClipData(TOcFormatData far& formatData)
{
  if (strcmp(OleStr(formatData.Format.GetRegName()), OleStr(DrawPadFormat)) != 0)
    return false; // not our clipboard format

  bool status = true;
  if (formatData.Paste) { // Pasting native data
    DrawDoc->SetHandle(ofReadWrite, formatData.Handle, false);
    DrawDoc->OpenSelection(ofRead, 0, formatData.Where);
    Invalidate();
    // Restore the original storage
    //
    DrawDoc->RestoreStorage();

  }
  else { // Copying native data
    HANDLE data = GlobalAlloc(GHND|GMEM_SHARE, 0);
    DrawDoc->SetHandle(ofReadWrite, data, true);

    // Copy the selection if the target format is "DrawPad"
    //
    if (formatData.UserData) {
      status = DrawDoc->CommitSelection(*this, formatData.UserData);
    }
    else {
      status = DrawDoc->Commit(true);
    }

    formatData.Handle = data;
    // Restore the original storage
    //
    DrawDoc->RestoreStorage();
  }

  return status;
}
```

EvOcViewGetItemName

Implement this event handler so that a name is associated with each line that is linked or embedded in a document.

```
bool
TDrawView::EvOcViewGetItemName(TOcItemName& item)
{
  if (item.Selection) {
    if (!Selected)
      return false;
    char name[32];
    itoa(DrawDoc->GetLines()->Find(*Selected), name, 10);
    item.Name = name;
  }
  else {
    item.Name = "content"; // item name representing the whole document
  }
  return true;
}
```

EvOcViewSetLink

Implement this event handler to create a *TOleLinkView* object for each linked or embedded line. (The *TOleLinkView* class is implemented later.)

```
bool
TDrawView::EvOcViewSetLink(TOcLinkView& view)
{
  // Attach a linked view to this document
  //
  new TDrawLinkView(GetDocument(), view);
  return true;
}
```

EvOcViewPartsize

Implement this event handler so a container can determine the size of each line that is linked or embedded.

```
bool
TDrawView::EvOcViewPartSize(TOcPartSize far& ps)
{
  TClientDC dc(*this);

  TRect rect(0, 0, 0, 0);
  TLine* line = 0;
  if (ps.Selection) {
    if (ps.Moniker) {
      if (strcmp(*ps.Moniker, OleStr(DocContent)) == 0)
        line = 0; // whole document
      else
        line = DrawDoc->GetLine(*ps.Moniker);
    }
    else{
      line = (TLine*) ps.UserData;
    }
  }
```

```
      if (line) {
        *(TPoint*)&rect.left    = line->GetBound().TopLeft();
        rect.right  = rect.left + line->GetBound().Width()  + 2 * Margin;
        rect.bottom = rect.top  + line->GetBound().Height() + 2 * Margin;
      }
      else {
        // a 2" x 2" extent for server
        //
        rect.right  = dc.GetDeviceCaps(LOGPIXELSX) * 2;
        rect.bottom = dc.GetDeviceCaps(LOGPIXELSY) * 2;
      }

      ps.PartRect = rect;
      return true;
    }
```

EvLButtonDown

Enhance this event handler so that lines are drawn when the view is in Pen mode and
lines are selected when the view is in Select mode.

```
    void
    TDrawView::EvLButtonDown(uint modKeys, TPoint& point)
    {
      TOleView::EvLButtonDown(modKeys, point);
      if (SelectEmbedded() || !DragDC)
        return;

      if (Tool == DrawSelect) { // selection
    //    Select(modKeys, point);
      }
      else if (Tool == DrawPen) {
        SetCapture();
        Pen = new TPen(Line->QueryColor(), Line->QueryPenSize());
        DragDC->SelectObject(*Pen);
        DragRect.SetNull();
        DragDC->MoveTo(point);
        Line->Add(point);
      }
    }
```

Adding a TOleLinkView class

Finally, you must add a *TOleLinkView* class. When a *TOleLinkView* object is associated
with a linked or embedded line, all documents containing the line are notified when the
line is changed or deleted (if you implement the *VnModify* and *VnDelete* event handlers).

The actual *TOleLinkView* objects are created in the *EvOcPasteLink* event handler.

```
    DEFINE_RESPONSE_TABLE1(TDrawLinkView, TOleLinkView)
      EV_VN_DRAWDELETE,
      EV_VN_DRAWMODIFY,
    END_RESPONSE_TABLE;
```

```
TDrawLinkView::TDrawLinkView(TDocument& doc, TOcLinkView& view) : TOleLinkView(doc
, view)
{
  DrawDoc = TYPESAFE_DOWNCAST(&doc, TDrawDocument);
  CHECK(DrawDoc);
}

TDrawLinkView::~TDrawLinkView()
{
}

//
// Line was modified
//
bool
TDrawLinkView::VnModify(uint index)
{
  // Get the selection corresponding to the moniker
  //
  TLine * line = DrawDoc->GetLine(GetMoniker());
  if (!line)
    return false;

  // Notify the container
  //
  if (index == DrawDoc->GetLines()->Find(*line)) {
    UpdateLinks();
}

  return true;
}

//
// Line was deleted
//
bool
TDrawLinkView::VnDelete(uint index)
{
  // Get the selection corresponding to the moniker
  //
  TLine * line = DrawDoc->GetLine(GetMoniker());
  if (!line)
    return false;

  // Notify the container
  //
  if (index == DrawDoc->GetLines()->Find(*line)) {
    UpdateLinks();
  }
  return true;
}
```

Adding non-OLE enhancements to the drawing application

Step 17 also demonstrates the following non-OLE features:

- Using the cursor to show the current mode.
- Dragging and dropping a selection.
- Zooming in on and out from a drawing document.
- Adding scroll bars to windows containing linked documents.

For more information, see the STEP17DV.CPP file.

18

For further study

As you can see, ObjectWindows packs a lot of functionality into its classes. With this tutorial, you've really only begun to scratch the surface of the things you can do with ObjectWindows. Here are a number of suggestions for things you can do to expand the tutorial application even more:

- You can add other Doc/View classes to the application. To do this, compile the document class, its view classes, and a list of document templates into an object file. Then add that object file to the application when you link it. Then, when you open a new document, you'll see the new document types appear in the File Open dialog box. Note that this works even though the application knows nothing about the Doc/View classes you added.

- A good source for Doc/View classes is the DOCVIEWX application in the EXAMPLES\OWL\OWLAPI\DOCVIEW directory. You can also try writing your own document and view classes.

- Try adding new GDI objects to the application. For example, you might try adding the ability to import bitmaps with the *TBitmap* class. Or add textured brushes with the *TBrush* class.

- Add different drawing operations, such as lines, boxes, circles, and so on. You can add menu choices for each of these operations. You can also set up exclusive state button gadgets on the control bar to let the user change the current operation just by pressing a button gadget.

- Try converting the control bar into a floating tool box by changing the *TControlBar* into a *TToolBox* in a *TFloatingFrame*. You can see an example of how this is done in the PAINT example in the EXAMPLES\OWL\OWLAPPS\PAINT directory.

- Try adding the ability to perform multiple undo operations. You can use container classes to hold all the lines that have been changed.

You can also go through the examples in the other ObjectWindows example directories. Many of these have features in them you may want to try to add to the Drawing Pad application.

II

ObjectWindows programmer's guide

This part presents topics in a task-oriented fashion, describing how to use functional groups of ObjectWindows classes to accomplish various tasks. This part is organized as follows:

Chapter 19, "Overview of ObjectWindows," presents a brief, nontechnical overview of the ObjectWindows hierarchy.

Chapter 20, "Application and module objects," describes application objects and the application class *TApplication*.

Chapter 21, "Interface objects," discusses the use of interface objects in the ObjectWindows programming model. Interface objects are instances of classes representing windows, dialog boxes, and controls; these classes are based on the class *TWindow*.

Chapter 22, "Event handling," explains response tables, the ObjectWindows method for event handling.

Chapter 23, "Command enabling," describes the ObjectWindows command-enabling mechanism for enabling and disabling command items such as menu choices and control bar buttons, setting menu item text, and checking and unchecking command items.

Chapter 24, "ObjectWindows exception handling," describes the ObjectWindows exception-handling mechanism.

Chapter 25, "Window objects," describes window objects, including how to use frame windows, layout windows, decorated frame windows, and MDI windows.

Chapter 26, "Menu objects," discusses the use of menu objects and the *TMenu* class.

Chapter 27, "Dialog box objects," explains how to use dialog box objects (such as *TDialog* and *TDialog*-derived objects) and also Windows common dialog boxes, which are based on the *TCommonDialog* class.

Chapter 28, "Doc/View objects," presents the ObjectWindows Doc/View programming model, which uses the *TDocument*, *TView*, and *TDocManager* classes.

Chapter 29, "Control objects," discusses the use of various controls, such as buttons, list boxes, edit boxes, and so on.

Chapter 30, "Gadget and gadget window objects," explains gadgets and gadget windows, including control bars, status bars, button gadgets, and so on.

Chapter 31, "Printer objects," describes how to use the printer and print preview classes.

Chapter 32, "Graphics objects," presents the classes that encapsulate Windows GDI.

Chapter 33, "Validator objects," describes the use of input validators in edit controls.

Chapter 34, "Visual Basic controls," discusses using Visual Basic controls and the *TVbxControl* class in your ObjectWindows application.

Chapter 35, "ObjectWindows dynamic-link libraries," explains the use of ObjectWindows-encapsulated dynamic-link libraries (DLLs).

Chapter 36, "Turning an application into an OLE and OCX container," explains how to turn applications OLE containers using Doc/View and ObjectWindows.

Chapter 37, "Turning an application into an OLE server," explains how to turn applications OLE servers using Doc/View and ObjectWindows. It also explains how to turn an ObjectWindows server into a DLL server.

Chapter 38, "Windows shell classes," describes how to use the windows shell classes.

Chapter 39, "Windows Socket classes," explains socket communications, socket modes, and socket classes.

Overview of ObjectWindows

This chapter presents an overview of the ObjectWindows hierarchy. It also describes the basic groupings of the ObjectWindows classes, explains how each class fits together with the others, and refers you to specific chapters for more detailed information about how to use each class.

Working with class hierarchies

This section describes some of the basic properties of classes, focusing specifically on ObjectWindows classes. It covers the following topics:

- What you can do with a class
- Inheriting members
- Types of member functions

Using a class

There are three basic things you can do with a class:

- Derive a new class from it
- Add its behavior to that of another class
- Create an instance of it (instantiate it)

Deriving new classes

To change or add behavior to a class, you derive a new class from it:

```
class TNewWindow : public TWindow
{
  puc:
    TNewWindow(...);
  // ...
};
```

When you derive a new class, you can do three things:

- Add new data members
- Add new member functions
- Override inherited member functions

Adding new members lets you add to or change the functionality of the base class. You can define a new constructor for your derived class to call the base classes' constructors and initialize any new data members you might have added.

Mixing object behavior

With ObjectWindows designed using multiple inheritance, you can derive new classes that inherit the behavior of more than one class. Such "mixed" behavior is different from the behavior you get from single inheritance derivation. Instead of inheriting the behavior of the base class and being able to add to and change it, you're inheriting *and combining* the behavior of several classes.

As with single inheritance derivation, you can add new members and override inherited ones to change the behavior of your new class.

Instantiating classes

To use a class, you must create an instance of it. There are a number of ways you can instantiate a class:

- You can use the standard declaration syntax. This is the same syntax you use to declare any standard variable such as an **int** or **char**. In this example, *app* is initialized by calling the *TMyApplication* constructor with no arguments:

  ```
  TMyApplication app;
  ```

  You can use this syntax only when the class has a default constructor or a constructor in which all the parameters have default values.

- You can also use the standard declaration syntax along with arguments to call a particular constructor. In this example, *app* is initialized by calling the *TMyApplication* constructor with a **char *** argument:

  ```
  TMyApplication app("AppName");
  ```

- You can use the **new** operator to allocate space for and instantiate an object. For example:

  ```
  TMyApplication *app;
  app = new TMyApplication;
  ```

- You can also use the **new** operator along with arguments. In this example, *app* is initialized by calling the *TMyApplication* constructor with a **char *** argument:

  ```
  TMyApplication* app = new TMyApplication("AppName");
  ```

The constructors call the base class' constructors and initialize any needed data members. You can only instantiate classes that aren't abstract; that is, classes that don't contain a pure virtual function.

Abstract classes

Abstract classes, which are classes with pure virtual member functions that you must override to provide some behavior, serve two main purposes. They provide a conceptual framework to build other classes on and, on a practical level, they reduce coding effort.

For example, the ObjectWindows *THSlider* and *TVSlider* classes could each be derived directly from *TScrollBar*. Although one is vertical and the other horizontal, they have similar functionality and responses. This commonality warrants creating an abstract class called *TSlider*. *THSlider* and *TVSlider* are then derived from *TSlider* with the addition of a few specialized member functions to draw the sliders differently.

You can't create an instance of an abstract class. Its pure virtual member functions must be overridden to make a useful instance. *TSlider*, for example, doesn't know how to paint itself or respond directly to mouse events.

If you wanted to create your own slider (for example, a circular slider), you might try deriving your slider from *TSlider* or it might be easier to derive from *THSlider* or *TVSlider*, depending on which best meets your needs. In any case, you add data members and add or override member functions to add the desired functionality. If you wanted to have diagonal sliders going both northwest-southeast and southwest-northeast, you might want to create an intermediate abstract class called *TAngledSlider*.

Inheriting members

The following figure shows the inheritance of *TInputDialog*. As you can see, *TInputDialog* is derived from *TDialog*, which is derived from *TWindow*, which is in turn derived from *TEventHandler* and *TStreamable*. Inheritance lets you add more specialized behavior as you move further along the hierarchy.

Figure 19.1   TDialog inheritance

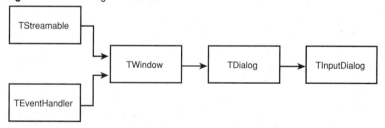

The following table shows the public data members of each class, including those inherited from the *TDialog* and *TWindow* base classes:

Table 19.1   Data member inheritance

TWindow	TDialog	TInputDialog
Status	Status	Status
HWindow	HWindow	HWindow
Title	Title	Title
Parent	Parent	Parent
Attr	Attr	Attr

Table 19.1 Data member inheritance (continued)

TWindow	TDialog	TInputDialog
DefaultProc	*DefaultProc*	*DefaultProc*
Scroller	*Scroller*	*Scroller*
	IsModal	*IsModal*
		Prompt
		Buffer
		BufferSize

TInputDialog inherits all the data members of *TDialog* and *TWindow* and adds the data members it needs to be an input dialog box.

To fully understand what you can do with *TInputDialog*, you have to understand its inheritance: a *TInputDialog* object is both a dialog box (*TDialog*) and a window (*TWindow*). *TDialog* adds the concept of modality to the *TWindow* class. *TInputDialog* extends that by adding the ability to store and retrieve user-input data.

Types of member functions

There are four (possibly overlapping) types of ObjectWindows member functions:

- Virtual
- Nonvirtual
- Pure virtual
- Default placeholder

Virtual functions

Virtual functions can be overridden in derived classes. They differ from pure virtual functions in that they don't *have* to be overridden in order to use the class. Virtual functions provide you with *polymorphism*, which is the ability to provide a consistent class interface, even when the functionality of your classes is quite different.

Nonvirtual functions

You should not override nonvirtual functions. Therefore, it's important to make virtual any member function that derived classes might need to override (an exception is the event-handling functions defined in your response tables). For example, *TWindow::CanClose* is virtual because derived classes should override it to verify whether the window should close. On the other hand, *TWindow::SetCaption* is nonvirtual because you usually don't need to change the way a window's caption is set.

The problem with overriding nonvirtual functions is that classes that are derived from your derived class might try to use the overridden function. Unless the new derived classes are *explicitly* aware that you have changed the functionality of the derived function, this can lead to faulty return values and run-time errors.

Pure virtual functions

You must override pure virtual functions in derived classes. Functions are marked as pure virtual using the = 0 initializer. For example, here's the declaration of *TSlider::PaintRuler*:

```
virtual void PaintRuler(TDC& dc) = 0;
```

You must override all of an abstract class' pure virtual functions in a derived class before you can create an instance of that derived class. In most cases, when using the standard ObjectWindows classes, you won't find this to be much of a problem; most of the ObjectWindows classes you might need to derive from are *not* abstract classes. In lieu of pure virtual functions, many ObjectWindows classes use default placeholder functions.

Default placeholder functions

Unlike pure virtual functions, default placeholder functions don't have to be overridden. They offer minimal default actions or no actions at all. They serve as placeholders, where you can place code in your derived classes. For example, here's the definition of *TWindow::EvLButtonDblClk*:

```
inline void
TWindow::EvLButtonDblClk (uint modKeys, TPoint &)
{
    DefaultProcessing();
}
```

By default, *EvLButtonDblClk* calls *DefaultProcessing* to perform the default message processing for that message. In your own window class, you could override *EvLButtonDblClk* by defining it in your class' response table. Your version of *EvLButtonDblClk* can provide some custom behavior you want to happen when the user clicks the left mouse button. You can also continue to provide the base class' default processing by calling the base class' version of the function.

Object typology

The ObjectWindows hierarchy has many different types of classes that you can use, modify, or add to. You can separate what each class does into the following groups:

- Windows
- Dialog boxes
- Controls
- Graphics
- Printing
- Modules and applications
- Doc/View applications
- Miscellaneous Windows elements

Window classes

An important part of any Windows application is, of course, the window. ObjectWindows provides several different window classes for different types of windows (not to be confused with the Windows "window class" registration types):

- Windows
- Frame windows
- MDI windows
- Decorated windows

Chapter 25 describes the window classes in detail.

Windows

TWindow is the base class for all window classes. It represents the functionality common to all windows, whether they are dialog boxes, controls, MDI windows, or so on.

Frame windows

TFrameWindow is derived from *TWindow* and adds the functionality of a frame window that can hold other client windows.

MDI windows

Multiple Document Interface (MDI) is the Windows standard for managing multiple documents or windows in a single application. *TMDIFrame*, *TMDIClient*, and *TMDIChild* provide support for MDI in ObjectWindows applications.

Decorated windows

Several classes, such as *TLayoutWindow* and *TLayoutMetrics*, work together to provide support for *decoration* controls like tool bars, status bars, and message bars. Using multiple inheritance, decoration support is added into frame windows and MDI frame windows in *TDecoratedFrame* and *TDecoratedMDIFrame*.

Dialog box classes

TDialog is a derived class of *TWindow*. It's used to create dialog boxes that handle a variety of user interactions. Dialog boxes typically contain controls to get user input. Dialog box classes are explained in detail in Chapter 27.

Common dialog boxes

In addition to specialized dialog boxes your own application might use, ObjectWindows supports Windows' common dialog boxes for:

- Choosing files (*TFileOpenDialog* and *TFileSaveDialog*)
- Choosing fonts (*TChooseFontDialog*)
- Choosing colors (*TChooseColorDialog*)
- Choosing printing options (*TPrintDialog*)
- Searching and replacing text (*TFindDialog* and *TReplaceDialog*)

Other dialog boxes

ObjectWindows also provides additional dialog boxes that aren't based on the Windows common dialog boxes:

- Inputting text (*TInputDialog*)
- Aborting print jobs (*TPrinterAbortDlg*, used in conjunction with the *TPrinter* and *TPrintout* classes)

Control classes

TControl is a class derived from *TWindow* to support behavior common to all controls. ObjectWindows offers four types of controls:

- Standard Windows controls
- Widgets
- Gadgets
- Decorations

All these controls are discussed in depth in Chapter 29, except for gadgets, which are discussed in Chapter 30.

Standard Windows controls

Standard Windows controls include list boxes, scroll bars, buttons, check boxes, radio buttons, group boxes, edit controls, static controls, and combo boxes. Member functions let you manipulate these controls.

Widgets

Unlike standard Windows controls, ObjectWindows widgets are specialized controls written entirely in C++. The widgets ObjectWindows offers include horizontal and vertical sliders (*THSlider* and *TVSlider*) and gauges (*TGauge*).

Gadgets

Gadgets are similar to standard Windows controls, in that they are used to gather input from or convey information to the user. But gadgets are implemented differently from controls. Unlike most other interface elements, gadgets are not windows: gadgets don't have window handles, they don't receive events and messages, and they aren't based on *TWindow*.

Instead, gadgets must be contained in a gadget window. The gadget window controls the presentation of the gadget, all message processing, and so on. The gadget receives its commands and direction from the gadget window.

Decorations

Decorations are specialized child windows that let the user choose a command, provide a place to give the user information, or somehow allow for specialized communication with the user.

- A control bar (*TControlBar*) lets you arrange a set of buttons on a bar attached to a window as shortcuts to using menus (the SpeedBar in the Borland C++ IDE is an example of this functionality).

- A tool box (*TToolBox*) lets you arrange a set of buttons on a floating palette.

- Message bars (*TMessageBar*) are bars, usually at the bottom of a window, where you can display information to the user. For example, the Borland C++ IDE uses a message bar to give you brief descriptions of what menu commands and SpeedBar buttons do as you press them.

- Status bars (*TStatusBar*) are similar to message bars, but have room for more than one piece of information. The status bar in the Borland C++ IDE shows your position in the edit window, whether you're in insert or overtype mode, and error messages.

Graphics classes

Windows offers a powerful but complex graphics library called the Graphics Device Interface (GDI). ObjectWindows encapsulates GDI to make it easier to use device context (DC) classes (*TDC*) and GDI objects (*TGDIObject*).

See Chapter 32 for full details on these classes.

DC classes

With GDI, instead of drawing directly on a device (like the screen or a printer), you draw on a bitmap using a device context (DC). A *device context* is a collection of tools, settings, and device information regarding a graphics device and its current drawing state. This allows for a high degree of device independence when using GDI functions. The following table lists the different types of DCs that ObjectWindows encapsulates.

Table 19.2   ObjectWindows-encapsulated device contexts

Type of device context	ObjectWindows DC class
Memory	*TMemoryDC*
Metafile	*TMetaFileDC*
Bitmap	*TDibDC*
Printer	*TPrintDC*
Window	*TWindowDC*
Desktop	*TDesktopDC*
Screen	*TScreenDC*
Client	*TClientDC*
Paint	*TPaintDC*

GDI objects

TGDIObject is a base class for several other classes that represent things you can use to draw with and to control drawings. The following table lists these classes and other ObjectWindows GDI support classes.

Table 19.3   GDI support classes

Type of GDI object	ObjectWindows GDI class
Pens	*TPen*
Brushes	*TBrush*
Fonts	*TFont*
Palettes	*TPalette*
Bitmaps	*TBitmap, TDib, TUIBitmap*
Icons	*TIcon*
Cursors	*TCursor*
Regions	*TRegion*
Points	*TPoint*
Size	*TSize*
Rectangles	*TRect*
Color specifiers	*TColor*
RGB triple color	*TRgbTriple*
RGB quad color	*TRgbQuad*
Palette entries	*TPaletteEntry*
Metafile	*TMetafilePict*

Printing classes

TPrinter makes printing significantly easier by encapsulating the communications with printer drivers. *TPrintout* encapsulates the task of printing a document. Chapter 31 discusses how to use the printing classes.

Module and application classes

A Windows application is responsible for initializing windows and ensuring that messages Windows sends to it are sent to the proper window. ObjectWindows encapsulates that behavior in *TApplication*. A DLL's behavior is encapsulated in *TModule*. For full details on module and application objects, see Chapter 20.

Doc/View classes

The Doc/View classes are a complete abstraction of a generic document-view model. The base classes of the Doc/View model are *TDocManager*, *TDocument*, and *TView*. The Doc/View model is a system in which data is contained in and accessed through a document object, and displayed and manipulated through a view object. Any number of views can be associated with a particular document type. You can use this to display the same data in a number of different ways.

For example, you can display a line both graphically (as a line in a window) and as sets of numbers indicating the coordinates of the points that make up the line. This would require one document that contains the data and two view classes: one view class to display the line onscreen and another view class to display the coordinates of the points in the line. You can also modify the data through the views so that, in this case, you could change the data in the line by either drawing in the graphical display or by typing in numbers to modify and add coordinates in the numerical display.

The Doc/View model is discussed in depth in Chapter 28.

Miscellaneous classes

Since Windows is so varied, not all the classes ObjectWindows provides fall into neat categories. This section discusses those miscellaneous classes.

Menus

Menus can be static or you can modify them or even load whole new menus. *TMenu* and its derived classes (*TSystemMenu* and *TPopupMenu*) let you easily manipulate menus. Chapter 26 discusses the menu classes in more detail.

Clipboard

The Windows Clipboard is one of the main ways users share data between applications. ObjectWindows' *TClipboard* object lets you easily provide Clipboard support in your applications. See Chapter 25 for details.

Application and module objects

This chapter describes how to use application objects, including

- Deriving an application object from the *TApplication* class

- Creating an application object

- Overriding base class functions in derived application objects to customize application behavior

- Using the Borland Custom Control and Microsoft Control 3-D libraries, including automatically subclassing custom controls as Microsoft Control 3-D controls

ObjectWindows encapsulates Windows applications and DLL modules using the *TApplication* and *TModule* classes, respectively. *TModule* objects

- Encapsulate the initialization and closing functions of a Windows DLL

- Contain the *hInstance* and *lpCmdLine* parameters, which are equivalent to the parameters of the same name that are passed to the *WinMain* function in a non-ObjectWindows application (note that both *WinMain* and *LibMain* have these two parameters in common)

TApplication objects build on the basic functionality provided by *TModule*. *TApplication* and *TApplication*-derived objects

- Encapsulate the initialization, run-time management, and closing functions of a Windows application

- Contain the values of the *hPrevInstance* and *nCmdShow* parameters, which are equivalent to the parameters of the same name that are passed to the *WinMain* function in a non-ObjectWindows application

The *TApplication* class is derived from the *TModule* class. You usually won't need to create a *TModule* object yourself, unless you're working with a DLL. See Chapter 35 for more information on using DLLs in an ObjectWindows application.

The minimum requirements

To use a *TApplication* object, you must first:

- Include the correct header file
- Create an application object
- Call the application object's *Run* function

Including the header file

TApplication is defined in the header file owl\applicat.h; you must include this header file to use *TApplication*. Because *TApplication* is derived from *TModule*, owl\applicat.h includes owl\module.h.

Creating an object

You can create a *TApplication* object using one of two constructors. The most commonly used constructor is this:

```
TApplication(const char far* name);
```

This version of the *TApplication* constructor takes a string, which becomes the application's name. If you don't specify a name, by default the constructor names it the null string. *TApplication* uses this string as the application name.

The second version of the *TApplication* constructor lets you specify a number of parameters corresponding to the parameters normally passed to the *WinMain* function:

```
TApplication(const char far* name,
             HINSTANCE instance,
             HINSTANCE prevInstance,
             const char far* cmdLine,
             int cmdShow);
```

You can use this constructor to pass command parameters to the *TApplication* object. This is discussed on page 198.

Calling the Run function

The most obvious thing that *TApplication::Run* function does is to start your application running. But in doing so it performs a number of other very important tasks, including

- Initializing the application
- Creating and displaying the main window
- Running the application's message loop

Each of these tasks is discussed later in this chapter. For the purposes of creating the basic ObjectWindows application, however, it is sufficient to know that *Run* is the function you call to make your application go.

Finding the object

You may need to access an application object from outside that object's scope. For example, you may need to call one of the application object's member functions from a function in a derived window class. But because the window object is not in the same scope as the application object, you have no way of accessing the application object. In this case, you must find the application object.

TApplication contains several member functions and data members you might need to call from outside the scope your application object. To find these easily, the *TWindow* class has a member function, *GetApplication*, that returns a pointer to the application object. You can then use this pointer to call *TApplication* member functions and access *TApplication* data members. The following listing shows a possible use of *GetApplication*.

```
void
TMyWindow::Error()
{
  // display message box containing the application name
  MessageBox("An error occurred!",
             GetApplication()->Name, MB_OK);
}
```

The *TWindow* class is discussed in Chapter 25.

Creating the minimum application

Here's the smallest ObjectWindows application you can create. It includes the correct header file, creates a *TApplication* object, and calls that object's *Run* function.

```
#include <owl\applicat.h>

int
OwlMain(int argc, char* argv[])
{
  return TApplication("Wow!").Run();
}
```

This creates a Windows application with a main window with the caption "Wow!". You can resize, move, minimize, maximize, and close this window. In a real application, you'd derive a new class for the application to add more functionality. Notice that the only function you have to call explicitly in this example is the *Run* function. Figure 20.1 shows how this application looks when it's running.

Figure 20.1   The basic ObjectWindows application

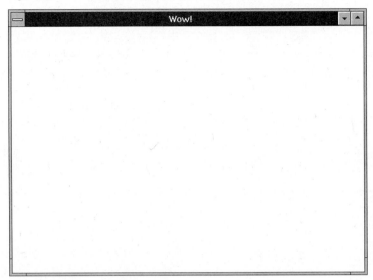

Initializing applications

Initializing an ObjectWindows application takes four steps:

- Construct the application object.
- Initialize the application.
- Initialize each new instance.
- Initialize the main window.

Constructing the application object

When you construct a *TApplication* object, it calls its *InitApplication*, *InitInstance*, and *InitMainWindow* member functions to start the application. You can override any of those members to customize how your application initializes. Since the base *InitMainWindow* function only creates a default window object with no way to customize its functionality, you must override *InitMainWindow* to start creating an application with the functionalty you want to create. To override a function in *TApplication* you need to derive your own application class from *TApplication*.

The constructor for the *TApplication*-derived class *TMyApplication* shown in the following examples takes the application name as its only argument; its default value is zero, for no name. The application name is used for the default main window title and in error messages. The application name is referenced by a **char far *** member of the *TModule* base class called *Name*. You can set the application name one of two ways:

- Your application class' constructor can explicitly call *TApplication*'s constructor, passing the application name onto *TApplication*. The following example shows this method:

```
#include <owl\applicat.h>

class TMyApplication: public TApplication
{
  public:
    // This constructor initializes the base class constructor
    TMyApplication(const char far* name = 0) : TApplication(name) {}
    ⋮
};
```

- Override one of *TApplication*'s initialization functions, usually *InitMainWindow*, and set the application name there. The following example shows this method:

```
#include <owl\applicat.h>

class TMyApplication: public TApplication
{
  public:
    // This constructor just uses the default base class constructor
    TMyApplication(const char far* name = 0) {}
    void InitMainWindow()
    {
      if (name)
      {
        Name = new char[strlen(name) + 1];
        strcpy(Name, name);
      }
    }
};
```

ObjectWindows applications don't require an explicit *WinMain* function; the ObjectWindows libraries provide one that performs error handling and exception handling. You can perform any initialization you want in the *OwlMain* function, which is called by the default *WinMain* function.

To construct an application object, create an instance of your application class in the *OwlMain* function. The following example shows a simple application object's definition and instantiation:

```
#include <owl\applicat.h>

class TMyApplication: public TApplication
{
public:
  TMyApplication(const char far* name = 0): TApplication(name) {}
};

int
OwlMain(int argc, char* argv[])
{
  return TMyApplication("Wow!").Run();
}
```

Using WinMain and OwlMain

ObjectWindows furnishes a default *WinMain* function that provides extensive error checking and exception handling. This *WinMain* function sets up the application and calls the *OwlMain* function.

Although you can use your own *WinMain* by placing it in a source file, there's little reason to do so. Everything you would otherwise do in *WinMain* you can do in *OwlMain* or in *TApplication* initialization member functions. The following example shows a possible use of *OwlMain* in an application. *OwlMain* checks to see whether the user specified any parameters on the application's command line. If so, *OwlMain* creates the application object using the first parameter as the application name. If not, *OwlMain* creates the application object using Wow! as the application name.

```
#include <owl\applicat.h>
#include <string.h>

class TMyApplication: public TApplication
{
public:
  TMyApplication(const char far* name = 0) : TApplication(name) {}
};

int
OwlMain(int argc, char* argv[])
{
  char title[30];
  if(argc >= 2)
    strcpy(title, argv[1]);
  else
    strcpy(title, "Wow!");
  return TMyApplication(title).Run();
}
```

If you do decide to provide your own *WinMain*, *TApplication* supports passing traditional *WinMain* function parameters with another constructor. The following example shows how to use that constructor to pass *WinMain* parameters to the *TApplication* object:

```
#include <owl\applicat.h>

class TMyApplication : public TApplication
{
public:
  TMyApplication (const char far* name,
                  HINSTANCE instance,
                  HINSTANCE prevInstance,
                  const char far* cmdLine,
                  int cmdShow)
    : TApplication (name, instance, prevInstance, cmdLine, cmdShow) {}
};

int
PASCAL WinMain(HINSTANCE hInstance, HINSTANCE hPrevInstance,
```

```
                    LPSTR lpszCmdLine, int nCmdShow)
{
   return TMyApplication("MyApp", hInstance, hPrevInstance,
                    lpszCmdLine, nCmdShow).Run();
}
```

Calling initialization functions

TApplication contains three initialization functions:

- *InitApplication* initializes the first instance of the application
- *InitInstance* initializes each instance of the application
- *InitMainWindow* initializes the application's main window

How these functions are called depends on whether this is the first instance of the application. *InitApplication* is called only for the first instance of the application on the system. *InitInstance* is the next function called for the first instance. It is the first function called by additional instances. *InitInstance* calls *InitMainWindow*.

If the application is a 32-bit application, each instance appears to be the first instance of the application, affecting this chain of execution. This is described in the next section.

Initializing the application

Users can run multiple copies of an application simultaneously. From the point of view of a 16-bit application, first-instance initialization happens only when another copy of the application is not currently running. Each-instance initialization happens every time the user runs the application. If a user starts and closes your application, starts it again, and so on, each instance is a first instance because the instances don't run at the same time.

In the case of 32-bit applications, each application runs in its own address space, with no shared instance data, so that each instance appears as a first instance. Therefore every time you start a 32-bit application, it performs both first-instance initialization and each-instance initialization.

If the current instance is a first instance (indicated by the data member *hPrevInstance* being set to zero), *InitApplication* is called. You can override *InitApplication* in your derived application class; the default *InitApplication* has no functionality.

For example, you could use first-instance initialization to make the main window's caption indicate whether it's the first instance. To do this,

1 Add a data member called *WindowTitle* in your derived application class.
2 In the application class' constructor, set *WindowTitle* to "Additional Instance."
3 Override *InitApplication* to set *WindowTitle* to "First Instance."

If your application is the first instance of the application, *InitApplication* is called and overwrites the value of *WindowTitle* that was set in the constructor. The following example shows how the code might look:

```
#include <owl\applicat.h>
#include <owl\framewin.h>
#include <cstring.h>

class TTestApp : public TApplication
```

```
{
  public:
    TTestApp() : TApplication("Instance Tester"), WindowTitle("Additional Instance")
{}

  protected:
    string WindowTitle;

    void InitApplication() { WindowTitle = string("First Instance"); }
    void InitMainWindow() { SetMainWindow(new TFrameWindow(0, WindowTitle.c_str())); }
};

int
OwlMain(int /* argc */, char* /* argv *//[])
{
  return TTestApp().Run();
}
```

Figure 20.2 shows a number of instances of this application open on the desktop. Note that the first instance—the upper left one—has the title "First Instance," while every other instance has the title "Additional Instance."

Figure 20.2   First-instance and each-instance initialization

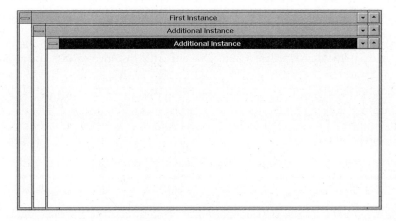

Again, this application doesn't function as you might expect when it's built as a 32-bit application. Because each instance of a 32-bit application perceives itself to be the first instance of the application, multiple copies running at the same time would all have the caption "First Instance."

Initializing each new instance

A user can run multiple instances (copies) of an application simultaneously. You can override *TApplication::InitInstance* to perform any initialization you need to do for each instance.

InitInstance calls *InitMainWindow* and then creates and shows the main window you set up in *InitMainWindow*. If you override *InitInstance*, be sure your new *InitInstance* calls

TApplication::InitInstance. The following example shows how to use *InitInstance* to load an accelerator table:

```
void
TTestApp::InitInstance()
{
  TApplication::InitInstance();
  HAccTable = LoadAccelerators(MAKEINTRESOURCE(MYACCELS));
}
```

Initializing the main window

By default, *TApplication::InitMainWindow* creates a frame window with the same name as the application object. This window isn't very useful, because it can't receive or process any user input. You must override *InitMainWindow* to create a window object that does process user input.

Normally, your *InitMainWindow* function creates a *TFrameWindow* or *TFrameWindow-* derived object and calls the *SetMainWindow* function. *SetMainWindow* takes one parameter, a pointer to a *TFrameWindow* object, and returns a pointer to the old main window (if this is a new application that hasn't yet set up a main window, the return value is zero). Chapter 25 describes window classes and objects in detail.

The following example shows a simple application that creates a *TFrameWindow* object and makes it the main window:

```
#include <owl\applicat.h>
#include <owl\framewin.h>

class TMyApplication: public TApplication
{
public:
  TMyApplication(): TApplication() {}
  void InitMainWindow();
};

void
TMyApplication::InitMainWindow()
{
  // Just sets the main window with a basic TFrameWindow object
  SetMainWindow(new TFrameWindow(0, "My First Main Window"));
}

int
OwlMain(int argc, char* argv[])
{
  return TMyApplication("Wow!").Run();
}
```

When you run this application, the caption bar is titled "My First Main Window," and not "Wow!". The application name passed in the *TApplication* constructor is used only when you do not provide a main window. Once again, this example doesn't do a lot; there is still no provision for the frame window to process any user input. But once you have derived a window class that does interact with the user, you use the same simple method to display the window.

Specifying the main window display mode

You can change how your application's main window is displayed by setting the *TApplication* data member *nCmdShow*, which corresponds to the *WinMain* parameter *nCmdShow*. You can set this variable as soon as the *Run* function begins, up until the time you call *TApplication::InitInstance*. This effectively means you can set *nCmdShow* in either the *InitApplication* or *InitMainWindow* function.

For example, suppose you want to display your window maximized whenever the user runs the application. You could set *nCmdShow* in your *InitMainWindow* function:

```
#include <owl\applicat.h>
#include <owl\framewin.h>

class TMyApplication : public TApplication
{
  public :
    TMyApplication(char far *name) : TApplication(name) {}
    void InitMainWindow();
};

void
TMyApplication::InitMainWindow()
{
  // Sets the main window
  SetMainWindow(new TFrameWindow(0, "Maximum Window"));

  // Sets nCmdShow so that the window is maximized when it's created
  nCmdShow = SW_SHOWMAXIMIZED;
}

int
OwlMain(int argc, char* argv[])
{
  return TMyApplication("Wow!").Run();
}
```

nCmdShow can be set to any value appropriate as a parameter to the *ShowWindow* Windows function or the *TWindow::Show* member function, such as SW_HIDE, SW_SHOWNORMAL, SW_NORMAL, and so on.

Changing the main window

You can use the *SetMainWindow* function to change your main window during the course of your application. *SetMainWindow* takes one parameter, a pointer to a *TFrameWindow* object, and returns a pointer to the old main window (if this is a new application that hasn't yet set up a main window, the return value is zero). You can use this pointer to keep the old main window in case you want to restore it. Alternatively, you can use this pointer to delete the old main window object.

Application message handling

Once your application is initialized, the application object's *MessageLoop* starts running. *MessageLoop* is responsible for processing incoming messages from Windows. There are two ways you can refine message processing in an ObjectWindows application:

- Extra message processing, by overriding default message handling functions
- Idle processing

Extra message processing

TApplication has member functions that provide the message-handling functionality for any ObjectWindows application. These functions are *MessageLoop*, *IdleAction*, *PreProcessMenu*, and *ProcessAppMsg*. See the *ObjectWindows Reference* for more information.

Idle processing

Idle processing lets your application take advantage of the idle time when there are no messages waiting (including user input). If there are no waiting messages, *MessageLoop* calls *IdleAction*.

To perform idle processing, override *IdleAction* to perform the actual idle processing. Remember that idle processing takes place while the user isn't doing anything. Therefore, idle processing should be short-lasting. If you need to do anything that takes longer than a few tenths of a second, you should split it up into several processes.

IdleAction's parameter (*idleCount*) is a **long** specifying the number of times *IdleAction* was called between messages. You can use *idleCount* to choose between low-priority and high-priority idle processing. If *idleCount* reaches a high value, you know that a long period without user input has passed, so it's safe to perform low-priority idle processing.

Return **true** from *IdleAction* to call *IdleAction* back sooner.

You should always call the base class *IdleAction* function in addition to performing your own processing. If you're writing applications for Windows NT, you can also use multiple threads for background processing.

Closing applications

Users usually close a Windows application by choosing File | Exit or pressing *Alt+F4*. It's important, though, that the application be able to intercept such an attempt, to give the user a chance to save any open files. *TApplication* lets you do that.

Changing closing behavior

TApplication and all window classes have or inherit a member function *CanClose*. Whenever an application tries to shut down, it queries the main window's and document manager's *CanClose* function. (The exception to this is when dialog boxes are cancelled by the user clicking the Cancel button or pressing *Esc*; in which case, the dialog box is simply destroyed, bypassing the *CanClose* function.) If either the application object or the document manager has children, it calls the *CanClose* function for each child. In turn, each child calls the *CanClose* function of each of their children if any, and so on.

The *CanClose* function gives each object a chance to prepare to be shut down. It also gives the object a chance to cancel the shutdown if necessary. When the object has completed its clean-up procedure, its *CanClose* function should return **true**.

If any of the *CanClose* functions called returns **false**, the shut-down procedure is cancelled.

Closing the application

The *CanClose* mechanism gives the application object, the main window, and any other windows a chance to either prepare for closing or prevent the closing from taking place. In the end, the application object approves the closing of the application. The normal closing sequence looks like this:

1 Windows sends a WM_CLOSE message to the main window.

2 The main window object's *EvClose* member function calls the application object's *CanClose* member function.

3 The application object's *CanClose* member function calls the main window object's *CanClose* member function.

4 The main window and document manager objects call *CanClose* for each of their child windows. The main window and document manager objects' *CanClose* functions return **true** only if all child windows' *CanClose* member functions return **true**.

5 If both the main window and document manager objects' *CanClose* functions return **true**, the application object's *CanClose* function returns **true**.

6 If the application object's *CanClose* function returns **true**, the *EvClose* function shuts down the main window and ends the application.

Modifying CanClose

CanClose should rarely return **false**. Instead, *CanClose* gives you a chance to perform any actions necessary to return **true**. If you override *CanClose* in your derived application objects, the function should return **false** *only* if it's unable to do something necessary for orderly shutdown or if the user wants to keep the application running.

For example, suppose you are creating a text editor. A possible procedure to follow in the *CanClose* member function would be to:

1 Check to see if the editor text had changed.

2 If so, prompt the user to ask whether the text should be saved before closing, using a message box with Yes, No, and Cancel buttons.

3 Check the return value from the message box:

- If the user clicks Yes, save the file, then return **true** from the *CanClose* function.
- If the user clicks No, simply return **true** from the *CanClose* function without saving the file.
- If the user clicks Cancel, indicating the user doesn't want to close the application yet, return **false** from the *CanClose* function without saving the file.

Using control libraries

TApplication has functions for loading the Borland Custom Controls Library (BWCC.DLL for 16-bit applications and BWCC32.DLL for 32-bit applications) and the Microsoft 3-D Controls Library (contained in the file CTL3DV2.DLL for 16-bit applications and CTL3D32.DLL for 32-bit applications). These DLLs are widely used to provide a standard look-and-feel for many applications.

Using the Borland Custom Controls Library

You can open and close the Borland Custom Controls Library using the function *TApplication::EnableBWCC*. *EnableBWCC* takes one parameter, a **bool**, and returns a **void**. When you pass **true** to *EnableBWCC*, the function loads the DLL if it's not already loaded. When you pass **false** to *EnableBWCC*, the function unloads the DLL if it's not already unloaded.

You can find out if the Borland Custom Controls Library DLL is loaded by calling the function *TApplication::BWCCEnabled*. *BWCCEnabled* takes no parameters. If the DLL is loaded, *BWCCEnabled* returns **true**; if not, *BWCCEnabled* returns **false**.

Once the DLL is loaded, you can use all the regular functionality of Borland Custom Controls Library. *EnableBWCC* automatically opens the correct library regardless of whether you have a 16- or a 32-bit application.

Figure 20.3 shows an example of a dialog box using the Borland Custom Controls Library.

Figure 20.3   Dialog box using the Borland Custom Controls Library

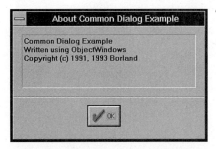

Using the Microsoft 3-D Controls Library

You can load and unload the Microsoft 3-D Controls Library using the function *TApplication::EnableCtl3d*. *EnableCtl3d* takes one parameter, a **bool**, and returns a **void**. When you pass **true** to *EnableCtl3d*, the function loads the DLL if it's not already loaded. When you pass **false** to *EnableCtl3d*, the function unloads the DLL if it's not already unloaded.

Figure 20.4 shows an example of a dialog box using the Microsoft 3-D Controls Library.

Figure 20.4   Dialog box using the Microsoft 3-D Controls Library

You can find out if the Microsoft 3-D Controls Library DLL is loaded by calling the function *TApplication::Ctl3dEnabled*. *Ctl3dEnabled* takes no parameters. If the DLL is loaded, *Ctl3dEnabled* returns **true**; if not, *Ctl3dEnabled* returns **false**.

To use the *EnableCtl3dAutosubclass* function, load the Microsoft 3-D Controls Library DLL using *EnableCtl3d*. *EnableCtl3dAutosubclass* takes one parameter, a **bool**, and returns a **void**. When you pass **true** to *EnableCtl3dAutosubclass*, autosubclassing is turned on. When you pass **false** to *EnableCtl3dAutosubclass*, autosubclassing is turned off.

When autosubclassing is on, any non-ObjectWindows dialog boxes you create have a 3-D effect. You can turn autosubclassing off immediately after creating the dialog box; it is not necessary to leave it on when displaying the dialog box.

21

Interface objects

Instances of C++ classes representing windows, dialog boxes, and controls are called *interface objects*. This chapter discusses the general requirements and behavior of interface objects and their relationship with the *interface elements*—the actual windows, dialog boxes, and controls that appear onscreen.

The following figure illustrates the difference between interface objects and interface elements:

Figure 21.1   Interface elements vs. interface objects

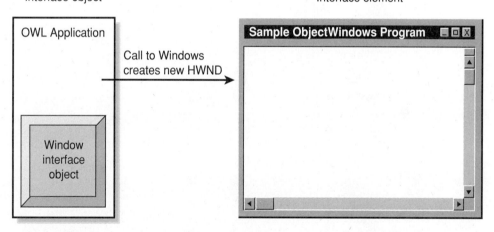

Notice how the interface object is actually inside the application object. The interface object is an ObjectWindows class that is created and stored on the application's heap or stack, depending on how the object is allocated. The interface element, on the other hand, is actually a part of Windows. It is the actual window displayed on the screen.

The information in this chapter applies to all interface objects. This chapter also explains the relationships between the different interface objects of an application, and describes the mechanism that interface objects use to respond to Windows messages.

Why interface objects?

One of the greatest difficulties of Windows programming is that controlling interface elements can be inconsistent and confusing. Sometimes you send a message to a window; other times you call a Windows API function. The conventions for similar types of operations often differ when those operations are performed with different kinds of elements.

ObjectWindows alleviates much of this difficulty by providing objects that encapsulate the interface elements. This insulates you from having to deal directly with Windows and provides a more uniform interface for controlling interface elements.

What do interface objects do?

An interface object provides member functions for creating, initializing, managing, and destroying its associated interface element. The member functions manage many of the details of Windows programming for you.

Interface objects also encapsulate the data needed to communicate with the interface element, such as handles and pointers to child and parent windows.

The relationship between an interface object and an interface element is similar to that between a file on disk and a C++ stream object. The stream object only represents an actual file on disk; you manipulate that file by manipulating the stream object. With ObjectWindows, interface objects represent the interface elements that Windows itself actually manages. You work with the object, and Windows takes care of maintaining the Windows element.

The generic interface object: TWindow

ObjectWindows' interface objects are all derived from *TWindow*, which defines behavior common to all window, dialog box, and control objects. Classes like *TFrameWindow*, *TDialog*, and *TControl* are derived from *TWindow* and refine *TWindow*'s generic behavior as needed.

As the common base class for all interface objects, *TWindow* provides uniform ways to:

- Maintain the relationship between interface objects and interface elements, including creating and destroying the objects and elements

- Handle parent-child relationships between interface objects

- Register new Windows window classes

Creating interface objects

Setting up an interface object with its associated interface element requires two steps:

1 Calling one of the interface object constructors, which constructs the interface object and sets its attributes.

2 Creating the interface element by telling Windows to create the interface object with a new interface element:

- When creating most interface elements, you call the interface object's *Create* member function. *Create* also indirectly calls *SetupWindow*, which initializes the interface object by creating an interface element, such as child windows.

- When creating a modal dialog box, you create the interface element by calling the interface object's *Execute* member function. See Chapter 27 for more information on modal dialog boxes.

The association between the interface object and the interface element is maintained by the interface object's *HWindow* data member, a handle to a window.

When is a window handle valid?

Normally under Windows, a newly created interface element receives a WM_CREATE message from Windows, and responds to it by initializing itself. ObjectWindows interface objects intercept the WM_CREATE message and call *SetupWindow* instead. *SetupWindow* is where you want to perform your own initialization.

Note   If part of the interface object's initialization requires the interface element's window handle, you must perform that initialization *after* you call the base class' *SetupWindow*. Prior to the time you call the base class' *SetupWindow*, the window and its child windows haven't been created; *HWindow* isn't valid and shouldn't be used. You can easily test the validity of *HWindow*: if it hasn't been initialized, it is set to NULL.

Although it might seem odd that you can't perform all initialization in the interface object's constructor, there's a good reason: once an interface element is created, you can't change many of its characteristics. Therefore, a two-stage initialization is required: before and after the interface element is created.

The interface object's constructor is the place for initialization before the element is created and *SetupWindow* is the place for initialization after the element is created. You can think of *SetupWindow* as the second part of the constructor.

Making interface elements visible

Creating an object and its corresponding element doesn't mean that you'll see something on the screen. When Windows creates the interface element, Windows checks to see if the element's style includes WS_VISIBLE. If it does, Windows displays the interface element; if it doesn't, the element is created but not displayed onscreen.

TWindow's constructor sets WS_VISIBLE, so most interface objects are visible by default. But if your object loads a resource, that resource's style depends on what is defined in its resource file. If WS_VISIBLE is turned on in the resource's style, WS_VISIBLE is turned on for the object. If WS_VISIBLE is *not* turned on in the resource's style, WS_VISIBLE is turned *off* in the object's style. You can set WS_VISIBLE and other window styles in the interface object in the *Attr.Style* data member.

For example, if you use *TDialog* to load a dialog resource that doesn't have WS_VISIBLE turned on, you must explicitly turn WS_VISIBLE before attempting to display the dialog using *Create*.

You can find out whether an interface object is visible by calling *IsWindowVisible*. *IsWindowVisible* returns **true** if the object is visible.

At any point after the interface element has been created, you can show or hide it by calling its *Show* member function with a value of **true** or **false**, respectively.

Object properties

In addition to the attributes of its interface element, the interface object possesses certain attributes as an ObjectWindows object. You can query and change these properties and characteristics using the following functions:

- *SetFlag* sets the specified flag for the object.
- *ClearFlag* clears the specified flag for the object.
- *IsFlagSet* returns **true** if the specified flag is set, **false** if the specified flag is not set.

You can use the following flags with these functions:

- *wfAlias* indicates whether the object is an alias; see Chapter 25.

- *wfAutoCreate* indicates whether automatic creation is enabled for this object.

- *wfFromResource* indicates whether the interface element is loaded from a resource.

- *wfShrinkToClient* indicates whether the frame window should shrink to fit the size of the client window.

- *wfMainWindow* indicates whether the window is the main window.

- *wfPredefinedClass* indicates whether the window is a predefined Windows class.

- *wfTransfer* indicates whether the window can use the data transfer mechanism. See Chapter 29 for transfer mechanism information.

Window properties

TWindow also provides a couple of functions that let you change resources and properties of the interface element. Because *TWindow* provides generic functionality for a large variety of objects, it doesn't provide very specific functions for resource and property manipulation. High-level objects provide much more specific functionality. But that specific functionality builds on and is in addition to the functionality provided by *TWindow*:

- *SetCaption* sets the window caption to the string that you pass as a parameter.

- *GetWindowTextTitle* returns a string containing the current window caption.

- *SetCursor* sets the cursor of the instance, identified by the *TModule* parameter, to the cursor passed as a resource in the second parameter.

- You can set the accelerator table for a window by assigning the resource ID (which can be a string or an integer) to *Attr.AccelTable*. For example, suppose you have an accelerator table resource called MY_ACCELS. You would assign the resource to *Attr.AccelTable* like this:

```
TMyWnd::TMyWnd(const char* title)
{
  Init(0, title);
  Attr.AccelTable = MY_ACCELS; // AccelTable can be assigned
}
```

For more specific information on these functions, refer to the *ObjectWindows Reference*.

Destroying interface objects

Destroying interface objects is a two-step process:

- Destroy the interface element.
- Delete the interface object.

You can destroy the interface element without deleting the interface object, if you need to create and display the interface element again.

Destroying the interface element

Destroying the interface element is the responsibility of the interface object's *Destroy* member function. *Destroy* destroys the interface elements by calling the *DestroyWindow* API function. When the interface element is destroyed, the interface object's *HWindow* data member is set to zero. Therefore, you can tell if an interface object is still associated with a valid interface element by checking its *HWindow*.

When a user closes a window on the screen, the following things happen:

- Windows notifies the window.

- The window goes through the *CanClose* mechanism to verify that the window should be closed.

- If *CanClose* approves the closing of the window, the interface element is destroyed and the interface object is deleted.

Deleting the interface object

If you destroy an interface element yourself so that you can redisplay the interface object later, you must make sure that you delete the interface object when you're done with it. Because an interface object is nothing more than a regular C++ object, you can delete it using the **delete** statement if you've dynamically allocated the object with **new**.

The following code illustrates how to destroy the interface element and the interface object.

```
TWindow *window = new TWindow(0, "My Window");

// ...

window->Destroy();
delete window;
```

Parent and child interface elements

In a Windows application, interface elements work together through parent-child links. A parent window controls its child windows, and Windows keeps track of the links. ObjectWindows maintains a parallel set of links between corresponding interface objects.

A child window is an interface element that is managed by another interface element. For example, list boxes are managed by the window or dialog box in which they appear. They are displayed only when their parent windows are displayed. In turn, dialog boxes are child windows managed by the windows that create them.

When you move or close the parent window, the child windows automatically close or move with it. The ultimate parent of all child windows in an application is the main window (there are a couple of exceptions: you can have windows and dialog boxes without parents and all main windows are children of the Windows desktop).

Child-window lists

When you construct a child-window object, you specify its parent as a parameter to its constructor. A child-window object keeps track of its parent through the *Parent* data member. A parent keeps track of its child-window objects in a private data member called *ChildList*. Each parent maintains its list of child windows automatically.

You can access an object's child windows using the window iterator member functions *FirstThat* and *ForEach*. See page 215 for more information on these functions.

Constructing child windows

As with all interface objects, child-window objects get created in two steps: constructing the interface object and creating the interface element. If you construct child-window objects in the constructor of the parent window, their interface elements are automatically created when the parent is, assuming that automatic creation is enabled for the child windows. By default, automatic creation is enabled for all ObjectWindows objects based on *TWindow*, with the exception of *TDialog*. See page 215 for more information on automatic creation.

For example, the constructor for a window object derived from *TWindow* that contains three button child windows would look like this:

```
TTestWindow::TTestWindow(TWindow *parent, const char far *title)
{
  Init(parent, title);

  button1 = new TButton(this, ID_BUTTON1, "Show",
                          190, 270, 65, 20, false);
  button2 = new TButton(this, ID_BUTTON2, "Hide",
                          275, 270, 65, 20, false);
  button3 = new TButton(this, ID_BUTTON3, "Transfer",
                          360, 270, 65, 20, false);
}
```

Note the use of the **this** pointer to link the child windows with their parent. Interface object constructors automatically add themselves to their parents' child window lists. When an instance of *TTestWindow* is created, the three buttons are automatically displayed in the window.

Creating child interface elements

If you don't construct child-window objects in their parent window object's constructor, they won't be automatically created and displayed when the parent is. You can then create them yourself using *Create* or, in the case of modal dialog boxes, *Execute*. In this context, creating means instantiating an interface element.

For example, suppose you have two buttons displayed when the main window is created, one labeled Show and the other labeled Hide. When the user presses the Show button, you want to display a third button labeled Transfer. When the user presses the Hide button, you want to remove the Transfer button:

```
class TTestWindow : public TFrameWindow
{
  public:
    TestWindow(TWindow *parent, const char far *title);

    void
    EvButton1()
    {
      if(!button3->HWindow)
        button3->Create();
    }

    void
    EvButton2()
    {
      if(button3->HWindow)
        button3->Destroy();
    }

    void
    EvButton3()
    {
      MessageBeep(-1);
    }
```

```
    protected:
      TButton *button1, *button2, *button3;

    DECLARE_RESPONSE_TABLE(TTestWindow);
};

DEFINE_RESPONSE_TABLE1(TTestWindow, TFrameWindow)
  EV_COMMAND(ID_BUTTON1, EvButton1),
  EV_COMMAND(ID_BUTTON2, EvButton2),
  EV_COMMAND(ID_BUTTON3, EvButton3),
END_RESPONSE_TABLE;

TTestWindow::TTestWindow(TWindow *parent, const char far *title)
{
  Init(parent, title);
  button1 = new TButton(this, ID_BUTTON1, "Show",
                        10, 10, 75, 25, false);
  button2 = new TButton(this, ID_BUTTON2, "Hide",
                        95, 10, 75, 25, false);
  button3 = new TButton(this, ID_BUTTON3, "Transfer",
                        180, 10, 75, 25, false);
  button3->DisableAutoCreate();
}
```

The call to *DisableAutoCreate* in the constructor prevents the Transfer button from being displayed when *TTestWindow* is created. The conditional tests in the *EvButton1* and *EvButton2* functions work by testing the validity of the *HWindow* data member of the *button3* interface object; if the Transfer button is already being displayed, *EvButton1* doesn't try to display it again, and *EvButton2* doesn't try to destroy the Transfer button if it isn't being displayed.

Destroying windows

Destroying a parent window also destroys all of its child windows. You do not need to explicitly destroy child windows or delete child-window interface objects. The same is **true** for the *CanClose* mechanism; *CanClose* for a parent window calls *CanClose* for all its children. The parent's *CanClose* returns **true** only if all its children return **true** for *CanClose*.

When you destroy an object's interface element, it enables automatic creation for all of its children, *regardless* of whether automatic creation was on or off before. This way, when you create the parent, all the children are restored in the state they were in before their parent was destroyed. You can use this to destroy an interface element, and then re-create it in the same state it was in when you destroyed it.

To prevent this, you must explicitly turn off automatic creation for any child objects you don't want to have created automatically.

Automatic creation

When automatic creation is enabled for a child interface object before its parent is created, the child is automatically created at the same time the parent is created. This is **true** for all the parent object's children.

To explicitly exclude a child window from the automatic create-and-show mechanism, call the *DisableAutoCreate* member function in the child object's constructor. To explicitly add a child window (such as a dialog box, which would normally be excluded) to the automatic create-and-show mechanism, call the *EnableAutoCreate* member function in the child object's constructor.

By default automatic creation is enabled for all ObjectWindows classes except for dialog boxes.

Manipulating child windows

TWindow provides two iterator functions, *ForEach* and *FirstThat*, that let you perform operations on either all the children in the parent's child list or a single child at a time. *TWindow* also provides a number of other functions that let you determine the number of children in the child list, move through them one at a time, or move to the top or bottom of the list.

Operating on all children: ForEach

You might want to perform some operation on each of a parent window's child windows. The iterator function *ForEach* takes a pointer to a function. The function can be either a member function or a stand-alone function. The function should take a *TWindow* * and a **void** * argument. *ForEach* calls the function once for each child. The child is passed as the *TWindow* *. The **void** * defaults to 0. You can use the **void** * to pass any arguments you want to your function.

After *ForEach* has called your function, you often need to be careful when dealing with the child object. Although the object is passed as a *TWindow* *, it is actually usually a descendant of *TWindow*. To make sure the child object is handled correctly, you should use the DYNAMIC_CAST macro to cast the *TWindow* * to a *TClass* *, where *TClass* is whatever type the child object is.

For example, suppose you want to check all the check box child windows in a parent window:

```
void
CheckTheBox(TWindow* win, void*)
{
  TCheckbox *cb = DYNAMIC_CAST(win, TCheckbox);
  if(cb)
    cb->Check();
}

void
TMDIFileWindow::CheckAllBoxes()
{
  ForEach(CheckTheBox);
}
```

If the class you're downcasting to (in this case from a *TWindow* to a *TCheckbox*) is virtually derived from its base, you *must* use the DYNAMIC_CAST macro to make the assignment. In this case, *TCheckbox* isn't virtually derived from *TWindow*, making the DYNAMIC_CAST macro superfluous in this case.

DYNAMIC_CAST returns 0 if the cast could not be performed. This is useful here, because not all of the children are necessarily of type *TCheckbox*. If a child of type *TControlBar* was encountered, the value of *cb* would be 0, thus assuring that you don't try to check a control bar.

Finding a specific child

You might also want to perform a function only on a specific child window. For example, if you wanted to find the first check box that's checked in a parent window with several check boxes, you would use *TWindow::FirstThat*:

```
bool
IsThisBoxChecked(TWindow* cb, void*)
{
   return cb ? (cb->GetCheck == BF_CHECKED) : false;
}


TCheckBox*
TMDIFileWindow::GetFirstChecked()
{
   return FirstThat(IsThisBoxChecked);
}
```

Working with the child list

In addition to the iterator functions *ForEach* and *FirstThat*, *TWindow* provides a number of functions that let you locate and manipulate a single child window:

- *NumChildren* returns an **unsigned**. This value indicates the total number of child windows in the child list.
- *GetFirstChild* returns a *TWindow* * that points to the first entry in the child list.
- *GetLastChild* returns a *TWindow* * that points to the last entry in the child list.
- *Next* returns a *TWindow* * that points to the next entry in the child list.
- *Previous* returns a *TWindow* * that points to the prior entry in the child list.

Registering window classes

Whenever you create an interface element from an interface object using the *Create* or *Execute* functions, the object checks to see if another object of the same type has registered with Windows. If so, the element is created based on the existing Windows registration class. If not, the object automatically registers itself, then is created based on the class just registered. This removes the burden from the programmer of making sure all window classes are registered before use.

22

Event handling

This chapter describes how to use ObjectWindows response tables. Response tables are the method you use to handle all events in an ObjectWindows application. There are four main steps to using ObjectWindows response tables:

1 Declare the response table.
2 Define the response table.
3 Define the response table entries.
4 Declare and define the response member functions.

To use any of the macros described in this chapter, the header file owl\eventhan.h must be included. This file is already included by owl\module.h (which is included by owl\applicat.h) and owl\window.h, so there is usually no need to explicitly include this file.

ObjectWindows response tables are a major improvement over other methods of handling Windows events and messages, including **switch** statements (such as those in standard C Windows programs) and schemes used in other types of application frameworks. Unlike other methods of event handling, ObjectWindows response tables provide:

- Automatic message "cracking" for predefined command messages, eliminating the need for manually extracting the data encoded in the WPARAM and LPARAM values.

- Compile-time error and type checking, which checks the event-handling function's return type and parameter types.

- Ability to have one function handle multiple messages.

- Support for multiple inheritance, enabling each derived class to build on top of the base class or classes' response tables.

- Portability across platforms by not relying on product-specific compiler extensions.

- Easy handling of command, registered, child ID notification, and custom messages, using the predefined response table macros.

Declaring response tables

Because the response table is a member of an ObjectWindows class, you must declare the response table when you define the class. ObjectWindows provides the DECLARE_RESPONSE_TABLE macro to hide the actual template syntax that response tables use.

The DECLARE_RESPONSE_TABLE macro takes a single argument, the name of the class for which the response table is being declared. Add the macro at the end of your class definition. For example, *TMyFrame*, derived from *TFrameWindow*, would be defined like this:

```
class TMyFrame : public TFrameWindow
{
  ⋮
  DECLARE_RESPONSE_TABLE(TMyFrame);
};
```

It doesn't matter what the access level is at the point where you declare the response table. That is, it doesn't matter if the declaration is in a position where it would public, protected, or private. The DECLARE_RESPONSE_TABLE macro sets up its own access levels when it's expanded by the preprocessor. By the same token, you must make certain that the DECLARE_RESPONSE_TABLE macro is the last element in your class declaration; otherwise, any members declared after the macro will have unpredictable access levels.

Defining response tables

Once you've declared a response table, you must define it. Response table definitions must appear outside the class definition.

ObjectWindows provides the DEFINE_RESPONSE_TABLE*X* macro to help define response tables. The value of *X* depends on your class' inheritance, and is a number equal to the number of immediate base classes your class has. END_RESPONSE_TABLE ends the event response table definition.

To define your response table,

1 Begin the response table definition for your class using the DEFINE_RESPONSE_TABLE*X* macro. DEFINE_RESPONSE_TABLE*X* takes *X* + 1 arguments:
  • The name of the class you're defining the response table for
  • The name of each immediate base class

2 Fill in the response table entries (see the next section for information on how to do this step).

3 End the response table definition using the END_RESPONSE_TABLE macro.

For example, the response table definition for *TMyFrame*, derived from *TFrameWindow*, would look like this:

```
DEFINE_RESPONSE_TABLE1(TMyFrame, TFrameWindow)
  EV_WM_LBUTTONDOWN,
  EV_WM_LBUTTONUP,
  EV_WM_MOUSEMOVE,
  EV_WM_RBUTTONDOWN,
END_RESPONSE_TABLE;
```

You must always place a comma after each response table entry and a semicolon after the END_RESPONSE_TABLE macro.

Defining response table entries

Response table entries associate a Windows event with a particular function. When a window or control receives a message, it checks its response table to see if there is an entry for that message. If there is, it passes the message on to that function. If not, it passes the message up to its parent. If the parent is not the main window, it passes the message up to *its* parent. Once the parent is the main window, it passes the message on to the application object. If the application object doesn't have a response entry for that particular message, the message is handled by ObjectWindows default processing. This is illustrated in Figure 22.1.

ObjectWindows provides a large number of macros for response table entries. These include:

- Command message macros that let you handle command messages and route them to a specified function.

- Standard Windows message macros for handling Windows messages.

- Registered messages (messages returned by *RegisterWindowMessage*).

- Child ID notification macros that let you handle child ID notification codes at the child or the parent.

- Control notification macros that handle messages from specialized controls such as buttons, combo boxes, edit controls, list boxes, and so on.

- Document manager message macros to notify the application that a document or view has been created or destroyed and to notify views about events from the document manager.

- VBX control notifications.

Figure 22.1 Window message processing

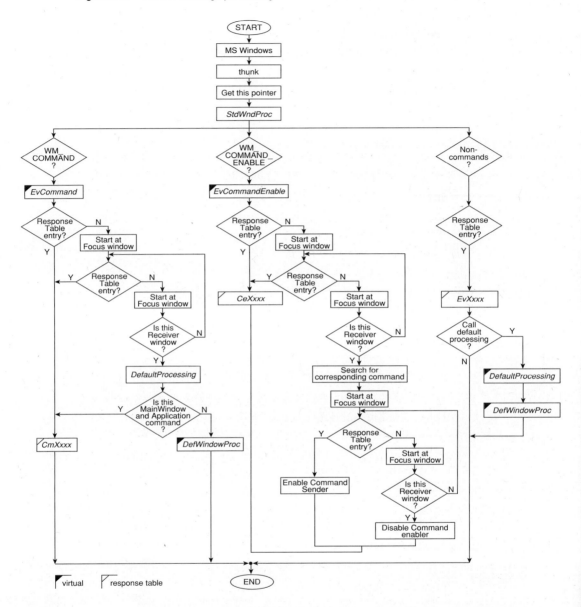

Command message macros

ObjectWindows provides a large number of macros, called *command message macros*, that let you assign command messages to any function. The only requirement is that the signature of the function you specify to handle a message must match the signature required by the macro for that message. The different types of command message macros and the corresponding function signatures are listed in Table 22.1:

Table 22.1   Command message macros

Macro	Prototype	Description
EV_COMMAND(CMD, UserName)	**void** *UserName*()	Calls *UserName* when the CMD message is received.
EV_COMMAND_AND_ID(CMD, UserName)	**void** *UserName*(WPARAM)	Calls *UserName* when the CMD message is received. Passes the command's ID (WPARAM parameter) to *UserName*.
EV_COMMAND_ENABLE(CMD,UserName)	**void** *UserName*(TCommandEnabler&)	Used to automatically enable and disable command controls such as menu items, tool bar buttons, and so on.

Table 22.2 lists other message macros that let you pass the raw, unprocessed message on to the event-handling function. These message macros handle any kind of generic message and registered message.

Table 22.2   Message macros

Macro	Prototype	Description
EV_MESSAGE(MSG, UserName)	LRESULT *UserName*(WPARAM, LPARAM)	Calls *UserName* when the user-defined message MSG is received. MSG is passed to *UserName* without modification.
EV_REGISTERED(MSG, UserName)	LRESULT *UserName*(WPARAM, LPARAM)	Calls *UserName* when the registered message MSG is received. MSG is passed to *UserName* without modification.

It is very important that you correctly match the function signature with the macro that you use in the response table definition. For example, suppose you have the following code:

```
class TMyFrame : public TFrameWindow
{
  public:
    TMyFrame(TWindow* parent, const char* name) : TFrameWindow(parent, name) {}

  protected:
    void CmAdvise();

  DECLARE_RESPONSE_TABLE(TMyFrame);
};
```

```
DEFINE_RESPONSE_TABLE(TMyFrame, TFrameWindow)
  EV_COMMAND_AND_ID(CM_ADVISE, CmAdvise),
END_RESPONSE_TABLE;

void
TMyFrame::CmAdvise()
{
  ⋮
}
```

This code produces a compile-time error because the EV_COMMAND_AND_ID macro requires a function that returns **void** and takes a single WPARAM parameter. In this example, the function correctly returns **void**, but incorrectly takes no parameters. To make this code compile correctly, change the member declaration and function definition of *TMyFrame::CmAdvise* to:

```
void TMyFrame::CmAdvise(WPARAM cmd);
```

Windows message macros

ObjectWindows provides predefined macros for all standard Windows messages. You can use these macros to handle standard Windows messages in one of your class' member functions.

To find the name of the macro to handle a particular predefined message, preface the message name with EV_. This macro passes the message on to a function with a predefined name. To determine the function name, remove the WM_ from the message name, add *Ev* to the remaining part of the message name, and convert the name to lowercase with capital letters at word boundaries. Table 22.3 shows some examples.

Table 22.3 Sample message macros and function names

Message	Response table macro	Function name
WM_PAINT	EV_WM_PAINT	*EvPaint*
WM_LBUTTONDOWN	EV_WM_LBUTTONDOWN	*EvLButtonDown*
WM_MOVE	EV_WM_MOVE	*EvMove*

The advantage to using these message macros is that the message is automatically "cracked," that is, the parameters that are normally encoded in the LPARAM and WPARAM parameters are broken out into their constituent parts and passed to the event-handling function as individual parameters.

For example, the EV_WM_CTLCOLOR macro passes the cracked parameters to an event-handling function with the following signature:

```
HBRUSH EvCtlColor(HDC hDCChild, HWND hWndChild, uint nCtrlType);
```

Message cracking provides for strict C++ compile-time type checking, and helps you catch errors as you compile your code rather than at run time. It also helps when migrating applications from 16-bit to 32-bit and vice versa. Part I of the *ObjectWindows Reference* lists each predefined message, its corresponding response table macro, and the signature of the corresponding event-handling function.

To use a predefined Windows message macro:

1 Add the macro to your response table.

2 Add the appropriate member function with the correct name and signature to your class.

3 Define the member function to handle the message however you want.

For example, suppose you wanted to perform some operation when your *TMyFrame* window object received the WM_ERASEBKGND message. The code would look like this:

```
class TMyFrame : public TFrameWindow {
public:
  bool EvEraseBkgnd(HDC);

  DECLARE_RESPONSE_TABLE(TMyFrame);
};

DEFINE_RESPONSE_TABLE(TMyFrame, TFrameWindow)
  EV_WM_ERASEBKGND,
END_RESPONSE_TABLE;

bool
TMyFrame::EvEraseBkgnd(HDC hdc)
{
  ⋮
}
```

Child ID notification message macros

The child ID notification message macros provide a number of different ways to handle child ID notification messages. You can

- Handle notification codes from multiple children with a single function
- Pass all notification codes from a child to a response window
- Handle the notification code at the child

Use these macros to facilitate controlling and communicating with child controls. The different types of child ID notification message macros are listed in the following table.

Table 22.4   Child notification message macros

Macro	Prototype	Description
EV_CHILD_NOTIFY(ID, Code, UserName)	**void** *UserName*()	Dispatches the message and notification code to the member function *UserName*.
EV_CHILD_NOTIFY_AND_CODE(Id, Code, UserName)	**void** *UserName*(WPARAM code)	Dispatches message *Id* with the notification code *Code* to the function *UserName*.

Table 22.4   Child notification message macros (continued)

Macro	Prototype	Description
EV_CHILD_NOTIFY_ALL_CODES(Id, UserName)	**void** *UserName*(WPARAM code)	Dispatches message *Id* to the function *UserName*, regardless of the message's notification code.
EV_CHILD_NOTIFY_AT_CHILD(Code, UserName)	**void** *UserName*()	Dispatches the notification code *Code* to the child-object member function *UserName*.

These macros provide different methods for handling child ID notification codes. There are described in the next sections.

EV_CHILD_NOTIFY

If you want child ID notifications to be handled at the child's parent window, use EV_CHILD_NOTIFY, which passes the notification code as a parameter and lets multiple child ID notifications be handled with a single function. This also prevents having to handle each child's notification message in separate response tables for each control. Instead, each message is handled at the parent, enabling, for example, a dialog box to handle all its controls in its response table.

For example, suppose you have a dialog box called *TTestDialog* that has four buttons. The buttons IDs are ID_BUTTON1, ID_BUTTON2, ID_BUTTON3, and ID_BUTTON4. When the user clicks a button, you want a single function to handle the event, regardless of which button was pressed. If the user double-clicks a button, you want a special function to handle the event. The code would look like this:

```
class TTestDialog : public TDialog
{
  public:
    TTestDialog(TWindow* parent, TResId resId);

    void HandleClick();
    void HandleDblClick1();
    void HandleDblClick2();
    void HandleDblClick3();
    void HandleDblClick4();

    DECLARE_RESPONSE_TABLE(TTestDialog);
};

DEFINE_RESPONSE_TABLE1(TTestDialog, TDialog)
    EV_CHILD_NOTIFY(ID_BUTTON1, BN_CLICKED, HandleClick),
    EV_CHILD_NOTIFY(ID_BUTTON2, BN_CLICKED, HandleClick),
    EV_CHILD_NOTIFY(ID_BUTTON3, BN_CLICKED, HandleClick),
    EV_CHILD_NOTIFY(ID_BUTTON4, BN_CLICKED, HandleClick),
    EV_CHILD_NOTIFY(ID_BUTTON1, BN_DOUBLECLICKED, HandleDblClick1),
    EV_CHILD_NOTIFY(ID_BUTTON2, BN_DOUBLECLICKED, HandleDblClick2),
    EV_CHILD_NOTIFY(ID_BUTTON3, BN_DOUBLECLICKED, HandleDblClick3),
    EV_CHILD_NOTIFY(ID_BUTTON4, BN_DOUBLECLICKED, HandleDblClick4),
END_RESPONSE_TABLE;
```

EV_CHILD_NOTIFY_ALL_CODES

If you want all notification codes from the child to be passed to the parent window, use EV_CHILD_NOTIFY_ALL_CODES, the generic handler for child ID notifications. For example, the sample program BUTTONX.CPP defines this response table:

```
DEFINE_RESPONSE_TABLE1(TTestWindow, TWindow)
  EV_COMMAND(ID_BUTTON, HandleButtonMsg),
  EV_COMMAND(ID_CHECKBOX, HandleCheckBoxMsg),
  EV_CHILD_NOTIFY_ALL_CODES(ID_GROUPBOX, HandleGroupBoxMsg),
END_RESPONSE_TABLE;
```

This table handles button, check box, and group box messages. In this case, the parent window (*TTestWindow*) gets all notification messages sent by the child (ID_GROUPBOX). The EV_CHILD_NOTIFY_ALL_CODES macro uses the user-defined function *HandleGroupBoxMsg* to process these messages. As a result, if the user clicks the mouse on one of the group box radio buttons, a message box appears that tells the user which button was selected.

EV_CHILD_NOTIFY_AND_CODE

You can use the macro EV_CHILD_NOTIFY_AND_CODE if you want the parent window to handle more than one message using the same function. For example:

```
DEFINE_RESPONSE_TABLE1(TTestWindow, TWindow)
  EV_CHILD_NOTIFY_AND_CODE(ID_GROUPBOX, SomeNotifyCode, HandleThisMessage),
  EV_CHILD_NOTIFY_AND_CODE(ID_GROUPBOX, AnotherNotifyCode, HandleThisMessage),
END_RESPONSE_TABLE;
```

If your window has several different messages to handle and uses several different functions to handle these messages, it's better to use EV_CHILD_NOTIFY_AND_CODE instead of EV_CHILD_NOTIFY because EV_CHILD_NOTIFY message-handling function receives no parameters and therefore doesn't know which message it's handling.

EV_CHILD_NOTIFY_AT_CHILD

To handle child ID notifications at the child window, use EV_CHILD_NOTIFY_AT_CHILD. The sample program NOTITEST.CPP contains the following response table:

```
DEFINE_RESPONSE_TABLE1(TBeepButton, TButton)
  EV_NOTIFY_AT_CHILD(BN_CLICKED, BnClicked),
END_RESPONSE_TABLE;
```

This response table uses the macro EV_NOTIFY_AT_CHILD to tell the child window (*TBeepButton*) to handle the notification code (BN_CLICKED) using the function, *BnClicked*.

Command enabling

This chapter discusses the ObjectWindows implementation of command enabling. Most applications provide menu items and control-bar or palette-button gadgets to access the application's functionality. Some of the commands accessed by these controls are not always available. The menu items and buttons that access these commands should somehow indicate to the application's user when the command isn't available. These menu items and button gadgets can also indicate an application state, such as the current character format, whether a feature is turned on or off, and so on.

ObjectWindows provides a mechanism, known as *command enabling*, that you can use to perform a number of important tasks. This chapter describes how to use ObjectWindows command enabling to:

- Turn menu choices and button gadgets on and off

- Set the state of toggled items such as checked menu items and control-bar buttons that can be clicked on and off

- Change the text of menu items

For information on menus, please see Chapter 26. For information on button gadgets, such as control-bar buttons or palette buttons, and gadget windows, such as control bars and status bars, see Chapter 30.

Handling command-enabling messages

The basic idea behind ObjectWindows command enabling is that the decision to enable or disable a function should be made by the object that handles the command. ObjectWindows does this by sending the WM_COMMAND_ENABLE message through the same command chain as a WM_COMMAND event. The event is then received by the window that implements the functionality that you are enabling or disabling. The command event chain is discussed in Chapter 22.

When a WM_COMMAND_ENABLE message is sent depends on the type of command item that is affected. *TFrameWindow* performs command enabling for menu items when the user clicks a menu, spawning a WM_INITMENUPOPUP message. Gadget windows perform command enabling for control-bar buttons during the window's idle processing.

To handle command-enabling messages for a particular function,

1 Add a member function to the window class to handle the command-enabling message. This function should return **void** and take a single parameter, a reference to a *TCommandEnabler* object. The abstract base class *TCommandEnabler* is declared in the ObjectWindows header file window.h.

2 Place the EV_COMMAND_ENABLE macro in the parent window's response table. This macro takes two parameters, the command identifier and the name of the handler function.

Suppose you have a frame window class that handles a File|Save menu command that uses the command identifier CM_FILESAVE. The class definition would look something like this:

```
class TMyFrame : pmeWindow
{
  public:
    TMyFrame(TWindow *parent = 0, char *title = 0)
      : TFrameWindow(parent, title), IsDirty(false) {}

  protected:
    void CmFileSave();

  DECLARE_RESPONSE_TABLE(TMyFrame);
};

DEFINE_RESPONSE_TABLE(TMyFrame)
  EV_COMMAND(CM_FILESAVE, CmFileSave),
END_RESPONSE_TABLE;
```

Suppose you don't want the user to be able to access the File|Save command if the file hasn't been modified since it was opened or last saved. Adding a handler function and response-table macro to affect the *CmFileSave* function looks something like this:

```
class TMyFrame : public TFrameWindow
{
  public:
    TMyFrame(TWindow *parent = 0, char *title = 0)
      : TFrameWindow(parent, title), IsDirty(false) {}

  protected:
    void CmFileSave();

    // This is the command-enabling handler function.
    void CeFileSave(TCommandEnabler& commandEnabler);

  DECLARE_RESPONSE_TABLE(TMyFrame);
};
```

```
DEFINE_RESPONSE_TABLE(TMyFrame)
  EV_COMMAND(CM_FILESAVE, CmFileSave),
  EV_COMMAND_ENABLE(CM_FILESAVE, CeFileSave),
END_RESPONSE_TABLE;
```

Notice that the EV_COMMAND macro and the EV_COMMAND_ENABLE macro both use the same command identifier. Often a single function can be accessed through multiple means. For example, many applications let you open a file through a menu item and also through a button on the control bar. Command enabling in ObjectWindows lets you do command enabling for all means of accessing a function through a single common identifier. The abstraction of command enabling through command-enabling objects saves a great deal of time by removing the need to write multiple command-enabling functions for each different command item.

Working with command-enabling objects

Once you have received a command-enabling message and the handler function has been called, you can perform a number of actions using the command-enabling object passed to the handler function. This section discusses the various types of ObjectWindows command-enabling objects.

ObjectWindows command-enabling objects

ObjectWindows provides three predefined command-enabling objects:

• *TCommandEnabler* is the abstract base class for command-enabling objects. It's declared in the ObjectWindows header file window.h.

• *TMenuItemEnabler* is the command-enabling class for menu items. This class enables and disables menu items, sets check marks by menu items, and changes menu-item text. This class is declared in the ObjectWindows source file FRAMEWIN.CPP.

• *TButtonGadgetEnabler* is the command-enabling class for button gadgets. This class enables and disables button gadgets and toggles boolean button gadgets. This class is declared in the ObjectWindows source file BUTTONGA.CPP.

TCommandEnabler: The command-enabling interface

Although in your command-enabling functions you always manipulate an object derived from *TCommandEnabler* as opposed to an actual *TCommandEnabler* object, in practice it appears as if you are working with a *TCommandEnabler* object. *TCommandEnabler* provides a consistent interface for the other command-enabling classes, which implement the appropriate functionality for the type of command object that each class services. Because you never create an instance of the *TMenuItemEnabler* and *TButtonGadgetEnabler* classes, they are declared in source files instead of header files. You don't need to be able to create one of these objects; instead you work with the basic *TCommandEnabler* interface, while your handler functions are ignorant of the specific command tool that is being handled.

This section describes the *TCommandEnabler* function interface. There are two approaches to the *TCommandEnabler* function interface:

- If you are using existing command-enabling classes, you need to be familiar with the basic interface as implemented in the *TCommandEnabler* class.

- If you are deriving new command-enabling classes, you need to be familiar with the actual implementation of functionality in the *TCommandEnabler* base class.

This section discusses both approaches and points out which aspects are relevant to using existing classes and which are relevant to creating new classes.

Functions

TCommandEnabler has a number of member functions:

- Because *TCommandEnabler* is an abstract class, its constructor is of interest only when you are deriving a new command-enabling class. The *TCommandEnabler* constructor takes two parameters, a uint and an HWND. The uint is the command identifier. The constructor initializes the *Id* data member with the value of the command identifier. The HWND is the handle to the window that received the command-enabling message. The constructor initializes *HWndReceiver* with the value of the HWND parameter.

- *Enable* takes a single bool parameter and returns **void**. The bool parameter indicates whether the command should be enabled or disabled; if it's true, the command is enabled, if it's false, the command is disabled.

  From the standpoint of deriving new classes, all that *TCommandEnabler::Enable* does is perform initialization of data members in the base class. Any other actions required for enabling or disabling a command item must be handled in the derived class. For example, *TMenuItemEnabler* performs all the work necessary to turn menu items on or off. Derived classes' *Enable* functions should always call *TCommandEnabler::Enable*.

- *SetText* takes a single parameter, a **const char far***, and returns **void**. This function sets the text of the command item to the string passed in the character array parameter. *SetText* has no effect on button gadgets.

  SetText is declared as a pure virtual; you *must* declare and define *SetText* in classes derived from *TCommandEnabler*. Whatever steps are needed to implement this functionality in your command item must be done in the derived *SetText* function. If, as is the case in *TButtonGadgetEnabler*, there is no valid application for the *SetText* function, you can simply implement it as an empty function.

- *SetCheck* takes a single **int** parameter and returns **void**. This function toggles the command item on or off, depending on the value of the **int** parameter. This parameter can be one of three enumerated values defined in the *TCommandEnabler* class, *Unchecked*, *Checked*, or *Indeterminate*. *Unchecked* sets the state of the command item to be unchecked, *Checked* sets the state of the command item to be checked, and *Indeterminate* sets the command item to its indeterminate state. The nature of the indeterminate state is defined by the command item:

- For menu items, the indeterminate state is the same as unchecked.
- For button gadgets, the indeterminate state is an intermediate state between checked and unchecked.

SetCheck is declared as a pure virtual; you *must* declare and define *SetCheck* in classes derived from *TCommandEnabler*. Whatever steps are needed to implement this functionality in your command item must be done in the derived *SetCheck* function.

- *GetHandled* takes no parameters and returns bool. This function returns true if the command enabler has been handled by calling the *Enable* function. Otherwise, it returns false.

- *IsReceiver* takes a single HWND parameter and returns a bool value. *IsReceiver* returns true if the HWND parameter matches the receiver HWND passed into the *TCommandEnabler* constructor and stored in *HWndReceiver*. Otherwise, it returns false.

Data members

TCommandEnabler contains three data members:

- *Id* is the only public data member. This member contains the identifier for the command. It is declared as a **const** uint and is initialized in the constructor. Once initialized, it cannot be modified.

- *HWndReceiver* contains the handle of the window that implements the command. This is a protected data member and cannot be directly accessed unless you are deriving a class from *TCommandEnabler*. *HWndReceiver* can be accessed indirectly by calling the *IsReceiver* function, which compares the value of the HWND parameter passed in to the value of *HWndReceiver*.

- *Handled* indicates whether the command-enabling object has been dealt with. It is initialized to false in the *TCommandEnabler* constructor and set to true in *TCommandEnabler::Enable*. This is a protected data member and cannot be directly accessed unless you are deriving a class from *TCommandEnabler*. *Handled* can be accessed indirectly by calling the *GetHandled* function, which returns the value of *Handled*.

Common command-enabling tasks

This section describes how to perform some of the more common tasks for which you'll use command enabling, including:

- Enabling and disabling command items
- Changing menu-item text
- Toggling command items

Enabling and disabling command items

Enabling and disabling command items is as simple as calling the *Enable* function in your handler function. You decide the criteria for enabling and disabling a particular item. For example, if a particular library is not available, you may want to disable any commands that access that library. If your application handles files in a number of different formats, you may want to disable commands that aren't appropriate to the current format.

To enable or disable a command,

1 Add the command-enabling handler function and response-table macro to your window class as described on page 227.

2 Define the handler function.

3 Inside the handler function, call the *Enable* member function of the command-enabling object passed into the handler function. The *Enable* function takes a single bool parameter. Call *Enable* with the value of the parameter as true to enable the command, and with the value of the parameter as false to disable the command.

Here's the earlier example class from page 228, but with a bool flag, *IsDirty*, added to tell if the file has been modified since it was opened or last saved, and the *CeFileSave* function added to enable and disable the File | Save command:

```
class TMyFrame : public TFrameWindow
{
  public:
    TMyFrame(TWindow *parent = 0, char *title = 0)
      : TFrameWindow(parent, title), IsDirty(false) {}

  protected:
    bool IsDirty;

    void CmFileSave();

    // This is the command-enabling handler function.
    void CeFileSave(TCommandEnabler& commandEnabler);

  DECLARE_RESPONSE_TABLE(TMyFrame);
};

DEFINE_RESPONSE_TABLE(TMyFrame)
  EV_COMMAND(CM_FILESAVE, CmFileSave),
  EV_COMMAND_ENABLE(CM_FILESAVE, CeFileSave),
END_RESPONSE_TABLE;

void
TMyFrame::CeFileSave(TCommandEnabler& ce)
{
  ce.Enable(IsDirty);
}
```

CeFileSave checks the *IsDirty* flag. If *IsDirty* is false (the file has not been modified), then disable the *CmFileSave* function by calling *Enable*, passing false as the parameter. If *IsDirty* is true (the file has been modified), then enable the *CmFileSave* function, passing true as the parameter. Because you want to call *Enable* with the true parameter when *IsDirty* is true, and vice versa, you can just pass *IsDirty* as the parameter to *Enable*.

This method of enabling and disabling a command works for both menu items and button gadgets. In the preceding example, if you have both a control bar button and a menu item that send the CM_FILESAVE command, both commands are implemented in the *CmFileSave* function. Similarly, command enabling for the control-bar button and the menu item is implemented in the *CeFileSave* function.

Changing menu-item text

Changing the text of a menu item is done with the *SetText* function. To change the text of a menu item,

1 Add the command-enabling handler function and response-table macro to your window class as described on page 227.

2 Define the handler function.

3 In the handler function, call the *SetText* member function of the command-enabling object passed into the handler function. *SetText* takes a single parameter, a **const far char***. This character array parameter should contain the new text for the menu item. *SetText* returns **void**.

Note   If you're setting the text for a menu item and turning on a check mark for that menu item in the same function, you must call *SetText* before you call *SetCheck*. Reversing this order removes the check mark. See page 234 for information on setting check marks for menu items.

Suppose your application supports three different file formats, text, binary, and encrypted. You want the File | Save menu item to reflect the format of the file being saved. Here's the example class from earlier on page 228, modified with an **enum** type, *TFormat*, and a *TFormat* data member called *Format*:

```
class TMyFrame : public TFrameWindow
{
  public:
    TMyFrame(TWindow *parent = 0, char *title = 0);
    enum TFormat {Text, Binary, Encrypted};

  protected:
    TFormat Format;

    void CmFileSave();

    // This is the command-enabling handler function.
    void CeFileSave(TCommandEnabler& commandEnabler);

  DECLARE_RESPONSE_TABLE(TMyFrame);
};

DEFINE_RESPONSE_TABLE(TMyFrame)
  EV_COMMAND(CM_FILESAVE, CmFileSave),
  EV_COMMAND_ENABLE(CM_FILESAVE, CeFileSave),
END_RESPONSE_TABLE;
```

```
void
TMyFrame::CeFileSave(TCommandEnabler& ce)
{
  switch(Format) {
    case Text:
      ce.SetText("Save as text file");
      break;
    case Binary:
      ce.SetText("Save as binary file");
      break;
    case Encrypted:
      ce.SetText("Save as encrypted file");
      break;
    default:
      ce.SetText("Save");
  }
}
```

Toggling command items

You can use command-item toggling to provide the users of your applications visual cues about what functions are enabled, various application states, and so on. Anything that can be presented in a boolean fashion, such as on and off, in and out, and so on, can be represented by command-item toggling.

There are two different types of toggling implemented in ObjectWindows, but both are implemented the same way.

- You can turn check marks by menu items on and off.

- You can also "check" and "uncheck" button gadgets so that the gadget stands out when it's off and is recessed and light when it's on.

There is also a third *indeterminate* state that indicates when something is not checked or unchecked. The meaning of this state is mostly up to you, but usually indicates a situation where the criteria for being enabled or disabled is mixed. For example, many word processors have control-bar buttons that indicate the current text format, such as a button with a "B" on it to indicate bold text. This button is unchecked when the current text format is not bold, and checked when the format is bold. But if a block of text contains text, some of which is bold and some not, the button is placed in its indeterminate state.

A variation of toggling button gadgets is that you can enable or disable an exclusive button gadget. Exclusive button gadgets function just like radio buttons. In a group of exclusive button gadgets only one button gadget can be on at a time. Enabling another button gadget in the group disables the previously enabled button gadget.

To toggle a command item,

1 Add the command-enabling handler function and response-table macro to your window class as described on page 227.

2 Define the handler function.

3 Inside the handler function, call the *SetCheck* member function of the command-enabling object passed into the handler function. The *SetCheck* function takes a single **int** parameter. Call *SetCheck* with one of the enumerated values defined in *TCommandEnabler*: *Checked*, *Unchecked*, or *Indeterminate*.

Note If you are turning on a check mark for a menu item and setting the text for that menu item in the same function, you must call *SetText* before you call *SetCheck*. Reversing this order removes the check mark. See page 234 for information on setting check marks for menu items.

A common use for toggling command items is to let the user of your application specify whether some feature should be active. For example, suppose your application provides both a menu item and control-bar button to access the *CmFileSave* function. Many applications provide "fly-over" hints, short descriptions that appear in the status bar when the pointer moves over a menu item or button gadget. You may want to let the user turn these hints off. To provide this option to the user,

1 Add a new command identifier to your application, such as CM_TOGGLEHINTS.

2 Add a new menu, perhaps named Options, with a menu item Fly-over Hints.

3 You can also add a new button to your button bar (see Chapter 30 for information on adding a new button gadget to your control bar).

4 Add a function to handle the CM_TOGGLEHINTS event and actually turn the hints on and off.

5 Add a command-enabling function to check and uncheck the command items.

Here's the example class from earlier on page 228, modified to use a decorated frame window. The user can toggle hints by choosing the command item set up for this.

```
class TMyDecFrame : public TDecoratedFrame
{
  public:
    TMyDecFrame(TWindow *parent = 0, char *title = 0, TWindow* client)
      : TDecoratedFrame(parent, title, client), hintMode (true) {}

    //Cb must be set by the application object during the InitMainWindow function.
    TControlBar* Cb;

  protected:
    // hintMode indicates whether the hints are currently on or off.
    bool HintMode;

    // This is the function that actually turns the hints on and off.
    void CmToggleHints();

    // This is the command-enabling handler function.
    void CeToggleHints(TCommandEnabler& commandEnabler);

  DECLARE_RESPONSE_TABLE(TMyDecFrame);
};

DEFINE_RESPONSE_TABLE(TMyDecFrame)
```

```
    EV_COMMAND(CM_TOGGLEHINTS, CmToggleHints),
    EV_COMMAND_ENABLE(CM_TOGGLEHINTS, CeToggleHints),
END_RESPONSE_TABLE;

void
TMyDecFrame::CmToggleHints()
{
  if(HintMode)
    Cb->SetHintMode(TGadgetWindow::EnterHints);
  else
    Cb->SetHintMode(TGadgetWindow::NoHints);
  HintMode = !HintMode;
}

void
TMyDecFrame::CeToggleHints(TCommandEnabler& ce)
{
  ce.SetChecked(HintMode);
}
```

Note that the control bar is set up by the application object in its *InitMainWindow* function. The code for this is not shown here. For an explanation of application objects and the *InitMainWindow* function see Chapter 20. For an explanation of button gadgets and control bars, see Chapter 30. For a working example of command item toggling, see the example EXAMPLES/OWL/OWLAPPS/MDIFILE.

24

ObjectWindows exception handling

ObjectWindows provides a robust exception-handling mechanism for dealing with exceptional situations. An exceptional situation is any situation that falls outside of your application's normal operating parameters. This can be something as innocuous as an unexpected user response or something as serious as an invalid handle or memory allocation failure. Exception handling provides a clean, efficient way to deal with these and other conditions.

This chapter describes the ObjectWindows exception-handling encapsulation, including

- Exception class hierarchy
- Exception resource identifiers
- Code macros, which make it easy to turn exception handling off and on

You should be thoroughly familiar with C++ exception handling before reading this chapter. C++ exception handling is described in Chapter 4 of the *Borland C++ Programmer's Guide*.

ObjectWindows exception hierarchy

ObjectWindows provides a number of classes that can be thrown as exceptions. Based on the *TXBase* and *TXOwl* classes, these exception classes can inform the user of the existing exceptional state, prompt the user for a course of action, create new exception objects, throw exceptions, and so on. There are four exception classes that are implemented as independent classes:

- *TXBase* is the base class for all ObjectWindows and ObjectComponents exception classes. *TXBase* is derived from the Borland C++ *xmsg* class. *xmsg* is described in Chapter 4 of the *Borland C++ Programmer's Guide*.

- *TXOwl* is derived from *TXBase*. *TXOwl* is the base class for the ObjectWindows exception classes.

- *TXCompatibility* describes exceptions that occur when *TModule::Status* is non-zero. This provides backwards compatibility between the ObjectWindows 1.0 method of detecting exceptional situations and the ObjectWindows 2.*x* exception hierarchy. *TXCompatibility* maps the value of *TModule::Status* to a resource string identifier.

- *TXOutOfMemory* describes an exception that occurs when an attempt to allocate memory space for an object fails. This is analogous to the *xalloc* object thrown when **new** fails to properly allocate memory.

Two other classes, *TXOle* and *TXAuto*, are derived from *TXBase*. These classes provide exception handling for the ObjectComponents classes. They are described in the *ObjectWindows Reference*.

Working with TXBase

As the base class for the ObjectWindows exception classes, *TXBase* provides the basic interface for working with ObjectWindows exceptions. *TXBase* can perform a number of functions:

- It can construct itself, initializing its base *xmsg* object.
- It can clone itself, making a copy of the exception object.
- It can throw itself as an exception object.

Constructing and destroying TXBase

TXBase provides two public constructors:

```
TXBase(const string& msg);
TXBase(const TXBase& src);
```

The first constructor initializes the *xmsg* base class with the value of the *string* parameter, calling the *xmsg* constructor that takes a *string* parameter. The second creates a new object that is a copy of the *TXBase* object passed in as a parameter.

Both constructors increment the *TXBase* data member *InstanceCount*. *InstanceCount* is a **static int**, meaning there is only a single instance of the member no matter how many actual *TXBase* or *TXBase*-derived objects exist in the application. The *TXBase* destructor decrements *InstanceCount*. The destructor is declared virtual to allow easy overriding of the destructor.

Because each new *TXBase* or *TXBase*-derived object increments *InstanceCount*, and each deleted *TXBase* or *TXBase*-derived object decrements *InstanceCount*, the value of *InstanceCount* reflects the total number of *TXBase* and *TXBase*-derived objects existing in the application at the time. To access *InstanceCount* from outside a *TXBase* or *TXBase*-derived class, qualify the name *InstanceCount* with a *TXBase::* scope qualifier.

Cloning exception objects

TXBase contains a function called *Clone*. This function takes no parameters and returns a *TXBase**. *Clone* creates a copy of the current exception object by allocating a new *TXBase* object with **new** and passing a dereferenced **this** pointer to the copy constructor.

```
TXBase*
TXBase::Clone()
```

```
  {
    return new TXBase(*this);
  }
```

It is important to note that any classes derived from *TXBase* must override this function to use the proper constructor. For example, the *TXOwl* class, which is derived from *TXBase*, implements the *Clone* function like this:

```
TXOwl*
TXOwl::Clone()
{
  return new TXOwl(*this);
}
```

Throwing TXBase exceptions

Once you have a *TXBase* object, either by creating it or cloning it, you can throw the object one of three ways.

- Use the **throw** keyword followed by the object name:

```
TXBase xobj("Some exception...");
throw xobj;
```

- Use the ObjectWindows THROW macro, which corresponds to the C++ keyword **throw**. See page 241 for an explanation of the ObjectWindows exception-handling macros. The previous example would look like this:

```
TXBase xobj("Some exception...");
throw xobj;
```

- Call the exception object's *Throw* function:

```
TXBase xobj("Some exception...");
xobj.Throw();
```

This method provides for strict type safety when you throw the exception. It also provides a polymorphic interface when throwing the exception, so that the function that catches a *TXBase*-derived exception object can treat the object as a *TXBase*, regardless of what it actually is.

Working with TXOwl

As the base class for the ObjectWindows exception classes, *TXOwl* provides the basic interface for working with ObjectWindows exceptions. In addition to the functionality provided in the *TXBase* class, *TXOwl* can perform a number of other functions.

- It can construct itself, initializing its base objects.
- It can clone itself, making a copy of the exception object.
- It can pass unhandled exceptions to the application object's *Error* function or to the global exception handler *HandleGlobalException* (*HandleGlobalException* is discussed later).

Constructing and destroying TXOwl

TXOwl has two constructors to provide flexibility in passing the exception message string:

```
TXOwl(const string& str, unsigned resId = 0);
TXOwl(unsigned resId, TModule* module = ::Module);
```

The first constructor initializes the *TXBase* base object with the value of the *string* parameter. The **unsigned** parameter is used as an error number.

The second constructor loads the string resource identified by *resId* and uses the string to initialize *TXBase*. The *TModule** identifies the module from which the resource should be loaded. It defaults to the global current module pointer *Module*, meaning the resource should be loaded from the current module or application.

The *TXOwl* destructor has no default functionality other than that inherited from *TXBase*.

Cloning TXOwl and TXOwl-derived exception objects

TXOwl also contains the *Clone* function. This function takes no parameters and returns a *TXOwl**. *Clone* creates a copy of the current exception object by allocating a new *TXOwl* object with **new** and passing a dereferenced **this** pointer to the automatic copy constructor.

```
TXOwl*
TXOwl::Clone()
{
    return new TXOwl(*this);
}
```

It is important to note that any classes derived from *TXOwl* must override this function to use the proper constructor. For example, the *TXOutOfMemory* class, which is derived from *TXOwl*, implements the *Clone* function like this:

```
TXOwl*
TXOutOfMemory::Clone()
{
    return new TXOutOfMemory(*this);
}
```

Note that the return type is still *TXOwl**. This lets the ObjectWindows exception-handling functions treat any exception object as a *TXOwl* object, in keeping with the polymorphic nature of the ObjectWindows hierarchy. But also note that the return type for *TXOwl::Close* differs from the *TXBase::Clone* function. That is because, while *TXBase* provides the basic functionality for the ObjectWindows and ObjectComponents exception classes, *TXOwl* provides the basic interface for the ObjectWindows exception classes.

Specialized ObjectWindows exception classes

A number of regular ObjectWindows classes implement specialized exception classes, all of which are based on *TXOwl* but are defined within the implementing class definition to provide name scoping. The following table describes these classes, along with the unique functionality of each class. The various IDS_* resources mentioned in the table, along with many others, are described in Chapter 2 of the *ObjectWindows Reference*.

Table 24.1 Specialized exception classes

Parent class	Exception class	Function
TApplication	*TXInvalidMainWindow*	Initializes the exception message with the IDS_INVALIDMAINWINDOW string resource. This object is thrown when the *MainWindow* member of *TApplication contains either an invalid pointer or a pointer to an invalid window.*
TModule	*TXInvalidModule*	Initializes the exception message with the IDS_INVALIDMODULE string resource. This exception is thrown in the *TModule* constructor when the module's *HInstance* is invalid.
TWindow	*TXWindow*	Initializes the exception message with the window title and with a string resource passed to the *TXWindow* constructor. This exception is thrown in situations where an error relating to a window object has occurred.
TMenu	*TXMenu*	Initializes the exception message with a string resource passed to the *TXMenu* constructor. By default this is the IDS_GDIFAILURE string resource. This exception is thrown when a menu object's handle is invalid.
TValidator	*TXValidator*	Initializes the exception message with a string resource passed to the *TXValidator* constructor. By default this is the IDS_VALIDATORSYNTAX string resource. This exception is thrown when a validator expression is corrupt or invalid.
TGdiBase	*TXGdi*	Initializes the exception message with a string resource passed to the *TXGdi* constructor, along with the GDI object handle. By default, the string resource is IDS_GDIFAILURE and the GDI object handle is 0. This exception is thrown in numerous situations when an error relating to a graphics object has occurred.
TPrinter	*TXPrinter*	Initializes the exception message with a string resource passed to the *TXPrinter* constructor. By default this is the IDS_PRINTERERROR string resource. This exception is thrown when the printer's device context is invalid.

ObjectWindows exception-handling macros

ObjectWindows provides a number of macros for implementing exception handling. Although you can use the standard C++ keywords such as **try**, **catch**, **throw**, and so on, the ObjectWindows macros enable you to turn exception handling on and off simply by defining or not defining a single symbol. The macros provided are

- TRY
- THROW(x)
- THROWX(x)
- RETHROW
- CATCH(x)

These macros are explained later in this section.

Turning ObjectWindows exceptions on and off

The symbol that switches exception handling on and off in ObjectWindows applications is NO_CPP_EXCEPTIONS. The value (or lack of value) assigned to NO_CPP_EXCEPTIONS doesn't matter. What matters is whether it is defined. If it's not, the exception-handling macros expand to implement exception handling. If it is defined, the macros provide only the barest functionality by aborting the application when an exception is thrown. The precise behaviors of the macros when exception handling is switched on and off is described later.

There are many different methods for defining NO_CPP_EXCEPTIONS. This list doesn't contain all the ways to define it, but makes a few suggestions.

- You can specify the -DNO_CPP_EXCEPTIONS option on the MAKE command line. This defines the macro, but with no specific value.

- You can define a symbol using a graphical development environments such as the Borland C++ IDE. Use the method provided in your graphical development to define the NO_CPP_EXCEPTIONS symbol.

- You can define NO_CPP_EXCEPTIONS in your source code. This is a less desirable method than the previous ones, mainly because if you're using some type of MAKE or dependency-checking program for building your application, modifying the source code modifies the time stamp on the file. You might or might not want the time stamp to change.

Macro expansion

The exception-handling macros in ObjectWindows behave differently depending on whether NO_CPP_EXCEPTIONS is defined. The following table explains how each macro is expanded depending on the state of NO_CPP_EXCEPTIONS:

Table 24.2 ObjectWindows exception-handling macro expansion

Macro	NO_CPP_EXCEPTIONS defined	NO_CPP_EXCEPTIONS not defined
TRY	Expands to nothing, removing the **try** statement.	Expands to **try**, allowing the code in the **try** block to be tested for thrown exceptions.
THROW(x)	Calls the *abort* function.	Expands to **throw**(x), throwing the x object if the exceptional conditions are met.
THROWX(x)	Calls the *abort* function.	Expands to x.Throw(), calling the object x's *Throw* function. This macro should only be used with *TXBase*-derived classes.
RETHROW	Expands to nothing, removing the **throw** statement.	Expands to **throw**. This macro should be used only inside of **catch** (or CATCH) clauses to rethrow the caught exception.
CATCH(x)	Expands to nothing, removing the **catch** statement.	Expands to **catch** x, catching exceptions thrown with objects of type x.

25

Window objects

ObjectWindows window objects provide an interface wrapper around windows, making dealing with windows and their children and controls much easier. ObjectWindows provides several different types of window objects:

- Layout windows (described starting on page 247)
- Frame windows (described starting on page 253)
- Decorated frame windows (described starting on page 256)
- MDI windows (described starting on page 259)

Another class of window objects, called gadget windows, is discussed in Chapter 30.

Using window objects

This section explains how to create, display, and fill window objects. It describes how to perform the following tasks:

- Constructing window objects
- Setting creation attributes
- Creating window interface elements

The different types of windows discussed in this chapter—frame windows, layout windows, decorated frame windows, and MDI windows—are all examples of window objects. The information in this section applies to all the different types of window objects.

Constructing window objects

Window objects represent interface elements. The object is connected to the element through a handle stored in the object's *HWindow* data member. *HWindow* is inherited from *TWindow*. When you construct a window object, its interface element doesn't yet exist. You must create it in a separate step. *TWindow* also has a constructor that you can use in a DLL to create a window object for an interface element that already exists.

Constructing window objects with virtual bases

Several ObjectWindows classes use *TWindow* or *TFrameWindow* as a virtual base. These classes are *TDialog, TMDIFrame, TTinyCaption, TMDIChild, TDecoratedFrame, TLayoutWindow, TClipboardViewer, TKeyboardModeTracker,* and *TFrameWindow*. In C++, virtual base classes are constructed first, which means that the derived class' constructor cannot specify default arguments for the base class constructor. There are two ways to handle this problem:

- Explicitly construct your immediate base class or classes and any virtual base classes when you construct your derived class.

- Use the virtual base's default constructor. Both *TWindow* and *TFrameWindow* have a default constructor. They also each have an *Init* function that lets you specify parameters for the base class; call this *Init* function in the constructor of your derived class to set any parameters you need in the base class.

Here are a couple of examples showing how to construct a window object using the each of the methods described above:

```
class TMyblic TFrameWindow
{
  public:
    // This constructor calls the base class constructors
    TMyWin(TWindow *parent, char *title)
      : TFrameWindow(parent, title),
        TWindow(parent, title) {}
}

TMyWin *myWin = new TMyWin(GetMainWindow(), "Child window");

class TNewWin : virtual public TWindow
{
  public:
    TNewWin(TWindow *parent, char *title);
}

TNewWin::TNewWin(TWindow *parent, char *title)
{
  // This constructor uses the default base class constructors and calls Init
  Init(parent, title, IDL_DEFAULT);
};

TNewWin *newWin = new TMyWin(GetMainWindow(), "Child window");
```

Setting creation attributes

A typical Windows application has many different types of windows: overlapped or pop-up, bordered, scrollable, and captioned, to name a few. The different types are selected with *style attributes*. Style attributes, as well as a window's title, are set during a window object's initialization and are used during the interface element's creation.

A window object's creation attributes, such as style and title, are stored in the object's *Attr* member, a *TWindowAttr* structure. Table 25.1 shows *TWindowAttr*'s members.

Table 25.1   Window creation attributes

Member	Type	Description
Style	*uint32*	Style constant.
ExStyle	*uint32*	Extended style constant.
X	**int**	The horizontal screen coordinate of the window's upper-left corner.
Y	**int**	The vertical screen coordinate of the window's upper-left corner.
W	**int**	The window's initial width in screen coordinates.
H	**int**	The window's initial height in screen coordinates.
Menu	*TResId*	ID of the window's menu resource. You should not try to directly assign a menu identifier to *Attr.Menu*! Use the *AssignMenu* function instead.
Id	**int**	Child window ID for communicating between a control and its parent. *Id* should be unique for all child windows of the same parent. If the control is defined in a resource, its *Id* should be the same as the resource ID. A window should never have both *Menu* and *Id* set, since these members actually occupy the same in the window's HWND structure.
Param	**char far ***	Used by *TMDIClient* to hold information about the MDI frame and child windows.
AccelTable	*TResId*	ID of the window's accelerator table resource.

Overriding default attributes

Table 25.2 lists the default window creation attributes. You can override those defaults in a derived window class' constructor by changing the values in the *Attr* structure. For example:

```
TTestWindow::TTestWindow(TWindow* parent, const char* title)
  : TFrameWindow(parent, title),
    TWindow(parent, title)
{
  Attr.Style &= (WS_SYSMENU | WS_MAXIMIZEBOX);
  Attr.Style |= WS_MINIMIZEBOX;
  Attr.X = 100;
  Attr.Y = 100;
  Attr.W = 415;
  Attr.H = 355;
}
```

Child-window attributes

You can set the attributes of a child window in the child window's constructor or in the code that creates the child window. When you change the attributes in the parent window object's constructor, you need to use a pointer to the child window object to get access to its *Attr* member.

```
TTestWindow::TTestWindow(TWindow* parent, const char* title)
  : TWindow(parent, title)
{
  TWindow helpWindow(this, "Help System");
```

```
    helpWindow.Attr.Style |= WS_POPUPWINDOW | WS_CAPTION;
    helpWindow.Attr.X = 100;
    helpWindow.Attr.Y = 100;
    helpWindow.Attr.W = 300;
    helpWindow.Attr.H = 300;
    helpWindow.SetCursor(0, IDC_HAND);
}
```

Table 25.2 shows some default values you might want to override for *Attr* members. A default value of 0 means to use the Windows default value.

Table 25.2   Default window attributes

Attr member	Default value
Style	WS_CHILD	WS_VISIBLE
ExStyle	0
X	0
Y	0
W	0
H	0
Menu	0
Id	0
Param	0
AccelTable	0

Creating window interface elements

Once you've constructed a window object, you need to tell Windows to create the associated interface element. Do this by calling the object's *Create* member function:

```
    window.Create();
```

Create does the following things:

- Creates the interface element

- Sets *HWindow* to the handle of the interface element

- Sets members of *Attr* to the actual state of the interface element (*Style, ExStyle, X, Y, H, W*)

- Calls *SetupWindow*

An application's main window is automatically created by *TApplication::InitInstance*. You don't need to call *Create* yourself to create the main window. See Chapter 18, "Application and module objects," for more information about main windows.

Two ObjectWindows exceptions can be thrown while creating a window object's interface element. You should therefore enclose calls to *Create* within a **try**/**catch** block to handle any memory or resource problems your application might encounter. *Create* throws a *TXInvalidWindow* exception when the window can't be created. *SetupWindow* throws *TXInvalidChildWindow* when a child window in the window can't be created.

Both exceptions are usually caused by insufficient memory or other resources. Here is an example of using exceptions to catch an error while creating a window object:

```
try
{
  TWindow* window = new TMyWindow(this);
  window->Create();
}
catch(TXOwl& exp)
{
  MessageBox(exp.why.c_str(), "Window creation error");
throw(exp);
}
```

ObjectWindows exception objects are described in Chapter 24.

Layout windows

This section discusses layout windows. Layout windows are encapsulated in the class *TLayoutWindow*, which is derived from *TWindow*. Along with *TFrameWindow*, *TLayoutWindow* provides the basis for decorated frame windows and their ability to arrange decorations in the frame area.

Layout windows are so named because they can lay out child windows in the layout window's client area. The children's locations are determined relative to the layout window or another child window (known as a *sibling*). The location of a child window depends on that window's *layout metrics*, which consist of a number of rules that describe the window's X and Y coordinates, its height, and its width. These rules are usually based on a sibling window's coordinates and, ultimately, on the size and arrangement of the layout window.

Figure 25.1 shows two shots of a sample layout window with a child window in the client area. In this example, the child's layout metrics specify that the child is to remain the same distance from each side of the layout window. Notice how, in the first shot, the child window is rather small. Then, in the second shot, the layout window has been enlarged. The child window, following its layout constraints, got larger so that each of its edges stayed the same distance from the edge of the layout window.

Figure 25.1 Sample layout windows

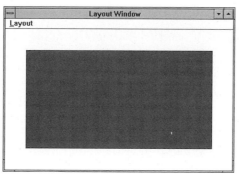

Layout metrics for a child window are contained in a class called *TLayoutMetrics*. A layout metrics object consists of a number of *layout constraints*. Each layout constraint describes a rule for finding a particular dimension, such as the X coordinate or the width of the window. It takes four layout constraints to fully describe a layout metrics object. Layout constraints are contained in a structure named *TLayoutConstraints*, but you usually use one of the *TLayoutConstraints*-derived classes, such as *TEdgeConstraint*, *TEdgeOrWidthConstraint*, or *TEdgeOrHeightConstraint*.

Layout constraints

Layout constraints specify a relationship between an edge or dimension of one window and an edge or dimension of a sibling window or the parent layout window. This relationship can be quite flexible. For example, you can set the width of a window to be a percentage of the width of the parent window, so that whenever the parent is resized, the child window is resized to take up the same relative window area. You can also set the left edge of a window to be the same as the right edge of another child, so that when the windows are moved around, they are tied together. You can even constrain a window to occupy an absolute size and position in the client area.

The three types of constraints most often used are *TEdgeConstraint*, *TEdgeOrWidthConstraint*, and *TEdgeOrHeightConstraint*. These structures constitute the full set of constraints used in the *TLayoutMetrics* class. *TEdgeOrWidthConstraint* and *TEdgeOrHeightConstraint* are derived from *TEdgeConstraint*. From the outside, these three objects look almost the same. When this section discusses *TEdgeConstraint*, it is referring to all three objects—*TEdgeConstraint*, *TEdgeOrWidthConstraint*, and *TEdgeOrHeightConstraint*—unless the other two classes are explicitly excluded from the statement.

Defining constraints

The most basic way to define a constraining relationship (that is, setting up a relationship between an edge or size of one window and an edge or size of another window) is to use the *Set* function. The *Set* function is defined in the *TEdgeConstraint* class and subsequently inherited by *TEdgeOrWidthConstraint* and *TEdgeOrHeightConstraint*.

Here is the *Set* function declaration:

```
void Set(TEdge edge, TRelationship rel,
        TWindow* otherWin, TEdge otherEdge,
        int value = 0);
```

where:

- *edge* specifies which part of the window you are constraining. For this, there is the **enum** *TEdge*, which has five possible values:
  - *lmLeft* specifies the left edge of the window.
  - *lmTop* specifies the top edge of the window.
  - *lmRight* specifies the right edge of the window.
  - *lmBottom* specifies the bottom edge of the window.

- *lmCenter* specifies the center of the window. The object that owns the constraint, such as *TLayoutMetrics,* decides whether this means the vertical center or the horizontal center.

- You can also specify the window's width or height as a constraint, but only with *TEdgeOrWidthConstraint* and *TEdgeOrHeightConstraint.* For this, there is the **enum** *TWidthHeight. TWidthHeight* has two possible values:
  - *lmWidth* specifies that the width of the window should be constrained.
  - *lmHeight* specifies that the height of the window should be constrained.

- *rel* specifies the relationship between the two edges:

Table 25.3   Default window attributes

rel	Relationship
lmAsIs	This dimension is constrained to its current value.
lmPercentOf	This dimension is constrained to a percentage of the constraining edge's size. This is usually used with a constraining width or height.
lmAbove	This dimension is constrained to a certain distance above its constraining edge.
lmLeftOf	This dimension is constrained to a certain distance to the left of its constraining edge.
lmBelow	This dimension is constrained to a certain distance below its constraining edge.
lmRightOf	This dimension is constrained to a certain distance to the right of its constraining edge.
lmSameAs	This dimension is constrained to the same value as its constraining edge.
lmAbsolute	This dimension is constrained to an absolute coordinate or size.

- *otherWin* specifies the window with which you are constraining your child window. You must use the value *lmParent* when specifying the parent window. Otherwise, pass a pointer to the *TWindow* or *TWindow*-derived object containing the other window.

- *otherEdge* specifies the particular edge of *otherWin* with which you are constraining your child window. *otherEdge* can have any of the same values that are allowed for *edge.*

- *value* means different things, depending on the value of *rel*:

rel	Meaning of *value*
lmAsIs	*value* has no meaning and should be set to 0.
lmPercentOf	*value* indicates what percent of the constraing measure the constrained measure should be.
lmAbove	*value* indicates how many units above the constraining edge the constrained edge should be.
lmLeftOf	*value* indicates how many units to the left of the constraining edge the constrained edge should be.
lmBelow	*value* indicates how many units below the constraining edge the constrained edge should be.
lmRightOf	*value* indicates how many units to the right of the constraining edge the constrained edge should be.

rel	Meaning of *value*
lmSameAs	*value* has no meaning and should be set to 0.
lmAbsolute	*value* is the absolute measure for the constrained edge:
	When *edge* is *lmLeft*, *lmRight*, or sometimes *lmCenter*, *value* is the X coordinate for the edge.
	When *edge* is *lmTop*, *lmBottom*, or sometimes *lmCenter*, *value* is the Y coordinate for the edge.
	When *edge* is *lmWidth* or *lmHeight*, *value* represents the size of the constraint.
	The owning object determines whether *lmCenter* represents an X or Y coordinate. See page 248.

- The meaning of *value* is also dependent on the value of *Units*. *Units* is a *TMeasurementUnits* member of *TLayoutConstraint*. *TMeasurementUnits* is an **enum** that describes the type of unit represented by *value*. *Units* can be either *lmPixels* or *lmLayoutUnits*. *lmPixels* indicates that *value* is meant to represent an absolute number of physical pixels. *lmLayoutUnits* indicates that *value* is meant to represent a number of logical units. These layout units are based on the size of the current font of the layout window.

TEdgeConstraint also contains a number of functions that you can use to set up predefined relationships. These correspond closely to the relationships you can specify in the *Set* function. In fact, these functions call *Set* to define the constraining relationship. You can use these functions to set up a majority of the constraint relationships you define.

The following four functions work in a similar way:

```
void LeftOf(TWindow* sibling, int margin = 0);
void RightOf(TWindow* sibling, int margin = 0);
void Above(TWindow* sibling, int margin = 0);
void Below(TWindow* sibling, int margin = 0);
```

Each of these functions place the child window in a certain relationship with the constraining window *sibling*. The edges are predefined, with the constrained edge being the opposite of the function name and the constraining edge being the same as the function name.

For example, the *LeftOf* function places the child window to the left of *sibling*. This means the constrained edge of the child window is *lmRight* and the constraining edge of *sibling* is *lmLeft*.

You can set an edge of your child window to an absolute value with the *Absolute* function:

```
void Absolute(TEdge edge, int value);
```

edge indicates which edge you want to constrain, and *value* has the same value as when used in *Set* with the *lmAbsolute* relationship.

There are two other shortcut functions you can use:

```
void SameAs(TWindow* otherWin, TEdge edge);
void PercentOf(TWindow* otherWin, TEdge edge, int percent);
```

These two use the same edge for the constrained window and the constraining window; that is, if you specify *lmLeft* for *edge*, the left edge of your child window is constrained to the left edge of *otherWin*.

Defining constraining relationships

A single layout constraint is not enough to lay out a window. For example, specifying that one window must be 10 pixels below another window doesn't tell you anything about the width or height of the window, the location of the left or right borders, or the location of the bottom border. It only tells you that one edge is located 10 pixels below another window.

A combination of layout constraints can define fully a window's location (there are some exceptions, as discussed on page 252). The class *TLayoutMetrics* uses four layout constraint structures—two *TEdgeConstraint* objects named *X* and *Y*, a *TEdgeOrWidthConstraint* named *Width*, and a *TEdgeOrHeightConstraint* named *Height*.

TLayoutMetrics is a fairly simple class. The constructor takes no parameters. The only thing it does is to set up each layout constraint member. For each layout constraint, the constructor

- Zeroes out the value for the constraining window.
- Sets the constraint's relationship to *lmAsIs*.
- Sets units to *lmLayoutUnits*.
- Sets the value to 0.

The only difference is to *MyEdge*, which indicates to which edge of the window this constraint applies. *X* is set to *lmLeft*, *Y* is set to *lmTop*, *Width* is set to *lmWidth*, and *Height* is set to *lmHeight*.

Once you have constructed a *TLayoutMetrics* object, you need to set the layout constraints for the window you want to lay out. You can use the functions described in the preceding section for setting each layout constraint.

It is important to realize that the labels *X*, *Y*, *Width*, and *Height* are more labels of convenience than strict rules on how the constraints should be used. *X* can represent the X coordinate of the left edge, the right edge, or the center. You can combine this with the *Width* constraint—which can be one of *lmCenter*, *lmRight*, or *lmWidth*—to completely define the window's X-axis location and width. Using all of the edge constraints is easy, and is useful in situations where tiling is performed.

The simplest way is to assign an X coordinate to *X* and a width to width. But you could also set the edge for *X* to *lmCenter* and the edge for *Width* to *lmRight*. So *Width* doesn't really represent a width, but the X-coordinate of the window's right edge. If you know the X-coordinate of the right edge and the center, it's easy to calculate the X-coordinate of the left edge.

To better understand how constraints work together to describe a window, try building and running the sample application LAYOUT in the directory EXAMPLES\OWL\ OWLAPI\LAYOUT. This application has a number of child windows in a layout window. A dialog box you can access from the menu lets you change the constraints of each of the windows and then see the results as the windows are laid out. Be careful, though. If you specify a set of layout constraints that doesn't fully describe a window, the application will probably crash, or, if diagnostics are on, a check will occur. The reason for this is discussed in the next section.

Indeterminate constraints

You must be careful about how you specify your layout constraints. The constraints available in the *TLayoutMetrics* class give you the ability to fully describe a window. But they do not guarantee that the constraints you use will fully describe a window. In cases where the constraints do not fully describe a window, the most likely result is an application crash.

Using layout windows

Once you've set up layout constraints, you're ready to create a layout window to contain your child windows. Here's the constructor for *TLayoutWindow*:

```
TLayoutWindow(TWindow* parent,
              const char far* title = 0,
              TModule* module = 0);
```

where:

- *parent* is the layout window's parent window.
- *title* is the layout window's title. This parameter defaults to a null string.
- *module* is passed to the *TWindow* base class constructor as the *TModule* parameter for that constructor. This parameter defaults to 0.

After the layout window is constructed and displayed, there are a number of functions you can call:

- The *Layout* function returns **void** and takes no parameters. This function tells the layout window to look at all its child windows and lay them out again. You can call this to force the window to recalculate the boundaries and locations of each child window. You usually want to call *Layout* after you've moved a child window, resized the layout window, or anything else that could affect the constraints of the child windows.

  Note that *TLayoutWindow* overrides the *TWindow* version of *EvSize* to call *Layout* automatically whenever a WM_SIZE event is caught. If you override this function yourself, you should be sure either to call the base class version of the function or call *Layout* in your derived version.

- *SetChildLayoutMetrics* returns **void** and takes a *TWindow* & and a *TLayoutMetrics* & as parameters. Use this function to associate a set of constraints contained in a *TLayoutMetrics* object with a child window. Here is an example of creating a *TLayoutMetrics* object and associating it with a child window:

```
TMyLayoutWindow::TMyLayoutWindow(TWindow* parent, char far* title)
  : TLayoutWindow(parent, title)
{
  TWindow MyChildWindow(this);

  TLayoutMetrics layoutMetrics;
```

```
layoutMetrics.X.Absolute(lmLeft, 10);
layoutMetrics.Y.Absolute(lmTop, 10);
layoutMetrics.Width.PercentOf(lmParent, lmWidth, 60);
layoutMetrics.Height.PercentOf(lmParent, lmHeight, 60);

SetChildLayoutMetrics(MyChildWindow, layoutMetrics);
}
```

Notice that the child window doesn't need any special functionality to be associated with a layout metrics object. The association is handled entirely by the layout window itself. The child window doesn't have to know anything about the relationship.

- *GetChildLayoutMetrics* returns **bool** and takes a *TWindow* **&** and a *TLayoutMetrics* **&** as parameters. This looks up the child window that is represented by the *TWindow* **&**. It then places the current layout metrics associated with that child window into the *TLayoutMetrics* object passed in. If *GetChildLayoutMetrics* doesn't find a child window that equals the window object passed in, it returns **false**.

- *RemoveChildLayoutMetrics* returns **bool** and takes a *TWindow* **&** for a parameter. This looks up the child window that is represented by the *TWindow* **&**. It then removes the child window and its associated layout metrics from the layout window's child list. If *RemoveChildLayoutMetrics* doesn't find a child window that equals the window object passed in, it returns **false**.

You must provide layout metrics for all child windows of a layout window. The layout window assumes that all of its children have an associated layout metrics object. Removing a child window from a layout window, or deleting the child window object automatically removes the associated layout metrics object.

Frame windows

Frame windows (objects of class *TFrameWindow*) are specialized windows that support a *client window*. Frame windows are the basis for MDI and SDI frame windows, MDI child windows, and, along with *TLayoutWindow*, decorated frame windows.

Frame windows have an important role in ObjectWindows development: frame windows manage application-wide tasks like menus and tool bars. Client windows within the frame can be specialized to perform a single task. Changes you make to the frame window (for example, adding tool bars and status bars) don't affect the client windows.

Constructing frame window objects

You can construct a frame window object using one of the two *TFrameWindow* constructors. These two constructors let you create new frame window objects along with new interface elements, and let you connect a new frame window object to an existing interface element.

Constructing a new frame window

The first *TFrameWindow* constructor is used to create an entirely new frame window object:

```
TFrameWindow(TWindow *parent,
             const char far *title = 0,
             TWindow *clientWnd = 0,
             bool shrinkToClient = false,
             TModule *module = 0);
```

where:

- The first parameter is the window's parent window object. Use zero if the window you're creating is the main window (which doesn't have a parent window object). Otherwise, use a pointer to the parent window object. This is the only parameter that you *must* provide.

- The second parameter is the window title. This is the string that appears in the caption bar of the window. If you don't specify anything for the second parameter, no title is displayed in the title bar.

- The third parameter lets you specify a client window for the frame window. If you don't specify anything for the third parameter, by default the constructor gets a zero, meaning that there is no client window. Otherwise, pass a pointer to the client window object.

- The fourth parameter lets you specify whether the frame window should shrink to fit the client window. If you don't specify anything, by default the constructor gets **false**, meaning that it should not fit the frame to the client window.

- The fifth parameter is passed to the base class constructor as the *TModule* parameter for that constructor. This parameter defaults to 0.

Here are some examples of using this constructor:

```
void
TMyApplication::InitMainWindow()
{
  // default is for no client window
  SetMainWindow(new TFrameWindow(0, "Main Window"));
}

void
TMyApplication::InitMainWindow()
{
  // client window is TMyClientWindow
  SetMainWindow(new TFrameWindow(0, "Main window with client",
                                 new TMyClientWindow, true));
}
```

Constructing a frame window alias

The second *TFrameWindow* constructor is used to connect an existing interface element to a new *TFrameWindow* object. This object is known as an *alias* for the existing window:

```
TFrameWindow(HWND hWnd, TModule *module);
```

where:

- The first parameter is the window handle of the existing interface element. This is the window the *TFrameWindow* object controls.

- The second parameter is passed to the base class constructor as the *TModule* parameter for that constructor. This parameter defaults to 0.

This is useful for creating window objects for existing windows. You can then manipulate any window as if it were an ObjectWindows-created window. This is useful in situations such as DLLs, when a non-ObjectWindows application calling into the DLL passes in an HWND. You can then construct a *TFrameWindow* alias for the HWND and proceed to call *TFrameWindow* member functions like normal.

The following example shows how to construct a *TFrameWindow* for an existing interface element and use that window as the main window:

```
void
TMyApplication::AddWindow(HWND hWnd)
{
  TFrameWindow* frame = new TFrameWindow(hWnd);
  TFrameWindow* tmp = SetMainWindow(frame);
  ShowWindow(GetMainWindow()->HWindow, SW_SHOW);
  tmp->ShutDownWindow();
}
```

When you use the second constructor for *TFrameWindow,* it sets the flag *wfAlias*. You can tell whether a window element was constructed from its window object or whether it's actually an alias by calling the function *IsFlagSet* with the *wfAlias* flag. For example, suppose you don't know whether the function *AddWindow* in the last example has executed yet. If your main window is *not* an alias, *AddWindow* hasn't executed. If your main window *is* an alias, *AddWindow* has executed:

```
void
TMyApplication::CheckAddExecute()
{
  if(GetMainWindow()->IsFlagSet(wfAlias))
    // MainWindow is an alias; AddWindow has executed
  else
    // MainWindow is not an alias; AddWindow has not executed
}
```

See page 32 for more information on window object attributes.

Modifying frame windows

Many frame window attributes can be set after the object has been constructed. You can change and query object attributes using the functions discussed in Chapter 21, "Interface objects." You can also use the *TWindow* functions discussed in Chapter 21. *TFrameWindow* provides an additional set of functions for modifying frame windows:

- *AssignMenu* is typically used to set up a window's menu before the interface element has been created, such as in the *InitMainWindow* function or the window object's constructor or *SetupWindow* function.

- *SetMenu* sets the window's menu handle to the HMENU parameter passed in.

- *SetMenuDescr* sets the window's menu description to the *TMenuDescr* parameter passed in.

- *GetMenuDescr* returns the current menu description.

- *MergeMenu* merges the current menu description with the *TMenuDescr* parameter passed in.

- *RestoreMenu* restores the window's menu from *Attr.Menu*.

- *SetIcon* sets the icon in the module passed as the first parameter to the icon passed as a resource in the second parameter.

For more specific information on these functions, refer to the *ObjectWindows Reference*.

Decorated frame windows

This section discusses decorated frame windows. Decorated frame windows are encapsulated in *TDecoratedFrame*, which is derived from *TFrameWindow* and *TLayoutWindow*. Decorated frame windows provide all the functionality of frame windows and layout, but in addition provide:

- Support for adding controls (known as *decorations*) to the frame of the window
- Automatic adjustment of child windows to accommodate the placement of decorations

Figure 25.2 shows a sample decorated frame window.

Figure 25.2   Sample decorated frame window

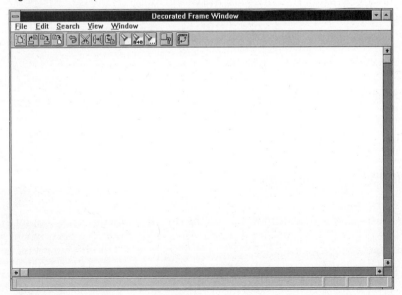

Constructing decorated frame window objects

TDecoratedFrame has only one constructor. Except for the fourth parameter, this constructor looks nearly identical to the first *TFrameWindow* constructor described on page 253.

```
TDecoratedFrame(TWindow* parent,
                const char far* title,
                TWindow* clientWnd,
                bool trackMenuSelection = false,
                TModule* module = 0);
```

where:

- The first parameter is the window's parent window object. Use zero if the window you're creating is the main window (which doesn't have a parent window object). Otherwise use a pointer to the parent window object. This is the only parameter that you *must* provide.

- The second parameter is the window title. This string appears in the caption bar of the window. If you don't specify anything for the second parameter, no title is displayed in the title bar.

- The third parameter lets you specify a pointer to a client window for the frame window. If you don't specify anything for the third parameter, by default the constructor gets a zero, meaning that there is no client window.

- The fourth parameter lets you specify whether menu commands should be tracked. When tracking is on, the window tries to pass a string to the window's status bar. The string passed has the same resource name as the currently selected menu choice. You should not turn on menu selection tracking unless you have a status bar in your window. If you don't specify anything, by default the constructor gets **false**, meaning that it should not track menu commands.

- The fifth parameter is passed to the base class constructor as the *TModule* parameter for that constructor. This parameter defaults to 0.

Adding decorations to decorated frame windows

You can use the methods for modifying windows described on page 78 and in Chapter 21, to modify the basic attributes of a decorated frame window. *TDecoratedFrame* provides the extra ability to add decorations using the *Insert* member function.

To use the *Insert* member function, you must first construct a control to be inserted. Valid controls include control bars (*TControlBar*), status bars (*TStatusBar*), button gadgets (*TButtonGadget*), and any other control type based on *TWindow*.

Once you have constructed the control, use the *Insert* function to insert the control into the decorated frame window. The *Insert* function takes two parameters: a reference to the control and a location specifier. *TDecoratedFrame* provides the **enum** *TLocation*. *TLocation* has four possible values: *Top*, *Bottom*, *Left*, and *Right*.

Suppose you want to construct a status bar to add to the bottom of your decorated frame window. The code would look something like this:

```
TStatusBar* sb = new TStatusBar(0, TGadget::Recessed,
                                TStatusBar::CapsLock |
                                TStatusBar::NumLock |
                                TStatusBar::Overtype);


TDecoratedFrame* frame = new TDecoratedFrame(0,
                                             "Decorated Frame",
                                             0,
                                             true);


frame->Insert(*sb, TDecoratedFrame::Bottom);
```

Docking Classes

The docking classes provide a simple way to add docking windows, such as tool bars, to ObjectWindows applications. Docking tool bars (such as those in Word for Windows) can be arranged by the user to suit his needs.

The *THarbor* class is the organizer for the whole docking system. *THarbor* is derived from *TWindow* in order to get mouse events, but it is never visible. Instead, it functions as an abstract interface, providing the following services to the application:

- Construction and setup of slips, whenever needed

- Insertion of dockables

- Dockable dragging and dropping

The *TDockable* class is an abstract base class. Any window that wants to be dockable must be derived from it. A small number of pure virtuals must then be overridden to provide information about the dockable window to the window that it is docked in, and to the harbor. Two predefined classes are provided that inherit from *TDockable*: *TDockableGadgetWindow,* and *TDockableControlBar.*

The *TDockingSlip* is also an abstract base class. Two predefined classes are provided that inherit from *TDockingSlip*: *TEdgeSlip* and *TFloatingSlip*. *TEdgeSlip* is used for docking slips along the edge of the frame. *TFloatingSlip* is used for a floating frame; it is also dockable in order to act as a proxy for its held dockables, when dragging.

The docking areas are contained, as decorations, in a *TDecoratedFrame*, or derived window.

To use the docking classes, follow these steps:

1 Create a decorated frame. This can be a *TDecoratedFrame*, a *TMDIDecoratedFrame*—or any frame derived from *TDecoratedFrame*.

```
TDecoratedMDIFrame* frame = new TDecoratedMDIFrame(Name, IDM_MAIN,
                                                   *MdiClient, true);
```

2 Create a harbor, passing the decorated frame to it:

```
Harbor = new THarbor(*frame);
```

3 Create a dockable control bar:

```
TDockableControlBar* cb = new TDockableControlBar(frame);
```

4 Set the caption and insert objects into the control bar:

```
cb->SetCaption("Toolbar with Combobox");
TComboBox* cBox = new TComboBox(0, 500, 0, 0, 180, 150, CBS_DROPDOWNLIST, 20);
cb->Insert(*new TControlGadget(*cBox));
cb->Insert(*new TSeparatorGadget);
cb->Insert(*new TButtonGadget(CM_FONTBOLD, CM_FONTBOLD)
cb->Insert(*new TButtonGadget(CM_FONTITALIC, CM_FONTITALIC));
```

5 Insert the control bar into the harbor, specifying the location for the tool bar:

```
Harbor->Insert(*cb, alTop);
```

MDI windows

Multiple-document interface, or MDI, windows are part of the MDI interface for managing multiple windows or views in a single frame window. MDI lets the user work with a number of child windows at the same time. Figure 25.3 shows a sample MDI application.

Figure 25.3 Sample MDI application

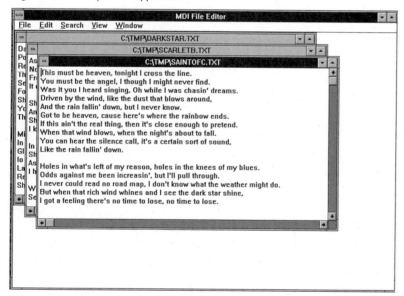

MDI applications

Certain components are present in every MDI application. Most evident is the main window, called the *MDI frame window*. Within the frame window's client area is the

MDI client window, which holds child windows called *MDI child windows*. When using the Doc/View classes, the application can put views into MDI windows. See Chapter 28 for more information on the Doc/View classes.

MDI Window menu

An MDI application usually has a menu item labeled Window that controls the MDI child windows. The Window menu usually has items like Tile, Cascade, Arrange, and Close All. The name of each open MDI child window is automatically added to the end of this menu, and the currently selected window is checked.

MDI child windows

MDI child windows have some characteristics of an overlapped window. An MDI child window can be maximized to the full size of its MDI client window, or minimized to an icon that sits inside the client window. MDI child windows never appear outside their client or frame windows. Although MDI child windows can't have menus attached to them, they can have a *TMenuDescr* that the frame window uses as a menu when that child is active. The caption of each MDI child window is often the name of the file associated with that window; this behavior is optional and under your control.

MDI in ObjectWindows

ObjectWindows defines classes for each type of MDI window:

- *TMDIFrame*
- *TMDIClient*
- *TMDIChild*

In ObjectWindows, the MDI frame window owns the MDI client window, and the MDI client window owns each of the MDI child windows.

TMDIFrame's member functions manage the frame window and its menu. ObjectWindows first passes commands to the focus window and then to its parent, so the client window can process the frame window's menu commands. Because *TMDIFrame* doesn't have much specialized behavior, you'll rarely have to derive your own MDI frame window class; instead, just use an instance of *TMDIFrame*. Since *TMDIChild* is derived from *TFrameWindow*, it can be a frame window with a client window. Therefore, you can create specialized windows that serve as client windows in a *TMDIChild*, or you can create specialized *TMDIChild* windows. The preferred style is to use specialized clients with the standard *TMDIChild* class. The choice is yours, and depends on your particular application.

Building MDI applications

Follow these steps to building an MDI application in ObjectWindows:

1 Create an MDI frame window
2 Add behavior to an MDI client window
3 Create MDI child windows

The ObjectWindows *TMDIXxx* classes handle the MDI-specific behavior for you, so you can concentrate on the application-specific behavior you want.

Creating an MDI frame window

The MDI frame window is always an application's main window, so you construct it in the application object's *InitMainWindow* member function. MDI frame windows differ from other frame windows in the following ways:

- An MDI frame is always a main window, so it never has a parent. Therefore, *TMDIFrame*'s constructor doesn't take a pointer to a parent window object as a parameter.

- An MDI frame must have a menu, so *TMDIFrame*'s constructor takes a menu resource identifier as a parameter. With non-MDI main frame windows, you'd call *AssignMenu* to set the windows menu. *TMDIFrame*'s constructor makes the call for you. Part of what *TMDIFrame::AssignMenu* does is search the menu for the child-window menu, by searching for certain menu command IDs. If it finds a Window menu, new child window titles are automatically added to the bottom of the menu.

A typical *InitMainWindow* for an MDI application looks like this:

```
void
TMDIApp::InitMainWindow()
{
   SetMainWindow(new TMDIFrame("MDI App", ID_MENU, *new TMyMDIClient));
}
```

The example creates an MDI frame window titled "MDI App" with a menu from the ID_MENU resource. The ID_MENU menu should have a child-window menu. The MDI client window is created from the *TMyMDIClient* class.

Adding behavior to an MDI client window

Since you usually use an instance of *TMDIFrame* as your MDI frame window, you need to add application-wide behavior to your MDI client window class. The frame window owns menus and tool bars but passes the commands they generate to the client window and to the application. A common message-response function would respond to the File | Open menu command to open another MDI child window.

Manipulating child windows

TMDIClient has several member functions for manipulating MDI child windows. Commands from an MDI application's child-window menu control the child windows. *TMDIClient* automatically responds to those commands and performs the appropriate action:

Table 25.4   Standard MDI child-window menu behavior

Action	Menu command ID	*TMDIClient* member function
Cascade	CM_CASCADECHILDREN	*CmCascadeChildren*
Tile	CM_TILECHILDREN	*CmTileChildren*
Tile Horizontally	CM_TILECHILDRENHORIZ	*CmTileChildrenHoriz*

Table 25.4   Standard MDI child-window menu behavior (continued)

Action	Menu command ID	*TMDIClient* member function
Arrange Icons	CM_ARRANGEICONS	*CmArrangeIcons*
Close All	CM_CLOSECHILDREN	*CmCloseChildren*

The header file owl\mdi.h includes owl\mdi.rh for your applications. owl\mdi.rh is a resource header file that defines the menu command IDs listed in Table 25.4. When you design your menus in your resource script, be sure to include owl\mdi.rh to get those IDs.

MDI child windows shouldn't respond to any of the child-window menu commands. The MDI client window takes care of them.

Creating MDI child windows

There are two ways to create MDI child windows: automatically in *TMDIClient::InitChild* or manually elsewhere.

Automatic child window creation

TMDIClient defines the *CmCreateChild* message response function to respond to the CM_CREATECHILD message. *CmCreateChild* is commonly used to respond to an MDI application's File | New menu command. *CmCreateChild* calls *CreateChild*, which calls *InitChild* to construct an MDI child window object, and finally calls that object's *Create* member function to create the MDI child window interface element.

If your MDI application uses CM_CREATECHILD as the command ID to create new MDI child windows, then you should override *InitChild* in your MDI client window class to construct MDI child window objects whenever the user chooses that command:

```
TMDIChild*
TMyMDIClient::InitChild()
{
  return new TMDIChild(*this, "MDI child window");
}
```

Since *TMDIChild*'s constructor takes a reference to its parent window object, and not a pointer, you need to dereference the **this** pointer.

Manual child window creation

You don't have to construct MDI child window objects in *InitChild*. If you construct them elsewhere, however, you must create their interface element yourself:

```
void
TMyMDIClient::CmFileOpen()
{
  new TMDIChild(*this, "")->Create();
}
```

26

Menu objects

ObjectWindows menu objects encapsulate menu resources and provide an interface for controlling and modifying the menu. Many applications use only a single menu assigned to the main window during its initialization. Other applications might require more complicated menu handling. ObjectWindows menu objects, encapsulated in the *TMenu, TSystemMenu, TPopupMenu*, and the *TMenuDescr* classes, give you an easy way to create and manipulate menus, from basic functionality to complex menu merging.

This chapter discusses the following tasks you can perform with menu objects:

- Constructing menu objects
- Modifying menu objects
- Querying menu objects
- Using system menu objects
- Using pop-up menu objects
- Using menu objects with frame windows

Constructing menu objects

TMenu has several constructors to create menu objects from existing windows or from menu resources. After the menu is created, you can add, delete, or modify it using *TMenu* member functions. Table 26.1 lists the constructors you can use to create menu objects.

Table 26.1   TMenu constructors for creating menu objects

TMenu constructor	Description
TMenu()	Creates an empty menu.
TMenu(HWND)	Creates a menu object representing the window's current menu.
TMenu(HMENU)	Creates a menu object from an already-loaded menu.
TMenu(LPCVOID*)	Creates a menu object from a menu template in memory.
TMenu(HINSTANCE, TResID)	Creates a menu object from a resource.

Modifying menu objects

After you create a menu object, you can use *TMenu* member functions to modify it. Table 26.2 lists the member functions you can call to modify menu objects.

Table 26.2   TMenu constructors for modifying menu objects

TMenu member function	Description
Adding menu items:	
AppendMenu(uint, uint, const char*)	Adds a menu item to the end of the menu.
AppendMenu(uint, uint, const TBitmap&)	Adds a bitmap as a menu item at the end of the menu.
InsertMenu(uint, uint, uint, const char*)	Adds a menu item to the menu after the menu item of the given ID.
InsertMenu(uint, uint, uint, const TBitmap&)	Adds a bitmap as a menu item after the menu item of the given ID.
Modifying menu items:	
ModifyMenu(uint, uint, uint, const char*)	Changes the given menu item.
ModifyMenu(uint, uint, uint, const TBitmap&)	Changes the given menu item to a bitmap.
Enabling and disabling menu items:	
EnableMenuItem(uint, uint)	Enables or disables the given menu item.
Deleting and removing menu items:	
DeleteMenu(uint, uint)	Removes the menu item from the menu it is part of. Deletes it if it's a pop-up menu.
RemoveMenu(uint, uint)	Removes the menu item from the menu but not from memory.
Checking menu items:	
CheckMenuItem(uint, uint)	Check or unchecks the menu item.
SetMenuItemBitmaps(uint, uint, const TBitmap*, const TBitmap*)	Specifies the bitmap to be displayed when the given menu item is checked and unchecked.
Displaying pop-up menus:	
TrackPopupMenu(uint, int, int, int, HWND, TRect*) TrackPopupMenu(uint, TPoint&, int, HWND, TRect*)	Displays the menu as a pop-up menu at the given location on the specified window.

After modifying the menu object, you should call the window object's *DrawMenuBar* member function to update the menu bar with the changes you've made.

Querying menu objects

TMenu has a number of member functions and member operators you can call to find out information about the menu object and its menu. You might need to call one of the query member functions before you call one of the modify member functions. For example, you need to call *GetMenuCheckmarkDimensions* before calling *SetMenuItemBitmaps*.

Table 26.3 lists the menu-object query member functions.

Table 26.3 TMenu constructors for querying menu objects

TMenu member function	Description
Querying the menu object as a whole:	
operator uint()	Returns the menu's handle as a uint.
operator HMENU()	Returns the menu's handle as an HMENU.
IsOK()	Checks whether the menu is OK (has a valid handle).
GetMenuItemCount()	Returns the number of items in the menu.
GetMenuCheckMarkDimensions(TSize&)	Gets the size of the bitmap used to display the check mark on checked menu items.
Querying items in the menu:	
GetMenuItemID(int)	Returns the ID of the menu item at the specified position.
GetMenuState(uint, uint)	Returns the state flags of the specified menu item.
GetMenuString(uint, char*, int, uint)	Gets the text of the given menu item.
GetSubMenu(int)	Returns the handle of the menu at the given position.

Using system menu objects

ObjectWindows' *TSystemMenu* class lets you modify a window's System menu. *TSystemMenu* is derived from *TMenu* and differs from it only in its constructor, which takes a window handle and a **bool** flag. If the flag is **true**, the current System menu is deleted and a menu object representing the unmodified menu that's put in its place is created. If the flag is **false**, the menu object represents the current System menu. By default this flag is **false**.

You can use all the member functions inherited from *TMenu* to manipulate the System menu. For example, the following example shows how to add an About menu choice to the System menu.

```
void
TSysMenuFrame::SetupWindow()
{
  TFrameWindow::SetupWindow();

  // Append about menu item to system menu.
  TSystemMenu sysMenu(HWindow);
  sysMenu.AppendMenu(MF_SEPARATOR, 0, (LPSTR)0);
  sysMenu.AppendMenu(MF_STRING, CM_ABOUT, "&About...");
}
```

Notice that the System menu is modified in the *SetupWindow* function of the window object. The System menu should be modified before the window is created. It's usually easiest to do this simply by overriding the base window class' *SetupWindow* function.

Using pop-up menu objects

You can use *TPopupMenu* to create a pop-up menu that you can add to an existing menu structure or pop up anywhere in the window. Like *TSystemMenu*, *TPopupMenu* is derived from *TMenu* and differs from it only in its constructor, which creates an empty pop-up menu. You can then add whatever menu items you like using the *AppendMenu* function.

Once you've created a pop-up menu, you can use *TrackPopupMenu* to display it as a "free-floating" menu. *TrackPopupMenu* creates a pop-up menu at a particular location in your window. There are two forms of this function.

```
bool TrackPopupMenu(uint flags, int x, int y, int rsvd, HWND wnd, TRect* rect = 0);
bool TrackPopupMenu(uint flags, TPoint& point, int rsvd, HWND wnd, TRect* rect = 0);
```

where:

- *flags* specifies the relative location of the pop-up menu. It can be one of the following values:
  - TPM_CENTERALIGN
  - TMP_LEFTALIGN
  - TPM_RIGHTALIGN
  - TPM_LEFTBUTTON
  - TPM_RIGHTBUTTON

- *x* and *y* specify the screen location of the pop-up menu. In the second form of *TrackPopupMenu*, *point* does the same thing, combining *x* and *y* into a single *TPoint* object. The menu is then created relative to this point, depending on the value of *flags*.

- *rsvd* is a reserved value and must be set to 0.

- *wnd* is the handle to the window that receives messages about the menu.

- *rect* defines the area that the user can click without dismissing the menu.

The following example shows a window class that displays a pop-up menu in response to a right mouse button click.

```
class TPopupMenuFrame : public TFrameWindow
{
  public:
    TPopupMenuFrame(TWindow* parent, const char *name);

  protected:
    TPopupMenu PopupMenu;
    void EvRButtonDown(uint modKeys, TPoint& point);

  DECLARE_RESPONSE_TABLE(TPopupMenuFrame);
};

DEFINE_RESPONSE_TABLE1(TSysMenuFrame, TFrameWindow)
  EV_WM_RBUTTONDOWN,
END_RESPONSE_TABLE;
```

```
TPopupMenuFrame::TPopupMenuFrame(TWindow* parent, const char *name)
  : TFrameWindow(parent, name)
{
  PopupMenu.AppendMenu(MF_STRING, CM_FILENEW, "Create new file");
  PopupMenu.AppendMenu(MF_STRING, CM_FILEOPEN, "Open file");
  PopupMenu.AppendMenu(MF_STRING, CM_FILESAVE, "Save file");
  PopupMenu.AppendMenu(MF_STRING, CM_FILESAVEAS, "Save file under new name");
  PopupMenu.AppendMenu(MF_STRING, CM_PENSIZE, "Change pen size");
  PopupMenu.AppendMenu(MF_STRING, CM_PENCOLOR, "Change pen color");
  PopupMenu.AppendMenu(MF_STRING, CM_ABOUT, "&About...");
  PopupMenu.AppendMenu(MF_STRING, CM_EXIT, "Exit Program");
}

void
TPopupMenuFrame::EvRButtonDown(uint /* modKeys */, TPoint& point)
{
  PopupMenu.TrackPopupMenu(TPM_LEFTBUTTON, point, 0, HWindow);
}
```

Using menu objects with frame windows

ObjectWindows frame window objects (*TFrameWindow* and *TFrameWindow*-derived classes) provide a number of functions that you can use to assign, change, and modify menus. There are two ways to manipulate frame window menus:

- Directly assigning or changing the frame window's main menu. This is typically how you work with menus when you have a single menu that doesn't use menu merging.

- Assigning and merging the frame window's menu descriptor with that of client and child windows. Menu descriptors are objects that divide the menu bar into functional groups and permit easy merging and removal of pop-up menus.

These methods of using menu objects are described in the next sections.

Adding menu resources to frame windows

It was fairly common practice in ObjectWindows 1.0 to assign a menu resource directly to the *Attr.Menu* member of a frame window; for example,

```
Attr.Menu = MENU_1;
```

ObjectWindows no longer permits this type of assignment; you should instead use the *AssignMenu* function. *AssignMenu* is defined in the *TFrameWindow* class, and is available in any class derived from *TFrameWindow*, such as *TMDIFrame*, *TMDIChild*, *TDecoratedFrame*, and *TFloatingFrame*.

The *AssignMenu* function takes a *TResId* for its only parameter and returns **true** if the assignment operation was successful. *AssignMenu* is declared **virtual**, so you can override it in your own *TFrameWindow*-derived classes. Here's what the previous example looks like when the *AssignMenu* function is used:

```
AssignMenu(MENU_1);
```

You can also change the menu after the frame window has been created. To change the frame window's menu, call the window object's *SetMenu* function.

```
SetMenu(MENU_2);
```

Using menu descriptors

Managing menus—adding menus for child windows, merging menus, and so on—can be a tedious and confusing chore. ObjectWindows simplifies menu management with objects known as menu descriptors. Menu descriptors divide the menu bar into six groups, which correspond to conventional ways of arranging functions on a menu bar:

- File
- Edit
- Container
- Object
- Window
- Help

Organizing menus into functional groups makes it easy to insert a new menu into an existing menu bar. For example, consider an MDI application, such as Step 11 of the ObjectWindows tutorial. The frame and client windows provide menus that let the user perform general application functions such as opening files, managing windows, and so on. The child windows handle the menu commands for functions specific to a particular drawing, such as setting the line width and color.

In the tutorial, the menu stays the same, but menu items handled by the child windows are grayed out when no child window is available to handle the command. Another way to handle this would be to have the menu bar populated only with the menus handled by the frame and client windows. Then, when a child window is opened, the menus handled by the child window would be merged into the existing menu bar. The figures below show how this looks to the user. Figure 26.1 shows the application with no child windows open. Notice that there are only four pop-up menus on the menu bar.

Figure 26.2 shows the application once one or more child windows have been opened. Notice the extra pop-up menu labeled Tools. The Tools menu is merged into the main menu bar only when there is a child window where the tools can be used.

Adding menu descriptors to an application is a simple process.

1 Set the menu descriptor for the frame window's menu bar by calling the frame window's *SetMenuDescr* function.

2 When creating a new child window, set the child's menu descriptor by calling the child's *SetMenuDescr* function. Once the child window is created, ObjectWindows automatically merges the menu from the child with the frame window's menu bar while the child is active. Note that different MDI child windows in the same application can have different menu descriptors. This is useful when the child windows contain different kinds of documents.

Creating menu descriptors and using the menu descriptor handling functions is described in the next sections.

Figure 26.1   Menu descriptor application without child windows open

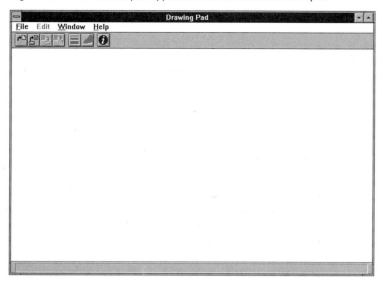

Figure 26.2   Menu descriptor application with child windows open

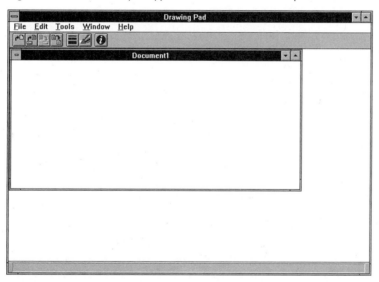

Creating menu descriptors

The *TMenuDescr* class implements the ObjectWindows menu descriptor functionality.
Menu descriptors take a menu resource and place the separate pop-up menus in the
resource into six functional groups. The naming of the groups is arbitrary in that you are
not restricted to putting only menus of a certain functional type into a particular group.
However, the naming convention does reflect standard conventions of menu item
placement. These names are contained in the *TGroup* **enum** defined in the *TMenuDescr*
class:

- *FileGroup*
- *EditGroup*
- *ContainerGroup*
- *ObjectGroup*
- *WindowGroup*
- *HelpGroup*

These groups are arranged consecutively on the menu bar from left to right. When another menu descriptor is merged with the existing menu bar, the new pop-up menus are merged according to their groups. For example, consider the examples shown in Figure 26.1 and Figure 26.2. The original three pop-up menus are placed in the following menu groups:

- The File menu is placed in the *FileGroup* group.
- The Edit menu is placed in the *EditGroup* group.
- The Window menu is placed in the *WindowGroup* group.
- The Help menu is placed in the *HelpGroup* group.

When the child window is created, its pop-up menu, called Tools, is placed in the *EditGroup* group. Then, when the menus are merged, the child window's menu is automatically placed between the File menu and the Window menu.

Constructing menu descriptor objects

There are a number of different constructors for *TMenuDescr*. These are described in Table 26.4.

Table 26.4   TMenuDescr constructors

Constructor	Function
TMenuDescr(TResId id, *TModule* module = ::Module)*	Creates a menu descriptor from the menu resource identified by *id*. The grouping of the pop-up menus are determined by the occurrence of separators at the menu level (that is, separators inside of a pop-up menu are disregarded for grouping purposes) in the menu resource. This is discussed in more detail in the next section.

TMenuDescr(TResId id,
        int fg, int eg, int cg,
        int og, int wg, int hg,
        TModule module = ::Module);*
 	
TMenuDescr(HMENU hMenu,
        int fg, int eg, int cg,
        int og, int wg, int hg,
        TModule module = ::Module);*
	Creates a menu descriptor from the menu resource identified by *id* or *hMenu*. The separate pop-ups in the resource are then placed in groups according to the values of *fg, eg, cg, og, wg,* and *hg*. The total of all the values of *fg, eg, cg, og, wg,* and *hg* should be equivalent to the number of pop-ups in the menu resource. The *fg, eg, cg, og, wg,* and *hg* parameters correspond to the groups defined in the *TMenuDescr::TGroup* **enum**.
	
	You can place more than one pop-up in a single group, and you don't have to place a pop-up in every group. For example, suppose you have a menu resource with a File menu, a Window menu, and a Help menu, all contained in the menu resource COMMANDS. You want to insert the File menu in the *FileGroup* group, the Window menu in the *WindowGroup* group, and the File menu in the *FileGroup* group. The constructor would look something like this:
	
	`TMenuDescr md(COMMANDS, 1, 0, 0, 0, 1, 1);`

TMenuDescr()	Creates a default menu constructor without menu resources or any group counts.
TMenuDescr(const TMenuDescr& original)	Creates a copy of the menu descriptor object *original*.

Creating menu groups in menu resources

The *TMenuDescr* class provides two ways to set up the groups that your various pop-up menus belong in:

- Explicitly numbering the menu resources in the *TMenuDescr* constructor
- Placing separators at the pop-up menu level in the menu resource

Earlier versions of ObjectWindows provided only the first method. The second method is new in ObjectWindows. This method is more flexible, eliminating the need to modify the *TMenuDescr* constructor whenever you add or remove a pop-up menu in your menu resource.

To set up groups in your menu resource, you need to put separators at the pop-up menu level. This means placing the separators *outside* of pop-up definitions. These separators have meaning only to the *TMenuDescr* constructor and don't cause any changes in the appearance of your menu bar. Separators inside pop-up menus are treated normally, that is, they appear in the pop-up menu as separator bars between menu choices.

The following example shows how a menu resource might be divided up into groups using separators in the menu resource. The menu resource is divided up into the requisite six groups, with four of the groups containing actual pop-up menus—the File menu, the Edit menu, the Window menu, and the Help menu. The other two groups are empty.

```
IDM_COMMANDS MENU
{
  POPUP "File"
  {
    MENUITEM "&New\aCtrl+N", CM_FILENEW
    MENUITEM "&Open\aCtrl+O", CM_FILEOPEN
    MENUITEM "&Save\aCtrl+S", CM_FILESAVE
    MENUITEM "Save &as...", CM_FILESAVEAS
    MENUITEM SEPARATOR
    MENUITEM "&Print\aCtrl+P", CM_FILEPRINT
  }
  MENUITEM SEPARATOR
  POPUP "&Edit"
  {
    MENUITEM "&Undo\aCtrl+Z", CM_EDITUNDO
    MENUITEM Separator
    MENUITEM "&Cut\aCtrl+X", CM_EDITCUT
    MENUITEM "C&opy\aCtrl+C", CM_EDITCOPY
    MENUITEM "&Paste\aCtrl+V", CM_EDITPASTE
    MENUITEM "&Delete\aDel", CM_EDITDELETE
  }
  MENUITEM SEPARATOR
  MENUITEM SEPARATOR
  MENUITEM SEPARATOR
  POPUP "&Window"
  {
    MENUITEM "&Cascade", CM_CASCADECHILDREN
    MENUITEM "&Tile", CM_TILECHILDREN
    MENUITEM "Arrange &Icons", CM_ARRANGEICONS
```

```
    MENUITEM "C&lose All", CM_CLOSECHILDREN
    MENUITEM "Add &View", CM_VIEWCREATE
  }
  MENUITEM SEPARATOR
  POPUP "&Help"
  {
    MENUITEM "&About", CM_ABOUT
  }
}
```

Merging menus with menu descriptors

To use menu descriptors for menu merging, you need to set your frame window's menu descriptor sometime before the creation of the window, usually during the *InitMainWindow* function. Then whenever you wish to merge a child window's menu or menus with that of its parent, you set the child window's menu descriptor before creating the child. When child is created, its menu descriptor is automatically merged with the parent.

You set a window's menu descriptor using the *SetMenuDescr* function. *SetMenuDescr* is inherited from *TFrameWindow*. It returns **void** and takes a **const** *TMenuDescr* reference as its only parameter. The following example shows how you might create and set the menu descriptors for the examples shown in Figure 26.1 and Figure 26.2.

```
class TMenuDescrApp : public TApplication
{
  public:
    TMenuDescrApp(const char* name) : TApplication(name) {}

    void InitMainWindow()
    {
      SetMainWindow(Frame = new TMDIFrame(Name, COMMANDS, *new
                                          TMenuDescrMDIClient));
      Frame->SetMenuDescr(TMenuDescr(COMMANDS));
    }

  protected:
    TMDIFrame* Frame;
};

void
TMenuDescrMDIClient::CmAddMenu1()
{
  TMDIChild *child = new TMDIChild(*this, "Child Window 1", new
                                   TMenuDescrWindow, true);
  child->SetMenuDescr(TMenuDescr(IDM_MENU1));
  child->Create();
}
```

27

Dialog box objects

Dialog box objects are interface objects that encapsulate the behavior of dialog boxes. The *TDialog* class supports the initialization, creation, and execution of all types of dialog boxes. As with window objects derived from *TWindow*, you can derive specialized dialog box objects from *TDialog* for each dialog box your application uses.

ObjectWindows also supplies classes that encapsulate Windows *common dialog boxes*. Windows provides common dialog boxes as a way to let users choose file names, fonts, colors, and so on.

This chapter covers the following topics:

- Using dialog box objects
- Using a dialog box as your main window
- Manipulating controls in dialog boxes
- Associating interface objects with controls
- Using common dialog boxes

Using dialog box objects

Using dialog box objects is a lot like using window objects. For simple dialog boxes that appear for only a short period of time, you can control the dialog box in one member function of the parent window. The dialog box object can be constructed, executed, and destroyed in the member function.

Using a dialog box object requires the following steps:

1 Construct the object
2 Execute the dialog box
3 Close the dialog box
4 Destroy the object

Constructing a dialog bbject

Dialog boxes are designed and created using a dialog box resource. You can use Borland's Resource Workshop or any other resource editor to create dialog box resources and bind them to your application. The dialog box resource describes the appearance and location of controls, such as buttons, list boxes, group boxes, and so on. The dialog box resource isn't responsible for the behavior of the dialog box; that's the responsibility of the application.

Each dialog box resource has an identifier that enables a dialog box object to specify which dialog box resource it uses. The identifier can be either a string or an integer. You pass this identifier to the dialog box constructor to specify which resource the object should use.

Calling the constructor

To construct a dialog box object, create it using a pointer to a parent window object and a resource identifier (the resource identifier can be either string or integer based) as the parameters to the constructor:

```
TDialog dialog1(this, "DIALOG_1");
    :
TDialog dialog2(this, IDD_MY_DIALOG);
```

The parent window is almost always **this**, since you normally construct dialog box objects in a member function of a window object. If you don't construct a dialog box object in a window object, use the application's main window as its parent, because that is the only window object always present in an ObjectWindows application:

```
TDialog mySpecialDialog(GetApplication()->GetMainWindow(), IDD_DLG);
```

The exception to this is when you specify a dialog box object as a client window in a *TFrameWindow* or *TFrameWindow*-based constructor. The constructor passes the dialog box object to the *TFrameWindow::Init* function, which automatically sets the dialog box's parent. See page 278.

Executing a dialog box

Executing a dialog box is analogous to creating and displaying a window. However, because dialog boxes are usually displayed for a shorter period of time, some of the steps can be abbreviated. This depends on whether the dialog box is a modal or modeless dialog box.

Modal dialog boxes

Most dialog boxes are *modal*. While a modal dialog box is displayed, the user can't select or use its parent window. The user must use the dialog box and close it before proceeding. A modal dialog box, in effect, freezes the operation of the rest of the application.

Use *TDialog::Execute* to execute a dialog box modally. When the user closes the dialog box, *Execute* returns an integer value indicating how the user closed the dialog box. The return value is the identifier of the control the user pressed, such as IDOK for the OK button or IDCANCEL for a Cancel button. If the dialog box object was dynamically allocated, be sure to delete the object.

The following example assumes you have a dialog resource IDD_MY_DIALOG, and that the dialog box has two buttons, an OK button that sends the identifier value IDOK and a Cancel button that sends some other value:

```
if (TMyDialog(this, IDD_MY_DIALOG).Execute() == IDOK)
  // User pressed OK
else
  // User pressed Cancel
```

Only the object is deleted when it goes out of scope, not the dialog box resource. You can create and delete any number of dialog boxes using only a single dialog box resource.

Modeless dialog boxes

Unlike a modal dialog box, you can continue to use other windows in your application while a modeless dialog box is open. You can use a modeless dialog box to let the user continue to perform actions, find information, and so on, while still using the dialog box.

Use *TDialog::Create* to execute a dialog box modelessly. When using *Create* to execute a dialog box, you must explicitly make the dialog box visible by either specifying the WS_VISIBLE flag for the resource style or using the *ShowWindow* function to force the dialog box to display itself.

For example, suppose your resource script file looks something like this:

```
DIALOG_1 DIALOG 18, 18, 142, 44
STYLE DS_MODALFRAME | WS_POPUP | WS_CAPTION | WS_SYSMENU
CAPTION "Dialog 1"
{
  PUSHBUTTON "Button", IDOK, 58, 23, 25, 16
}
```

Now suppose that you try to create this dialog box modelessly using the following code:

```
    ⋮
TDialog dialog1(this, "DIALOG_1");
  dialog1.Create();
    ⋮
```

This dialog box wouldn't appear on your screen. To make it appear, you'd have to do one of two things:

- Change the style of the dialog box to have the WS_VISIBLE flag set:

  ```
  STYLE DS_MODALFRAME | WS_POPUP | WS_CAPTION | WS_SYSMENU | WS_VISIBLE
  ```

- Add the *ShowWindow* function after the call to *Create*:

  ```
      ⋮
  TDialog dialog1(this, "DIALOG_1");
    dialog1.Create();
    dialog1.ShowWindow(SW_SHOW);
      ⋮
  ```

The *TDialog::CmOk* and *TDialog::CmCancel* functions close the dialog box and delete
the object. These functions handle the IDOK and IDCANCEL messages, usually sent
by the OK and Cancel buttons, in the *TDialog* response table. The *CmOk* function calls
CloseWindow to close down the modeless dialog box. The *CmCancel* function calls
Destroy with the IDCANCEL parameter. Both of these functions close the dialog box. If
you override either *CmOk* or *CmCancel*, you need to either call the base class *CmOk* or
CmCancel function in your overriding function or perform the closing and cleanup
operations yourself.

Alternately, you can create your dialog box object in the dialog box's parent's
constructor. This way, you create the dialog box object just once. Furthermore, any
changes made to the dialog box state, such as its location, active focus, and so on, are
kept the next time you open the dialog box.

Like any other child window, the dialog box object is automatically deleted when its
parent is destroyed. This way, if you close down the dialog box's parent, the dialog box
object is automatically destroyed; you don't need to explicitly delete the object.

In the following code fragment, a parent window constructor constructs a dialog box
object, and another function actually creates and displays the dialog box modelessly:

```
class TParentWindow : public TFrameWindow
{
  public:
    TParentWindow(TWindow* parent, const char* title);
    void CmDOIT();

  protected:
    TDialog *dialog;
};
    ⋮
void
TParentWindow::CmDO_IT()
{
   dialog = new TDialog(this, IDD_EMPLOYEE_INFO);
   dialog->Create();
}
```

Using autocreation with dialog boxes

You can use autocreation to let ObjectWindows do the work of explicitly creating your
child dialog objects for you. By creating the objects in the constructor of a *TWindow*-
derived class and specifying the **this** pointer as the parent, the *TWindow*-derived class
builds a list of child windows. This also happens when the dialog box object is a data
member of the parent class. Then, when the *TWindow*-derived class is created, it
attempts to create all the children in its list that have the *wfAutoCreate* flag turned on.
This results in the children appearing onscreen at the same time as the parent window.

Turn on the *wfAutoCreate* flag using the function *EnableAutoCreate*. Turn off the
wfAutoCreate flag using the function *DisableAutoCreate*.

TWindow uses *Create* for autocreating its children. Thus any dialog boxes created with autocreation are modeless dialog boxes.

Just as with regular modeless dialog boxes, if you're using autocreation to turn your dialog boxes on, you must make your dialog box visible. But with autocreation you must turn the WS_VISIBLE flag on in the resource file. You can't use the *ShowWindow* function to enable autocreation.

The following code shows how to enable autocreation for a dialog box:

```
class TMyFrame : public TFrameWindow
{
  public:
    TDialog *dialog;
    TMyFrame(TWindow *, const char far *);
};

TMyFrame::TMyFrame(TWindow *parent, const char far *title)
{
  Init(parent, true);
  dialog = new TDialog(this, "MYDIALOG");

  // For the next line to work properly, the WS_VISIBLE attribute
  // must be specified for the MYDIALOG resource.

  dialog->EnableAutoCreate();
}
```

When you execute this application, the dialog box is automatically created for you. See page 37 for more information on autocreation.

Managing dialog boxes

Dialog boxes differ from other child windows, such as windows and controls, in that they are often displayed and destroyed many times during the life of their parent windows but are rarely displayed or destroyed at the same time as their parents. Usually, an application displays a dialog box in response to a menu selection, mouse click, error condition, or other event.

Therefore, you must be sure to not repeatedly construct new dialog box objects without deleting previous ones. Remember that when you construct a dialog box object in its parent window object's constructor or include the dialog box as a data member of the parent window object, the dialog box object is inserted into the child-window list of the parent and deleted when the parent is destroyed.

You can retrieve data from a dialog box at any time, as long as the dialog box object still exists. You'll do this most often in the dialog box object's *CmOK* member function, which is called when the user presses the dialog box's OK button.

Handling errors executing dialog boxes

Like window objects, a dialog box object's *Create* and *Execute* member functions can throw the C++ exception *TXWindow*. This exception is usually thrown when the dialog box can't be created, usually because the specified resource doesn't exist or because of insufficient memory.

You can rely on the global exception handler that ObjectWindows installs when your application starts to catch *TXWindow*, or you can install your own exception handler. To install your own exception handler, place a **try**/**catch** block around the code you want to protect. For example, if you want to know if your function *DoStuff* produces an error, the code would look something like this:

```
try
{
  DoStuff();
}

catch(TWindow::TXWindow& e)
{
  // You can do whatever exception handling you like here.
  MessageBox(0, e.why().c_str(),
              "Error", MB_OK);
}
```

ObjectWindows exception handling is explained in more detail in Chapter 24.

Closing the dialog box

Every dialog box must have a way for the user to close it. For modal dialog boxes, this is usually an OK or Cancel button, or both. *TDialog* has the event response functions *CmOk* and *CmCancel* to respond to those buttons.

CmOk calls *CloseWindow*, which calls *CanClose* to see if it's OK to close the dialog box. If *CanClose* returns **true**, *CloseWindow* transfers the dialog's data and closes the dialog box by calling *CloseWindow*.

CmCancel calls *Destroy*, which closes the dialog box. No checking of *CanClose* is performed, and no transfer is done.

To verify the input in a dialog box, you can override the dialog box object's *CanClose* member function. Also see the description of the *TInputValidator* classes in Chapter 33. If you override *CanClose*, be sure to call the parent *TWindow::CanClose* function, which handles calling *CanClose* for child windows.

Using a dialog box as your main window

To use a dialog box as your main window, it's best to make the main window a frame window that has your dialog box as a client window. To do this, derive an application class from *TApplication*. Aside from a constructor, the only function necessary for this purpose is *InitMainWindow*. In the *InitMainWindow* function, construct a frame window object, specifying a dialog box as the client window. In the five-parameter *TFrameWindow* constructor, pass a pointer to the client window as the third parameter. Your code should look something like this:

```
#include <owl\applicat.h>
#include <owl\framewin.h>
#include <owl\dialog.h>

class TMyApp : public TApplication
{
  public:
    TMyApp(char *title) : TApplication(title) {}
    void InitMainWindow();
};

void
TMyApp::InitMainWindow()
{
  SetMainWindow(new TFrameWindow(0, "My App",
                               new TDialog(0, "MYDIALOG"), true));
}

int
OwlMain(int argc, char* argv[])
{
  return TMyApp("My App").Run();
}
```

The *TFrameWindow* constructor turns autocreation on for the dialog box object that you pass as a client, regardless of the state you pass it in. For more information on autocreation for dialog boxes, see page 276.

You also must make sure the dialog box resource has certain attributes:

- Destroying your dialog object does not destroy the frame. You must destroy the frame explicitly.

- You can no longer dynamically add resources directly to the dialog, because it isn't the main window. You must add the resources to the frame window. For example, suppose you added an icon to your dialog using the *SetIcon* function. You now must use the *SetIcon* function for your frame window.

- You can't specify the caption for your dialog in the resource itself anymore. Instead, you must set the caption through the frame window.

- You must set the style of the dialog box as follows:
  - Visible (WS_VISIBLE)
  - Child window (WS_CHILD)
  - No Minimize and Maximize buttons, drag bars, system menus, or any of the other standard frame window attributes

Manipulating controls in dialog boxes

Almost all dialog boxes have (as child windows) controls such as edit controls, list boxes, buttons, and so on. Those controls are created from the dialog box's resource.

There is a two-way communication between a dialog box object and its controls. In one direction, the dialog box needs to manipulate its controls; for example, to fill a list box. In the other direction, it needs to process and respond to the messages the controls generate; for example, when the user selects an item from a list box. To learn about responding to controls, see Chapter 21.

Chapter 29 describes using controls in more detail, and also discusses how to use controls in windows instead of dialog boxes.

Communicating with controls

Windows defines a set of control messages that are sent from the application back to Windows. For example, list-box messages include LB_GETTEXT, LB_GETCURSEL, and LB_ADDSTRING. Control messages specify the specific control and pass along information in *wParam* and *lParam* arguments. Each control in a dialog resource has an identifier, which you use to specify the control to receive the message. To send a control message, you can call *SendDlgItemMessage*. For example, the following member function adds the specified string to the list box using the LB_ADDSTRING message:

```
void
TTestDialog::FillListBox(const char far* string)
{
    SendDlgItemMessage(ID_LISTBOX, LB_ADDSTRING, 0, (LPARAM)string);
}
```

It's rarely necessary to communicate with controls like this; ObjectWindows control classes provide member functions to perform the same actions. This section discusses the mechanisms used to perform this communication only to enhance your understanding of the process. Although *TListBox::AddString* does basically the same thing as this function and is easier to understand, this shows how you can use *SendDlgItemMessage* to force actions.

Associating interface objects with controls

Because a dialog box is created from its resource, you don't use C++ code to specify what it looks like or the controls in it. Although this lets you create the dialog box visually, it makes it harder to manipulate the controls from your application. ObjectWindows lets you "connect" or *associate* controls in a dialog box with interface objects. Associating controls with control objects lets you do two things:

- Provide specialized responses to messages. For example, you might want an edit control that allows only digits to be entered, or you might want a button that changes styles when it's pressed.

- Use member functions and data members to manipulate the control. This is easier and more object-oriented than using control messages.

Control objects

To associate a control object with a control element, you can define a pointer to a control object as a data member and construct a control object in the dialog box object's constructor. Control classes such as *TButton* have a constructor that takes a pointer to the parent window object and the control's resource identifier. In the following example, *TTestDialog*'s constructor creates a *TButton* object from the resource ID_BUTTON:

```
TTestDialog::TTestDialog(TWindow* parent, const char* resID)
  : TDialog(parent, resID), TWindow(parent)
{
  new TButton(this, ID_BUTTON);
}
```

You can also define your own control class, derived from an existing control class (if you want to provide specialized behavior). In the following example, *TBeepButton* is a specialized *TButton* that overrides the default response to the BN_CLICKED notification code. A *TBeepButton* object is associated with the ID_BUTTON button resource.

```
class TBeepButton : public TButton
{
  public:
    TBeepButton(TWindow* parent, int resId) : TButton(parent, resId) {}

    void BNClicked();  // BN_CLICKED

  DECLARE_RESPONSE_TABLE(TBeepButton);
};

DEFINE_RESPONSE_TABLE1(TBeepButton, TButton)
  EV_NOTIFY_AT_CHILD(BN_CLICKED, BNClicked),
END_RESPONSE_TABLE;

void
TBeepButton::BNClicked()
{
  MessageBeep(-1);
}
   :
TBeepDialog::TBeepDialog(TWindow* parent, const char* name)
  : TDialog(parent, name), TWindow(parent)
{
  button = new TBeepButton(this, ID_BUTTON);
}
```

Unlike setting up a window object, which requires two steps (construction and creation), associating an interface object with an interface element requires only the construction step. This is because the interface element already exists: it's loaded from the dialog box resource. You just have to tell the constructor which control from the resource to use, using its resource identifier.

Setting up controls

You can't manipulate controls by, for example, adding strings to a list box or setting the font of an edit control until the dialog box object's *SetupWindow* member function executes. Until *TDialog::SetupWindow* has called *TWindow::SetupWindow*, the dialog box's controls haven't been associated with the corresponding objects. Once they're associated, the objects' *HWindow* data members are valid for the controls.

In this example, the *AddString* function isn't called until the base class *SetupWindow* function is called:

```
class TDerivedDialog : public TDialog
{
  public:
    TDerivedDialog(TWindow* parent, TResId resId)
      : TDialog(parent, resId), TWindow(parent)
    {
      listbox = new TListBox(this, IDD_LISTBOX);
    }

  protected:
    TListBox* listbox;
};

void
TDerivedDialog::SetupWindow()
{
  TDialog::SetupWindow();
  listbox->AddString("First entry");
}
```

Using dialog boxes

A Windows application often needs to prompt the user for file names, colors, or fonts. ObjectWindows provides classes that make it easy to use dialog boxes, including Windows' common dialog boxes. The following table lists the different types of dialog boxes and the ObjectWindows class that encapsulates each one.

Table 27.1   ObjectWindows-encapsulated dialog boxes

Type	ObjectWindows class
Color	*TChooseColorDialog*
Font	*TChooseFontDialog*
File open	*TFileOpenDialog*
File save	*TFileSaveDialog*
Find string	*TFindDialog*
Input from user	*TInputDialog*
Printer abort dialog	*TPrinterAbortDlg*

Table 27.1 ObjectWindows-encapsulated dialog boxes (continued)

Type	ObjectWindows class
Printer control	*TPrintDialog*
Replace string	*TReplaceDialog*

Using input dialog boxes

Input dialog boxes are simple dialog boxes that prompt the user for a single line of text input. You can run input dialog boxes as either modal or modeless dialog boxes, but you'll usually run them modally. Input dialog box objects have a dialog box resource associated with them, provided in the resource script file owl\inputdia.rc. Your application's .RC file must include owl\inputdia.rc.

When you construct an input dialog box object, you specify a pointer to the parent window object, caption, prompt, and the text buffer and its size. The contents of the text buffer is the default input text. When the user chooses OK or presses *Enter*, the line of text entered is automatically transferred into the character array. Here's an example:

```
char patientName[33] = "";

TInputDialog(this, "Patient name",
            "Enter the patient's name:",
            patientName, sizeof(patientName)).Execute();
```

In this example, *patientName* is a text buffer that gets filled with the user's input when the user chooses OK. It's initialized to an empty string for the default text.

Using common dialog boxes

The common dialog boxes encapsulate the functionality of the Windows common dialog boxes. These dialog boxes let the user choose colors, fonts, file names, find and replace strings, print options, and more. You construct, execute, and destroy them similarly. The material in this section describes the common tasks; the material in the following sections describes the tasks specific to each type of common dialog box.

Constructing common dialog boxes

Each common dialog box class has a nested class called *TData*. *TData* contains some common housekeeping members and data specific to each type of common dialog box. For example, *TChooseColorDialog::TData* has members for the color being chosen and an array for a set of custom colors. Table 27.2 lists the two members common to all *TData* nested classes.

Table 27.2 Common dialog box TData members

Name	Type	Description
Flags	*uint32*	A set of common dialog box-specific flags that control the appearance and behavior of the dialog box. For example, CC_SHOWHELP is a flag that tells the color selection common dialog box to display a Help button the user can press to get context-sensitive Help. Full information about the various flags is available in the *ObjectWindows Reference Guide*.
Error	*uint32*	This is an error code if an error occurred while processing a common dialog box; it's zero if no error occurred. *Execute* returns IDCANCEL both when the user chose Cancel and when an error occurred, so you should check *Error* to determine whether an error actually occurred.

Each common dialog box class has a constructor that takes a pointer to a parent window object, a reference to that class' *TData* nested class, and optional parameters for a custom dialog box template, title string, and module pointer.

Here's a sample fragment that constructs a common color selection dialog box:

```
TChooseColorDialog::TData colors;
static TColor custColors[16] =
{
  0x010101L, 0x101010L, 0x202020L, 0x303030L,
  0x404040L, 0x505050L, 0x606060L, 0x707070L,
  0x808080L, 0x909090L, 0xA0A0A0L, 0xB0B0B0L,
  0xC0C0C0L, 0xD0D0D0L, 0xE0E0E0L, 0xF0F0F0L
};

colors.CustColors = custColors;
colors.Flags = CC_RGBINIT;
colors.Color = TColor::Black;
if (TChooseColorDialog(this, colors).Execute() == IDOK)
  SetColor(colors.Color);
```

Once the user has chosen a new color in the dialog box and pressed OK, that color is placed in the *Color* member of the *TData* object.

Executing common dialog boxes

Once you've constructed the common dialog box object, you should execute it (for a modal dialog box) or create it (for a modeless dialog box). The following table lists whether each type of common dialog box must be modal or modeless.

Table 27.3 Common dialog box TData members

Type	Modal or modeless	Run by calling
Color	Modal	*Execute*
Font	Modal	*Execute*
File open	Modal	*Execute*
File save	Modal	*Execute*
Find	Modeless	*Create*

Table 27.3   Common dialog box TData members (continued)

Type	Modal or modeless	Run by calling
Find/replace	Modeless	*Create*
Printer	Modal	*Execute*

You must check *Execute*'s return value to see whether the user chose OK or Cancel, or to determine if an error occurred:

```
TChooseColorDialog::TData colors;
TChooseColorDialog colorDlg(this, colors);

if (colorDlg.Execute() == IDOK)
  // OK: data.Color == the color the user chose
  : // Some code here.
else if (data.Error)
  // error occurred
  : // Some code here.

MessageBox("Error in color dialog box!", GetApplication()->Name,
           MB_OK | MB_ICONSTOP);
```

Using color common dialog boxes

The color common dialog box lets you choose and create colors for use in your application. For example, a paint application might use the color common dialog box to choose the color of a paint bucket.

TChooseColorDialog::TData has several members you must initialize before constructing the dialog box object:

Table 27.4   Color common dialog box TData data members

TData member	Type	Description
Color	*TColor*	The selected color. When you execute the dialog box, this specifies the default color. When the user closes the dialog box, this specifies the color the user chose.
CustColors	*TColor**	A pointer to an array of sixteen custom colors. On input, it specifies the default custom colors. On output, it specifies the custom colors the user chose.

In the following example, a color common dialog box is used to set the window object's *Color* member, which is used elsewhere to paint the window. Note the use of the *TWindow::Invalidate* member function to force the window to be repainted in the new color.

```
void
TCommDlgWnd::CmColor()
{
  // use static to keep custom colors around between
  // executions of the color common dialog box
  static TColor custColors[16];
  TChooseColorDialog::TData choose;
```

```
choose.Flags = CC_RGBINIT;
choose.Color = Color;
choose.CustColors = custColors;

if(TChooseColorDialog(this, choose).Execute() == IDOK)
  Color = choose.Color;
Invalidate();
}
```

For details about *TData::Flags* in the *TChooseColorDialog* class, see the *Object WIndows Reference*.

Using font common dialog boxes

The font common dialog box lets you choose a font to use in your application, including its typeface, size, style, and so on. For example, a word processor might use the font common dialog box to choose the font for a paragraph.

TChooseFontDialog::TData has several members you must initialize before constructing the dialog box object:

Table 27.5 Font common dialog box TData data members

TData member	Type	Description
DC	*HDC*	A handle to the device context of the printer whose fonts you want to select, if you specify CF_PRINTERFONTS in *Flags*. Otherwise ignored.
LogFont	*LOGFONT*	A handle to a *LOGFONT* that specifies the font's appearance. When you execute the dialog box and specify the flag CF_INITTOLOGFONTSTRUCT, the dialog box appears with the specified font (or the closest possible match) as the default. When the user closes the dialog box, *LogFont* is filled with the selections the user made.
PointSize	**int**	The point size of the selected font (in tenths of a point). On input, it sets the size of the default font. On output, it returns the size the user selected.
Color	*TColor*	The color of the selected font, if the CF_EFFECTS flag is set. On input, it sets the color of the default font. On output, it holds the color the user selected.
Style	**char far***	Lets you specify the style of the dialog.
FontType	*uint16*	A set of flags describing the styles of the selected font. Set only on output.
SizeMin	**int**	Specifies the minimum and maximum
SizeMax	**int**	Point sizes (in tenths of a point) the user can select, if the CF_LIMITSIZE flag is set.

In this example, a font common dialog box is used to set the window object's *Font* member, which is used elsewhere to paint text in the window. Note how a new font object is constructed, using *TFont*.

```
void
TCommDlgWnd::CmFont()
```

```
  {
    TChooseFontDialog::TData FontData;

    FontData.DC = 0;
    FontData.Flags = CF_EFFECTS | CF_FORCEFONTEXIST | CF_SCREENFONTS;
    FontData.Color = Color;
    FontData.Style = 0;
    FontData.FontType = SCREEN_FONTTYPE;

    FontData.SizeMin = 0;
    FontData.SizeMax = 0;

    if (TChooseFontDialog(this, FontData).Execute() == IDOK) {
      delete Font;
      Color = FontData.Color;
      Font = new TFont(&FontData.LogFont);
    }
    Invalidate();
  }
```

Using file open common dialog boxes

The file open common dialog box serves as a consistent replacement for the many different types of dialog boxes applications have used to open files.

TOpenSaveDialog::TData has several members you must initialize before constructing the dialog box object. You can either initialize them by assigning values, or you can use *TOpenSaveDialog::TData*'s constructor, which takes *Flags*, *Filter*, *CustomFilter*, *InitialDir*, and *DefExt* (the most common) as parameters with default arguments of zero.

Table 27.6 File open and save common dialog box TData data members

TData member	Type	Description
FileName	char*	The selected file name. On input, it specifies the default file name. On output, it contains the selected file name.
Filter	char*	The file name filters and filter patterns. Each filter and filter pattern is in the form: `filter|filter pattern|...` where *filter* is a text string that describes the filter and *filter pattern* is a DOS wildcard file name. You can repeat *filter* and *filter pattern* for as many filters as you need. You must separate them with	characters.
CustomFilter	char*	Lets you specify custom filters.
FilterIndex	int	Specifies which of the filters specified in *Filter* should be displayed by default.
InitialDir	char*	The directory to be displayed on opening the file dialog box. Use zero for the current directory.
DefExt	char*	Default extension appended to *FileName* if the user doesn't type an extension. If *DefExt* is zero, no extension is appended.

In this example, a file open common dialog box prompts the user for a file name. If an error occurred (*Execute* returns IDCANCEL and *Error* returns nonzero), a message box is displayed.

```
void
TCommDlgWnd::CmFileOpen()
{
  TFileOpenDialog::TData FilenameData
    (OFN_FILEMUSTEXIST | OFN_HIDEREADONLY | OFN_PATHMUSTEXIST,
    "All Files (*.*)|*.*|Text Files (*.txt)|*.txt|",
    0, "", "*");

  if (TFileOpenDialog(this, FilenameData).Execute() != IDOK) {
    if (FilenameData.Errval) {
      char msg[50];
      wsprintf(msg, "GetOpenFileName returned Error #%ld", Errval);
      MessageBox(msg, "WARNING", MB_OK | MB_ICONSTOP);
    }
  }
}
```

Using file save common dialog boxes

The file save common dialog box serves as a single, consistent replacement for the many different types of dialog boxes that applications have previously used to let users choose file names.

TOpenSaveDialog::TData is used by both file open and file save common dialog boxes.

In the following example, a file save common dialog box prompts the user for a file name to save under. The default directory is WINDOWS and the default extension is .BMP.

```
void
TCanvasWindow::CmFileSaveAs()
{
  TOpenSaveDialog::TData data
    (OFN_HIDEREADONLY | OFN_OVERWRITEPROMPT,
    "Bitmap Files (*.BMP)|*.bmp|",
    0,
    "\windows",
    "BMP");

  if (TFileSaveDialog(this, data).Execute() == IDOK) {
    // save data to file
    ifstream is(FileData->FileName);

    if (!is)
      MessageBox("Unable to open file", "File Error", MB_OK | MB_ICONEXCLAMATION);
    else
      // Do file output
  }
}
```

Using find and replace common dialog boxes

The find and replace common dialog boxes let you search and optionally replace text in your application's data. These dialog boxes are flexible enough to be used for documents or even databases. The simplest way to use the find and replace common dialog boxes is to use the *TEditSearch* or *TEditFile* edit control classes; they implement an edit control that you can search and replace text in. If your application is text-based, you can also use the find and replace common dialog boxes manually.

Constructing and creating find and replace common dialog boxes

Since the find and replace dialog boxes are modeless, you normally keep a pointer to them as a data member in your parent window object. This makes it easy to communicate with them.

The find and replace common dialog boxes are modeless. You should construct and create them in response to a command (for example, a menu item Search | Find or Search | Replace). This displays the dialog box and lets the user enter the search information.

TFindReplaceDialog::TData has the standard *Flags* members, plus members for holding the find and replace strings. See the *ObjectWindows Reference Guide* for more details about *Flags*.

The following example shows the pointer to the find dialog box in the parent window object and shows the command event response function that constructs and creates the dialog box.

```
class TDatabaseWindow : public TFrameWindow
{
    ⋮
    TFindReplaceDialog::TData SearchData;
    TFindReplaceDialog* SearchDialog;
    ⋮
};

void
TDatabaseWindow::CmEditFind()
{
  // If the find dialog box isn't already
  // constructed, construct and create it now
  if (!SearchDialog) {
    SearchData.Flags |= FR_DOWN; // default to searching down
    SearchDialog = new TFindDialog(this, SearchData)
    SearchDialog->Create();
  }
}
```

Processing find-and-replace messages

Since the find and replace common dialog boxes are modeless, they communicate with their parent window object by using a registered message *FINDMSGSTRING*. You must write an event response function that responds to *FINDMSGSTRING*. That event response function takes two parameters—a *WPARAM* and an *LPARAM*—and returns an *LRESULT*. The *LPARAM* parameter contains a pointer that you must pass to the dialog box object's *UpdateData* member function.

After calling *UpdateData*, you must check for the FR_DIALOGTERM flag. The common dialog box code sets that flag when the user closes the modeless dialog box. Your event response function should then zero the dialog box object pointer because it's no longer valid. You must construct and create the dialog box object again.

As long as the FR_DIALOGTERM flag wasn't set, you can process the *FINDMSGSTRING* message by performing the actual search. This can be as simple as an edit control object's *Search* member function or as complicated as triggering a search of a Paradox or dBASE table.

In this example, *EvFindMsg* is an event response function for a registered message. *EvFindMsg* calls *UpdateData* and then checks the FR_DIALOGTERM flag. If it wasn't set, *EvFindMsg* calls another member function to perform the search.

```
DEFINE_RESPONSE_TABLE1(TDatabaseWindow, TFrameWindow)
   ⋮
  EV_REGISTERED(FINDMSGSTRING, EvFindMsg),
END_RESPONSE_TABLE;
   ⋮
LRESULT TDatabaseWindow::EvFindMsg(WPARAM, LPARAM lParam)
{
  if (SearchDialog) {
    SearchDialog->UpdateData(lParam);
    // is the dialog box closing?
    if (SearchData.Flags & FR_DIALOGTERM) {
      SearchDialog = 0;
      SearchCmd = 0;
    } else
      DoSearch();
  }
  return 0;
}
```

Handling a Find Next command

The find and replace common dialog boxes have a Find Next button that users can use while the dialog boxes are visible. Most applications also support a Find Next command from the Search menu, so users can find the next occurrence in one step instead of having to open the find dialog box and click the Find Next button. *TFindDialog* and *TReplaceDialog* make it easy for you to offer the same functionality.

Setting the FR_FINDNEXT flag has the same effect as clicking the Find Next button:

```
void
TDatabaseWindow::CmEditFindNext()
{
  SearchDialog->UpdateData();
  SearchData.Flags |= FR_FINDNEXT;
  DoSearch();
}
```

Using printer common dialog boxes

There are two printer common dialog boxes. The *print job* dialog box lets you choose what to print, where to print it, the print quality, the number of copies, and so on. The *print setup* dialog box lets you choose among the installed printers on the system, the page orientation, and paper size and source.

TPrintDialog::TData's members let you control the appearance and behavior of the printer common dialog boxes:

Table 27.7 Printer common dialog box TData data members

TData member	Type	Description
FromPage	**int**	The first page of output, if the PD_PAGENUMS flag is specified. On input, it specifies the default first page. On output, it specifies the first page the user chose.
ToPage	**int**	The last page of output, if the PD_PAGENUMS flag is specified. On input, it specifies the default last page number. On output, it specifies the last page number the user chose.
MinPage	**int**	The fewest number of pages the user can choose.
MaxPage	**int**	The largest number of pages the user can choose.
Copies	**int**	The number of copies to print. On input, the default number of copies. On output, the number of copies the user actually chose.

In the following example, *CmFilePrint* executes a standard print job common dialog box and uses the information in *TPrintDialog::TData* to determine what to print. *CmFilePrintSetup* adds a flag to bring up the print setup dialog box automatically.

```
void
TCanvas::CmFilePrint()
{
  if (TPrintDialog(this, data).Execute() == IDOK)
    // Use TPrinter and TPrintout to print the drawing
}

void
TCanvas::CmFilePrintSetup()
{
  static TPrintDialog::TData data;
  data.Flags |= PD_PRINTSETUP;

  if (TPrintDialog(this, data, 0).Execute() == IDOK)
    // Print
}
```

28

Doc/View objects

ObjectWindows provides a flexible and powerful way to contain and manipulate data: the Doc/View model. The Doc/View model consists of three parts:

- Document objects, which can contain many different types of data and provide methods to access that data.

- View objects, which form an interface between a document object and the user interface and control how the data is displayed and how the user can interact with the data.

- An application-wide document manager that maintains and coordinates document objects and the corresponding view objects.

How documents and views work together

This section describes the basic concept of the Doc/View model. If you're already familiar with these concepts or if you want more technical information, refer to the programming sections beginning on page 297.

The Doc/View model frees the programmer and the user from worrying about what type of data a file contains and how that data is presented on the screen. Doc/View associates data file types with a document class and a view class. The document manager keeps a list of associations between document classes and view classes. Each association is called a *document template* (note that document templates are *not* related to C++ templates).

A document class handles data storage and manipulation. It contains the information that is displayed on the screen. A document object controls changes to the data and when and how the data is transferred to persistent storage (such as the hard drive, RAM disk, and so on).

When the user opens a document, whether by creating a new document or opening an existing document, the document is displayed using an associated view class. The view class manages how the data is displayed and how the user interacts with the data onscreen. In effect, the view forms an interface between the display window and the document. Some document types might have only one associated view class; others might have several. Each different view type can be used to let the user interact with the data in a different way.

Figure 28.1 illustrates the interaction between the document manager, a document class, and the document's associated views:

Figure 28.1   Doc/View model diagram

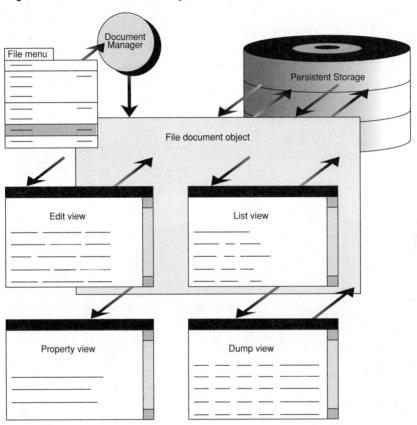

This figure shows a file document object from the *TFileDocument* class, along with some associated views. The *TFileDocument* class is shown in the DOCVIEWX example. This example is in the directory *BC 5*\EXAMPLES\OWL\OWLAPI\DOCVIEW, where *BC5* is the directory in which you installed Borland C++ 5.0.

Documents

The traditional concept of a document and the Doc/View concept of a document differ in several important ways. The traditional concept of a document is generally like that of a word-processing file. It consists of text mixed with the occasional graphic, along with embedded commands to assist the word-processing program in formatting the document.

A Doc/View document differs quite significantly from the traditional concept of a document:

- The first distinction is between the contents of the two types of documents. Whereas the traditional document is mostly text with a few other bits of data, a Doc/View document can contain literally any type of data, such as text, graphics, sounds, multimedia files, and even other documents.

- The next distinction is in terms of presentation. Whereas the format of the traditional document is usually designed with the document's presentation in mind, a Doc/View document is completely independent of how it is displayed.

- The last distinction is that a document from a particular word-processing program is generally dependent on the format demanded by that program; documents are usually portable between different word-processing programs only after a tedious porting process. The intention of Doc/View documents is to let data be easily ported between different applications, even applications whose basic functions are highly divergent.

The basic functionality for a document object is provided in the ObjectWindows class *TDocument*. A more in-depth discussion of *TDocument* and how to use it as a basis for your own document classes is presented later in this chapter on page 305.

Views

View objects enable document objects to present themselves to the world. Without a view object, you can't see or manipulate the document. But when you pair a document with a view object into a document template, you've got a functional piece of data and code that provides a graphic representation of the data stored in the document and a way to interact with and change that data.

The separation between the document and view also permits flexibility in when and how the data in document is modified. Although the data is manipulated through the view, the view only relays those changes on to the document. It is then up to the document to determine whether to change the data in the document (known as *committing* the changes) or discarding the changes (known as *reverting* back to the document).

Another advantage of using view objects instead of some sort of fixed-display method (such as a word-processing program) is that view objects offer the programmer and the user a number of different ways to display and manipulate the same document. Although you might need to provide only one view for a document type, you might also want to provide three or four views.

For example, suppose you create a document class to store graphic information, such as a picture or drawing. For a basic product, you might want to provide only one type of view, such as a view that draws the picture in a window and then lets the user "paint" and modify the picture. For a more advanced version, you might want to provide extra views; for example, the drawing could be displayed as a color separation, as a hexadecimal file, or even as a series of equations if the drawing was mathematically generated. To access these other views, users choose the type of view desired when they open the document. In all these scenarios, the document itself never changes.

The basic functionality for a view is provided in the ObjectWindows class *TView*. A more in-depth discussion of *TView* and how to use it as a basis for your own view classes is presented on page 310.

Associating document and view classes

A document class is associated with its view class (or classes) by a document template. Document templates are created in two steps:

1 Define a template class by associating a document class with a view class.
2 Instantiate a template from a defined class.

The difference between these two steps is important. After you've defined a template class, you can create any number of instances of that template class. Each template associates *only* a document class and a view class. Each instance has a name, a default file extension, directory, flags, and file filters. Thus you could provide a single template class that associates a document with a view. You could then provide a number of different *instances* of that template class, where each instance handles files in a different default directory, with different extensions, and so on, still using the same document and view classes.

Managing Doc/View

The document manager maintains the list of template instances used in your application and the list of current documents. Every application that uses Doc/View documents must have a document manager, but each application can have only one document manager at a time.

The document manager brings the Doc/View model together: document classes, view classes, and templates. The document manager provides a default File menu and default handling for each of the choices on the File menu:

Table 28.1   Document manager's File menu

Menu choice	Handling
New	Creates a new document.
Open...	Opens an existing document.
Save	Saves the current document.
As...	Saves the current document with a new name.
Revert To Saved	Reverts changes to the last document saved.

Table 28.1   Document manager's File menu (continued)

Menu choice	Handling
Close	Closes the current document.
Exit	Quits the application, prompts to save documents.

Once you've written your document and view classes, defined any necessary templates, and made instances of the required templates, all you still need to do is to create your document manager. When the document manager is created, it sets up its list of template instances and (if specified in the constructor) sets up its menu. Then whenever it receives one of the events that it handles, it performs the command specified for that event. The example on page 306 shows how to set up document manager for an application.

Document templates

Document templates join together document classes and view classes by creating a new class. The document manager maintains a list of document templates that it uses when creating a new Doc/View instance. This section explains how to create and use document templates, including

- Designing document template classes
- Creating document registration tables
- Creating instances of document template classes
- Modifying existing document template classes

Designing document template classes

You create a document template class using the DEFINE_DOC_TEMPLATE_CLASS macro. This macro takes three arguments:

- Document class
- View class
- Template class name

The document class should be the document class you want to use for data containment. The view class should be the view class you want to use to display the data contained in the document class. The template class name should be indicative of the function of the template. It cannot be a C++ keyword (such as **int**, **switch**, and so on) or the name of any other type in the application.

For example, suppose you've two document classes—one called *TPlotDocument*, which contains graphics data, and another called *TDataDocument*, which contains numerical data. Now suppose you have four view classes, two for each document class. For *TPlotDocument*, you have *TPlotView*, which displays the data in a *TPlotDocument* object as a drawing, and *THexView*, which displays the data in a *TPlotDocument* object as arrays of hexadecimal numbers. For *TDataDocument*, you have *TSpreadView*, which displays the data in a *TDataDocument* object much like a spreadsheet, and *TCalcView*, which displays the data in a *TDataDocument* object after performing a series of calculations on the data.

To associate the document classes with their views, you would use the DEFINE_DOC_TEMPLATE_CLASS macro. The code would look something like this:

```
DEFINE_DOC_TEMPLATE_CLASS(TPlotDocument, TPlotView, TPlotTemplate);
DEFINE_DOC_TEMPLATE_CLASS(TPlotDocument, THexView, THexTemplate);
DEFINE_DOC_TEMPLATE_CLASS(TDataDocument, TSpreadView, TSpreadTemplate);
DEFINE_DOC_TEMPLATE_CLASS(TDataDocument, TCalcView, TCalcTemplate);
```

As you can see from the first line, the existing document class *TPlotDocument* and the existing view class *TPlotView* are brought together and associated in a new class called *TPlotTemplate*. The same thing happens in all the other lines, so that you have four new classes, *TPlotTemplate*, *THexTemplate*, *TSpreadTemplate*, and *TCalcTemplate*. The next section describes how to use these new classes you've created.

Creating document registration tables

Once you've defined a template class, you can create any number of instances of that class. You can use template class instances to provide different descriptions of a template, search for different default file names, look in different default directories, and so on. Each of these attributes of a template class instance is affected by the document registration table passed to the template class constructor.

Document registration tables let you specify the various attributes and place them in a single object. The object type is *TRegList*, although in normal cirsumstances, you shouldn't ever have to access this object directly. To create a registration table,

1 You always start a registration table definition with the BEGIN_REGISTRATION macro. This macro takes a single parameter, the name of the registration object. This name can be whatever you want it to be, although it should be somewhat descriptive of the particular template instance you want to create with it.

2 Once you've started the table you need to register a number of data items in the table. You can place these items in the table using the REGDATA macro. REGDATA takes two parameters. The first is a key that identifies the type of data, while the second is a string containing the actual data. The key should be a string composed of alphanumeric characters; you don't need to place quotes around this value. The actual data string can be any legal string; you *do* need to place quotes around this value. Also, you don't need to use commas or semicolons after the macros. There are three data items you need to enter in the table for an instance of a document template:

    1 The *description* value should be a short text description of the template class. It should be indicative of the type of data handled by the document class and how that data is displayed by the view class.

    2 The *extension* value should indicate the default file extension for documents of this type.

    3 The *docfilter* value should indicate the file name masks that should be applied to documents when searching through file names.

3 You also need to register a number of flags describing how this document type is to be opened or created. These document flags can be registered with the REGDOCFLAGS macro. REGDOCFLAGS takes a single parameter, the flags themselves. The flags specified can be one or more of the following:

Table 28.2   Document creation mode flags

Flag	Function
dtAutoDelete	Close and delete the document object when the last view is closed.
dtNoAutoView	Do not automatically create a default view.
dtSingleView	Allow only one view per document.
dtAutoOpen	Open a document upon creation.
dtHidden	Hide template from list of user selections.

4 Once you've registered the necessary data items and the document mode flags, you can end the table definition with the END_REGISTRATION macro. This macro takes no parameters. You don't need to append a semicolon at the end of the line either.

The code below shows a sample registration table declaration. The resulting registration table, called *ListReg*, applies to a document template class described as a Line List, which has the default extension PTS and the default file-name mask *.pts. *ListReg* is set to be automatically deleted when the last view on the document is closed and is hidden from the list of documents available to the user.

```
BEGIN_REGISTRATION(ListReg)
  REGDATA(description,"Line List")
  REGDATA(extension,   ".PTS")
  REGDATA(docfilter,   "*.pts")
  REGDOCFLAGS(dtAutoDelete | dtHidden)
END_REGISTRATION
```

Creating template class instances

Once you've created a document template class and a registration table, you're ready to create an actual instance of the template class. An instance of a document template class serves as an entry in the document manager's list of possible document and view combinations that can be opened. Once this is in place, you can open documents of the type defined in the document template class and display the document in the specified view.

The signature of a template class constructor is always the same:

```
TplName name(TRegList& regTable);
```

where:

- *TplName* is the name you gave the template class when defining it.

- *name* is the name you want to give this instance (this name isn't very useful until you want to revise an existing template class instance).

- *regTable* is a registration table created using the BEGIN/END_REGISTRATION macros.

For example, suppose you've got the following template class definition:

```
DEFINE_DOC_TEMPLATE_CLASS(TPlotDocument, TPlotView, TPlotTemplate);
```

Now suppose you want to create three instances of this template class:

- One instance should have the description "Approved plots", for document files with the extension .PLT. You want to allow only a single view of the document and to automatically delete the document when the view is closed.

- Another instance should have the description "In progress", for document files with the extension .PLT. You want to automatically delete the document when the last view is closed.

- Another instance should have the description "Proposals", for document files with the extensions .PLT or .TMP (but with the default extension of .PLT). You want to keep this template hidden until the user has entered a password, and delete the document object when the last view is closed.

The code for creating these instances would look something like this:

```
BEGIN_REGISTRATION(aReg)
   REGDATA(description, "Approved plots",
   REGDATA(docfilter, "*.PLT",
   REGDATA(extension, "PLT",
   REGDOCFLAGS(dtSingleView | dtAutoDelete)
END_REGISTRATION

TPlotTemplate atpl(aReg);

BEGIN_REGISTRATION(bReg)
   REGDATA(description, "In progress",
   REGDATA(docfilter,"*.PLT",
   REGDATA(extension, "PLT",
   REGDOCFLAGS(dtAutoDelete);
END_REGISTRATION

TPlotTemplate btpl(bReg);

BEGIN_REGISTRATION(cReg)
   REGDATA(description, "Proposals",
   REGDATA(docfilter, "*.PLT; *.TMP",
   REGDATA(extension, "PLT",
   REGDOCFLAGS(dtHidden | dtAutoDelete);
END_REGISTRATION

TPlotTemplate *ctpl = new TPlotTemplate(cReg);
```

Just as in any other class, you can create both static and dynamic instances of a document template.

Modifying existing templates

Once you've created an instance of a template class, you usually don't need to modify the template object. However, you might occasionally want to modify the properties with which you constructed the template. You can do this using these access functions:

- Use the *GetFileFilter* and *SetFileFilter* functions to get and set the string used to filter file names in the current directory.

- Use the *GetDescription* and *SetDescription* functions to get and set the text description of the template class.

- Use the *GetDirectory* and *SetDirectory* functions to get and set the default directory.

- Use the *GetDefaultExt* and *SetDefaultExt* functions to get and set the default file extension.

- Use the *GetFlags*, *IsFlagSet*, *SetFlag*, and *ClearFlag* functions to get and set the flag settings.

Using the document manager

The document manager, an instance of *TDocManager* or a *TDocManager*-derived class, performs a number of tasks:

- Manages the list of current documents and registered templates

- Handles the standard File menu command events CM_FILENEW, CM_FILEOPEN, CM_FILESAVE, CM_FILESAVEAS, CM_FILECLOSE, and optionally CM_FILEREVERT

- Provides the file selection interface

To support the Doc/View model, a document manager must be attached to the application. This is done by creating an instance of *TDocManager* and making it the document manager for your application. The following code shows an example of how to attach a document manager to your application:

```
class TMyApp : public TApplication
{
  public:
    TMyApp() : TApplication() {}

    void InitMainWindow() {
       ⋮
      SetDocManager(new TDocManager(dmMDI | dmMenu));
       ⋮
    }
};
```

You can set the document manager to a new object using the *SetDocManager* function. *SetDocManager* takes a *TDocManager* & and returns **void**.

The document manager's public data and functions can be accessed through the document's *GetDocManager* function. *GetDocManager* takes no parameters and returns a *TDocManager* &. The document manager provides the following functions for creating documents and views:

- *CreateAnyDoc* presents all the visible templates, whereas the *TDocTemplate* member function *CreateDoc* presents only its own template.

- *CreateAnyView* filters the template list for those views that support the current document and presents a list of the view names, whereas the *TDocTemplate* member function *CreateView* directly constructs the view specified by the document template class.

Specialized document managers can be used to support other needs. For example, an OLE 2.0 server needs to support class factories that create documents and views through interfaces that are not their own. If the server is invoked with the embedded command-line flags, it doesn't bring up its own user interface and can attach a document manager that replaces the interface with the appropriate OLE support.

Constructing the document manager

The constructor for *TDocManager* takes a single parameter that's used to set the mode of the document manager. You can open the document manager in one of two modes:

- In single-document interface (SDI) mode, you can have only a single document open at any time. If you open a new document while another document is already open, the document manager attempts to close the first document and replace it with the new document.

- In multiple-document interface (MDI) mode, you can have a number of documents and views open at the same time. Each view is contained in its own client window. Furthermore, each document can be a single document type presented by the same view class, a single document presented with different views, or even entirely different document types.

To open the document manager in SDI mode, call the constructor with the *dmSDI* parameter. To open the document manager in MDI mode, call the constructor with the *dmMDI* parameter.

There are three other parameters you can also specify:

- *dmMenu* specifies that the document manager should install its own File menu, which provides the standard document manager File menu and its corresponding commands.

- *dmSaveEnabled* enables the Save command on the File menu even if the document has not been modified.

- *dmNoRevert* disables the Revert command on the File menu.

Once you've constructed the document manager you cannot change the mode. The following example shows how to open the document manager in either SDI or MDI mode. It uses command-line arguments to let the user specify whether the document manager should open in SDI or MDI mode.

```
class TMyApp : public TApplication
{
  public:
    TMyApp() : TApplication() {}
    void InitMainWindow();
    int DocMode;
};

void
TMyApp::InitMainWindow()
{
  switch ((_argc > 1 && _argv[1][0]=='-' ? _argv[1][1] : (char)0) | ('S'^'s'))
  {
    case 's': DocMode = dmSDI; break; // command line: -s
    case 'm': DocMode = dmMDI; break; // command line: -m
    default : DocMode = dmMDI; break; // no command line
  }

  SetDocManager(new TDocManager(DocMode | dmMenu));
};
```

Thus, if the user starts the application with the **-s** option, the document manager opens in SDI mode. If the user starts the application with the **-m** option or with no option at all, the document manager opens in MDI mode.

TDocManager event handling

If you specify the *dmMenu* parameter when you construct your *TDocManager* object, the document manager handles certain events on behalf of the documents. It does this by using a response table to process standard menu commands. These menu commands are provided by the document manager even when no documents are opened and regardless of whether you explicitly add the resources to your application. The File menu is also provided by the document manager.

The events that the document manager handles are

- CM_FILECLOSE
- CM_FILENEW
- CM_FILEOPEN
- CM_FILEREVERT
- CM_FILESAVE
- CM_FILESAVEAS
- CM_VIEWCREATE

In some instances, you might want to handle these events yourself. Because the document manager's event table is the last to be searched, you can handle these events at the view, frame, or application level. Another option is to construct the document manager without the *dmMenu* parameter. You must then provide functions to handle these events, generally through the application object or your interface object.

You can still call the document manager's functions through the *DocManager* member of the application object. For example, suppose you want to perform some action before opening a file. Providing the function through your window class *TMyWindow* might look something like this:

```
class TMyApp : public TApplication
{
  public:
    TMyApp() : TApplication() {}
    void InitMainWindow();
    int DocMode;
};

void
TMyApp::InitMainWindow()
{
  // Don't specify dmMenu when constructing TDocManager
  SetDocManager(new TDocManager(dmMDI));
};

class TMyWindow : public TDecoratedMDIFrame
{
  public:
    TMyWindow();
    void CmFileOpen();

    // You also need to provide the other event handlers
    // provided by the document manager.
      ⋮

  DECLARE_RESPONSE_TABLE(TMyWindow);
};

DEFINE_RESPONSE_TABLE1(TMyWindow, TDecoratedMDIFrame)
  EV_COMMAND(CM_FILEOPEN, CmFileOpen),
    ⋮
END_RESPONSE_TABLE;

void
TMyWindow::CmFileOpen()
{
  // Do your extra work here.
  GetApplication()->GetDocManager()->CmFileOpen();
}
```

Creating a document class

The primary function of a document class is to provide callbacks for requested data changes in a view, to handle user actions as relayed through associated views, and to tell associated views when data has been updated. *TDocument* provides the framework for this functionality. The programmer needs only to add the parts needed for a specific application of the document model.

Constructing TDocument

TDocument is an abstract base class that cannot be directly instantiated. Therefore you implement document classes by deriving them from *TDocument*.

You must call *TDocument*'s constructor when constructing a *TDocument*-derived class. The *TDocument* constructor takes only one parameter, a *TDocument* * that points to the parent document of the new document. If the document has no parent, you can either pass a 0 or pass no parameters; the default value for this parameter is 0.

Adding functionality to documents

As a standard procedure, you should avoid overriding *TDocument* functions that aren't declared **virtual**. The document manager addresses all *TDocument*-derived objects as if they were actually *TDocument* objects. If you override a nonvirtual function, it isn't called when the document manager calls that function. Instead, the document manager calls the *TDocument* version of the function. But if you override a virtual function, the document manager correctly calls your class' version of the function.

The following functions are declared **virtual** in *TDocument*:

~TDocument	InStream
OutStream	Open
Close	Commit
Revert	RootDocument
SetDocPath	SetTitle
GetProperty	IsDirty
IsOpen	CanClose
AttachStream	DetachStream

You can override these functions to provide your own custom interpretation of the function. But when you do override a **virtual** function, you should be sure to find out what the base class function does. Where the base class performs some sort of essential function, you should call the base class version of the function from your own function; the base class versions of many functions perform a check of the document's hierarchy, including checking or notifying any child documents, all views, any open streams, and so on.

Data access functions

TDocument provides a number of functions for data access. You can access data as a simple serial stream or in whatever way you design into your derived classes. The following sections describe the helper functions you can use to control when the document attempts data access operations.

Stream access

TDocument provides two functions, *InStream* and *OutStream*, that return pointers to a *TInStream* and a *TOutStream*, respectively. The *TDocument* versions of these function both return a 0, because the functions actually perform no actions. To provide stream access for your document class you must override these functions, construct the appropriate stream class, and return a pointer to the stream object.

TInStream and *TOutStream* are abstract stream classes, derived from *TStream* and *istream* or *ostream*, respectively. *TStream* provides a minimal functionality to connect the stream to a document. *istream* and *ostream* are standard C++ iostreams. You must derive document-specific stream classes from *TInStream* and *TOutStream*. The *TInStream* and *TOutStream* classes are documented in the *ObjectWindows Reference*. Here, though, is a simple description of the *InStream* and *OutStream* member functions. Both *InStream* and *OutStream* take two parameters in their constructors:

```
XXXStream(int mode, LPCSTR strmId = 0);
```

where *XXX* is either *In* or *Out*, *mode* is a stream opening mode identical to the *open_mode* flags used for *istream* and *ostream*, and *strmId* is a pointer to an existing stream object. Passing a valid pointer to an existing stream object in *strmId* causes that stream to be used as the document's stream object. Otherwise, the object opens a new stream object.

There are also two stream-access functions called *AttachStream* and *DetachStream*. Both of these functions take a reference to an existing (that is, already constructed and open) *TStream*-derived object. *AttachStream* adds the *TStream*-derived object to the document's list of stream objects, making it available for access. *DetachStream* searches the document's list of stream objects and deletes the *TStream*-derived object passed to it. Both of these functions have protected access and thus can be called only from inside the document object.

Stream list

Each document maintains a list of open streams that is updated as streams are added and deleted. This list is headed by the *TDocument* data *StreamList*. *StreamList* is a *TStream** that points to the first stream in the list. If there are no streams in the list, *StreamList* is 0. Each *TStream* object in the list has a member named *NextStream*, which points to the next stream in the stream list.

When a new stream is opened in a document object or an existing stream is attached to the object, it is added to the document's stream list. When an existing stream is closed in a document object or detached from the object, it is removed from the document's stream list.

Complex data access

Streams can provide only simple serial access to data. In cases where a document contains multimedia files, database tables, or other complex data, you probably want more sophisticated access methods. For this purpose, *TDocument* uses two more access functions, *Open* and *Close*, which you can override to define your own opening and closing behavior.

The *TDocument* version of *Open* performs no actions; it always returns **true**. You can write your own version of *Open* to work however you want. There are no restrictions placed on how you define opening a document. You can make it as simple as you like or as complex as necessary. *Open* lets you open a document and keep it open, instead of opening the document only on demand from one of the document's stream objects.

The *TDocument* version of *Close* provides a little more functionality than does *Open*. It checks any existing children of your document and tries to close them before closing your document. If you provide your own *Close*, the first thing you should do in that function is call the *TDocument* version of *Close* to ensure that all children have been closed before you close the parent document. Other than this one restriction, you are free to define the implementation of the *Close* function. Just as with *Open*, *Close* lets you close a document when you want it closed, as opposed to permitting the document's stream objects to close the document.

Data access helper functions

TDocument also provides a number of functions that you can use to help protect your data:

IsDirty first checks to see whether the document itself is "dirty" (that is, modified but not updated) by checking the state of the data member *DirtyFlag*. It then checks whether any child documents are dirty, then whether any views are dirty. *IsDirty* returns **true** if any children or views are dirty.

IsOpen checks to see whether the document is held open or has any streams in its stream list. If the document is not open, *IsOpen* returns **false**. Otherwise, *IsOpen* returns **true**.

Commit commits any changes to your data to storage. Once you've called *Commit*, you cannot back out of any changes made. The *TDocument* version of this function checks any child documents and commits them to their changes. If any child document returns **false**, the *Commit* is aborted and returns **false**. All child documents must return **true** before the *Commit* function commits its own data. After all child documents have returned **true**, *Commit* flushes all the views for operations that might have taken place since the document last checked the views. Data in the document is updated according to the changes in the views and then saved. *Commit* then returns **true**.

Revert performs the opposite function from *Commit*. Instead of updating changes and saving the data, *Revert* clears any changes that have been made since the last time the data was committed. *Revert* also polls any child documents and aborts if any of the children return **false**. If all operations are successful, *Revert* returns **true**.

Closing a document

Like most other objects, *TDocument* provides functions that let you safely close and destroy the object.

~TDocument does a lot of cleanup. First it destroys its children and closes all open streams and other resources. Then, in order, it detaches its attached template, closes all associated views, deletes its stream list, and removes itself from its parent's list of children if the document has a parent or, if it doesn't have a parent, removes itself from the document manager's document list.

In addition to a destructor, *TDocument* also provides a *CanClose* function to make sure that it's OK to close. *CanClose* first checks whether all its children can close. If any child returns **false**, *CanClose* returns **false** and aborts. If all child documents return **true**, *CanClose* calls the document manager function *FlushDoc*, which checks to see if the document is dirty. If the document is clean, *FlushDoc* and *CanClose* return **true**. If the document is dirty, *FlushDoc* opens a message box that prompts the user to either save the data, discard any changes, or cancel the close operation.

Expanding document functionality

The functions described in this section include most of what you need to know to make a functioning document class. It is up to you to expand the functionality of your document class. Your class needs special functions for manipulating data, understanding and acting on the information obtained from the user through the document's associated view, and so on. All this functionality goes into your *TDocument*-derived class.

Because the Doc/View model is so flexible, there are no requirements or rules as to how you should approach this task. A document can handle almost any type of data because the Doc/View data-handling mechanism is a primitive framework, intended to be extended by derived classes. The base classes provided in ObjectWindows provide the functionality to support your extensions to the Doc/View model.

Working with the document manager

TDocument provides two functions for accessing the document manager, *GetDocManager* and *SetDocManager*. *GetDocManager* returns a pointer to the current document manager. You can then use this pointer to access the data and function members of the document manager. *SetDocManager* lets you assign the document to a different document manager. All other document manager functionality is contained in the document manager itself.

Working with views

TDocument provides two functions for working with views, *NotifyViews* and *QueryViews*. Both functions take three parameters, an **int** corresponding to an event, a **long** item, and a *TView* *. The meaning of the **long** item is dependent on the event and is essentially a parameter to the event. The *TView* * lets you exclude a view from your query or notification by passing a pointer to that view to the function. These two functions are your primary means of communicating information between your document and its views.

Both functions call views through the views' response tables. The general-purpose macro used for ObjectWindows notification events is EV_OWLNOTIFY. The response functions for EV_OWLNOTIFY events have the following signature:

```
bool FnName(long);
```

The **long** item used in the *NotifyViews* or *QueryViews* function call is used for the **long** parameter for the response function.

You can use *NotifyViews* to notify your child documents, their associated views, and the associated views of your root document of a change in data, an update, or any other event that might need to be reflected onscreen. The meaning of the event and the accompanying item passed as a parameter to the event are implementation defined.

NotifyViews first calls all the document's child documents' *NotifyViews* functions, which are called with the same parameters. Once all the children have been called, *NotifyViews* passes the event and item to all of the document's associated views. *NotifyViews* returns a **bool**. If any child document or associated view returns **false**, *NotifyViews* returns **false**. Otherwise *NotifyViews* returns **true**.

QueryViews sends an event and accompanying parameter just like *NotifyViews*. The difference is that, whereas *NotifyViews* returns **true** when any child or view returns **true**, *QueryViews* returns a pointer to the first view that returns **true**. This lets you find a view that meets some condition and then perform some action on that view. If no views return **true**, *QueryViews* returns 0.

Another difference between *NotifyViews* and *QueryViews* is that *NotifyViews* always sends the event and its parameter to *all* children and associated views, whereas *QueryViews* stops at the first view that returns **true**.

For example, suppose you have a document class that contains graphics data in a bitmap. You want to know which of your associated views is displaying a certain area of the current bitmap. You can define an event such as WM_CHECKRECT. Then you can set up a *TRect* structure containing the coordinates of the rectangle you want to check for. The excerpted code for this would look something like this:

```
DEFINE_RESPONSE_TABLE1(TMyView, TView)
    ⋮
    EV_OWLNOTIFY(WM_CHECKREST, EvCheckRest),
    ⋮
END_RESPONSE_TABLE;

void
MyDocClass::Function()
{
    // Set up a TRect * with the coordinates you want to send.
    TRect *rect = new TRect(100, 100, 300, 300);

    // QueryViews
```

```
        TView *view = QueryViews(WM_CHECKRECT, (long) rect);

        // Clear all changes from the view
        if(view)
          view->Clear();
      }

      // The view response function gets the pointer to the rectangle
      // as the long parameter to its response function.
      bool
      TMyView::EvCheckRest(long item)
      {
        TRect *rect = (TRect *) item;

        // Check to see if rect is equal to this view's.
        if(*rect == this->rect)
          return true;
        else
          return false;
      }
```

You can also set up your own event macros to handle view notifications. See page 313.

Creating a view class

The user almost never interacts directly with a document. Instead the user works with an interface object, such as a window, a dialog box, or whatever type of display is appropriate for the data being presented and the method in which it is presented. But this interface object doesn't stand on its own. A window knows nothing about the data it displays, the document that contains that data, or about how the user can manipulate and change the data. All this functionality is handled by the view object.

A view forms an interface between an interface object (which can only do what it's told to do) and a document (which doesn't know how to tell the interface object what to do). The view's job is to bridge the gap between the two objects, reading the data from the document object and telling the interface object how to display that data.

This section discusses how to write a view class to work with your document classes.

Constructing TView

You cannot directly create an instance of *TView*. *TView* contains a number of pure **virtual** functions and placeholder functions whose functionality must be provided in any derived classes. But you must call the *TView* constructor when you are constructing your *TView*-derived object. The *TView* constructor takes one parameter, a reference to the view's associated document. You must provide a valid reference to a *TDocument*-derived object.

Adding functionality to views

TView contains some pure **virtual** functions that you must provide in every new view class. It also contains a few placeholder functions that have no base class functionality. You need to provide new versions of these functions if you plan to use them for anything.

Much like *TDocument*, you should not override a *TView* function unless that function is a virtual. When functions in *TDocument* call functions in your view, they address the view object as a *TView*. If you override a nonvirtual function and the document calls that function, the document actually calls the *TView* version of that function, rendering your function useless in that context.

TView virtual functions

The following functions are declared **virtual** so you can override them to provide some useful functionality. But most are not declared as pure **virtuals**; you are not *required* to override them to construct a view. Instead, you need to override these functions only if you plan to view them.

GetViewName returns the static name of the view. This function is declared as a *pure* **virtual** function; you *must* provide a definition of this function in your view class.

GetWindow returns a *TWindow* * that should reference the view's associated interface object if it has one; otherwise, *GetWindow* returns 0.

SetDocTitle sets the view window's caption. It should be set to call the *SetDocTitle* function in the interface object.

Adding a menu

TView contains the *TMenuDescr* * data member *ViewMenu*. You can assign any existing *TMenuDescr* object to this member. The menu should normally be set up in the view's constructor. This menu is then merged with the frame window's menu when the view is activated.

Adding a display to a view

TView itself makes no provision for displaying data—it has no pointer to a window, no graphics functions, no text display functions, and no keyboard handling. You need to provide this functionality in your derived classes; you can use one of the following methods to do so:

- Add a pointer to an interface object in your derived view class.
- Mix in the functionality of an interface object with that of *TView* when deriving your new view class.

Each of these methods has its advantages and drawbacks, which are discussed in the following sections. You should weigh the pros and cons of each approach before deciding how to build your view class.

Adding pointers to interface objects

To add a pointer to an interface object to your *TView*-derived class, add the member to the new class and instantiate the object in the view class' constructor. Access to the interface object's data and function members is through the pointer.

The advantage of this method is that it lets you easily attach and detach different interface objects. It also lets you use different types of interface objects by making the pointer a pointer to a common base class of the different objects you might want to use. For example, you can use most kinds of interface objects by making the pointer a *TWindow* *.

The disadvantage of this method is that event handling must go through either the interface object or the application first. This basically forces you to either use a derived interface object class to add your own event-handling functions that make reference to the view object, or handle the events through the application object. Either way, you decrease your flexibility in handling events.

Mixing TView with interface objects

Mixing *TView* or a *TView*-derived object with an interface object class gives you the ability to display data from a document, and makes that ability integral with handling the flow of data to and from the document object. To mix a view class with an interface object class is a fairly straightforward task, but one that must be undertaken with care.

To derive your new class, define the class based on your base view class (*TView* or a *TView*-derived class) and the selected interface object. The new constructor should call the constructors for both base classes, and initialize any data that needs to be set up. At a bare minimum, the new class must define any functions that are declared pure **virtual** in the base classes. It should also define functions for whatever specialized screen activities it needs to perform, and define event-handling functions to communicate with both the interface element and the document object.

The advantage of this approach is that the resulting view is highly integrated. Event handling is performed in a central location, reducing the need for event handling at the application level. Control of the interface elements does not go through a pointer but is also integrated into the new view class.

However, if you use this approach, you lose the flexibility you have with a pointer. You cannot quickly detach and attach new interface objects; the interface object is an organic part of the whole view object. You also cannot exchange different types of objects by using a base pointer to a different interface object classes. Your new view class is locked into a single type of interface element.

Closing a view

Like most other objects, *TView* provides functions that let you safely close and destroy the object.

~*TView* does fairly little. It calls its associated document's *DetachView* function, thus removing itself from the document's list of views.

TView also provides a *CanClose* function, which calls its associated document's *CanClose* function. Therefore the view's ability to close depends on the document's ability to close.

Doc/View event handling

You should normally handle Doc/View events through both the application object and your view's interface element. You can either control the view's display through a pointer to an interface object or mix the functionality of the interface object with a view class (see page 311 for details on constructing an interface element).

You can find more information about event handling and response tables in an ObjectWindows application in Chapter 22.

Doc/View event handling in the application object

The application object generally handles only a few events, indicating when a document or a view has been created or destroyed. The *dnCreate* event is posted whenever a view or document is created. The *dnClose* event is posted whenever a view or document is closed.

To set up response table entries for these events, add the EV_OWLDOCUMENT and EV_OWLVIEW macros to your response table:

1 Use the EV_OWLDOCUMENT macro to check for:

- The *dnCreate* event when a new document object is created. The standard name used for the handler function is *EvNewDocument*. *EvNewDocument* takes a reference to the new *TDocument*-derived object and returns **void**.

- The *dnClose* event when a document object is about to be closed. The standard name used for the handler function is *EvCloseDocument*. *EvCloseDocument* takes a reference to the *TDocument*-derived object that is being closed and returns **void**.

The response table entries and function declarations for these two macros would look like this:

```
DEFINE_RESPONSE_TABLE1(MyDVApp, TApplication)
    ⋮
    EV_OWLDOCUMENT(dnCreate, EvNewDocument),
    EV_OWLDOCUMENT(dnClose, EvCloseDocument),
    ⋮
END_RESPONSE_TABLE;

void EvNewDocument(TDocument& document);
void EvCloseDocument(TDocument& document);
```

2 Use the EV_OWLVIEW macro to check for:

- The *dnCreate* event when a new view object is constructed. The standard name used for the handler function is *EvNewView*. *EvNewView* takes a reference to the new *TView*-derived object and returns **void**.

If the view contains a window interface element, either by inheritance or through a pointer, the interface element typically has not been created when the view is constructed. You can then modify the interface element's creation attributes before actually calling the *Create* function.

- The *dnClose* event when a view object is destroyed. The standard name used for the handler function is *EvCloseView*. *EvCloseView* takes a reference to the *TView*-derived object that is being destroyed and returns **void**.

The response table entries and function declarations for these two macros would look like this:

```
DEFINE_RESPONSE_TABLE1(MyDVApp, TApplication)
  ⋮
  EV_OWLVIEW(dnCreate, EvNewView),
  EV_OWLVIEW(dnClose,  EvCloseView),
  ⋮
END_RESPONSE_TABLE;

void EvNewView(TView &view);
void EvCloseView(TView &view);
```

Doc/View event handling in a view

The header file docview.h provides a number of response table macros for predefined events, along with the handler function names and type checking for the function declarations. You can also define your own events and functions to handle those events using the NOTIFY_SIG and VN_DEFINE macros.

Handling predefined Doc/View events

There are a number of predefined Doc/View events. Each event has a corresponding response table macro and handler function signature defined. Note that the Doc/View model doesn't provide versions of these functions. You must declare the functions in your view class and provide the appropriate functionality for each function.

Table 28.3   Predefined Doc/View event handlers

Response table macro	Event name	Event handler	Event
EV_VN_VIEWOPENED	*vnViewOpened*	*VnViewOpened*(*TView* *)	Indicates that a new view has been constructed.
EV_VN_VIEWCLOSED	*vnViewClosed*	*VnViewClosed*(*TView* *)	Indicates that a view is about to be destroyed.
EV_VN_DOCOPENED	*vnDocOpened*	*VnDocOpened*(**int**)	Indicates that a new document has been opened.
EV_VN_DOCCLOSED	*vnDocClosed*	*VnDocClosed*(**int**)	Indicates that a document has been closed.
EV_VN_COMMIT	*vnCommit*	*VnCommit*(**bool**)	Indicates that changes made to the data in the view should be committed to the document.
EV_VN_REVERT	*vnRevert*	*VnRevert*(**bool**)	Indicates that changes made to the data in the view should be discarded and the data should be restored from the document.
EV_VN_ISDIRTY	*vnIsDirty*	*VnIsDirty*(**void**)	Should return **true** if changes have been made to the data in the view and not yet committed to the document, otherwise returns **false**.
EV_VN_ISWINDOW	*vnIsWindow*	*VnIsWindow*(HWND)	Should return **true** if the HWND parameter is the same as that of the view's display window.

All the event-handling functions used for these messages return **bool**.

Adding custom view events

You can use the VN_DEFINE and NOTIFY_SIG macros to post your own custom view events and to define corresponding response table macros and event-handling functions. This section describes how to define an event and set up the event-handling function and response table macro for that event.

First you must define the name of the event you want to handle. By convention, this name should begin with the letters *vn* followed by the event name. A custom view event should be defined as a **const int** greater than the value *vnCustomBase*. You can define your event values as being *vnCustomBase* plus some offset value. For example, suppose you are defining an event called *vnPenChange*. The code would look something like this:

```
const int vnPenChange = vnCustomBase + 1;
```

Next use the NOTIFY_SIG macro to specify the signature of the event-handling function. The NOTIFY_SIG macro takes two parameters, the first being the event name and the second being the exact parameter type to be passed to the function. The size of this parameter can be no larger than type **long**; if the object being passed is larger than a **long**, you must pass it by pointer. For example, suppose for the *vnPenChange* event, you want to pass a *TPen* object to the event-handling function. Because a *TPen* object is quite a bit larger than a **long**, you must pass the object by pointer. The macro would look something like this:

```
NOTIFY_SIG(vnPenChange, TPen *)
```

Now you need to define the response table macro for your event. By convention, the macro name uses the event name, in all uppercase letters, preceded by EV_VN_. Use the **#define** macro to define the macro name. Use the VN_DEFINE macro to define the macro itself. This macro takes three parameters:

- Event name

- Event-handling function name (by convention, the same as the event name preceded by *Vn* instead of the *vn* used for the event name)

- Size of the parameter for the event-handling function; this can have four different values:
  - void
  - int (size of an int parameter depends on the platform)
  - long (32-bit integer or far pointer)
  - pointer (size of a pointer parameter depends on the memory model)

  You should specify the value that most closely corresponds to the event-handling function's parameter type.

The definition of the response table macro for the *vnPenChange* event would look something like this:

```
#define EV_VN_PENCHANGE \
  VN_define (vnPenChange, VnPenChange, pointer)
```

Note that the third parameter of the VN_DEFINE macro in this case is pointer. This indicates the size of the value passed to the event-handling function.

Doc/View properties

Every document and view object contains a list of properties, along with functions you can use to query and change those properties. The properties contain information about the object and its capabilities. When the document manager creates or destroys a document or view object, it sends a notification event to the application. The application can query the object's properties to determine how to proceed. Views can also access the properties of their associated document.

Property values and names

TDocument and *TView* each have some general properties. These properties are available in any classes derived from *TDocument* and *TView*. These properties are indexed by a list of enumerated values. The first property for every *TDocument*- and *TView*-derived class should be *PrevProperty*. The last value in the property list should be *NextProperty*. These two values delimit the property list of every document and view object; they ensure that your property list starts at the correct value and doesn't overstep another property's value, and allows derived classes to ensure that their property lists start at a suitable value. *PrevProperty* should be set to the value of the most direct base class' *NextProperty* − 1.

For example, a property list for a class derived from *TDocument* might look something like this:

```
enum
{
  PrevProperty = TDocument::NextProperty-1,
  Size,
  StorageSize,
  NextProperty,
};
```

Note the use of the scope operator (::) when setting *PrevProperty*. This ensures that you set *PrevProperty* to the correct value for *NextProperty*.

Property names are usually contained in an array of strings, with the position of each name in the array corresponding to its enumerated property index. But, when adding properties to a derived class, you can store and access the strings in whatever style you want. Because you have to write the functions to access the properties, complicated storage schemes aren't recommended. A property name should be a simple description of the property.

Property attributes are likewise usually contained in an array, this time an array on **int**s. Again, you can handle this however you like. But the usual practice is to have the attributes for a property contained in an array corresponding to the value of its property index. The attributes indicate how the property can be accessed:

Table 28.4   Doc/View property attributes

Attribute	Function
pfGetText	Property accessible as text format.
pfGetBinary	Property accessible as native non-text format.

Table 28.4   Doc/View property attributes (continued)

Attribute	Function
pfConstant	Property cannot be changed once the object is created.
pfSettable	Property settable, must supply native format.
pfUnknown	Property defined but unavailable in **this** object.
pfHidden	Property should be hidden from normal browse (don't let the user see its name or value).
pfUserDef	Property has been user-defined at run time.

Accessing property information

There are a number of functions provided in both *TDocument* and *TView* for accessing Doc/View object property information. All of these functions are declared virtual. Because the property access functions are virtual, the function in the most derived class gets called first, and can override properties defined in a base class. It's the responsibility of each class to implement property access and to resolve its property names.

You normally access a property by its index number. Use the *FindProperty* function with the property name. *FindProperty* takes a **char** * parameter and searches the property list for a property with the same name. It returns an **int**, which is used as the property index for succeeding calls.

You can also use the *PropertyName* function to find the property name from the index. *PropertyName* takes an **int** parameter and returns a **char** * containing the name of the property.

You can get the attributes of a property using the *PropertyFlags* function. This function takes an **int** parameter, which should be the index of the desired property, and returns an **int**. You can determine whether a flag is set by using the **&** operator. For example, to determine whether you can get a property value in text form, you should check to see whether the *pfGetText* flag is set:

```
if(doc->PropertyFlags() & pfGetText)
{
  // Get property as text....
}
```

Getting and setting properties

You can use the *GetProperty* and *SetProperty* functions to query and modify the values of a Doc/View object's properties.

The *GetProperty* function lets you find out the value of a property:

```
int GetProperty(int index, void far* dest, int textlen = 0);
```

where:

• *index* is the property index.

• *dest* is used by *GetProperty* to contain the property data.

- *textlen* indicates the size of the memory array pointed to by *dest*. If *textlen* is 0, the property data is returned in binary form; otherwise the data is returned in text form. Data can be returned in binary form only if the *pfGetBinary* attribute is set; it can be returned in text form only if the *pfGetText* attribute is set. To get or set the binary data of properties, the data type and the semantics must be known by the caller.

The *SetProperty* function lets you set the value of a property:

```
bool SetProperty(int index, const void far* src)
```

where:

- *index* is the property index.

- *src* contains the data to which the property should be set; *src* must be in the correct native format for the property.

A derived class that duplicates property names should provide the same behavior and data type.

Chapter

29

Control objects

Windows provides a number of *controls*, which are standard user-interface elements with specialized behavior. ObjectWindows provides several *custom controls*; it also provides interface objects for controls so you can use them in your applications. Interface objects for controls are called *control objects*.

To learn more about interface objects, see Chapter 21, "Interface objects." This chapter covers the following topics:

- Tasks common to all control objects
    - Constructing and destroying control objects
    - Communicating with control objects
- Using each of the different control objects
- Setting and reading control values

Control classes

The following table lists all the control classes ObjectWindows provides.

Table 29.1   Controls and their ObjectWindows classes

Class	Control name	Description
TAnimateCtrl	Animate	Used to play simple animation loops in a window.
TButton	Button	A button with an associated text label.
TCheckBox	Check box	A box that can be checked (on) or unchecked (off), with an associated text label.
TColumnHeader	Header Window	Displays labels above columnar lists. Also accepts user input to control column widths and sorting order.
TComboBox	Combo box	A combined list box and edit or static control.
TControlBar	Control bar	Contains a row of gadgets.

Table 29.1   Controls and their ObjectWindows classes

Class	Control name	Description
TDragList	Drag List Box	An augmented listbox that lets the user arrange list items with the mouse.
TEdit	Edit control	A field for the user to type text in.
TGauge	Progress Bar	Static controls that display a range of process completion.
TGlyphButton		A button with a bitmap in addition to text.
TGroupBox	Group box	A static rectangle with optional text in the upper-left corner.
THotKey	Hot Key	A simple edit-like control for accepting hot-key strokes from the user.
THSlider and TVSlider	Trackbar	Horizontal and vertical controls that let the user choose from an upper and lower range (similar to scroll bars).
TListBox	List box	A list of items to choose from.
TListWindow	List View	Displays items in four ways: large (regular) icons, small icons, as a list, or as a report. (Right pane of Win95 Explorer).
TPropertySheet	Property Sheet	Allows multipage windows to be displayed. The user switches between pages using a built-in tab control.
TRadioButton	Radio button	A button that can be checked (on) or unchecked (off), usually in mutually exclusive groups.
TRichEdit	Rich Edit	This control is a full-featured rich text format (RTF) editor. The Win95 WordPad editor is essentially a frame around this control.
TScrollBar	Scroll bar	A scroll bar (like those in scrolling windows and list boxes) with direction arrows and an elevator thumb.
TStatic	Static control	Visible text the user cannot change.
TStatusBar	Status bar	Provides support for status bars, inserted gadgets, hint text, and keyboard modes.
TTabControl	Tab	Presents a number of tabbed pages in a dialog box. Provides emulation functionality when the common control is not available.
TToolTip	Tool Tip	Provides small popup help tip windows.
TTreeWindow	Tree View	Provides hierarchical tree display in a list. (Left pane of Win95 Explorer).
TUpDown	Up-Down	Used to manipulate information in a single step, up and down manner. (Sometimes called a spinner or spin button).

Control object example programs can be found in EXAMPLES\OWL\OWLAPI and EXAMPLES\OWL\OWLAPPS.

What are control objects?

To Windows, controls are just specialized windows. In ObjectWindows, *TControl* is derived from *TWindow*. Control objects and window objects are similar in how they behave as child windows, and in how you create and destroy them. Standard controls differ from other windows, however, in that Windows handles their event messages and is responsible for painting them. Custom ObjectWindows controls handle these tasks themselves because the ObjectWindows control classes contain the code needed to paint the controls and handle events.

In many cases, you can directly use instances of the classes listed in the previous table. However, sometimes you might need to create derived classes for specialized behavior. For example, you might derive a specialized list box class from *TListBox* called *TFontListBox* that holds the names of all the fonts available to your application and automatically displays them when you create an instance of the class.

Implementation of Controls

ObjectWindows provides two types of implementation for controls: those which encapsulate a Windows control (either a standard control or a common control), and those which are implemented internally. The *TGauge* control, for example, can use the Progress Bar common control, or an internal implementation (which has more options).

If a control encapsulates a Windows 95 control, and also provides an internal implementation, the internal implementation can be used to provide emulation of the Windows 95 control in Windows 16.

Table 29.2   Control Implementation

Control	Encapsulates	Internal Implementation
TAnimateCtrl	Common control	No
TButton	Standard control	No
TCheckBox	Standard control	No
TColumnHeader	Common control	No
TComboBox	Standard control	No
TControlBar	None	Yes
TDragList	Common control	No
TEditTEdit	Standard control	No
TGlyphButton	None	Yes
TGauge	Common control	Yes
TGroupBox	Standard control	No
THotKey	Common control	No
TListBox	Standard control	No
TListWindow	Common control	No
TPropertySheet	Common control	Yes
TRadioButton	Standard control	No
TRichEdit	Common control	No
TScrollBar	Standard control	No
TSlider	Common control	Yes
TStatic	Standard control	No
TStatusBar	None	Yes
TTabControl	Common control	Yes

Table 29.2 Control Implementation

Control	Encapsulates	Internal Implementation
TToolTip	Common control	Yes
TTreeWindow	Common control	Yes
TUpDown	Common control	Yes

Constructing and destroying control objects

Regardless of the type of control object you're using, there are several tasks you need to perform for each:

- Constructing the control object
- Showing the control
- Destroying the control

Constructing control objects

Constructing a control object is no different from constructing any other child window. Generally, the parent window's constructor calls the constructors of all its child windows. Notifications are described in Chapter 21. Controls communicate with parent windows in special ways (called *notifications*) in addition to the usual links between parent and child.

To construct and initialize a control object:

1 Add a control object pointer data member to the parent window.
2 Call the control object's constructor.
3 Change any control attributes.
4 Initialize the control in *SetupWindow*.

Each of these steps is described in the following sections.

Adding the control object pointer data member

Often when you construct a control in a window, you want to keep a pointer to the control in a window object data member. This is for convenience in accessing the control's member functions. Here's a fragment of a parent window object with the declaration for a pointer to a button control object:

```
class TMyWindow : public TWindow
{
  TButton *OkButton;
    ⋮
};
```

Controls that you rarely manipulate, like static text and group boxes, don't need these pointer data members. The following example constructs a group box without a data member and a button with a data member (*OkButton*):

```
TMyWindow::TMyWindow(TWindow *parent, const char far *title)
  : TWindow(parent, title)
```

```
{
    new TGroupBox(this, ID_GROUPBOX, "Group box", 10, 10, 100, 100);
    OkButton = new TButton(this, IDOK, "OK", 10, 200, 50, 50, true);
}
```

Calling control object constructors

Some control object constructors are passed parameters that specify characteristics of the control object. These parameters include

- A pointer to the parent window object
- A resource identifier
- The x-coordinate of the upper-left corner
- The y-coordinate of the upper-left corner
- The width
- The height
- Optional module pointer

For example, one of *TListBox*'s constructors is declared as follows:

```
TListBox(TWindow *parent, int resourceId,
         int x, int y, int w, int h,
         TModule* module = 0);
```

There are also constructors for associating a control object with an interface element (for example, a dialog box) created from a resource definition:

```
TListBox(TWindow* parent, int resourceId, TModule* module = 0);
```

Changing control attributes

All control objects get the default window styles WS_CHILD, WS_VISIBLE, WS_GROUP, and WS_TABSTOP. If you want to change a control's style, you manipulate its *Attr.Style*, as described in Chapter 25, "Window objects." Each control type also has other styles that define its particular properties.

Each control object inherits certain window styles from its base classes. You should rarely assign a value to *Attr.Style*. Instead, you should use the bitwise assignment operators (| = and &=) to "mask" in or out the window style you want. For example:

```
// Mask in the WS_BORDER window style
Attr.Style |= WS_BORDER;

// Mask out the WS_VSCROLL style
Attr.Style &= ~WS_VSCROLL;
```

Using the bitwise assignment operators helps ensure that you don't inadvertently remove a style.

Initializing the control

A control object's interface element is automatically created by the *SetupWindow* member function inherited by the parent window object. Make sure that when you derive new window classes, you call the base class' *SetupWindow* member function before attempting to manipulate its controls (for example, by calling control object member functions, sending messages to those controls, and so on).

You must not initialize controls in their parent window object's constructor. At that time, the controls' interface elements haven't yet been created.

Here's a typical *SetupWindow* function:

```
void
TMyWindow::SetupWindow()
{
  TWindow::SetupWindow(); // Lets TWindow create any child controls

  list1->AddString("Item 1");
  list1->AddString("Item 2");
}
```

Showing controls

It's not necessary to call the Windows function *Show* to display controls. Controls are child windows, and Windows automatically displays and repaints them along with the parent window. You can use *Show*, however, to hide or reveal controls on demand.

Destroying the control

Destroying controls is the parent window's responsibility. The control's interface element is automatically destroyed along with the parent window when the user closes the window or application. The parent window's destructor automatically destroys its child window objects (including child control objects).

Communicating with control objects

Communication between a window object and its control objects is similar in some ways to the communication between a dialog box object and its controls. Like a dialog box, a window needs a mechanism for manipulating its controls and for responding to control events, such as a list box selection.

Manipulating controls

One way dialog boxes manipulate their controls is by sending them messages using member functions inherited from *TWindow* (see Chapter 25), with a control message like LB_ADDSTRING. Control objects greatly simplify this process by providing member functions that send control messages for you. *TListBox::AddString*, for example, takes a string as its parameter and adds it to the list box by calling the list box object's *HandleMessage* member function:

```
int
TListBox::AddString(const char far* str)
{
```

```
       return (int)HandleMessage(LB_ADDSTRING, 0, (LPARAM)str);
   }
```

This example shows how you can call the control objects' member functions via a pointer:

```
   ListBox1->AddString("Atlantic City"); //where ListBox1 is a TListBox *
```

Responding to controls

When a user interacts with a control, Windows sends various control messages. To learn how to respond to control messages, see Chapter 21.

Making a window act like a dialog box

A dialog box lets the user use the *Tab* key to cycle through all of the dialog box's controls. It also lets the user use the arrow keys to select radio buttons in a group box. To emulate this keyboard interface for windows with controls, call *EnableKBHandler* in the window object's constructor.

Using particular controls

Each type of control operates somewhat differently from the others. In this section, you'll find specific information on how to use the objects for each of the standard Windows controls and the custom controls supplied with ObjectWindows.

Using the animate control

The *TAnimateCtrl* class encapsulates the Animation Control (a window that silently displays an AVI (Audio Video Interleaved) clip.

Note   The animation control can only play silent clips from an uncompressed .AVI file or from an .AVI file that was compressed using run-length encoding (RLE).

Creating a new control

To create a new control, use the *TAnimateCtrl(parent, id, x, y, w, h, module)* constructor. For example, you could use the following code within the constructor of a parent window:

```
   TClientWindow::TClientWindow(TWindow* parent) : TWindow(parent)
   {
     AnimateCtrl = new TAnimateCtrl(this, 0x100, 5, 10, 50, 60);
   };
```

This creates an animation control with the ID of 0x100, at location (5,10), 50 pixels wide and 60 pixels high within the client area of the *TClientWindow* window.

Aliasing a control

To alias an animation control which is part of a dialog resource, use the
TAnimateCtrl(parent, resourceId, module) constructor.

The following resource definition creates a dialog containing an animation control:

```
IDD_ANIMATE DIALOG 45, 56, 176, 99
STYLE DS_MODALFRAME | WS_POPUP | WS_VISIBLE | WS_CAPTION |
  WS_SYSMENU
CAPTION "Animation Dialog"
{
CONTROL "Sample_Avi", IDC_ANIMATE, "SysAnimate32", ACS_CENTER |
  ACS_TRANSPARENT | WS_CHILD | WS_VISIBLE | WS_BORDER, 16, 10, 145, 61
}
```

The following code shows how to alias an animation control within the constructor of a
Tdialog-derived class:

```
TAnimDialog::TAnimDialog(TWindow* parent, TResId res)
  :TDialog(parent, res)
{
  AnimCtrl = new TAnimateCtrl(this, IDC_ANIMATE);
}
```

Additional information

The specified caption of the control may contain the name of an .AVI resource to be
opened automatically by the control.

Passing -1 as the third argument to the *Play* method instructs the control to replay the
clip indefinitely.

Using the animate control

1 Create the control.

2 Invoke the *Open* method to open an .AVI clip and load it into memory:

```
AnimateCtrl->Open(MAKEINTRESOURCE(SAMPLE_ONE));
```

Note The parameter to the *Open* method can contain the path to an .AVI file or the name
of an AVI resource.

3 Use the *Play* method to play the current AVI clip in the animation window. The
control plays the clip in the background while the thread continues executing.

4 Use the *Seek* method to seek to a particular frame of the current AVI clip.

5 Use the *Stop* method to stop playing an AVI clip.

Using the column header control

The *TColumnHeader* class creates a horizontal window that is used above columns of text
or numbers, containing titles for each column. The right panel of the Windows 95
Explorer, for example, uses this type of window for file name, size, and type. Column
Header windows are generally used over a List Window window.

A header window contains parts called *header items*. The user can adjust the width of each item. Items can also behave like push buttons: clicking on the Size item in the Windows 95 Explorer, for example, sorts the files by size. Each item can have a string, a bit-mapped image, and a 32-bit application-defined value associated with it.

The native control for Windows 95 is the Header Window common control.

Creating a column header control

To create a Column Header Control, simply create a *TColumnHeader* object within the constructor of the parent object specifying the *parent* and the *id* of the control. For example,

```
TMyWindow::TMyWindow() {
  // ...
  TColumnHeader* hdrCtl = new TColumnHeader(this, ID_XX);
}
```

When constructed within the constructor of the parent object, it is not necessary to invoke the *Create* method of the *TColumnHeader* object. The *AutoCreate* feature of ObjectWindows will ensure that the control is created once the parent object is created. However, if you are constructing the *TColumnHeader* object after its parent has been created, you will also need to invoke it's *Create* method.

Note Although you can specify the screen coordinates of the control, these parameters are typically left out in favour of the *Layout* capabilities of the *TColumnHeader* object; as described in the section titled, "Sizing and positioning a column header control."

Adding items to a column header control

Once the control has been created, you can add items using the *Add* or *Insert* methods of the *TColumnHeader* class.

The *THdrItem* class holds information about an item of a Column Header Control. To add/insert an item you must first construct a *THdrItem* instance. After initializing the *THdrItem* instance, you can invoke the *Add* or *Insert* method of the *TColumnHeader* object.

For example:

```
THdrItem item("&Name of Employee");
hdrCtl->Add(item);
```

Responding to column header control notification messages

The Column Header Control sends notification messages to its parent window whenever the user manipulates the Column Header Control. For example, if the user clicks an item, the control sends a HDN_ITEMCLICK notification message.

ObjectWindows provides several macros which can be used in the definition of a Message Response Table, allowing a member function to be invoked when particular notification messages are received by the parent. The following list shows the macros pertinent to the Column Header Control:

```
EV_HDN_BEGINTRACK(id, method)        // User starts dragging divider
EV_HDN_DIVIDERDBLCLICK(id, method)   // User double clicked divider
```

```
EV_HDN_ENDTRACK(id, method)          // User ends drag operation
EV_HDN_ITEMCHANGED(id,method)        // Attribute of an item changed
EV_HDN_ITEMCHANGING(id,method)       // Attribute about to change
EV_HDN_ITEMCLICK(id, method)         // User clicked on item
EV_HDN_TRACK(id, method)             // User dragged a divider
```

Sizing and positioning a column header control

A Column Header Control is typically docked to the upper side of its parent's client area. The control provides an API which allows the control to specify a desired size and position within the boundary of a specified rectangle. The *bool Layout(TRect& boundingRect, WINDOWPOS& winPos)* method can be used to retrieve the appropriate size and position values in a WINDOWPOS structure.

The overloaded *bool Layout(uint swpFlags = 0)* method provides an higher abstraction of this API: the desired size of the control is retrieved by specifying the client area of its parent as the bounding rectangle and the control is then repositioned accordingly. The *swpFlags* are used when the call *SetWindowPos* is used to reposition the control.

Using the drag list control

The *TDragList* class creates an augmented list box that lets the user rearrange items with a mouse. It is best used for displaying a list of items that the user can reorder.

A major advantage this control has over the list box is the support for multiple columns. The right pane of the Windows 95 Explorer uses this type of window.

The native control for Windows 95 is the Drag List Box common control.

To use the drag list control, follow these steps:

1 `#include <owl/draglist.h>` for declarations of *TDragList* and *TDragListEventHandler* classes.

2 Derive a class from *TDragList* and override any of the following virtual functions:
```
virtual bool        BeginDrag(int item, const TPoint& point);
virtual TCursorType Dragging(int item, const TPoint& point);
virtual void        Dropped(int item, const TPoint& point);
virtual void        CancelDrag(int item, const TPoint& point);
```

3 Construct the control.
```
DragList = new TExampleDragList(this, DragListId, x, y, x + 200, y + 100);
```

4 In the parent window class that uses the drag list as a child, mix-in the *TDragListEventHandler* class and add it as a base for the response table.
```
DEFINE_RESPONSE_TABLE2(TDragListParentWindow, TWindow, TDragListEventHandler)
END_RESPONSE_TABLE;
```

5 As you would any listbox, add items to the drag list box after *TDragList::SetupWindow()* has been called.
```
DragList->AddString("Soyeun");
DragList->AddString("Valerie");
```

6 The virtual functions will be called at the proper time whenever the user does something. For example:

BeginDrag() will be called when the user clicks the left mouse button on an item to begin the drag transaction. When the user moves the mouse, the *Dragging* function will be called. The return type for dragging is an enum that specifies what cursor should be displayed. The *Dropped* function will be called when the user finishes a drag transaction by releasing the left mouse button. Each of the virtual functions is passed the item index the user wants to drag.

Using the glyph button control

The *TGlyphButton* class creates a button with a bitmap in addition to text.

Using the Hotkey control

The *THotKey* class encapsulates the hot-key control from the Common Control Library. A hot key is a key combination that the user can press to perform an action quickly. The key combination can consist of a modifier key, such as CTRL, ALT or SHIFT, and an accompanying key, such as a character key, an arrow key or a function key.

THotKey has two constructors: one for creating a new hot key object and one for aliasing a hot-key control which was defined in a dialog resource.

Creating a hotkey object

To create a new control, use the *THotKey(TWindow* parent, int id, int x, int y, int w, int h, TModule* module = 0)* constructor.

The following code fragment shows how to create a new hot-key control within a window represented by the class *TMyWindow*.

```
TMyWindow::TMyWindow(TWindow* parent) : TWindow(parent)
{
  HotKey = new THotKey(this, ID_HOTKEY, 10, 10, 40, 40);
}
```

Note Since the control is newed within the constructor of it's parent object, you need not explictly invoke its *Create* method. ObjectWindows' autocreate feature will ensure that the control is created after the creation of the parent window.

Aliasing a hotkey object

To alias a hot-key control from a dialog resource, use the *THotKey(TWindow* parent, int resourceId, TModule* module = 0)* constructor.

The following code fragment illustrates this:

```
TMyDialog::TMyDialog(TWindow* parent, TResId resId):TDialog(parent, resId)
{
  HotKey = new THotKey(this, IDC_HOTKEY);
}
```

Setting and retrieving the key combination

The *SetHotKey* and *GetHotKey* methods of *THotKey* allow you to set and retrieve the virtual key code and modifier flags of a hot-key from a hot-key control.

The value returned from the *GetHotKey* method can be used with the WM_SETHOTKEY message to associate a window with a hot-key. When user presses the hot-key, the system activates the window.

Additional information

The value retrieved from the hot-key control is not usable with the *RegisterHotKey* API.

You can customize a hot-key control by specifying invalid key combinations and providing the default modifier. See the *SetRules* method for more information.

Using the list window control

The *TListWindow* class creates a list view that displays items in four ways: large (regular) icons, small icons, as a list, or as a report. In-place editing of item names is supported. The right pane of the Windows 95 Explorer uses this type of window.

The native control for Windows 95 is the List View common control.

To use the list window control, follow these steps:

1 `#include <owl/listwind.h>` for declarations of *TListWindow, TListWindItem*, and *TListWindColumn* classes.

2 Create the control.

```
ListWind = new TListWindow(this, ListWindId, 40, 40, 400, 200);
```

3 Set the style for the control.

```
ListWind->Attr.Style |= LVS_SHAREIMAGELISTS | LVS_REPORT;
```

4 Optionally associate an image list with the control. If you are using an image list, do not forget to `#include <owl/imagelst.h>`.

```
ListWind->SetImageList(*ImageList, TListWindow::State);
```

5 Depending on the style of the control, add the appropriate columns.

```
TListWindColumn column("Column", 100);
ListWind->InsertColumn(0, column);
```

6 Add the items into the control.

```
for (int i = 0; i < ImageList->GetImageCount(); i++) {
  sprintf(Buffer, "Item %d", i);
  TListWindItem item(Buffer);
  item.SetStateImage(i);
  ListWind->InsertItem(item);
}
```

7 The parent window of the control may respond to events sent by the control.

Using the property sheet control

The *TPropertySheet* class creates a property sheet, which may be thought of as a kind of loose-leaf binder, containing a number of pages. Each page is indexed by a tab control. When a tab is selected, the corresponding page is brought to the front of the window.

The native control for Windows 95 is the Property Sheet common control.

Using the rich edit control

The *TRichEdit* class creates a full-featured rich text format (RTF) editor. The Windows 95 WordPad editor is essentially a frame around this control.

The native control for Windows 95 is the Rich Edit common control.

Using the tab control

The *TTabControl* class creates tabs that switch between the pages in a property sheet. When a tab is selected, the corresponding property sheet page is brought to the front of the window.

The native control for Windows 95 is the Tab Control common control.

Using the tool tip control

The *TToolTip* encapsulates a tooltip control: a small pop-up window that displays a single line of descriptive text giving the purpose of a tool in an application. The tool is either a window, such as a child window or control, or an application-defined rectangular area within a window's client area.

The tooltip control appears only when the user puts the cursor on a tool and leaves it there for approximately one-half second. It appears near the cursor and disappears when the user clicks a mouse button or moves the cursor away from the tool.

The *TTooltip* class offers two constructors: one for creating a new control and one for aliasing an existing control.

Creating a tooltip object

The following code fragment shows how to create a tooltip control.

```
void TMyWindow::SetupWindow()
{
  TWindow::SetupWindow();
  tooltip = new TTooltip(this);
  tooltip->Create();
}
```

Specifying tools to the tooltip control

Once you have created a tooltip control, you must specify the tools that it will work with. You do this by creating a *TToolInfo* for each tool. For example, the following code designates a rectangular area of a window as a tool:

```
void TMyWindow::AddTopLeftTool()
{
  uint toolId = ID_TOPLEFT_TOOL;        // Tool ID
  TRect rect(0, 0, 20, 20);             // Tool Rectangle
  TToolInfo ti(this, rect, ID_TOPLEFT_TOOL);
  tooltip->AddTool(ti);
}
```

Providing the tooltip text

When adding a tool, you may provide the text to be used when describing the tool as the last parameter to the constructor of the *TToolInfo* structure. For example, the following code specifies "Top Left" as the tooltip text:

```
TToolInfo ti(this, rect, ID_TOPLEFT_TOOL, "Top Left");
tooltip->AddTool(ti);
```

However, you may opt to provide the text on demand. This allows you to customize the message display to the user. The EV_TTN_NEEDTEXT macro allows you to specify a member function which can provide the text at runtime. The following code fragement illustrates:

```
class TMyWindow : public TWindow {
// Additional definitions ommitted for clarity
protected:
void HandleTooltipText(TTooltipText& tiTxt);
};

DEFINE_RESPONSE_TABLE1(TMyWindow, TWindow)
  EV_TTN_NEEDTEXT(ID_TOPLEFT_TOOL, HandleTooltipText),
END_RESPONSE_TABLE;

void
TMyWindow::HandleTooltipText(TTooltipText& tiTxt)
{
tiTxt.CopyText("Top Left square");
}
```

Additional information

The notification handler of the ObjectWindows *TDecoratedFrame* class enhances the mechanism for specifying the tooltip text by sending a *TTooltipEnabler* up the command chain. This allows the context window to provide the text even if it did not setup the tool. For example, a grid control in focus can customize the cut, paste, and copy tools to specify the data type being manipulated ("Copy Cell" instead of just "Copy").

The *EvCommandEnable* handler of *TDecoratedFrame* attempts to provide the tooltip text by looking in two locations:

1 First the window's menu is scanned for a menuitem with an id corresponding to that of the tool. If found, the menustring is provided.

2 Next, *TDecoratedFrame* attempts to load a string resource with an id corresponding to that of the tool. If found, the string is scanned for a line-feed character. If successful, *TDecoratedFrame* provides the string following the line-feed as tooltip text.

Note   You should structure your hint text string using the following format:

```
<string to be displayed on statusbar>\n<tooltip hint text>
```

Using the tree window control

The *TTreeWindow* class creates a hierarchical tree list display. This control should be used to represent data with parent-child relationships. This control can be seen as the left pane of the Windows 95 Explorer.

The native control for Windows 95 is the Tree View common control.

To use the tree window control, follow these steps:

1 `#include <owl/treewind.h>` for declarations of *TTreeWindow*, *TTreeNode*, and *TTreeItem*.

2 Determine the style of the control.

```
TTreeWindow::TStyle style = TTreeWindow::twsHasLines |
    TTreeWindow::twsHasButtons;
```

3 Construct the control.

```
TreeWind = new TTreeWindow(this, TreeWindId, 10, 10, 400, 200, style);
```

4 Add items into the control after *TTreeWindow::SetupWindow()* has been called.

```
TTreeNode root = TreeWind->GetRoot();
root.AddChild(TTreeItem("Child 8"));
TTreeNode parent1 = root.AddChild(TTreeItem("Parent 1"));
TTreeNode child1  = parent1.AddChild(TTreeItem("Child 1"));
    parent1.AddChild(TTreeItem("Child 2 (with some longer text)"));
```

5 Call *TTreeWindow::Update()* after adding items into the control.

```
TreeWind->Update();
```

6 The parent window of the control may respond to events sent by the control.

Using the up-down control

The *TUpDown* class creates pair of arrows to increment or decrement the value in an adjacent edit control. Support is provided for automatic updating of integer edit controls.

The native control for Windows 95 is the Up-Down common control.

Using list box controls

Using a list box is the simplest way to ask the user to pick something from a list. The *TListBox* class encapsulates list boxes. *TListBox* defines member functions for:

- Creating list boxes
- Modifying the list of items
- Inquiring about the list of items
- Finding out which item the user selected

Constructing list box objects

One of *TListBox*'s constructors takes seven parameters: a parent window, a resource identifier, the control's *x, y, h,* and *w* dimensions, and an module pointer:

```
TListBox(TWindow *parent,
         int resourceId,
         int x, int y, int w, int h,
         TModule* module = 0);
```

TListBox gets the default control styles (WS_CHILD, WS_VISIBLE, WS_GROUP, and WS_TABSTOP; see page 323) and adds LBS_STANDARD, which is a combination of LBS_NOTIFY (to receive notification messages), WS_VSCROLL (to have a vertical scroll bar), LBS_SORT (to sort the list items alphabetically), and WS_BORDER (to have a border). If you want a different list box style, you can modify *Attr.Style* in the list box object's constructor or in its parent's constructor. For example, for a list box that doesn't sort its items, use the following code:

```
listbox = new TListBox(this, ID_LISTBOX, 20, 20, 340, 100);
listbox->Attr.Style &= ~LBS_SORT;
```

Modifying list boxes

After you create a list box, you need to fill it with list items (which must be strings). Later, you can add, insert, or remove items or clear the list completely. The following table summarizes the member functions you use to perform these actions.

Table 29.3   TListBox member functions for modifying list boxes

Member function	Description
ClearList	Delete every item.
DirectoryList	Put file names in the list.
AddString	Add an item.
InsertString	Insert an item.
DeleteString	Delete an item.
SetSelIndex, *SetSel*, or *SetSelString*	Select an item.
SetSelStrings, *SetSelIndexes*, or *SetSelItemRange*	Select multiple items.
SetTopIndex	Scroll the list box so the specified item is visible.
SetTabStops	Set tab stops for multicolumn list boxes.
SetHorizontalExtent	Set number of pixels by which the list box can scroll horizontally.
SetColumnWidth	Set width of all columns in multicolumn list boxes.

Table 29.3   TListBox member functions for modifying list boxes (continued)

Member function	Description
SetCaretIndex	Set index of the currently focused item.
SetItemData	Set a *uint32* value to be associated with the specified index.
SetItemHeight	Set the height of item at the specified index or height of all items.

Querying list boxes

There are several member functions you can call to find out information about the list box or its item list. The following table summarizes the list box query member functions.

Table 29.4   TListBox member functions for querying list boxes

Member function	Description
GetCount	Number of items in the list.
FindString or *FindExactString*	Find string index.
GetTopIndex	Index of the item at the top of the list box.
GetCaretIndex	Index of the currently focused item.
GetHorizontalExtent	Number of pixels the list box can scroll horizontally.
GetItemData	*uint32* data set by *SetItemData*.
GetItemHeight	Height, in pixels, of the specified item.
GetItemRect	Rectangle used to display the specified item.
GetSelCount	Number of selected items (either 0 or 1).
GetSelIndex or *GetSel*	Index of the selected item.
GetSelString	Selected item.
GetSelStrings or *GetSelIndexes*	Selected items.
GetString	Item at a particular index.
GetStringLen	Length of a particular item.

Responding to list boxes

The member functions for modifying and querying list boxes let you set values or find out the status of the control at any given time. To know what a user is doing to a list box at run time, however, you have to respond to notification messages from the control.

There are only a few things a user can do with a list box: scroll through the list, click an item, and double-click an item. When the user does one of these things, Windows sends a *list box notification* message to the list box's parent window. Normally, you define notification-response member functions in the parent window object to handle notifications for each of the parent's controls.

The following table summarizes the most common list box notifications:

Table 29.5   List box notification messages

Event response table macro	Description
EV_LBN_SELCHANGE	An item has been selected with a single mouse click.
EV_LBN_DBLCLK	An item has been selected with a double mouse click.

Table 29.5   List box notification messages (continued)

Event response table macro	Description
EV_LBN_SELCANCEL	The user has deselected an item.
EV_LBN_SETFOCUS	The user has given the list box the focus by clicking or double-clicking an item, or by using *Tab*. Precedes LBN_SELCHANGE notification.
EV_LBN_KILLFOCUS	The user has removed the focus from the list box by clicking another control or pressing *Tab*.

Here's a sample parent window object member function to handle an LBN_SELCHANGE notification:

```
DEFINE_RESPONSE_TABLE1(TLBoxWindow, TFrameWindow)
  EV_LBN_SELCHANGE(ID_LISTBOX, EvListBoxSelChange),
END_RESPONSE_TABLE;

void
TLBoxWindow::EvListBoxSelChange()
{
  int index = ListBox->GetSelIndex();
  if (ListBox->GetStringLen(index) < 10) {
    char string[10];
    ListBox->GetSelString(string, sizeof(string));
    MessageBox(string, "You selected:", MB_OK);
  }
}
```

Using static controls

Static controls are usually unchanging units of text or simple graphics. The user doesn't interact with static controls, although your application can change the static control's text. See EXAMPLES\OWL\OWLAPI\STATIC for an example showing static controls.

Constructing static control objects

Because the user never interacts directly with a static control, the application doesn't receive control-notification messages from static controls. Therefore, you can construct most static controls with –1 as the control ID. However, if you want to use *TWindow::SendDlgItemMessage* to manipulate the static control, you need a unique ID.

One of *TStatic*'s constructors is declared as follows:

```
TStatic(TWindow* parent,
        int resourceId,
        const char far* title,
        int x, int y, int w, int h,
        UINT textLen = 0,
        TModule* module = 0);
```

It takes the seven parameters commonly found in this form of a control object constructor (a parent window, a resource ID, the control's x, y, h, and w dimensions, and an optional module pointer), and two parameters specific to static controls: the text string the static control displays and its maximum length (including the terminating NULL). A typical call to construct a static control looks like this:

```
new TStatic(this, -1, "Sample &Text", 170, 20, 200, 24);
```

If you want to be able to change the static control's text, you need to assign the control object to a data member in the parent window object so you can call the static control object's member function. If the static control's text doesn't need to change, you don't need a data member.

TStatic gets the default control styles (WS_CHILD, WS_VISIBLE, WS_GROUP, and WS_TABSTOP; see page 323), adds SS_LEFT (to left-align the text), and removes the WS_TABSTOP style (to prevent the user from selecting the control using *Tab*). To change the style, modify *Attr.Style* in the static control object's constructor. For example, the following code centers the control's text:

```
Attr.Style = (Attr.Style & ~SS_LEFT) | SS_CENTER;
```

To indicate a mnemonic for a nearby control, you can underline one or more characters in the static control's text string. To do this, insert an ampersand & in the string immediately preceding the character you want underlined. For example, to underline the *T* in *Text*, use *&Text*. If you want to use an ampersand in the string, use the static style SS_NOPREFIX.

Modifying static controls

TStatic has two member functions for altering the text of a static control: *SetText* sets the text to the passed string, and *Clear* erases the text. You can't change the text of static controls created with the SS_SIMPLE style.

Querying static controls

TStatic::GetTextLen returns the length of the static control's text. To get the text itself, use *TStatic::GetText*.

Using button controls

Buttons (sometimes called push buttons or command buttons) perform a task each time the button is pressed. There are two kinds of buttons: default buttons and non-default buttons. A default button, distinguished by the button style BS_DEFPUSHBUTTON, has a bold border that indicates the default user response. Nondefault buttons have the button style BS_PUSHBUTTON.

See EXAMPLES\OWL\OWLAPI\BWCC for an example of button controls.

Constructing buttons

One of *TButton*'s constructors takes the seven parameters commonly found in a control object constructor (a parent window, a resource identifier, the control's *x, y, h,* and *w* dimensions, and an optional module pointer), plus a text string that specifies the button's label, and a **bool** flag that indicates whether the button should be a default button. Here's the constructor declaration:

```
TButton(TWindow *parent,
```

```
      int resourceId,
      const char far *text,
      int X, int Y, int W, int H,
      bool isDefault = false,
      TModule *module = 0);
```

A typical button would be constructed like this:

```
btn = new TButton(this, ID_BUTTON, "DO_IT!", 38, 48, 316, 24, true);
```

Responding to buttons

When the user clicks a button, the button's parent window receives a notification message. If the parent window object intercepts the message, it can respond to these events by displaying a dialog box, saving a file, and so on.

To intercept and respond to button messages, define a command response member function for the button. The following example uses ID ID_BUTTON to handle the response to the user clicking the button:

```
DEFINE_RESPONSE_TABLE1(TTestWindow, TFrameWindow)
  EV_COMMAND(ID_BUTTON, HandleButtonMsg),
END_RESPONSE_TABLE;

void
TTestWindow::HandleButtonMsg()
{
  // Button was pressed
}
```

Using check box and radio button controls

A *check box* generally presents the user with a two-state option. The user can check or uncheck the control, or leave it as is. In a group of check boxes, any or all might be checked. For example, you might use a check box to enable or disable the use of sound in your application.

Radio buttons, on the other hand, are used for selecting one of several mutually exclusive options. For example, you might use radio buttons to choose between a number of sounds in your application.

TCheckBox is derived from *TButton* and represents check boxes. Since radio buttons share some behavior with check boxes, *TRadioButton* is derived from *TCheckBox*.

Check boxes and radio buttons are sometimes collectively referred to as *selection boxes*. While displayed on the screen, a selection box is either checked or unchecked. When the user clicks a selection box, it's an event, generating a Windows notification. As with other controls, the selection box's parent window usually intercepts and acts on these notifications.

See EXAMPLES\OWL\OWLAPI\BUTTON for radio button and check box control examples.

Constructing check boxes and radio buttons

TCheckBox and *TRadioButton* each have a constructor that takes the seven parameters commonly found in a control object constructor (a parent window, a resource identifier, the control's *x*, *y*, *h*, and *w* dimensions, and an optional module pointer). They also take a text string and a pointer to a group box object that groups the selection boxes. If the group box object pointer is zero, the selection box isn't part of a group box. Here are one each of their constructors:

```
TCheckBox(TWindow *parent,
          int resourceId,
          const char far *title,
          int x, int y, int w, int h,
          TGroupBox *group = 0,
          TModule *module = 0);


TRadioButton(TWindow *parent,
             int resourceId,
             const char far *title,
             int x, int y, int w, int h,
             TGroupBox *group = 0,
             TModule *module = 0);
```

The following listing shows some typical constructor calls for selection boxes.

```
CheckBox = new TCheckBox(this, ID_CHECKBOX, "Check Box Text", 158, 12, 150, 26);
GroupBox = new TGroupBox(this, ID_GROUPBOX, "Group Box", 158, 102, 176, 108);

RButton1 = new TRadioButton(this, ID_RBUTTON1, "Radio Button 1",
                            174, 128, 138, 24, GroupBox);
RButton2 = new TRadioButton(this, ID_RBUTTON2, "Radio Button 2",
                            174, 162, 138, 24, GroupBox);
```

Check boxes by default have the BS_AUTOCHECKBOX style, which means that Windows handles a click on the check box by toggling the check box. Without BS_AUTOCHECKBOX, you'd have to set the check box's state manually. Radio buttons by default have the BS_AUTORADIOBUTTON style, which means that Windows handles a click on the radio button by checking the radio button and unchecking the other radio buttons in the group. Without BS_AUTORADIOBUTTON, you'd have to intercept the radio button's notification messages and do this work yourself.

Modifying selection boxes

Checking and unchecking a selection box seems like a job for the application user, not your application. But in some cases, your application needs control over a selection box's state. For example, if the user opens a text file, you might want to automatically check a check box labeled "Save as ANSI text." *TCheckBox* defines several member functions for modifying a check box's state:

Table 29.6 TCheckBox member functions for modifying selection boxes

Member function	Description
Check or *SetCheck (BF_CHECKED)*	Check
Uncheck or *SetCheck (BF_UNCHECKED)*	Uncheck

Table 29.6 TCheckBox member functions for modifying selection boxes (continued)

Member function	Description
Toggle	Toggle
SetState	Highlight
SetStyle	Change the button's style

When you use these member functions with radio buttons, ObjectWindows ensures that only one radio button per group is checked, as long as the buttons are assigned to a group.

Querying selection boxes

Querying a selection box is one way to find out and respond to its state. Radio buttons have two states: checked (BF_CHECKED) and unchecked (BF_UNCHECKED). Check boxes can have an additional (and optional) third state: grayed (BF_GRAYED). The following table summarizes the selection-box query member functions.

Table 29.7 TCheckBox member functions for querying selection boxes

Member function	Description
GetCheck	Return the check state.
GetState	Return the check, highlight, or focus state.

Using group boxes

In its simplest form, a group box is a labeled static rectangle that visually groups other controls.

Constructing group boxes

TGroupBox has a constructor that takes the seven parameters commonly found in a control object constructor (a parent window, a resource identifier, the control's x, y, h, and w dimensions, and an optional module pointer), and also takes a text string parameter to label the group:

```
TGroupBox(TWindow *parent,
          int resourceId,
          const char far *text,
          int X, int Y, int W, int H,
          TModule *module = 0);
```

Grouping controls

Usually a group box visually associates a group of other controls; however, it can also logically associate a group of selection boxes (check boxes and radio buttons). This logical group performs the automatic unchecking (BS_AUTOCHECKBOX, BS_AUTORADIOBUTTON) discussed on page 339.

To add a selection box to a group box, pass a pointer to the group box object in the selection box's constructor call.

Responding to group boxes

When an event occurs that might change the group box's selections (for example, when a user clicks a button or the application calls *Check*), Windows sends a notification message to the group box's parent window. The parent window can intercept the message for the group box as a whole, rather than responding to the individual selection boxes in the group box. To find out which control in the group was affected, you can read the current status of each control.

Using scroll bars

Scroll bars are the primary mechanism for changing the user's view of an application window, a list box, or a combo box. However, you might want a separate scroll bar to perform a specialized task, such as controlling the temperature on a thermostat or the color in a drawing program. Use *TScrollBar* objects when you need a separate, customizable scroll bar.

See EXAMPLES\OWL\OWLAPI\SCROLLER for a scroll bar control example.

Constructing scroll bars

TScrollBar has a constructor that takes the seven parameters commonly found in a control object constructor (a parent window, a resource identifier, the control's *x, y, h,* and *w* dimensions, and an optional module pointer), and also takes a **bool** flag parameter that specifies whether the scroll bar is horizontal. Here's a *TScrollBar* constructor declaration:

```
TScrollBar(TWindow *parent,
           int resourceId,
           int x, int y, int w, int h,
           bool isHScrollBar,
           TModule *module = 0);
```

If you specify a height of zero for a horizontal scroll bar or a width of zero for a vertical scroll bar, Windows gives it a standard height and width. This code creates a standard-height horizontal scroll bar:

```
new TScrollBar(this, ID_THERMOMETER, 100, 150, 180, 0, true);
```

TScrollBar's constructor constructs scroll bars with the style SBS_HORZ for horizontal scroll bars and SBS_VERT for vertical scroll bars. You can specify additional styles, such as SBS_TOPALIGN, by changing the scroll bar object's *Attr.Style*.

Controlling the scroll bar range

One attribute of a scroll bar is its *range*, which is the set of all possible *thumb* positions. The thumb is the scroll bar's sliding box that the user drags or scrolls. Each position is associated with an integer. The parent window uses this integer, the *position*, to set and query the scroll bar. By default, a scroll bar object's range is 1 to 100.

The thumb's minimum position (at the top of a vertical scroll bar and the left of a horizontal scroll bar) corresponds to position 1, and the thumb's maximum position corresponds to position 100. Use *SetRange* to set the range differently.

Controlling scroll amounts

A scroll bar has two other important attributes: its *line magnitude* and *page magnitude*. The line magnitude, initialized to 1, is the distance, in range units, the thumb moves when the user clicks the scroll bar's arrows. The page magnitude, initialized to 10, is the distance, also in range units, the thumb moves when the user clicks the scrolling area. You can change these values by changing the *TScrollBar* data members *LineMagnitude* and *PageMagnitude*.

Querying scroll bars

TScrollBar has two member functions for querying scroll bars:

- *GetRange* gets the upper and lower ranges.
- *GetPosition* gets the current thumb position.

Modifying scroll bars

Modifying scroll bars is usually done by the user, but your application can also modify a scroll bar directly:

- *SetRange* sets the scrolling range.
  - *SetPosition* sets the thumb position.
  - *DeltaPos* moves the thumb position.

Responding to scroll-bar messages

When the user moves a scroll bar's thumb or clicks the scroll arrows, Windows sends a scroll bar notification message to the parent window. If you want your window to respond to scrolling events, respond to the notification messages.

Scroll bar notification messages are slightly different from other control notification messages. They're based on the WM_HSCROLL and WM_VSCROLL messages, rather than WM_COMMAND command messages. Therefore, to respond to scroll bar notification messages, you need to define *EvHScroll* or *EvVScroll* event response functions, depending on whether the scroll bar is horizontal or vertical:

```
class TTestWindow : public TFrameWindow
{
  public:
    TTestWindow(TWindow* parent, const char* title);
    virtual void SetupWindow();

    void EvHScroll(UINT code, UINT pos, HWND wnd);

  DECLARE_RESPONSE_TABLE(TTestWindow);
};

DEFINE_RESPONSE_TABLE1(TTestWindow, TFrameWindow)
  EV_WM_HSCROLL,
END_RESPONSE_TABLE;
```

Usually, you respond to all the scroll bar notification messages by retrieving the current thumb position and taking appropriate action. In that case, you can ignore the notification code:

```
void
TTestWindow::EvHScroll(UINT code, UINT pos, HWND wnd)
{
  TFrameWindow::EvHScroll(); // perform default WM_HSCROLL processing
  int newPos = ScrollBar->GetPosition();
  // do some processing with newPos
}
```

Avoiding thumb tracking messages

You might not want to respond to the scroll bar notification messages while the user is dragging the scroll bar's thumb, because the user is usually dragging the thumb quickly, generating many notification messages. It's more efficient to wait until the user has stopped moving the thumb, and then respond. To do this, screen out the notification messages that have the SB_THUMBTRACK code.

Specializing scroll bar behavior

You might want a scroll bar object respond to its own notification messages. *TWindow* has built-in support for dispatching scroll bar notification messages back to the scroll bar. *TWindow::EvHScroll* or *TWindow::EvVScroll* execute the appropriate *TScrollBar* member function based on the notification code. For example:

```
class TSpecializedScrollBar : public TScrollBar
{
  public:
    virtual void SBTop();
};

void
TSpecializedScrollBar::SBTop()
{
  TScrollBar::SBTop();
  ::sndPlaySound("AT-TOP.WAV", SND_ASYNC); // play sound
}
```

Be sure to call the base member functions first. They correctly update the scroll bar to its new position.

The following table associates notification messages with the corresponding *TScrollBar* member function:

Table 29.8   Notification codes and TScrollBar member functions

Notification message	*TScrollBar* member function
SB_LINEUP	*SBLineUp*
SB_LINEDOWN	*SBLineDown*
SB_PAGEUP	*SBPageUp*
SB_PAGEDOWN	*SBPageDown*
SB_THUMBPOSITION	*SBThumbPosition*

Table 29.8 Notification codes and TScrollBar member functions (continued)

Notification message	*TScrollBar* member function
SB_THUMBTRACK	*SBThumbTrack*
SB_TOP	*SBTop*
SB_BOTTOM	*SBBottom*

Using sliders

An abstract base class derived from *TScrollBar*, *TSlider* defines the basic behavior of sliders (controls that are used for providing nonscrolling, position information). Like scroll bars, sliders have minimum and maximum positions as well as line and page magnitude. Sliders can be moved using either the mouse or the keyboard. If you use a mouse to move the slider, you can drag the thumb position, click on the slot on either side of the thumb position to move the thumb by a specified amount (*PageMagnitude*), or click on the ruler to position the thumb at a specific spot on the slider. The keyboard's Home and End keys move the thumb position to the minimum (*Min*) and maximum (*Max*) positions on the slider.

You can use *TSlider*'s member functions to cause the thumb positions to automatically align with the nearest tick positions. (This is referred to as snapping.) You can also specify the tick gaps (the space between the lines that separate the major divisions of the X- or Y-axis).

THSlider (horizontal slider) and *TVSlider* (vertical slider) are derived from *Tslider*.

The native control for Windows 95 is the Trackbar common control. If the common controls are available, *ClassNativeUse* is set to *nuAlways*.

To use the slider control, follow these steps:

1 `#include <owl/slider.h>` in the .cpp files for declarations of *THSlider* and *TVSlider*.

2 `#include <owl/slider.rc>` as a resource in the .rc file. This file contains the bitmaps used to draw the slider.

3 Construct the control. Use *THSlider* for a horizontal slider. Use *TVSlider* for a vertical slider.

```
Thermostat = new THSlider(this, IDC_THERMOSTAT, 70, 130, 240, 40);
OutsideTemp = new TVSlider(this, IDC_OUTSIDETEMP, 330, 30, 32, 160);
```

4 Set the properties after *THSlider::SetupWindow* or *TVSlider::SetupWindow* has been called.

```
Thermostat->SetRange(40, 120);
Thermostat->SetRuler(5, false);
Thermostat->SetPosition(75);
OutsideTemp->SetRange(20, 90);
OutsideTemp->SetRuler(5, false);
OutsideTemp->SetPosition(40);
```

5 To retrieve the position from the slider, use *TSlider::GetPosition()*.

```
sprintf(str, "%d\xB0 %s", OutsideTemp->GetPosition(), "Outside");
```

Using gauges

Gauges are controls that display duration or other information about an ongoing process. Class *TGauge* implements gauges, and is derived from class *TControl*. Horizontal gauges are usually used to display process information, and vertical gauges are usually used to display analog information.

Generally, a broken bar gauge is recommended for processes lasting less than 10 seconds. A solid bar (with text) is recommended for longer processes.

The internal implementation can create a solid bar with text, and it can also have a vertical orientation. This implementation is used for the upper gauge in the illustration below.

The native control for Windows 95 is the Progress Bar common control.

To use the gauge control, follow these steps:

1 Construct the control.

Use the general constructor to construct a solid bar, a bar with text, or a vertical bar:

```
SolidGauge = new TGauge(this, "%d%%", IDC_SOLIDGAUGE, 20, 20, 240, 34, true);
```

Use the common control constructor to construct a horizontal LED bar:

```
LedGauge = new TGauge(this, IDC_LEDGAUGE, 20, 60, 240, 40);
```

2 Set the options:

```
SolidGauge->SetRange(0, 100);
LedGauge->SetRange(0, 100);
LedGauge->SetLed(4, 80);
LedGauge->SetStep(8);
```

3 Periodically update the gauge, using the control properties:

```
SolidGauge->SetValue(Setting);
LedGauge->SetValue(Setting);
```

Using edit controls

Edit controls are interactive static controls. They're rectangular areas that can be filled with text, modified, and cleared by the user or application. Edit controls are very useful as fields for data entry screens. They support the following operations:

- User text input
- Dynamic display of text (by the application)
- Cutting, copying, and pasting to the Clipboard
- Multiline editing (good for text editors)

See EXAMPLES\OWL\OWLAPI\VALIDATE for an edit controls example.

Constructing edit controls

One of *TEdit*'s constructors takes parameters for an initial text string, maximum string length (including the terminating NULL), and a **bool** flag specifying whether or not it's a multiline edit control (in addition to the parent window, resource identifier, and placement coordinates). This *TEdit* constructor is declared as follows:

```
TEdit(TWindow *parent,
      int resourceId,
      const char far *text,
      int x, int y, int w, int h,
      UINT textLen,
      bool multiline = false,
      TModule *module = 0);
```

By default, the edit control has the styles ES_LEFT (for left-aligned text), ES_AUTOHSCROLL (for automatic horizontal scrolling), and WS_BORDER (for a visible border surrounding the edit control). Multiline edit controls get the additional styles ES_MULTILINE (specifies a multiline edit control), ES_AUTOVSCROLL (automatic vertical scrolling), WS_VSCROLL (vertical scroll bar), and WS_HSCROLL (horizontal scroll bar).

The following are typical edit control constructor calls, one for a single-line control, the other multiline:

```
Edit1 = new TEdit(this, ID_EDIT1, "Default Text", 20, 50, 150, 30, MAX_TEXTLEN, false);
Edit2 = new TEdit(this, ID_EDIT2, "", 260, 50, 150, 30, MAX_TEXTLEN, true);
```

Using the Clipboard and the Edit menu

You can directly transfer text between an edit control object and the Windows Clipboard using *TEdit* member functions. You probably want to give users access to these member functions by giving your window an Edit menu.

Edit control objects have built-in responses to menu items like Edit | Copy and Edit | Undo. *TEdit* has command response member functions, such as *CmEditCopy* and *CmEditUndo*, which ObjectWindows invokes in response to users choosing items from the parent window's Edit menu.

The table below shows the Clipboard and editing member functions and the menu commands that invoke them.

Table 29.9   TEdit member functions and Edit menu commands

Member function	Menu command	Description
Copy	CM_EDITCOPY	Copy text to Clipboard.
Cut	CM_EDITCUT	Cut text to Clipboard.
Undo	CM_EDITUNDO	Undo last edit.
Paste	CM_EDITPASTE	Paste text from Clipboard.
DeleteSelection	CM_EDITDELETE	Delete selected text.
Clear	CM_EDITCLEAR	Clear entire edit control.

To add an editing menu to a window that contains edit control objects, define a menu resource for the window using the menu commands listed above. You don't need to write any new member functions.

Querying edit controls

Often, you want to query an edit control to store the entry for later use. *TEdit* has a number of querying member functions. Many of the edit control query and modification member functions return, or require you to specify, a line number or a character's position in a line. All of these indexes start at zero. In other words, the first line is line zero and the first character of a line is character zero. The following table summarizes *TEdit*'s query member functions.

Table 29.10   TEdit member functions for querying edit controls

Member function	Description
IsModified	Find out if text has changed.
GetText	Retrieve all text.
GetLine	Retrieve a line.
GetNumLines	Get number of lines.
GetLineLength	Get length of a given line.
GetSelection	Get index of selected text.
GetSubText	Get a range of characters.
GetLineIndex	Count characters before a line.
GetLineFromPos	Find the line containing an index.
GetRect	Get formatting rectangle.
GetHandle	Get memory handle.
GetFirstVisibleLine	Get index of first visible line.
GetPasswordChar	Get character used in passwords.
GetWordBreakProc	Get word-breaking procedure.
CanUndo	Find out if edit can be undone.

Text that spans lines in a multiline edit control contains two extra characters for each line break: a carriage return (\r) and a line feed (\n). *TEdit*'s member functions retain the text's formatting when they return text from a multiline edit control. When you insert this text back into an edit control, paste it from the Clipboard, write it to a file, or print it to a printer, the line breaks appear as they did in the edit control. When you use query member functions to get a specified number of characters, be sure to account for the two extra characters in a line break.

Modifying edit controls

Many uses of edit controls require that your application explicitly substitute, insert, clear, or select text. *TEdit* supports those operations, plus the ability to force the edit control to scroll.

Table 29.11   TEdit member functions for modifying edit controls

Member function	Description
Clear	Delete all text.
DeleteSelection	Delete selected text.
DeleteSubText	Delete a range of characters.
DeleteLine	Delete a line of text.
Insert	Insert text.
Paste	Paste text from Clipboard.
SetText	Replace all text.
SetSelection	Select a range of text.
Scroll	Scroll text.
ClearModify	Clear the modified flag.
Search	Search for text.
SetRect or *SetRectNP*	Set formatting rectangle.
FormatLines	Turn on or off soft line breaks.
SetTabStops	Set tab stops.
SetHandle	Set local memory handle.
SetPasswordChar	Set password character.
SetReadOnly	Make the edit control read-only.
SetWordBreakProc	Set word-breaking procedure.
EmptyUndoBuffer	Empty undo buffer.

Using combo boxes

A combo box control is a combination of two other controls: a list box and an edit or static control. It serves the same purpose as a list box—it lets the user choose one text item from a scrollable list of text items by clicking the item with the mouse. The edit control, grafted to the top of the list box, provides another selection mechanism, allowing users to type the text of the desired item. If the list box area of the combo box is displayed, the desired item is automatically selected. *TComboBox* is derived from *TListBox* and inherits its member functions for modifying, querying, and selecting list items. In addition, *TComboBox* provides member functions for manipulating the list part of the combo box, which, in some types of combo boxes, can *drop down* on request.

See EXAMPLES\OWL\OWLAPI\COMBOBOX for a combo box control example.

Varieties of combo boxes

There are three types of combo boxes: simple, drop down, and drop down list. All combo boxes show their edit area at all times, but some can show and hide their list box areas. The following table summarizes the properties of each type of combo box.

Table 29.12 Summary of combo box styles

Style	Can hide list?	Text must match list?
Simple	No	No
Drop down	Yes	No
Drop down list	Yes	Yes

From a user's perspective, these are the distinctions between the different styles of combo boxes:

- A simple combo box cannot hide its list box area. Its edit area behaves just like an edit control; the user can enter and edit text, and the text doesn't need to match one of the items in the list. If the text does match, the corresponding list item is selected.

- A drop down combo box behaves like a simple combo box, with one exception. In its initial state, its list area isn't displayed. It appears when the user clicks on the icon to the right of the edit area. When drop down combo boxes aren't being used, they take up less space than a simple combo box or a list box.

- The list area of a drop down list combo box behaves like the list area of a drop down combo box—it appears only when needed. The two combo box types differ in the behavior of their edit areas. Whereas drop down edit areas behave like regular edit controls, drop down list edit areas are limited to displaying only the text from one of their list items. When the edit text matches the item text, no more characters can be entered.

Choosing combo box types

Drop down list combo boxes are useful in cases where no other selection is acceptable besides those listed in the list area. For example, when choosing a printer, you can only choose a printer accessible from your system.

On the other hand, drop down combo boxes can accept entries other than those found in the list. A typical use of drop down combo boxes is selecting disk files for opening or saving. The user can either search through directories to find the appropriate file in the list, or type the full path name and file name in the edit area, regardless of whether the file name appears in the list area.

Constructing combo boxes

TComboBox has two constructors. The first constructor takes the seven parameters commonly found in a control object constructor (a parent window, a resource identifier, the control's *x*, *y*, *h*, and *w* dimensions, and an optional module pointer), and also style and maximum text length parameters. This constructor is declared like this:

```
TComboBox(TWindow *parent,
          int resourceId,
          int x, int y, int w, int h,
```

```
          uint32 style,
          uint16 textLen,
          TModule *module = 0);
```

All combo boxes have the styles WS_CHILD, WS_VISIBLE, WS_GROUP, WS_TABSTOP, CBS_SORT (to sort the list items), CBS_AUTOHSCROLL (to let the user enter more text than fits in the visible edit area), and WS_VSCROLL (vertical scroll bar). The style parameter you supply is one of the Windows combo box styles CBS_SIMPLE, CBS_DROPDOWN, or CBS_DROPDOWNLIST. The text length specifies the maximum number of characters allowed in the edit area.

The second *TComboBox* constructor lets you create an ObjectWindows object that serves as an alias for an existing combo box. This constructor looks like this:

```
TComboBox(TWindow* parent,
          int resourceId,
          UINT textLen = 0,
          TModule* module = 0);
```

The following lines show a typical combo box constructor call, constructing a drop down list combo box with an unsorted list:

```
Combo1 = new TComboBox(this, ID_COMBO1, 190, 30, 150, 100, CBS_SIMPLE, 20);
Combo1->Attr.Style &= ~CBS_SORT;
```

Modifying combo boxes

TComboBox defines several member functions for modifying a combo box's list and edit areas. The following table summarizes these member functions.

Because *TComboBox* is derived from *TListBox*, you can also use *TListBox* member functions to manipulate a combo box's list area.

Table 29.13   TComboBox member functions for modifying combo boxes

Member function	Description
SetText	Replace all text in the edit area.
SetEditSel	Select text in the edit area.
Clear	Delete all text in the edit area.
ShowList or *ShowList(true)*	Show the list area.
HideList or *ShowList(false)*	Hide the list area.
SetExtendedUI	Set the extended combo box UI.

Querying combo boxes

TComboBox adds several member functions to those inherited from *TListBox* for querying the contents of a combo box's edit and list areas. The following table summarizes these member functions.

Table 29.14   TComboBox member functions for querying combo boxes

Member function	Description
GetTextLen	Get length of text in edit area.
GetText	Retrieve all text in edit area.

Table 29.14 TComboBox member functions for querying combo boxes (continued)

Member function	Description
GetEditSel	Get indexes of selected text in edit area.
GetDroppedControlRect	Get rectangle of dropped-down list.
GetDroppedState	Determine if list area is visible.
GetExtendedUI	Determine if combo box has extended UI.

Setting and reading control values

To manage complex dialog boxes or windows with many child-window controls, you might create a derived class to store and retrieve the state of the dialog box or window controls. The state of a control includes the text of an edit control, the position of a scroll bar, and whether a radio button is checked.

Using transfer buffers

As an alternative to creating a derived class, you can use a structure to represent the state of the dialog box's or window's controls. This structure is called a *transfer buffer* because control states are transferred to the buffer from the controls and to the controls from the buffer.

For example, your application can bring up a modal dialog box and, after the user closes it, extract information from the transfer buffer about the state of each control. Then, if the user brings up the dialog box again, you can transfer the control states from the transfer buffer. In addition, you can set the initial state of each control based on the transfer buffer. You can also explicitly transfer data in either direction at any time, such as to reset the states of the controls to their previous values. A window or modeless dialog box with controls can also use the transfer mechanism to set or retrieve state information at any time.

The transfer mechanism requires the use of ObjectWindows objects to represent the controls for which you'd like to transfer data. To use the transfer mechanism, you have to do three things:

- Define the transfer buffer, with an instance variable for each control for which you want to transfer data.
- Define the corresponding window or dialog box.
- Transfer the data.

Defining the transfer buffer

The transfer buffer is a structure with one member for each control participating in the transfer. These members are known as *instance variables*. A window or dialog box can also have controls with no states to transfer. For example, by default, buttons, group boxes, and static controls don't participate in transfer. The type of the control determines the type of member needed in the transfer buffer.

To define a transfer buffer, define an instance variable for each participating control in the dialog box or window. It isn't necessary to define an instance variable for every control, only for those controls you want to transfer values to and from. The transfer buffer stores one of each type of control, except buttons, group boxes, and static controls. For example:

```
struct TSampleTransferStruct
{
  char editCtl[sizeOfEditCtl]; // edit control
  uint16 checkBox;             // check box
  uint16 radioButton;          // radio button
  TListBoxData listBox;     // list box
  TComboBoxData comboBox;   // combo box
  TScrollBarData scrollBar; // scroll bar
};
```

Each type of control has different information to store. The following table explains the transfer buffer for each of ObjectWindows' controls.

Table 29.15   Transfer buffer members for each type of control

Control type	Type	Description
Static	**char** *array*	A character array up to the maximum length of text allowed, plus the terminating NULL. By default, static controls don't participate in transfer, but you can explicitly enable them.
Edit	**char** *array*	A character array up to the maximum length of text allowed, plus the terminating NULL.
List box	*TListBoxData*	An instance of the *TListBoxData* class; *TListBoxData* has several members for holding the list box strings, item data, and the selected indexes.
Combo box	*TComboBoxData*	An instance of the *TComboBoxData* class; *TComboBoxData* has several members for holding the combo box list area strings, item data, the selection index, and the contents of the edit area.
Check box or radio button	*uint16*	BF_CHECKED, BF_UNCHECKED, or BF_GRAYED, indicating the selection box state.
Scroll bar	*TScrollBarData*	An instance of *TScrollBarData*; *TScrollBarData* has three **int** members: *LowValue* to hold the minimum range; *HighValue* to hold the maximum range; and *Position* to hold the current thumb position.

List box transfer

Because list boxes need to transfer several pieces of information (strings, item data, and selection indexes), the transfer buffer uses a class called *TListBoxData*. *TListBoxData* has several data members to hold the list box information:

Table 29.16 TListBoxData data members

Data member	Type	Description
ItemDatas	*TUint32Array**	Contains the item data *uint32* for each item in the list box.
SelIndices	*TIntArray**	Contains the indexes of each selected string (in a multiple-selection list box).
Strings	*TStringArray**	Contains all the strings in the list box.

TListBoxData also has member functions to manipulate the list box data:

Table 29.17 TListBoxData member functions

Member function	Description
AddItemData	Adds item data to the *ItemDatas* array.
AddString	Adds a string to the *Strings* array, and optionally selects it.
AddStringItem	Adds a string to the *Strings* array, optionally selects it, and adds item data to the *ItemDatas* array.
GetSelString	Get the selected string at the given index.
GetSelStringLength	Returns the length of the selected string at the given index.
ResetSelections	Removes all selections from the *SelIndices* array.
Select	Selects the string at the given index.
SelectString	Selects the given string.

Combo box transfer

Combo boxes need to transfer several pieces of information (strings, item data, selected item, and the index of the selected item). The transfer buffer for combo boxes is a class called *TComboBoxData*. *TComboBoxData* has several data members to hold the combo box information:

Table 29.18 TComboBoxData data members

Data member	Type	Description
ItemDatas	*TUint32Array**	Contains the item data *uint32* for each item in the list box.
Selection	**char***	Contains the selected string.
Strings	*TStringArray**	Contains all the strings in the list box.

TComboBoxData also has several member functions to manipulate the combo box information:

Table 29.19 TComboBoxData member functions

Member function	Description
AddString	Adds a string to the *Strings* array, and optionally selects it.
AddStringItem	Adds a string to the *Strings* array, optionally selects it, and adds item data to the *ItemDatas* array.
Clear	Clears all data.
GetItemDatas	Returns a reference to *ItemDatas*.
GetSelCount	Returns number of selected items.
GetSelection	Returns a reference to the current selection.
GetSelIndex	Returns the index of the current selection.
GetSelString	Places a copy of the current selection into a character buffer.
GetSelStringLength	Returns the length of the currently selected string.
GetStrings	Returns a reference to the entire array of strings in the combobox.
ResetSelections	Sets the current selection to a null string and sets the index to CB_ERR.
Select	Sets a string in *Strings* to be the current selection, based on an index parameter.
SelectString	Sets a string in *Strings* to be the current selection, based on matching a **const char far*** parameter.

Defining the corresponding window or dialog box

A window or dialog box that uses the transfer mechanism must construct its participating control objects in the exact order in which the corresponding transfer buffer members are defined. To enable transfer for a window or dialog box object, call *SetTransferBuffer* and pass a pointer to the transfer buffer.

Using transfer with a dialog box

Because dialog boxes get their definitions and the definitions of their controls from resources, you should construct control objects using the constructors that take resource IDs. For example:

```
struct TTransferBuffer
{
  char edit[30];
  TListBoxData listBox;
  TScrollBarData scrollBar;
}
    ⋮
TTransferDialog::TTransferDialog(TWindow* parent, int resId)
  : TDialog(parent, resId),
    TWindow(parent)
{
  new TEdit(this, ID_EDIT, 30);
  new TListBox(this, ID_LISTBOX);
  new TScrollBar(this, ID_SCROLLBAR);
```

```
        SetTransferBuffer(&TTransferBuffer);
    }
```

Control objects you construct like this automatically have transfer enabled (except for button, group box, and static control objects). To explicitly exclude a control from the transfer mechanism, call its *DisableTransfer* member function after constructing it.

Using transfer with a window

Controls constructed in a window have transfer disabled by default. To enable transfer, call the control object's *EnableTransfer* member function:

```
ListBox = new TListBox(this, ID_LISTBOX, 20, 20, 340, 100);
ListBox->EnableTransfer();
```

Transferring the data

In most cases, transferring data to or from a window is automatic, but you can also explicitly transfer data at any time.

Transferring data to a window

Transfer to a window happens automatically when you construct a window object. The constructor calls *SetupWindow* to create an interface element to represent the window object; it then calls *TransferData* to load any data from the transfer buffer. The window object's *SetupWindow* calls *SetupWindow* for each of its child windows as well, so each of the child windows has a chance to transfer its data. Because the parent window sets up its child windows in the order it constructed them, the data in the transfer buffer must appear in that same order.

Transferring data from a dialog box

When a modal dialog box receives a command message with a control ID of IDOK, it automatically transfers data from the controls into the transfer buffer. Usually this message indicates that the user chose OK to close the dialog box, so the dialog box automatically updates its transfer buffer. Then, if you execute the dialog box again, it transfers from the transfer buffer to the controls.

Transferring data from a window

You can explicitly transfer data in either direction at any time. For example, you might want to transfer data out of controls in a window or modeless dialog box. Or you might want to reset the state of the controls using the data in the transfer buffer in response to the user clicking a Reset or Revert button.

Use the *TransferData* member function in either case, passing the *tdSetData* enumeration to transfer from the transfer buffer to the controls or *tdGetData* to transfer from the controls to the transfer buffer. For example, you might want to call *TransferData* in the *CloseWindow* member function of a window object:

```
void
TMyWindow::CloseWindow()
{
  TransferData(tdGetData);
```

```
    TWindow::CloseWindow();
}
```

Supporting transfer for customized controls

You might want to modify the way a particular control transfers its data, or to include a new control you define in the transfer mechanism. In either case, all you need to do is to write a *Transfer* member function for your control object. See the following table to interpret the meaning of the transfer flag parameter.

Table 29.20   Transfer flag parameters

Transfer flag parameter	Description
tdGetData	Copy data from the control to the location specified by the supplied pointer. Return the number of bytes transferred.
tdSetData	Copy the data from the transfer buffer at the supplied pointer to the control. Return the number of bytes transferred.
tdSizeData	Return the number of bytes that would be transferred.

30

Gadget and gadget window objects

This chapter discusses the use of gadgets and gadget windows. In function, gadgets are similar to controls, in that they are used to gather input from or convey information to the user. But gadgets are implemented differently from controls. Unlike most other interface elements, gadgets are not windows: gadgets don't have window handles, they don't receive events and messages, and they aren't based on *TWindow*.

Instead, gadgets must be contained in a gadget window that controls the presentation of the gadget, all message processing, and so on. The gadget receives its commands and direction from the gadget window.

This chapter discusses the various kinds of gadgets implemented in ObjectWindows. It then describes the different kinds of gadget windows available for use with the gadgets.

Gadgets

This section discusses a number of gadgets. It begins with a discussion of *TGadget*, the base class for ObjectWindows gadgets. It then discusses the other gadget classes, *TSeparatorGadget*, *TBitmapGadget*, *TControlGadget*, *TTextGadget*, and *TButtonGadget*.

Class TGadget

All gadgets are based on the *TGadget* class. The *TGadget* class contains the basic functionality required by all gadgets, including controlling the gadget's borders and border style, setting the size of the gadget, enabling and disabling the gadget, and so on.

Constructing and destroying TGadget
Here is the *TGadget* constructor:

```
TGadget(int id = 0, TBorderStyle style = None);
```

where:

- *id* is an arbitrary value as the ID number for the gadget. You can use the ID to identify a particular gadget in a gadget window. Other uses for the gadget ID are discussed in the next section.

- *style* is an **enum** *TBorderStyle*. There are five possible values for *style*:
  - *None* makes the gadget with no border style; that is, it has no visible borders.
  - *Plain* makes the gadget borders visible as lines, much like the border of a window frame.
  - *Raised* makes the gadget look as if it is raised up from the gadget window.
  - *Recessed* makes the gadget look as if it is recessed into the gadget window.
  - *Embossed* makes the gadget border look as if it has an embossed ridge as a border.

The *TGadget* destructor is declared **virtual**. The only thing it does is to remove the gadget from its gadget window if that window is still valid.

Identifying a gadget

You can identify a gadget by using the *GetId* function to access its identifier. *GetId* takes no parameters and returns an **int** that is the gadget identifier. The identifier comes from the value passed in as the first parameter of the *TGadget* constructor.

There are a number of uses for the gadget identifier:

- You can use the identifier to identify a particular gadget. If you have a large number of gadgets in a gadget window, the easiest way to determine which gadget is which is to use the gadget identifier.

- You can set the identifier to the desired event identifier when the gadget is used to generate a command. For example, a button gadget used to open a file usually has the identifier CM_FILEOPEN.

- You can set the identifier to a string identifier if you want display a text string in a message bar or status bar when the gadget is pressed. For example, suppose you have a string identifier named IDS_MYSTRING that describes your gadget. You can set the gadget identifier to IDS_MYSTRING. Then, assuming your window has a message or status bar and you've turned menu tracking on, the string IDS_MYSTRING is displayed in the message or status bar whenever you press the gadget IDS_MYSTRING.

The last two techniques are often combined. Suppose you have a command identifier CM_FILEOPEN for the File Open menu command. You can also give the gadget the identifier CM_FILEOPEN. Then when you press the gadget, the gadget window posts the CM_FILEOPEN event. Then if you have a string with the resource identifier CM_FILEOPEN, that string is displayed in the message or status bar when you press the gadget. You can see an illustration of this technique in Step 10 of the ObjectWindows tutorial.

Modifying and accessing gadget appearance

You can modify and check the margin width, border width, and border style of a gadget using the following functions:

```
void SetBorders(TBorders& borders);
TBorders &GetBorders();
void SetMargins(TMargins& margins);
TMargins &GetMargins();
void SetBorderStyle(TBorderStyle style);
TBorderStyle GetBorderStyle();
```

The border is the outermost boundary of a gadget. The *TBorders* structure used with the *SetBorders* and *GetBorders* functions has four data members. These **unsigned** data members, *Left*, *Right*, *Top*, and *Bottom*, contain the width of the respective borders of the gadget.

The margin is the area between the border of the gadget and the inner rectangle of the gadget. The *TMargins* structure used with the *SetMargins* and *GetMargins* functions has four data members. These **int** data members, *Left*, *Right*, *Top*, and *Bottom*, contain the width of the respective margins of the gadget.

The *TBorderStyle* **enum** used with the *SetBorderStyle* and *GetBorderStyle* functions is the same one used with the *TGadget* constructor. The various border style effects are achieved by painting the sides of the gadget borders and margins differently for each style.

Bounding the gadget

The gadget's bounding rectangle is the entire area occupied by a gadget. It is contained in a *TRect* structure and is composed of the relative X and Y coordinates of the upper-left and lower-right corners of the gadget in the gadget window. The gadget window uses the bounding rectangle of the gadget to place the gadget. The gadget's bounding rectangle is also important in determining when the user has clicked the gadget.

To find and set the bounding rectangle of a gadget, use the following functions:

```
TRect &GetBounds();
virtual void SetBounds(TRect& rect);
```

Note that *SetBounds* is declared **virtual**. The default *SetBounds* updates only the bounding rectangle data. A derived class can override *SetBounds* to monitor changes and update the gadget's internal state.

Shrink wrapping a gadget

You can use the *SetShrinkWrap* function to specify whether you want the gadget window to "shrink wrap" a gadget. When shrink wrapping is on for an axis, the overall size required for the gadget is calculated automatically based on the border size, margin size, and inner rectangle. This saves you from having to calculate the bounds size of the gadget manually.

You can turn shrink wrapping on and off independently for the width and height of the gadget:

```
void SetShrinkWrap(bool shrinkWrapWidth, bool shrinkWrapHeight);
```

where:

- *shrinkWrapWidth* turns horizontal shrink wrapping on or off, depending on whether *true* or *false* is passed in.

- *shrinkWrapHeight* turns vertical shrink wrapping on or off, depending on whether *true* or *false* is passed in.

Setting gadget size

The gadget's size is the size of the bounding rectangle of the gadget. The size differs from the bounding rectangle in that it is independent of the position of the gadget. Thus, you can adjust the size of the gadget without changing the location of the gadget.

You can set the desired size of a gadget using the *SetSize* function:

```
void SetSize(TSize& size);
```

You can get use the *GetDesiredSize* function to get the size the gadget would like to be:

```
virtual void GetDesiredSize(TSize& size);
```

Even if you've set the desired size of the gadget with the *SetSize* function, you should still call the *GetDesiredSize* function to get the gadget's desired size. Gadget windows can change the desired size of a gadget during the layout process.

Matching gadget colors to system colors

To make your interface consistent with your application user's system, you should implement the *SysColorChange* function. The gadget window calls the *SysColorChange* function of each gadget contained in the window when the window receives a WM_SYSCOLORCHANGE message, which has this syntax:

```
virtual void SysColorChange();
```

The default version of *SysColorChange* does nothing. If you want your gadgets to follow changes in system colors, you should implement this function. You should make sure to delete and reallocate any resources that are dependent on system color settings.

TGadget public data members

There are two public data members in *TGadget*; both are **bool**s:

```
bool Clip;
bool WideAsPossible;
```

The value of *Clip* indicates whether a clipping rectangle should be applied before painting the gadget.

The value of *WideAsPossible* indicates whether the gadget should be expanded to fit the available room in the window. This is useful for such things as a text gadget in a message bar.

Enabling and disabling a gadget

You can enable and disable a gadget using the following functions:

```
virtual void SetEnabled(bool);
bool GetEnabled();
```

Changing the state of a gadget using the default *SetEnabled* function causes the gadget's bounding rectangle to be invalidated, but not erased. A derived class can override *SetEnabled* to modify this behavior.

If your gadget generates a command, you should implement the *CommandEnable* function:

```
virtual void CommandEnable();
```

The default version of *CommandEnable* does nothing. A derived class can override this function to provide command enabling. The gadget should send a WM_COMMAND_ENABLE message to the gadget window's parent with a command-enabler object representing the gadget.

For example, here's how the *CommandEnable* function might be implemented:

```
void
TMyGadget::CommandEnable()
{
  Window->Parent->HandleMessage(WM_COMMAND_ENABLE,
                          0,
                          (LPARAM) &TMyGadgetEnabler(*Window->Parent, this));
}
```

Deriving from TGadget

TGadget provides a number of **protected** access functions that you can use when deriving a gadget class from *TGadget*.

Initializing and cleaning up

TGadget provides a couple **virtual** functions that give a gadget a chance to initialize or clean up:

```
virtual void Inserted();
virtual void Removed();
```

Inserted is called after inserting a gadget into a gadget window. *Removed* is called before removing the gadget from its gadget window. The default versions of these function do nothing.

Painting the gadget

The *TGadget* class provides two different paint functions: *PaintBorder* and *Paint*.

The *PaintBorder* function paints the border of the gadget. This **virtual** function takes a single parameter, a *TDC &*, and returns **void**. *PaintBorder* implements the standard border styles. If you want to create a new border style, you need to override this function and provide the functionality for the new style. If you want to continue to provide the standard border styles, you should also call the *TGadget* version of this function. *PaintBorder* is called by the *Paint* function.

The *Paint* function is similar to the *TWindow* function *Paint*. This function takes a single parameter, a *TDC* **&**, and returns **void**. *Paint* is declared **virtual**. *TGadget*'s *PaintGadgets* function calls each gadget's *Paint* function when painting the gadget window. The default *Paint* function only calls the *PaintBorder* function. To paint the inner rectangle of the gadget's bounding rectangle, you should override this function to provide the necessary functionality.

If you're painting the gadget yourself in the *Paint* function, you often need to find the area inside the borders and margins of the gadget. This area is called the inner rectangle. You can find the inner rectangle using the *GetInnerRect* function:

```
void GetInnerRect(TRect& rect);
```

GetInnerRect places the coordinates of the inner rectangle into the *TRect* reference passed into it.

Invalidating and updating the gadget

Just like a window, a gadget can be invalidated. *TGadget* provides two functions to invalidate the gadget:

```
void Invalidate(bool erase = true);
void InvalidateRect(const TRect& rect, bool erase = true);
```

These functions are similar to the *TWindow* functions *InvalidateRect* and *Invalidate*. *InvalidateRect* looks and functions much like its Windows API version, except that it omits its HWND parameters. *Invalidate* invalidates the entire bounding rectangle of the gadget. *Invalidate* takes a single parameter, a **bool** indicating whether the invalid area should be erased when it's updated. By default, this parameter is *true*. So to erase the entire area of your gadget, you need only call *Invalidate*, either specifying *true* or nothing at all for its parameter.

A related function is the *Update* function, which attempts to force an immediate update of the gadget. It is similar to the Windows API *UpdateWindow* function.

```
void Update();
```

Mouse events in a gadget

You can track mouse events that happen inside and outside of a gadget. This happens through a number of "pseudo-event handlers" in the *TGadget* class. These functions look much like standard ObjectWindows event-handling functions, except that the names of the functions are not prefixed with *Ev*.

Gadgets don't have response tables like other ObjectWindows classes. This is because a gadget is not actually a window. All of a gadget's communication with the outside is handled through the gadget window. When a mouse event takes place in the gadget window, the window tries to determine which gadget is affected by the event. To find out if an event took place inside a particular gadget, you can call the *PtIn* function:

```
virtual bool PtIn(TPoint& point);
```

The default behavior for this function is to return *true* if *point* is within the gadget's bounding rectangle. You could override this function if you were designing an oddly shaped gadget.

When the mouse enters the bounding rectangle of a gadget, the gadget window calls the function *MouseEnter*. This function looks like this:

```
virtual void MouseEnter(uint modKeys, TPoint& point);
```

modKeys contains virtual key information identical to that passed-in in the standard ObjectWindows *EvMouseMove* function. This indicates whether various virtual keys are pressed. This parameter can be any combination of the following values: MK_CONTROL, MK_LBUTTON, MK_MBUTTON, MK_RBUTTON, or MK_SHIFT. See the *Object Windows Reference* for a full explanation of these flags. *point* tells the gadget where the mouse entered the gadget.

Once the gadget window calls the gadget's *MouseEnter* function to inform the gadget that the mouse has entered the gadget's area, the gadget captures mouse movements by calling the gadget window's *GadgetSetCapture* to guarantee that the gadget's *MouseLeave* function is called.

Once the mouse leaves the gadget bounds, the gadget window calls *MouseLeave*. This function looks like this:

```
virtual void MouseLeave(uint modKeys, TPoint& point);
```

There are also a couple of functions to detect left mouse button clicks, *LButtonDown* and *LButtonUp*. The default behavior for *LButtonDown* is to capture the mouse if the **bool** flag *TrackMouse* is set. The default behavior for *LButtonUp* is to release the mouse if the **bool** flag *TrackMouse* is set. By default *TrackMouse* is not set.

```
virtual void LButtonDown(uint modKeys, TPoint& point);
virtual void LButtonUp(uint modKeys, TPoint& point);
```

When the mouse is moved inside the bounding rectangle of a gadget while mouse movements are being captured by the gadget window, the window calls the gadget's *MouseMove* function. This function looks like this:

```
virtual void MouseMove(uint modKeys, TPoint& point);
```

Like with *MouseEnter*, *modKeys* contains virtual key information. *point* tells the gadget where the mouse stopped moving.

ObjectWindows gadget classes

ObjectWindows provides a number of classes derived from *TGadget*. These gadgets provide versatile and easy-to-use decorations and new ways to communicate with the user of your application. The gadget classes included in ObjectWindows are:

- *TSeparatorGadget*
- *TTextGadget*
- *TButtonGadget*
- *TControlGadget*
- *TBitmapGadget*

These gadgets are discussed in the following sections.

Class TSeparatorGadget

TSeparatorGadget is a very simple gadget. Its only function is to take up space in a gadget window. You can use it when laying other gadgets out in a window to provide a margin of space between gadgets that would otherwise be placed border-to-border in the window.

The *TSeparatorGadget* constructor looks like this:

```
TSeparatorGadget(int size = 6);
```

The separator disables itself and turns off shrink wrapping. The *size* parameter is used for both the width and the height of the gadget. This lets you use the separator gadget for both vertical and horizontal spacing.

Class TTextGadget

TTextGadget is used to display text information in a gadget window. You can specify the number of characters you want to be able to display in the gadget. You can also specify how the text should be aligned in the text gadget.

Constructing and destroying TTextGadget

Here is the constructor for *TTextGadget*:

```
TTextGadget(int id = 0,
            TBorderStyle style = Recessed,
            TAlign alignment = Left,
            uint numChars = 10,
            const char* text = 0);
```

where:

- *id* is the gadget identifier.

- *style* is the gadget border style.

- *align* specifies how text should be aligned in the gadget. There are three possible values for the **enum** *TAlign*: *Left*, *Center*, and *Right*.

- *numChars* specifies the number of characters to be displayed in the gadget. This parameter determines the width of the gadget. The gadget calculates the required gadget width by multiplying the number of characters by the maximum character width of the current font. The height of the gadget is based on the maximum character height of the current font, plus space for the margin and border.

- *text* is a default message to be displayed in the gadget.

~TTextGadget automatically deletes the storage for the gadget's text string.

Accessing the gadget text

You can get and set the text in the gadget using the *GetText* and *SetText* functions.

GetText takes no parameters and returns a **const char** *. You shouldn't attempt to modify the gadget text through the use of the returned pointer.

The *SetText* function takes a **const char** * and returns **void**. The gadget makes a copy of the text and stores it internally.

Class TBitmapGadget

TBitmapGadget is a simple gadget that can display an array of bitmap images, one at a time. You should store the bitmaps as an array. To do this, the bitmaps should be drawn side by side in a single bitmap resource. The bitmaps should each be the same width.

Constructing and destroying TBitmapGadget

Here is the constructor for *TBitmapGadget*:

```
TBitmapGadget(TResId bmpResId,
              int id,
              TBorderStyle style,
              int numImages,
              int startImage);
```

where:

- *bmResId* is the resource identifier for the bitmap resource.

- *id* is the gadget identifier.

- *style* is the gadget border style.

- *numImages* is the total number of images contained in the bitmap. The gadget figures the width of each single bitmap in the resource by dividing the width of the resource bitmap by *numImages*.

  For example, suppose you pass a bitmap resource to the *TBitmapGadget* constructor that is 400 pixels wide by 200 pixels high, and you specify *numImages* as 4. The constructor would divide the bitmap resource into four separate bitmaps, each one 100 pixels wide by 200 pixels high.

- *startImage* specifies which bitmap in the array should be initially displayed in the gadget.

~TBitmapGadget deletes the storage for the bitmap images.

Selecting a new image

You can change the image being displayed in the gadget with the *SelectImage* function:

```
int SelectImage(int imageNum, bool immediate);
```

The *imageNum* parameter is the array index of the image you want displayed in the gadget. Specifying *true* for *immediate* causes the gadget to update the display immediately. Otherwise, the area is invalidated and updated when the next WM_PAINT message is received.

Setting the system colors

TBitmapGadget implements the *SysColorChange* function so that the bitmaps track the system colors. It deletes the bitmap array, calls the *MapUIColors* function on the bitmap resource, then re-creates the array. For more information on the *MapUIColors* function, see page 237.

Class TButtonGadget

Button gadgets are the only type of gadget included in ObjectWindows that the user interacts with directly. Control gadgets, which are discussed in the next section, also provide a gadget that receives input from the user, but it does so through a control class. The gadget in that case only acts as an intermediary between the control and gadget window.

There are three normal button gadget states: up, down, and indeterminate. In addition the button can be highlighted when pressed in all three states.

There are two basic type of button gadgets, command gadgets and setting gadgets. Setting gadgets can be exclusive (like a radio button) or non-exclusive (like a check box). Commands can only be in the "up" state. Settings can be in all three states.

A button gadget is pressed when the left mouse button is pressed while the cursor position is inside the gadget's bounding rectangle. The gadget is highlighted when pressed.

Once the gadget has been pressed, it then captures the mouse's movements. When the mouse moves outside of the gadget's bounding rectangle without the left mouse button being released, highlighting is canceled but mouse movements are still captured by the gadget. The gadget is highlighted again when the mouse comes back into the gadget's bounding rectangle without the left mouse button being released.

When the left mouse button is released, mouse movements are no longer captured. If the cursor position is inside the bounding rectangle when the button is released, the gadget identifier is posted as a command message by the gadget window.

Constructing and destroying TButtonGadget

Here is the *TButtonGadget* constructor:

```
TButtonGadget(TResId bmpResId,
              int id,
              TType type = Command,
              bool enabled = false,
              TState state = Up,
              bool repeat = false);
```

where:

- *bmpResId* is the resource identifier for the bitmap to be displayed in the button. The size of the bitmap determines the size of the gadget, because shrink wrapping is turned on.

- *id* is the gadget identifier. This is also the command that is posted when the gadget is pressed.

- *type* specifies the type of the gadget. The *TType* **enum** has three possible values:

  - *Command* specifies that the gadget is a command.

- *Exclusive* specifies that the gadget is an exclusive setting button. Exclusive button gadgets that are adjacent to each other work together. You can set up exclusive groups by inserting other gadgets, such as separator gadgets or text gadgets, on either side of the group.

- *NonExclusive* specifies that the gadget is a nonexclusive setting button.

- *enabled* specifies whether the button gadget is enabled or not when it is first created. If the corresponding command is enabled when the gadget is created, the button is automatically enabled.

- *state* is the default state of the button gadget. The **enum** *TState* can have three values: *Up*, *Down*, or *Indeterminate*.

- *repeat* indicates whether the button repeats when held down. If *repeat* is *true*, the button repeats when it is clicked and held.

The *~TButtonGadget* function deletes the bitmap resources and, if the resource information is contained in a string, deletes the storage for the string.

Accessing button gadget information

There are a number of functions you can use to access a button gadget. These functions let you set the state of the gadget to any valid *TState* value, get the state of the button gadget, and get the button gadget type, respectively.

- You can set the button gadget's state with the *SetButtonState* function:

      void SetButtonState(TState);

- You can find the button gadget's current state using the *GetButtonState* function:

      TState GetButtonState();

- You can find out what type of button a gadget is using the *GetButtonType* function:

      TType GetButtonType();

Setting button gadget style

You can modify the appearance of a button gadget using the following functions:

- You can turn corner notching on and off using the *SetNotchCorners* function:

      void SetNotchCorners(bool notchCorners=true);

- You can turn antialiasing of the button bevels on and off using the *SetAntialiasEdges* function:

      void SetAntialiasEdges(bool anti=true);

- You can change the style of the button shadow using the *SetShadowStyle* function. There are two options for the shadow style, using the **enum** *TShadowStyle*, *SingleShadow* and *DoubleShadow*:

      void SetShadowStyle(TShadowStyle style=DoubleShadow);

Command enabling

TButtonGadget overrides the *TGadget* function *CommandEnable*. It is implemented to initiate a WM_COMMAND_ENABLE message for the gadget.

Here is the signature of the *TButtonGadget::CommandEnable* function:

```
void CommandEnable();
```

Setting the system colors

TButtonGadget implements the *SysColorChange* function so that the gadget's bitmaps track the system colors. It rebuilds the gadget using the system colors. If the system colors have changed, these changes are reflected in the new button gadget. This is *not* set up to automatically track the system colors; that is, it is not necessarily call in response to a WM_SYSCOLORCHANGE event.

Class TControlGadget

The *TControlGadget* is a fairly simple class that serves as an interface between a regular Windows control (such as a button, edit box, list box, and so on) and a gadget window. This lets you use a standard Windows control in a gadget window, like a control bar, status bar, and so on.

Constructing and destroying TControlGadget

Here's the constructor for *TControlGadget*:

```
TControlGadget(TWindow& control, TBorderStyle style = None);
```

where:

- *control* is a reference to an ObjectWindows window object. This object should be a valid constructed control object.

- *style* is the gadget border style.

The *~TControlGadget* function destroys the control interface element, then deletes the storage for the control object.

Gadget windows

Gadget windows are based on the class *TGadgetWindow*, which is derived from *TWindow*. Gadget windows are designed to hold a number of gadgets, lay them out, and display them in another window.

Gadget window provide a great deal of the functionality of the gadgets they contain. Because gadgets are not actually windows, they can't post or receive events, or directly interact with windows, or call Windows function for themselves. Anything that a gadget needs to be done must be done through the gadget window.

A gadget has little or no control over where it is laid out in the gadget window. The gadget window is responsible for placing and laying out all the gadgets it contains. Gadgets are generally laid in a line, either vertically or horizontally.

Gadget windows generally do not stand on their own, but instead are usually contained in another window. The most common parent window for a gadget window is a decorated frame window, such as *TDecoratedFrame* or *TDecoratedMDIFrame*, although the class *TToolBox* usually uses a *TFloatingFrame*.

Constructing and destroying TGadgetWindow

Here is the constructor for *TGadgetWindow*:

```
TGadgetWindow(TWindow* parent = 0,
            TTileDirection direction = Horizontal,
            TFont* font = new TGadgetWindowFont,
            TModule* module = 0);
```

where:

- *parent* is a pointer to the parent window object.

- *direction* is an **enum** *TTileDirection*. There are two possible values for *direction*: *Horizontal* or *Vertical*.

- *font* is a pointer to a *TFont* object. This contains the font for the gadget window. By default, this is set to *TGadgetWindowFont*, which is a variable-width sans-serif font, usually Helvetica.

- *module* is passed as the *TModule* parameter for the *TWindow* base constructor. This parameter defaults to 0.

The ~*TGadgetWindow* function deletes each of the gadgets contained in the gadget window. It then deletes the font object.

Creating a gadget window

TGadgetWindow overrides the default *TWindow* member function *Create*. The *TGadgetWindow* version of this function chooses the initial size based on a number of criteria:

- Whether shrink wrapping was requested by any of the gadgets in the window
- The size of the gadgets contained in the window
- The direction of tiling in the gadget window
- Whether the gadget window has a border, and the size of that border

The *Create* function determines the proper size of the window based on these factors, sets the window size attributes, then calls the base *TWindow::Create* to actually create the window interface element.

Inserting a gadget into a gadget window

For a gadget window to be useful, it needs to contain some gadgets. To place a gadget into the gadget window, use the *Insert* function:

```
virtual void Insert(TGadget& gadget,
                TPlacement placement = After,
                TGadget* sibling = 0);
```

where:

- *gadget* is a reference to the gadget to be inserted into the gadget window.

- *placement* indicates where the gadget should be inserted. The **enum** *TPlacement* can have two values, *Before* and *After*. If a sibling gadget is specified by the *sibling* parameter, the gadget is inserted *Before* or *After* the sibling, depending on the value of *placement*. If *sibling* is 0, the gadget is placed at the beginning of the gadgets in the window if *placement* is *Before*, and at the end of the gadgets if *placement* is *After*.

- *sibling* is a pointer to a sibling gadget.

If the gadget window has already been created, you need to call *LayoutSession* after calling *Insert*. Any gadget you insert will not appear in the window until the window has been laid out.

Removing a gadget from a gadget window

To remove a gadget from your gadget window, use the *Remove* function:

```
virtual TGadget* Remove(TGadget& gadget);
```

where *gadget* is a reference to the gadget you want to remove from the window.

This function removes *gadget* from the gadget window. The gadget is returned as a *TGadget* *. The gadget object is not deleted. *Remove* returns 0 if the gadget is not in the window.

As with the *Insert* function, if the gadget window has already been created, you need to call *LayoutSession* after calling *Remove*. Any gadget you remove will not disappear from the window until the window has been laid out.

Setting window margins and layout direction

You can change the margins and the layout direction either before the window is created or afterwards. To do this, use the *SetMargins* and *SetDirection* functions:

```
void SetMargins(TMargins& margins);
virtual void SetDirection(TTileDirection direction);
```

Both of these functions set the appropriate data members, then call the function *LayoutSession*, which is described in the next section.

You can find out in which direction the gadgets are laid out by calling the *GetDirection* function:

```
TTileDirection GetDirection() const;
```

Laying out the gadgets

To lay out a gadget window, call the *LayoutSession* function.

```
virtual void LayoutSession();
```

The default behavior of the *LayoutSession* function is to check to see if the window interface element is already created. If not, the function returns without taking any further action; the window is laid out automatically when the window element is created. But if the window element has already been created, *LayoutSession* tiles the gadgets and then invalidates the modified area of the gadget window.

A layout session is typically initiated by a change in margins, inserting or removing gadgets, or a gadget or gadget window changing size.

The actual work of tiling the gadgets is left to the function *TileGadgets*:

```
virtual TRect TileGadgets();
```

TileGadgets determines the space needed for each gadget and lays each gadget out in turn. It returns a *TRect* containing the area of the gadget window that was modified by laying out the gadgets.

TileGadgets calls the function *PositionGadget*. This lets derived classes adjust the spacing between gadgets to help in implementing a custom layout scheme.

```
virtual void PositionGadget(TGadget* previous, TGadget* next, TPoint& point);
```

This function takes the gadgets pointed to by *previous* and *next*, figures the required spacing between the gadgets, then fills in *point*. If you're tiling horizontally, then the relevant measure is contained in *point.x*. If you're tiling vertically, then the relevant measure is contained in *point.y*.

Notifying the window when a gadget changes size

When a gadget changes size, it should call the *GadgetChangedSize* function for its gadget window. Here's the signature for this function:

```
void GadgetChangedSize(TGadget& gadget);
```

gadget is a reference to the gadget that changed size. The default version of this function simply initiates a layout session.

Shrink wrapping a gadget window

You can specify whether you want the gadget window to "shrink wrap" a gadget using the *SetShrinkWrap* function. Shrink wrapping for a gadget window has a slightly different meaning than for a gadget. When a gadget window is shrink wrapped for an axis, the axis' size is calculated automatically based on the desired sizes of the gadgets laid out on that axis.

You can turn shrink wrapping on and off independently for the width and height of the gadget window:

```
void SetShrinkWrap(bool shrinkWrapWidth, bool shrinkWrapHeight);
```

where:

- *shrinkWrapWidth* turns horizontal shrink wrapping on or off, depending on whether *true* or *false* is passed in.

- *shrinkWrapHeight* turns vertical shrink wrapping on or off, depending on whether *true* or *false* is passed in.

Accessing window font

You can find out the current font and font size using the *GetFont* and *GetFontHeight* functions:

```
TFont& GetFont();
uint GetFontHeight() const;
```

Capturing the mouse for a gadget

A gadget is always notified when the left mouse button is pressed down within its bounding rectangle. After the button is pressed, you need to capture the mouse if you want to send notification of mouse movements. You can do this using the *GadgetSetCapture* and *GadgetReleaseCapture* functions:

```
bool GadgetSetCapture(TGadget& gadget);
void GadgetReleaseCapture(TGadget& gadget);
```

The *gadget* parameter for both functions indicates for which gadget the window should set or release the capture. The **bool** returned by *GadgetSetCapture* indicates whether the capture was successful.

These functions are usually called by a gadget in the window through the gadget's *Window* pointer to its gadget window.

Setting the hint mode

The hint mode of a gadget dictates when hints about the gadget are displayed by the gadget window's parent. You can set the hint mode for a gadget using the *SetHintMode* function:

```
void SetHintMode(THintMode hintMode);
```

The **enum** *THintMode* has three possible values:

Table 30.1   Hint mode flags

hintMode	Hint displayed
NoHints	Hints are not displayed.
PressHints	Hints are displayed when the gadget is pressed until the button is released.
EnterHints	Hints are displayed when the mouse passes over the gadget; that is, when the mouse enters the gadget.

You can find the current hint mode using the *GetHintMode* function:

```
THintMode GetHintMode();
```

Another function, the *SetHintCommand* function, determines when a hint is displayed:

```
void SetHintCommand(int id);
```

This function is usually called by a gadget through the gadget's *Window* pointer to its gadget window, but the gadget window could also call it. Essentially, *SetHintCommand* simulates a menu choice, making pressing the gadget the equivalent of selecting a menu choice.

For *SetHintCommand* to work properly with the standard ObjectWindows classes, a number of things must be in place:

- The decorated frame window parent of the gadget window must have a message or status bar.

- Hints must be on in the frame window.

- There must be a string resource with the same identifier as the gadget; that is, if the gadget identifier is CM_MYGADGET, you must also have a string resource defined as CM_MYGADGET.

Idle action processing

Gadget windows have default idle action processing. The *IdleAction* function attempts to enable each gadget contained in the window by calling each gadget's *CommandEnable* function. The function then returns *false*.

```
bool IdleAction(long idleCount);
```

Searching through the gadgets

Use one of the following functions to search through the gadgets contained in a gadget window:

```
TGadget* FirstGadget() const;
TGadget* NextGadget(TGadget& gadget) const;
TGadget* GadgetFromPoint(TPoint& point) const;
TGadget* GadgetWithId(int id) const;
```

- *FirstGadget* returns a pointer to the first gadget in the window's gadget list.

- *NextGadget* returns a pointer to the next gadget in the window's gadget list. If the current gadget is the last gadget in the window, *NextGadget* returns 0.

- *GadgetFromPoint* returns a pointer to the gadget that the point *point* is in. If *point* is not in a gadget, *GadgetFromPoint* returns 0.

- *GadgetWithId* returns a pointer to the gadget with the gadget identifier *id*. If no gadget in the window has that gadget identifier, *GadgetWithId* returns 0.

Deriving from TGadgetWindow

You can derive from *TGadgetWindow* to make your own specialized gadget window. *TGadgetWindow* provides a number of **protected** access functions that you can use when deriving a gadget class from *TGadgetWindow*.

Painting a gadget window

Just as with regular windows, *TGadgetWindow* implements the *Paint* function:

```
void Paint(TDC& dc, bool erase, TRect& rect);
```

This implementation of the *Paint* function selects the window's font into the device context and calls the function *PaintGadgets*:

```
virtual void PaintGadgets(TDC& dc, bool erase, TRect& rect);
```

PaintGadgets iterates through the gadgets in the window and asks each one to draw itself. Override *PaintGadgets* to implement a custom look for your window, such as separator lines, a raised look, and so on.

Size and inner rectangle

Use the *GetDesiredSize* and *GetInnerRect* functions to find the overall desired size (that is, the size needed to accommodate the borders, margins, and the widest or highest gadget) and the size and location of the window's inner rectangle.

```
virtual void GetDesiredSize(TSize& size);
```

If shrink wrapping was requested for the window, *GetDesiredSize* calculates the size the window needs to be to accommodate the borders, margins, and the widest or highest gadget. If shrink wrapping was not requested, *GetDesiredSize* uses the current width and height. The results are then placed into *size*.

```
virtual void GetInnerRect(TRect& rect);
```

GetInnerRect calculates the area inside the borders and margins of the window. The results are then placed into *rect*.

You can override *GetDesiredSize* and *GetInnerRect* to leave extra room for a custom look for your window. If you override either one of these functions, you probably also need to override the other.

Layout units

You can use three different units of measurement in a gadget window:

- Pixels, which are based on a single screen pixel
- Layout units, which are logical units defined by dividing the window font "em" into eight vertical and eight horizontal segments.
- Border units are based on the thickness of a window frame. This is usually equivalent to one pixel, but it could be greater at higher screen resolutions.

It is usually better to use layout units; because they are based on the font size, you don't have to worry about scaling your measures when you change window size or system metrics.

If you need to convert layout units to pixels, use the *LayoutUnitsToPixels* function:

```
int LayoutUnitsToPixels(int units);
```

where *units* is the layout unit measure you want to convert to pixels. *LayoutUnitsToPixels* returns the pixel equivalent of *units*.

You can also convert a *TMargins* object to actual pixel measurements using the *GetMargins* function:

```
void GetMargins(TMargins& margins,
                int& left,
                int& right,
                int& top,
                int& bottom);
```

where:

- *margins* is the object containing the measurements you want to convert. The measurements contained in *margins* can be in pixels, layout units, or border units.

- *left*, *right*, *top*, and *bottom* are the results of the conversion are placed.

Message response functions

TGadgetWindow catches the following events:

- WM_CTLCOLOR
- WM_LBUTTONDOWN
- WM_LBUTTONUP
- WM_MOUSEMOVE
- WM_SIZE
- WM_SYSCOLORCHANGE

It also implements the corresponding event-handling functions.

ObjectWindows gadget window classes

ObjectWindows provides a number of classes derived from *TGadgetWindow*. These windows provide a number of ways to display and lay out gadgets. The gadget window classes included in ObjectWindows are:

- *TControlBar*
- *TMessageBar*
- *TStatusBar*
- *TToolBox*

These classes are discussed in the following sections.

Class TControlBar

The class *TControlBar* implements a control bar similar to the "tool bar" or "control bar" found along the top of the window of many popular applications. You can place any type of gadget in a control bar.

Here's the constructor for *TControlBar*:

```
TControlBar(TWindow* parent = 0,
            TTileDirection direction = Horizontal,
            TFont* font = new TGadgetWindowFont,
            TModule* module = 0);
```

where:

- *parent* is a pointer to the control bar's parent window.

- *direction* is an **enum** *TTileDirection*. There are two possible values for *direction*: *Horizontal* or *Vertical*.

- *font* is a pointer to a *TFont* object. This contains the font for the gadget window. By default, this is set to *TGadgetWindowFont*, which is a variable-width sans-serif font, usually Helvetica.

- *module* is passed as the *TModule* parameter for the *TWindow* base constructor. This parameter defaults to 0.

Class TMessageBar

The *TMessageBar* class implements a message bar with no border and one text gadget as wide as the window. It positions itself horizontally across the bottom of its parent window.

Constructing and destroying TMessageBar

Here's the constructor for *TMessageBar*:

```
TMessageBar(TWindow* parent = 0,
            TFont* font = new TGadgetWindowFont,
            TModule* module = 0);
```

where:

- *parent* is a pointer to the control bar's parent window.

- *font* is a pointer to a *TFont* object. This contains the font for the gadget window. By default, this is set to *TGadgetWindowFont*, which is a variable-width sans-serif font, usually Helvetica.

- *module* is passed as the *TModule* parameter for the *TWindow* base constructor. This parameter defaults to 0.

The *~TMessageBar* function deletes the object's text storage.

Setting message bar text

Use the *SetText* function to set the text for the message bar text gadget:

```
void SetText(const char* text);
```

This function causes the string *text* to be displayed in the message bar.

Setting the hint text

Use the *SetHintText* function to set the menu or command item hint text to be displayed in a raised field over the message bar:

```
virtual void SetHintText(const char* text);
```

If you pass *text* as 0, the hint text is cleared.

Class TStatusBar

TStatusBar is similar to *TMessageBar*. The difference is that status bars have more options than a plain message bar, such as multiple text gadgets and reserved space for keyboard mode indicators such as Caps Lock, Insert or Overwrite, and so on.

Constructing and destroying TStatusBar

Here's the constructor for *TStatusBar*:

```
TStatusBar(TWindow* parent = 0,
          TGadget::TBorderStyle borderStyle = TGadget::Recessed,
          uint modeIndicators = 0,
          TFont* font = new TGadgetWindowFont,
          TModule* module = 0);
```

where:

- *parent* is a pointer to the parent window object.

- *style* is an **enum** *TBorderStyle*.

- *modeIndicators* indicates which keyboard modes can be displayed in the status bar. A defined **enum** type called *TModeIndicator* provides the following valid values for this parameter:
  - ExtendSelection
  - CapsLock
  - NumLock
  - ScrollLock
  - Overtype
  - RecordingMacro

  These values can be ORed together to indicate multiple keyboard mode indicators.

- *font* is a pointer to a *TFont* object that contains the font for the gadget window.

- *module* is passed as the *TModule* parameter for the *TWindow* base constructor. This parameter defaults to 0.

Inserting gadgets into a status bar

TStatusBar overrides the default *Insert* function. By default, the *TStatusBar* version adds the new gadget after the existing text gadgets but before the mode indicator gadgets.

You can place a gadget next to an existing gadget in the status bar by passing a pointer to the existing gadget in the *Insert* function as the new gadget's sibling. You can't insert a gadget beyond the mode indicators, however.

Displaying mode indicators

For a particular mode indicator to appear on the status bar, you must have specified the mode when the status bar was constructed. But once the mode indicator is on the status bar, it is up to you to make any changes in the indicator. *TStatusBar* provides a number of functions to modify the mode indicators.

You can change the status of a mode indicator to any valid arbitrary state with the *SetModeIndicator* function:

```
void SetModeIndicator(TModeIndicator indicator, bool state);
```

where:

- *indicator* is the mode indicator you want to set. This can be any value from the **enum** *TModeIndicator* used in the constructor.

- *state* is the state to which you want to set the mode indicator.

You can also toggle a mode indicator with the *ToggleModeIndicator* function:

```
void ToggleModeIndicator(TModeIndicator indicator);
```

where *indicator* is the mode indicator you want to toggle. This can be any value from the **enum** *TModeIndicator* used in the constructor.

Spacing status bar gadgets

You can vary the spacing between mode indicator gadgets on the status bar using the *SetSpacing* function:

```
void SetSpacing(TSpacing& spacing);
```

where *spacing* is a reference to a *TSpacing* object. *TSpacing* is a **struct** defined in the *TStatusBar* class. It has two data members, a *TMargins::TUnits* member named *Units* and an **int** named *Value*. The *TSpacing* constructor sets *Units* to *TMargins::LayoutUnits* and *Value* to 0.

The *TSpacing* **struct** lets you specify a unit of measurement and a number of units in a single object. When you pass this object into the *SetSpacing* command, the spacing between mode indicator gadgets is set to *Value Units*. You need to lay out the status bar before any changes take effect.

Class TToolBox

TToolBox differs from the other ObjectWindows gadget window classes discussed so far in that it doesn't arrange its gadgets in a single line. Instead, it arranges them in a matrix. The columns of the matrix are all the same width (as wide as the widest gadget) and the rows of the matrix are all the same height (as high as the highest gadget). The gadgets are arranged so that the borders overlap and are hidden under the tool box's border.

TToolBox can be created as a client window in a *TFloatingFrame* to produce a palette-type tool box. For an example of this, see the PAINT example in the directory EXAMPLES\ OWL\OWLAPPS\PAINT.

Constructing and destroying TToolBox

Here's the constructor for *TToolBox*:

```
TToolBox(TWindow* parent,
         int numColumns = 2,
         int numRows = AS_MANY_AS_NEEDED,
```

```
TTileDirection direction = Horizontal,
TModule* module = 0);
```

where:

- *parent* is a pointer to the parent window object.

- *numColumns* is the number of columns in the tool box.

- *numRows* is the number of rows in the tool box.

- *direction* is an **enum** *TTileDirection*. There are two possible values for *direction*: *Horizontal* or *Vertical*. If *direction* is *Horizontal*, the gadgets are tiled starting at the upper left corner and moving from left to right, going down one row as each row is filled. If *direction* is *Vertical*, the gadgets are tiled starting at the upper left corner and moving down, going right one column as each column is filled.

- *module* is passed as the *TModule* parameter for the *TWindow* base constructor. This parameter defaults to 0.

You can specify the constant AS_MANY_AS_NEEDED for either *numColumns* or *numRows*, but not both. When you specify AS_MANY_AS_NEEDED for either parameter, the toolbox figures out how many divisions are needed based on the opposite dimension. For example, if you have 20 gadgets and you requested 4 columns, you would get 5 rows.

Changing tool box dimensions

You can switch the dimensions of your tool box using the *SetDirection* function:

```
virtual void SetDirection(TTileDirection direction);
```

where *direction* is an **enum** *TTileDirection*. There are two possible values for *direction*: *Horizontal* or *Vertical*.

If *direction* is not equal to the current direction for the tool box, the tool box switches its rows and columns count. For example, suppose you have a tool box that has three columns and five rows, and is laid out vertically. If you call *SetDirection* and set *direction* to *Horizontal*, the tool box switches rows and columns, giving it five columns and three rows.

31

Printer objects

This chapter describes ObjectWindows classes that help you complete the following printing tasks:

- Creating a printer object
- Creating a printout object
- Printing window contents
- Printing a document
- Choosing and configuring a printer

Two ObjectWindows classes make these tasks easier:

- *TPrinter* encapsulates printer behavior and access to the printer drivers. It brings up a dialog box that lets the user select the desired printer and set the current settings for printing.

- *TPrintout* encapsulates the actual printout. Its relationship to the printer is similar to *TWindow*'s relationship to the screen. Drawing on the screen happens in the *Paint* member function of the *TWindow* object, whereas writing to the printer happens in the *PrintPage* member function of the *TPrintout* object. To print something on the printer, the application passes an instance of *TPrintout* to an instance of *TPrinter*'s *Print* member function.

Creating a printer object

The easiest way to create a printer object is to declare a *TPrinter** within your window object that other objects in the program can use for their printing needs.

```
class MyWindow: public TFrameWindow
{
    ⋮
  protected:
    TPrinter* Printer;
    ⋮
};
```

To make the printer available, make *Printer* point to an instance of *TPrinter*. This can be done in the constructor:

```
MyWindow::MyWindow(TWindow* parent, char *title)
{
    ⋮
  Printer = new TPrinter;
}
```

You should also eliminate the printer object in the destructor:

```
MyWindow::~MyWindow()
{
    ⋮
  delete Printer;
}
```

Here's how it's done in the PRINTING.CPP example from directory OWLAPI\
PRINTING:

```
class TRulerWin : public TFrameWindow
{
    ⋮
  protected:
     TPrinter* Printer;
};

TRulerWin::TRulerWin(TWindow* parent, const char* title, TModule* module)
   : TFrameWindow(parent, title, 0, false, module), TWindow(parent, title, module)
{
    ⋮
  Printer = new TPrinter;
}
```

For most applications, this is sufficient. The application's main window initializes a printer object that uses the default printer specified in WIN.INI. In some cases, however, you might have applications that use different printers from different windows simultaneously. In that case, construct a printer object in the constructors of each of the appropriate windows, then change the printer device for one or more of the printers. If the program uses different printers but not at the same time, it's probably best to use the same printer object and select different printers as needed.

Although you might be tempted to override the *TPrinter* constructor to use a printer other than the system default, the recommended procedure is to always use the default constructor, then change the device associated with the object (see page 387).

Creating a printout object

Creating a printout object is similar to writing a *Paint* member function for a window object: you use Windows' graphics functions to generate the image you want on a device context. The window object's display context manages interactions with the screen device; the printout object's device context insulates you from the printer device in much the same way. Windows graphics functions are explained in Chapter 32.

To create a printout object,

1 Derive a new object type from *TPrintout* that overrides the *PrintPage* member function. In very simple cases, that's all you need to do. See the *ObjectWindows Reference Guide* for a description of the *TPrintout* class.

2 If the document has more than one page, you must also override the *HasPage* member function. It must return non-zero while there is another page to be printed. The current page number is passed as a parameter to *PrintPage*.

The printout object has fields that hold the size of the page and a device context that is already initialized to render to the printer. The printer object sets those values by calling the printout object's *SetPrintParams* member function. You should use the printout object's device context in any calls to Windows graphics functions.

Here is the class *TWindowPrintout*, derived from *TPrintout*, from the example program PRINTING.CPP:

```
class TWindowPrintout : public TPrintout
{
  public:
    TWindowPrintout(const char* title, TWindow* window);

    void GetDialogInfo(int& minPage, int& maxPage,
                       int& selFromPage, int& selToPage);
    void PrintPage(int page, TRect& rect, unsigned flags);
    void SetBanding(bool b) {Banding = b;}
    bool HasPage(int pageNumber) {return pageNumber == 1;}

  protected:
    TWindow* Window;
    bool Scale;
};
```

GetDialogInfo retrieves page-range information from a dialog box if page selection is possible. Since there is only one page, *GetDialogInfo* for *TWindowPrintout* looks like this:

```
void
TWindowPrintout::GetDialogInfo(int& minPage, int& maxPage,
                               int& selFromPage, int& selToPage)
{
  minPage = 0;
  maxPage = 0;
  selFromPage = selToPage = 0;
}
```

PrintPage must be overridden to print the contents of each page, band (if banding is enabled), or window. *PrintPage* for *TWindowPrintout* looks like this:

```
void
TWindowPrintout::PrintPage(int, TRect& rect, unsigned)
{
  // Conditionally scale the DC to the window so the printout
  // will resemble the window
  int prevMode;
  TSize oldVExt, oldWExt;
  if (Scale) {
    prevMode = DC->SetMapMode(MM_ISOTROPIC);
    TRect windowSize = Window->GetClientRect();
    DC->SetViewportExt(PageSize, &oldVExt);
    DC->SetWindowExt(windowSize.Size(), &oldWExt);
    DC->IntersectClipRect(windowSize);
    DC->DPtoLP(rect, 2);
  }

  // Call the window to paint itself
  Window->Paint(*DC, false, rect);

  // Restore changes made to the DC
  if (Scale) {
    DC->SetWindowExt(oldWExt);
    DC->SetViewportExt(oldVExt);
    DC->SetMapMode(prevMode);
  }
}
```

SetBanding is called with banding enabled:

```
printout.SetBanding(true);
```

HasPage is called after every page is printed, and by default returns *false*, which means only one page will be printed. This function must be overridden to return *true* while pages remain in multipage documents.

Printing window contents

The simplest kind of printout to generate is a copy of a window, because windows don't have multiple pages, and window objects already know how to draw themselves on a device context.

To create a window printout object, construct a window printout object and pass it a title string and a pointer to the window you want printed:

```
TWindowPrintout printout("Ruler Test", this);
```

Often, you'll want a window to create a printout of itself in response to a menu command. Here is the message response member function that responds to the print command in PRINTING.CPP:

```
void
TRulerWin::CmFilePrint()        // Execute File:Print command
{
  if (Printer) {
    TWindowPrintout printout("Ruler Test", this);
    printout.SetBanding(true);
    Printer->Print(this, printout, true);
  }
}
```

This member function calls the printer object's *Print* member function, which passes a pointer to the parent window and a pointer to the printout object, and specifies whether or not a printer dialog box should be displayed.

TWindowPrintout prints itself by calling your window object's *Paint* member function (within *TWindowPrintout::PrintPage*), but with a printer device context instead of a display context.

Printing a document

Windows sees a printout as a series of pages, so your printout object must turn a document into a series of page images for Windows to print. Just as you use window objects to paint images for Windows to display on the screen, you use printout objects to paint images on the printer.

Your printout object needs to be able to do these things:

- Set print parameters
- Calculate the total number of pages
- Draw each page on a device context
- Indicate if there are more pages

Setting print parameters

To enable the document to paginate itself, the printer object (derived from class *TPrinter*) calls two of the printout object's member functions: *SetPrintParams* and then *GetDialogInfo*.

The *SetPrintParams* function initializes page-size and device-context variables in the printout object. It can also calculate any information needed to produce an efficient printout of individual pages. For example, *SetPrintParams* can calculate how many lines of text in the selected font can fit within the print area (using Windows API *GetTextMetrics*). If you override *SetPrintParams*, be sure to call the inherited member function, which sets the printout object's page-size and device-context defaults.

Counting pages

After calling *SetPrintParams*, the printer object calls *GetDialogInfo*, which retrieves user page-range information from the printer dialog box. It can also be used to calculate the total number of pages based on page-size information calculated by *SetPrintParams*.

Printing each page

After the printer object has given the document a chance to paginate itself, it calls the printout object's *PrintPage* member function for each page to be printed. The process of printing out just the part of the document that belongs on the given page is similar to deciding which portion gets drawn on a scrolling window.

When you write *PrintPage* member functions, keep these two issues in mind:

- *Device independence*. Make sure your code doesn't make assumptions about scale, aspect ratio, or colors. Those properties can vary between different video and printing devices, so you should remove any device dependencies from your code.

- *Device capabilities*. Although most video devices support all GDI operations, some printers do not. For example, many print devices, such as plotters, do not accept bitmaps at all. Others support only certain operations. When performing complex output tasks, your code should call the Windows API function *GetDeviceCaps*, which returns important information about the capabilities of a given output device.

Indicating further pages

Printout objects have one last duty: to indicate to the printer object whether there are printable pages beyond a given page. The *HasPage* member function takes a page number as a parameter and returns a Boolean value indicating whether further pages exist. By default, *HasPage* returns *true* for the first page only. To print multiple pages, your printout object needs to override *HasPage* to return *true* if the document has more pages to print and *false* if the parameter passed is the last page.

Be sure that *HasPage* returns *false* at some point. If *HasPage* always returns *true*, printing goes into an endless loop.

Other printout considerations

Printout objects have several other member functions you can override as needed. *BeginPrinting* and *EndPrinting* are called before and after any documents are printed, respectively. If you need special setup code, you can put it in *BeginPrinting* and undo it in *EndPrinting*.

Printing of pages takes place sequentially. That is, the printer calls *PrintPage* for each page in sequence. Before the first call to *PrintPage*, however, the printer object calls *BeginDocument*, passing the numbers of the first and last pages it prints. If your document needs to prepare to begin printing at a page other than the first, you should override *BeginDocument*. The corresponding member function, *EndDocument*, is called after the last page prints.

If multiple copies are printed, the multiple *BeginDocument*/*EndDocument* pairs can be called between *BeginPrinting* and *EndPrinting*.

Choosing a different printer

You can associate the printer objects in your applications with any printer device installed in Windows. By default, *TPrinter* uses the Windows default printer, as specified in the [devices] section of the WIN.INI file.

There are two ways to specify an alternate printer: directly (in code) and through a user dialog box.

By far the most common way to assign a different printer is to bring up a dialog box that lets you choose from a list of installed printer devices. *TPrinter* does this automatically when you call its *Setup* member function. *Setup* displays a dialog box based on *TPrinterDialog*.

One of the buttons in the printer dialog box lets the user change the printer's configuration. The Setup button brings up a configuration dialog box defined in the printer's device driver. Your application has no control over the appearance or function of the driver's configuration dialog box.

In some cases, you might want to assign a specific printer device to your printer object, without user input. *TPrinter* has a *SetPrinter* member function that does just that. *SetPrinter* takes three strings as parameters: a device name, a driver name, and a port name.

Graphics objects

This chapter discusses the ObjectWindows encapsulation of the Windows GDI. ObjectWindows makes it easier to use GDI graphics objects and functions because it simplifies how you create and manipulate GDI objects. From simple objects such as pens and brushes to more complex objects such as fonts and bitmaps, the GDI encapsulation of the ObjectWindows library provides a simple, consistent model for graphical programming in Windows.

GDI class organization

There are a number of ObjectWindows classes used to encapsulate GDI functionality. Most are derived from the *TGdiObject* class. *TGdiObject* provides the common functionality for all ObjectWindows GDI classes.

TGdiObject is the abstract base class for ObjectWindows GDI objects. It provides a base destructor, an HGDIOBJ conversion operator, and the base *GetObject* function. It also provides orphan control for true GDI objects (that is, objects derived from *TGdiObject*; other GDI objects, such as *TRegion*, *TIcon*, and *TDib*, which are derived from *TGdiBase*, are known as *pseudo-GDI objects*).

The other classes in the ObjectWindows GDI encapsulation are:

- *TDC* is the root class for encapsulating ObjectWindows GDI device contexts. You can create a *TDC* object directly or—for more specialized behavior—you can use derived classes.

- *TPen* contains the functionality of Windows pen objects. You can construct a pen object from scratch or from an existing pen handle, pen object, or logical pen (LOGPEN) structure.

- *TBrush* contains the functionality of Windows brush objects. You can construct a custom brush, creating a solid, styled, or patterned brush, or you can use an existing brush handle, brush object, or logical brush (LOGBRUSH) structure.

- *TFont* lets you easily use Windows fonts. You can construct a font with custom specifications, or from an existing font handle, font object, or logical font (LOGFONT) structure.

- *TPalette* encapsulates a GDI palette. You can construct a new palette or use existing palettes from various color table types that are used by DIBs.

- *TBitmap* contains Windows bitmaps. You can construct a bitmap from many sources, including files, bitmap handles, application resources, and more.

- *TRegion* defines a region in a window. You can construct a region in numerous shapes, including rectangles, ellipses, and polygons. *TRegion* is a pseudo-GDI object; it isn't derived from *TGdiObject*.

- *TIcon* encapsulates Windows icons. You can construct an icon from a resource or explicit information. *TIcon* is a pseudo-GDI object.

- *TCursor* encapsulates the Windows cursor. You can construct a cursor from a resource or explicit information.

- *TDib* encapsulates the device-independent bitmap (DIB) class. DIBs have no Windows handle; instead they are just a structure containing format and palette information and a collection of bits (pixels). This class provides a convenient way to work with DIBs like any other GDI object. A DIB is what is really inside a .BMP file, in bitmap resources, and what is put on the Clipboard as a DIB. *TDib* is a pseudo-GDI object.

Changes to encapsulated GDI functions

Many of the functions in the ObjectWindows GDI classes might look familiar to you; this is because many of them have the same names and very nearly, if not exactly, the same function signature as regular Windows API functions. Because the ObjectWindows GDI classes replicate the functionality of so many Windows objects, there was no need to alter the existing terminology. Therefore, function names and signatures have been deliberately kept as close as possible to what you are used to in the standard Windows GDI functions.

Some improvements, however, have been made to the functions. These improvements, many of which are discussed in this section, include such things as cracking packed return values and using ObjectWindows objects in place of Windows-defined structures.

Note None of these changes are hard and fast rules; just because a function can somehow be converted doesn't mean it necessarily has been. But if you see an ObjectWindows function with the same name as a Windows API function that looks a little different, one of the following reasons should explain the change to you:

- API functions that take an object handle as a parameter often omit the handle in the ObjectWindows version. The *TGdiObject* base object maintains a handle to each object. The ObjectWindows version then uses that handle when passing the call on to Windows. For example, when selecting an object in a device context, you would normally use the *SelectObject* API function, as shown here:

```
void
SelectPen(HDC& hdc, HPEN& hpen)
{
  HPEN hpenOld;
  hpenOld = SelectObject(hdc, hpen);

  // Do something with the new pen.
  ⋮

  // Now select the old pen again.
  SelectObject(hdc, hpenOld);
}
```

The ObjectWindows version of this function is encapsulated in the *TDC* class, which is derived from *TGdiObject*. The following example shows how the previous function would appear in a member function of a *TDC*-derived class. Notice the difference between the two calls to *SelectObject*:

```
void
SelectPen(TDC& dc, TPEN& pen)
{
  dc.SelectObject(pen);

  // Do something with the new pen.
  ⋮

  // Now select the old pen again.
  dc.RestorePen();
}
```

- ObjectWindows GDI functions usually substitute an ObjectWindows type in place of a Windows type:

  - Windows API functions use individual parameters to specify x and y coordinate values; ObjectWindows GDI functions use *TPoint* objects.

  - Windows API functions use RECT structures to specify a rectangular area; ObjectWindows GDI functions use *TRect* objects.

  - Windows API functions use RGN structures to specify a region; ObjectWindows GDI functions use *TRegion* objects.

  - Windows API functions take HLOCAL or HGLOBAL parameters to pass an object that doesn't have a predefined Windows structure; ObjectWindows GDI functions use references to ObjectWindows objects.

- Some Windows functions return a *uint32* with data encoded in it. The *uint32* must then must be cracked to get the data from it. The ObjectWindows versions of these functions take a reference to some appropriate object as a parameter. The function then places the data into the object, relieving the programmer from the responsibility of cracking the value. These functions usually return a **bool**, indicating whether the function call was successful.

For example, the Windows version of *SetViewportOrg* returns a *uint32*, with the old value for the viewport origin contained in it. The ObjectWindows version of *SetViewportOrg* takes a *TPoint* reference in place of the two **int**s the Windows version takes as parameters. It also takes a second parameter, a *TPoint* *, in which the old viewport origins are placed.

Working with device contexts

When working with the Windows GDI, you use a *device context* to access all devices, from windows to printers to plotters. The device context is a structure maintained by GDI that contains essential information about the device with which you are working, such as the default foreground and background colors, font, palette, and so on. ObjectWindows encapsulates device-context information in a number of device context classes, all of which are based on the *TDC* class.

TDC contains most of the device-context functionality you might require. The other DC-related classes are derived from *TDC* or *TDC*-derived classes. These derived classes only specialize the functionality of the *TDC* class and apply it to a discrete set of operations. Here is a description of each of the device-context classes:

- *TDC* is the root class for all GDI device contexts for ObjectWindows; it can be instantiated itself or specialized subclasses can be used to get specific behavior.
- *TWindowDC* provides access to the entire area owned by a window; this is the base for any device context class that releases its handle when done.
- *TScreenDC* provides direct access to the screen bitmap using a device context for window handle 0, which is for the whole screen with no clipping.
- *TDesktopDC* provides access to the desktop window's client area, which is the screen behind all other windows.
- *TClientDC* provides access to the client area owned by a window.
- *TPaintDC* wraps *BeginPaint* and *EndPaint* calls for use in a WM_PAINT response function.
- *TMetaFileDC* provides a device context with a metafile loaded for use.
- *TCreatedDC* lets you create a device context for a specified device.
- *TIC* lets you create an information context for a specified device.
- *TMemoryDC* provides access to a memory device context.
- *TDibDC* provides access to DIBs using the DIB.DRV driver.
- *TPrintDC* provides access to a printer device context.

TDC class

Although the specialized device-context classes provide extra functionality tailored to each class' specific purpose, the *TDC* class provides *most* of each class' functionality. This section discusses this base functionality.

Because of the large number of functions contained in *TDC*, this section doesn't discuss every function in detail. Instead, areas of functionality contained in the *TDC* class are described, with ObjectWindows-specific functions and the most important API-like functions discussed in detail; the other functions are described in the *ObjectWindows Reference Guide*. In particular, many of the *TDC* functions look much like Windows API functions and are therefore described only briefly in this section. You can find general information on the difference between the Windows API functions and the ObjectWindows versions of those functions on page 390.

Constructing and destroying TDC

TDC provides one public constructor and one public destructor. The public constructor takes an HDC, a handle to a device context. Essentially this means that you must have an existing device context before constructing a *TDC* object. Usually you don't construct a *TDC* directly, even though you can. Instead you usually use a *TDC* object when passing some device context as a function parameter or a pointer to a *TDC* to point to some device context contained in either a *TDC* or *TDC*-derived object.

~TDC restores all the default objects in the device context and discards the objects.

TDC also provides two **protected** constructors for use by derived classes. The first is a default constructor so that derived classes don't have to explicitly call *TDC*'s constructor. The second takes an HDC and a *TAutoDelete* flag. *TAutoDelete* is an **enum** that can be *NoAutoDelete* or *AutoDelete*. The *TAutoDelete* parameter is used to initialize the *ShouldDelete* member, which is inherited from *TGdiObject* (the public *TDC* constructor initializes this to *NoAutoDelete*).

Device-context operators

TDC provides one conversion operator, HDC, that lets you return the handle to the device context of your particular *TDC* or *TDC*-derived object. This operator is most often invoked implicitly. When you use a *TDC* object where you would normally use an HDC, such as in a function call or the like, the compiler tries to find a way to cast the object to the required type. Thus it uses the HDC conversion operator even though it is not explicitly called.

For example, suppose you want to create a device context in memory that is compatible with the device associated with a *TDC* object. You can use the *CreateCompatibleDC* Windows API function to create the new device context from your existing *TDC* object:

```
HDC
GetCompatDC(TDC& dc, TWindow& window)
{
  HDC compatDC;

  if(!(compatDC = CreateCompatibleDC(dc))) {
    window.MessageBox("Couldn't create compatible device context!",
                   "Failure", MB_OK | MB_ICONEXCLAMATION);
    return NULL;
  } else return compatDC;
}
```

Notice that *CreateCompatibleDC* takes a single parameter, an HDC. Thus the function parameter *dc* is implicitly cast to an HDC in the *CreateCompatibleDC* call.

Device-context functions

The functions in this section are used to access information about the device context itself. They are equivalent to the Windows API functions of the same names.

You can save and restore a device context much like normal using the functions *SaveDC* and *RestoreDC*. The following code sample shows how these functions might be used. Notice that *RestoreDC*'s single parameter uses a default value instead of specifying the **int** parameter:

```
void
TMyDC::SomeFunc(TDC& dc, int x1, int y1, int x2, int y2)
{
  dc.SaveDC();
  dc.SetMapMode(MM_LOENGLISH);
  :
  dc.Rectangle(x1, -y1, x2, -y2);
  dc.RestoreDC();
}
```

You can also reset a device context to the settings contained in a DEVMODE structure using the *ResetDC* function. The only parameter *ResetDC* takes is a reference to a DEVMODE structure.

You can use the *GetDeviceCaps* function to retrieve device-specific information about a given display device. This function takes one parameter, an **int** index to the type of information to retrieve from the device context. The possible values for this parameter are the same as for the Windows API function.

You can use the *GetDCOrg* function to locate the current device context's logical coordinates within the display device's absolute physical coordinates. This function takes a reference to a *TPoint* structure and returns a **bool**. The **bool** indicates whether the function call was successful, and the *TPoint* object contains the coordinates of the device context's translation origin.

Selecting and restoring GDI objects

You can use the *SelectObject* function to place a GDI object into a device context. There are four versions of the *SelectObject* function; all of them return **void**, but each takes different parameters. The version you should use depends on the type of object you are selecting into the device context. The different versions are:

```
SelectObject(const TBrush& brush);
SelectObject(const TPen& pen);
SelectObject(const TFont& font);
SelectObject(const TPalette& palette, bool forceBG=false);
```

In addition, *TMemoryDC* lets you select a bitmap.

Graphics objects that you can select into a device context normally exist as logical objects, which contain the information required for the creation of the object. The graphics objects are connected to the logical objects through a Windows handle. When the graphics object is selected into the device context, a physical tool (created using the attributes contained in the logical pen) is created inside the device context.

You can also select a stock object using the function *SelectStockObject*. *SelectStockObject* takes one parameter, an **int** that is equivalent to the parameter used to call the API function *GetStockObject*. Essentially the *SelectStockObject* function takes the place of two calls: a call to *GetStockObject* to actually get a stock object, then a call to *SelectObject* to place the stock object into the device context.

TDC provides functions to restore original objects in a device context. There are normally four versions of this function, *RestoreBrush*, *RestorePen*, *RestoreFont*, and *RestorePalette*. A fifth, *RestoreTextBrush*, exists only for 32-bit applications. The *RestoreObjects* function calls all four functions (or five, under 32 bits), and restores all original objects in the device context. All of these functions return **void** and take no parameters.

Drawing tool functions

GetBrushOrg takes one parameter, a reference to a *TPoint* object. It places the coordinates of the brush origin into the *TPoint* object. *GetBrushOrg* returns **true** if the operation was successful.

SetBrushOrg takes two parameters: a reference to a *TPoint* object and a *TPoint* *. This sets the device context's brush origin to the x and y values in the first *TPoint* object. If you don't specify a value for the second parameter, it defaults to 0. If you do pass a pointer to a *TPoint* object as the second parameter, *TDC::SetBrushOrg* places the old values for the brush origin into the x and y members of the object. The return value indicates whether the operation was successful.

Color and palette functions

TDC provides a number of functions you can use to manipulate the colors and palette of a device context.

GetNearestColor	RealizePalette
GetSystemPaletteEntries	SetSystemPaletteUse
GetSystemPaletteUs	UpdateColorse

Drawing attribute functions

Use drawing attribute functions to set the device context's drawing mode. All of these functions are analogous to the API functions of the same names, except that the HDC parameter is omitted in each.

GetBkColor	SetBkColor
GetBkMode	SetBkMode
GetPolyFillMode	SetPolyFillMode
GetROP2	SetROP2
GetStretchBltMode	SetStretchBltMode
GetTextColor	SetTextColor

Another function, *SetMiterLimit*, is available only for 32-bit applications.

Viewport and window mapping functions

Use these functions to set the viewport and window mapping modes:

GetMapMode   GetViewportExt
GetViewportExt   OffsetWindowOrg
GetViewportOrg   ScaleViewportExt
GetViewportOrg   ScaleWindowExt
GetWindowExt   SetMapMode
GetWindowExt   SetViewportExt
GetWindowOrg   SetViewportOrg
GetWindowOrg   SetWindowExt
OffsetViewportOrg   SetWindowOrg

The following viewport and window mapping functions are available only for 32-bit applications:

ModifyWorldTransform   SetWorldTransform

Coordinate functions

Coordinate functions convert logical coordinates to physical coordinates and vice versa:

DPtoLP   LPtoDP

Clip and update rectangle and region functions

Use clip and update rectangle and region functions to set up and retrieve simple or complex areas in a device context's clipping region:

ExcludeClipRect   OffsetClipRgn
ExcludeUpdateRgn   PtVisible
GetBoundsRect   RectVisible
GetClipBox   SelectClipRgn
GetClipRgn   SetBoundsRect
IntersectClipRect

Metafile functions

Use the metafile functions to access metafiles:

EnumMetaFile   PlayMetaFileRecord
PlayMetaFile

Current position functions

Use these functions to move to the current point in the device context. Three versions of *MoveTo* are provided:

• *MoveTo*(**int** *x*, **int** *y*) moves the pen to the point *x, y*.

- *MoveTo(TPoint &point)* moves the pen to the point *point.x, point.y*.
- *MoveTo(TPoint &point, TPoint &oldPoint)* moves the pen to the point *point.x, point.y* and places the old location of the pen into *oldPoint*.

GetCurrentPosition takes a reference to a *TPoint* object. It places the coordinates of the current position into the *TPoint* object and returns **true** if the function call was successful.

Font functions

Use *TDC*'s font functions to access and manipulate fonts:

EnumFontFamilies	GetCharWidth
EnumFonts	GetFontData
GetAspectRatioFilter	SetMapperFlags
GetCharABCWidths	

Path functions

Path functions are available only to 32-bit applications. The *TDC* path functions are the same as the Win32 versions, with the exception that the *TDC* versions don't take an HDC parameter.

BeginPath	PathToRegion
CloseFigure	SelectClipPath
EndPath	StrokeAndFillPath
FillPath	StrokePath
FlattenPath	WidenPath

Output functions

TDC provides a great variety of output functions for all different kinds of objects that a standard device context can handle, including:

- Icons
- Rectangles
- Regions
- Shapes
- Bitmaps
- Text

Nearly all of these functions provide a number of versions: one version that provides functionality nearly identical to that of the corresponding API function (with the exception of omitting the HDC parameter) and alternate versions that use *TPoint, TRect, TRegion,* and other ObjectWindows data encapsulations to make the calls more concise and easier to understand. These functions are discussed in further detail in the *ObjectWindows Reference Guide*.

- Current position

GetCurrentPosition	MoveTo

- Icons

  DrawIcon

- Rectangles

DrawFocusRect	FillRect
FrameRect	TextRect
InvertRect	

- Regions

FillRgn	FrameRgn
InvertRgn	PaintRgn

- Shapes

Arc	Chord
Ellipse	LineDDA
LineTo	Pie
Polygon	Polyline
PolyPolygon	Rectangle
RoundRect	

- Bitmaps and blitting

BitBlt	ExtFloodFill
FloodFill	GetDIBits
GetPixel	PatBlt
ScrollDC	SetDIBits
SetDIBitsToDevice	SetPixel
StretchBlt	StretchDIBits

- Text

DrawText	ExtTextOut
GrayString	TabbedTextOut
TextOut	

The following functions are available for 32-bit applications only:

- Shapes

AngleArc	PolyDraw
PolyBezier	PolylineTo
PolyBezierTo	PolyPolyline

- Bitmaps and blitting

MaskBlt	PlgBlt

32

Object data members and functions

These data members and functions are used to administer the device context object itself. The functions and data members discussed in this section are **protected** and can be accessed only by a *TDC*-derived class.

- *ShouldDelete* indicates whether the object should delete its handle to the device context when the destructor is invoked.

- *Handle* contains the actual handle of the device context.

- *OrgBrush, OrgPen, OrgFont,* and *OrgPalette* are the handles to the original objects when the device context was created; *OrgTextBrush* is also present in 32-bit applications.

- *CheckValid* throws an exception if the device context object is not valid.

- *Init* sets the *OrgBrush, OrgPen, OrgFont,* and *OrgPalette* when the object is created; if you're creating a *TDC*-derived class without explicitly calling a *TDC* constructor, you should call the *TDC::Init* first in your constructor.

- *GetHDC* returns an HDC using *Handle*.

- *GetAttributeHDC*, like *GetHDC*, returns an HDC using *Handle*; if you're creating an object with more than one device context, you should override this function and not *GetHDC* to provide the proper return.*OWLFastWindowFrame* draws a frame that is often used for window borders. This function uses the undocumented Windows API function *FastWindowFrame* if available, or *PatBlt* if not.

TPen class

The *TPen* class encapsulates a logical pen. It contains a color for the pen's "ink" (encapsulated in a *TColor* object), a pen width, and the pen style.

Constructing TPen

You can construct a *TPen* either directly, specifying the color, width, and style of the pen, or indirectly, by specifying a *TPen* & or pointer to a LOGPEN structure. Directly constructing a pen creates a new object with the specified attributes. Here is the constructor for directly constructing a pen:

```
TPen(TColor color, int width=1, int style=PS_SOLID);
```

The *style* parameter can be one of the following values: PS_SOLID, PS_DASH, PS_DOT, PS_DASHDOT, PS_DASHDOTDOT, PS_NULL, or PS_INSIDEFRAME. These values are discussed in the *ObjectWindows Reference*.

Indirectly creating a pen creates a new object, but copies the attributes of the object passed to it into the new pen object. Here are the constructors for indirectly creating a pen:

```
TPen(const LOGPEN far* logPen);
TPen(const TPen&);
```

You can also create a new *TPen* object from an existing HPEN handle:

```
TPen(HPEN handle, TAutoDelete autoDelete = NoAutoDelete);
```

This constructor is used to obtain an ObjectWindows object as an alias to a regular Windows handle received in a message.

Two other constructors are available only for 32-bit applications. You can use these constructors to create cosmetic or geometric pens:

```
TPen(uint32 penStyle,
    uint32 width,
    const TBrush& brush,
    uint32 styleCount,
    LPDWORD style);
TPen(uint32 penStyle,
    uint32 width,
    const LOGBRUSH& logBrush,
    uint32 styleCount,
    LPDWORD style);
```

where:

- *penStyle* is a combination of type, style, end cap, and join of the pen, where:

  - Type is either PS_GEOMETRIC or PS_COSMETIC.

  - Style can be any one of the following values:

PS_ALTERNATE	PS_DASH
PS_DASHDOT	PS_DASHDOTDOT
PS_DOT	PS_INSIDEFRAME
PS_NULL	PS_SOLID
PS_USERSTYLE	

  - End cap is specified only for geometric pens, and can be one of the following values:

PS_ENDCAP_FLAT	PS_ENDCAP_ROUND
PS_ENDCAP_SQUARE	

  - Join is specified only for geometric pens, and can be one of the following values:

PS_JOIN_BEVEL	PS_JOIN_MITER
PS_JOIN_ROUND	

- *width* is the pen width.

- *brush* or *logBrush* is a reference to an existing *TBrush* or *LOGBRUSH* object.

- *styleCount* is the size (in *uint32*s) of the *style* array; *styleCount* should be 0 unless the pen style is PS_USERSTYLE.

- *style* is a pointer to an array of *uint32*s that specifies the pattern of the pen; *style* should be NULL unless the pen style is PS_USERSTYLE.

Accessing TPen

You can access *TPen* through an HPEN or as a LOGPEN structure. To get an HPEN from a *TPen* object, use the HPEN operator with the *TPen* object as the parameter. The HPEN operator is almost never explicitly invoked:

```
HPEN
GetHPen(TPen& pen)
{
   return pen;
}
```

This code automatically invokes the HPEN conversion operator to cast the *TPen* object to the correct type.

To convert a *TPen* object to a LOGPEN structure, use the *GetObject* function:

```
bool
GetLogPen(LOGPEN far& logPen)
{
   TPen pen(TColor::LtMagenta, 10);
   return pen.GetObject(logPen);
}
```

The following example shows how to use a pen with a *TDC* to draw a line:

```
void
TPenDemo::DrawLine(TDC& dc, const TPoint& point, TColor& color)
{
   TPen BrushPen(color, PenSize);
   dc.SelectObject(BrushPen);
   dc.LineTo(point);
}
```

TBrush class

The *TBrush* class encapsulates a logical brush. It contains a color for the brush's ink (encapsulated in a *TColor* object), a brush width, and, depending on how the brush is constructed, the brush style, pattern, or bitmap.

Constructing TBrush

You can construct a *TBrush* either directly, specifying the color, width, and style of the brush, or indirectly, by specifying a *TBrush* & or pointer to a LOGBRUSH structure. Directly constructing a brush creates a new object with the specified attributes. Here are the constructors for directly constructing a brush:

```
TBrush(TColor color);
TBrush(TColor color, int style);
TBrush(const TBitmap& pattern);
TBrush(const TDib& pattern);
```

The first constructor creates a solid brush with the color contained in *color*.

The second constructor creates a hatched brush with the color contained in *color* and the hatch style contained in *style*. *style* can be one of the following values:

HS_BDIAGONAL	HS_CROSS
HS_DIAGCROSS	HS_FDIAGONAL
HS_HORIZONTAL	HS_VERTICAL

The third and fourth constructors create a brush from the bitmap or DIB passed as a parameter. The width of the brush depends on the size of the bitmap or DIB.

Indirectly creating a brush creates a new object, but copies the attributes of the object passed to it into the new brush object. Here are the constructors for indirectly creating a brush:

```
TBrush(const LOGBRUSH far* logBrush);
TBrush(const TBrush& src);
```

You can also create a new *TBrush* object from an existing HBRUSH handle:

```
TBrush(HBRUSH handle, TAutoDelete autoDelete = NoAutoDelete);
```

This constructor is used to obtain an ObjectWindows object as an alias to a regular Windows handle received in a message.

Accessing TBrush

You can access *TBrush* through an HBRUSH or as a LOGBRUSH structure. To get an HBRUSH from a *TBrush* object, use the HBRUSH operator with the *TBrush* object as the parameter. The HBRUSH operator is almost never explicitly invoked:

```
HBRUSH
GetHBrush(TBrush& brush)
{
  return brush;
}
```

This code automatically invokes the HBRUSH conversion operator to cast the *TBrush* object to the correct type.

To convert a *TBrush* object to a LOGBRUSH structure, use the *GetObject* function:

```
bool
GetLogBrush(LOGBRUSH far& logBrush)
{
  TBrush brush(TColor::LtCyan, HS_DIAGCROSS);
  return brush.GetObject(logBrush);
}
```

To reset the origin of a brush object, use the *UnrealizeObject* function. *UnrealizeObject* resets the brush's origin and returns nonzero if successful.

The following code shows how to use a brush to paint a rectangle in a window:

```
void
TMyWindow::PaintRect(TDC& dc, TPoint& p, TSize& size)
{
  TBrush brush(TColor(5,5,5));
  dc.SelectObject(brush);
```

```
        dc.Rectangle(p, size);
        dc.RestoreBrush();
    }
```

TFont class

The *TFont* class lets you easily create and use Windows fonts in your applications. The *TFont* class encapsulates all attributes of a logical font.

Constructing TFont

You can construct a *TFont* either directly, specifying all the attributes of the font in the constructor, or indirectly, by specifying a *TFont* & or pointer to a LOGFONT structure. Directly constructing a pen creates a new object with the specified attributes. Here are the constructors for directly constructing a font:

```
TFont(const char far* facename=0,
      int height=0, int width=0, int escapement=0,
      int orientation=0, int weight=FW_NORMAL,
      uint8 pitchAndFamily=DEFAULT_PITCH|FF_DONTCARE,
      uint8 italic=false, uint8 underline=false,
      uint8 strikeout=false,
      uint8 charSet=1,
      uint8 outputPrecision=OUT_DEFAULT_PRECIS,
      uint8 clipPrecision=CLIP_DEFAULT_PRECIS,
      uint8 quality=DEFAULT_QUALITY);

TFont(int height, int width, int escapement=0,
      int orientation=0,
      int weight=FW_NORMAL,
      uint8 italic=false, uint8 underline=false,
      uint8 strikeout=false,
      uint8 charSet=1,
      uint8 outputPrecision=OUT_DEFAULT_PRECIS,
      uint8 clipPrecision=CLIP_DEFAULT_PRECIS,
      uint8 quality=DEFAULT_QUALITY,
      uint8 pitchAndFamily=DEFAULT_PITCH|FF_DONTCARE,
      const char far* facename=0);
```

The first constructor lets you conveniently plug in the most commonly used attributes for a font (such as name, height, width, and so on) and let the other attributes (which generally have the same value time after time) take their default values. The second constructor has the parameters in the same order as the *CreateFont* Windows API call so you can easily cut and paste from existing Windows code.

Indirectly creating a font creates a new object, but copies the attributes of the object passed to it into the new font object. Here are the constructors for indirectly creating a font:

```
TFont(const LOGFONT far* logFont);
TFont(const TFont&);
```

You can also create a new *TFont* object from an existing HFONT handle:

```
TFont(HFONT handle, TAutoDelete autoDelete = NoAutoDelete);
```

This constructor is used to obtain an ObjectWindows object as an alias to a regular Windows handle received in a message.

Accessing TFont

You can access *TFont* through an HFONT or as a LOGFONT structure. To get an HFONT from a *TFont* object, use the HFONT operator with the *TFont* object as the parameter. The HFONT operator is almost never explicitly invoked:

```
HFONT
GetHFont(TFont& font)
{
    return font;
}
```

This code automatically invokes the HFONT conversion operator to cast the *TFont* object to the correct type.

To convert a *TFont* object to a LOGFONT structure, use the *GetObject* function:

```
bool
GetLogFont(LOGFONT far& logFont)
{
    TFont font("Times Roman", 20, 8);
    return font.GetObject(logFont);
}
```

TPalette class

The *TPalette* class encapsulates a Windows color palette that can be used with bitmaps and DIBs. *TPalette* lets you adjust the color table, match individual colors, move a palette to the Clipboard, and more.

Constructing TPalette

You can construct a *TPalette* object either directly, passing an array of color values to the constructor, or indirectly, by specifying a *TPalette* &, a pointer to a LOGPALETTE structure, a pointer to a bitmap header, and so on. Directly constructing a palette creates a new object with the specified attributes. Here is the constructor for directly constructing a palette:

```
TPalette(const PALETTEENTRY far* entries, int count);
```

entries is an array of PALETTEENTRY objects. Each PALETTEENTRY object contains a color value specified by three separate values, one each of red, green, and blue, plus a flags variable for the entry. *count* specifies the number of values contained in the *entries* array.

Indirectly creating a palette creates a new object, but copies the attributes of the object passed to it into the new palette object. Here are the constructors for indirectly creating a palette:

```
TPalette(const TClipboard&);
TPalette(const TPalette& palette);
TPalette(const LOGPALETTE far* logPalette);
TPalette(const BITMAPINFO far* info, uint flags=0);
TPalette(const BITMAPCOREINFO far* core, uint flags=0);
TPalette(const TDib& dib, uint flags=0);
```

Each of these constructors copies the color values contained in the object passed into the constructor into the new object. The objects passed to the constructor are not necessarily palettes themselves; many of them are objects that use palettes and contain a palette themselves. In these cases, the *TPalette* constructor extracts the palette from the object and copies it into the new palette object.

You can also create a new *TPalette* object from an existing HPALETTE handle:

```
TPalette(HPALETTE handle, TAutoDelete autoDelete = NoAutoDelete);
```

This constructor is used to obtain an ObjectWindows object as an alias to a regular Windows handle received in a message.

Accessing TPalette

You can access *TPalette* through an HPALETTE or as a LOGPALETTE structure. To get an HPALETTE from a *TPalette* object, use the HPALETTE operator with the *TPalette* object as the parameter. The HPALETTE operator is almost never explicitly invoked:

```
HPALETTE
GetHPalette(TPalette& palette)
{
  return palette;
}
```

This code automatically invokes the HPALETTE conversion operator to cast the *TPalette* object to the correct type.

The *GetObject* function for *TPalette* functions the same way the Windows API call *GetObject* does when passed a handle to a palette: it places the number of entries in the color table into the *uint16* reference passed to it as a parameter. *TPalette::GetObject* returns **true** if successful.

Member functions

TPalette also encapsulates a number of standard API calls for manipulating palettes:

- You can match a color with an entry in a palette using the *GetNearestPaletteIndex* function. This function takes a single parameter (a *TColor* object) and returns the index number of the closest match in the palette's color table.

- *GetNumEntries* takes no parameters and returns the number of entries in the palette's color table.

- You can get the values for a range of entries in the palette's color table using the *GetPaletteEntries* function. *TPalette::GetPaletteEntries* functions just like the Windows API call *GetPaletteEntries*, except that *TPalette::GetPaletteEntries* omits the HPALETTE parameter.

- You can set the values for a range of entries in the palette's color table using the *SetPaletteEntries* function. *TPalette::SetPaletteEntries* functions just like the Windows API call *SetPaletteEntries*, except that *TPalette::SetPaletteEntries* omits the HPALETTE parameter.

- The *GetPaletteEntry* and *SetPaletteEntry* functions work much like *GetPaletteEntries* and *SetPaletteEntries*, except that they work on a single palette entry at a time. Both functions take two parameters: the index number of a palette entry and a reference to a PALETTEENTRY object. *GetPaletteEntry* places the color value of the desired palette entry into the PALETTEENTRY object. *SetPaletteEntry* sets the palette entry indicated by the index to the value of the PALETTEENTRY object.

- You can use the *ResizePalette* function to resize a palette. *ResizePalette* takes a uint parameter, which specifies the number of entries in the resized palette. *ResizePalette* functions exactly like the Windows API *ResizePalette* call.

- The *AnimatePalette* function lets you replace entries in the palette's color table. *AnimatePalette* takes three parameter,: two UINTs and a pointer to an array of PALETTEENTRY objects. The first UINT specifies the first entry in the palette to be replaced. The second uint specifies the number of entries to be replaced. The entries indicated by these two UINTs are replaced by the values contained in the array of PALETTEENTRYs.

- You can also use the *UnrealizeObject* function for your palette objects. *UnrealizeObject* matches the palette to the current system palette. *UnrealizeObject* takes no parameters and functions just like the Windows API call.

- You can move a palette to the Clipboard using the *ToClipboard* function. *ToClipboard* takes a reference to a *TClipboard* object as a parameter. Because the *ToClipboard* function actually removes the object from your application, you should usually use a *TPalette* constructor to create a temporary object:

```
TClipboard clipBoard;
TPalette (tmpPalette).ToClipboard(clipBoard);
```

Extending TPalette

TPalette contains two **protected**-access functions, both called *Create*. The two functions differ in that one takes BITMAPINFO * as its first parameter and the other takes a BITMAPCOREINFO * as its first parameter. These functions are called from the *TPalette* constructors that take a BITMAPINFO *, a BITMAPCOREINFO *, or a *TDib* &. The BITMAPINFO * and BITMAPCOREINFO * constructors call the corresponding *Create* functions. The *TDib* & constructor extracts a BITMAPCOREINFO * or a BITMAPINFO * from its *TDib* object and calls the appropriate *Create* function.

Both *Create* functions take a uint for their second parameter. This parameter is equivalent to the *peFlags* member of the PALETTEENTRY structure and should be passed either as a 0 or with values compatible with *peFlags*: PC_EXPLICIT, PC_NOCOLLAPSE, and PC_RESERVED. A palette entry must have the PC_RESERVED flag set to use that entry with the *AnimatePalette* function.

The *Create* functions create a LOGPALETTE using the color table from the bitmap header passed as its parameter. You can use *Create* for 2-, 16-, and 256-color bitmaps. It fails for all other types, including 24-bit DIBs. It then uses the LOGPALETTE to create the HPALETTE.

TBitmap class

The *TBitmap* class encapsulates a Windows device-dependent bitmap, providing a number of different constructors, plus member functions to manipulate and access the bitmap.

Constructing TBitmap

You can construct a *TBitmap* object either directly or indirectly. Using direct construction, you can specify the bitmap's width, height, and so on. Using indirect construction, you can specify an existing bitmap object, pointer to a BITMAP structure, a metafile, a *TDC* device context, and more.

Here is the constructor for directly constructing a bitmap object:

```
TBitmap(int width, int height, uint8 planes=1, uint8 count=1, void* bits=0);
```

width and *height* specify the width and height in pixels of the bitmap. *planes* specifies the number of color planes in the bitmap. *count* specifies the number of bits per pixel. Either *plane* or *count* must be 1. *bits* is an array containing the bits to be copied into the bitmap. *bits* can be 0, in which case the bitmap is left uninitialized.

You can create bitmap objects from existing bitmaps, either encapsulated in a *TBitmap* object or contained in a BITMAP structure.

```
TBitmap(const TBitmap& bitmap);
TBitmap(const BITMAP far* bitmap);
```

TBitmap provides two constructors you can use to create bitmap objects that are compatible with a given device context. The first constructor creates an uninitialized bitmap of the size *height* by *width*. Specifying **true** for the *discardable* parameter makes the bitmap discardable. A bitmap should never be discarded if it is the currently selected object in a device context.

```
TBitmap(const TDC& Dc, int width, int height, bool discardable = false);
```

The second constructor creates a bitmap compatible with the device represented by the device context from a DIB. The *usage* parameter should be CBM_INIT for 16-bit applications. CBM_INIT indicates that the bitmap should be initialized with the bits contained in the DIB object. If you don't specify CBM_INIT, the bitmap is created, but is left empty. CBM_INIT is the default.

32-bit applications can also specify CBM_CREATEDIB. The CBM_CREATEDIB flag indicates that the color format of the new bitmap should be compatible with the color format contained in the DIB's BITMAPINFO structure. If the CBM_CREATEDIB flag isn't specified, the bitmap is assumed to be compatible with the given device context.

```
TBitmap(const TDC& Dc, const TDib& dib, uint32 usage);
```

You can also create bitmaps from the Windows Clipboard, from a metafile, or from a DIB object. To create a bitmap from the Clipboard, you only need to pass a reference to a *TClipboard* object to the constructor. The constructor gets the handle of the bitmap in the Clipboard and constructs a bitmap object from the handle:

```
TBitmap(const TClipboard& clipboard);
```

To create a bitmap from a metafile, you need to pass a *TMetaFilePict* &, a *TPalette* &, and a *TSize* &. The constructor initializes a device-compatible bitmap (based on the palette) and plays the metafile into the bitmap:

```
TBitmap(const TMetaFilePict& metaFile, TPalette& palette, const TSize& size);
```

To create a bitmap from a device-independent bitmap, you need to pass a *TDib* & to the constructor. You can also specify an optional palette. The constructor creates a device context and renders the DIB into a device-compatible bitmap:

```
TBitmap(const TDib& dib, const TPalette* palette = 0);
```

You can create a bitmap object by loading it from a module. This constructor takes two parameters, first the HINSTANCE of the module containing the bitmap and second the resource ID of the bitmap you want to load:

```
TBitmap(HINSTANCE, TResId);
```

You can also create a new *TBitmap* object from an existing HBITMAP handle:

```
TBitmap(HBITMAP handle, TAutoDelete autoDelete = NoAutoDelete);
```

This constructor is used to obtain an ObjectWindows object as an alias to a regular Windows handle received in a message.

Accessing TBitmap

You can access *TBitmap* through an HBITMAP or as a BITMAP structure. To get an HBITMAP from a *TBitmap* object, use the HBITMAP operator with the *TBitmap* object as the parameter. The HBITMAP operator is almost never explicitly invoked:

```
HBITMAP
GetHBitmap(TBitmap &bitmap)
{
  return bitmap;
}
```

This code automatically invokes the HBITMAP conversion operator to cast the *TBitmap* object to the correct type.

To convert a *TBitmap* object to a BITMAP structure, use the *GetObject* function:

```
bool
GetBitmap(BITMAP far& dest)
{
  TBitmap bitmap(200, 100);
  return bitmap.GetObject(dest);
}
```

The *GetObject* function fills out only the width, height, and color format information of the BITMAP structure. You can get the actual bitmap bits with the *GetBitmapBits* function.

Member functions

TBitmap also encapsulates a number of standard API calls for manipulating palettes:

- You can get the same information as you get from *GetObject*, except one item at a time, using the following functions. Each function returns a characteristic of the bitmap object:

  ```
  int Width();
  int Height();
  uint8 Planes();
  uint8 BitsPixel();
  ```

- The *GetBitmapDimension* and *SetBitmapDimension* functions let you find out and change the dimensions of the bitmap. *GetBitmapDimension*, which takes a reference to a *TSize* object as its only parameter, places the size of the bitmap into the *TSize* object. *SetBitmapDimension* can take two parameters, the first a reference to a *TSize* object containing the new size for the bitmap and a pointer to a *TSize*, in which the function places the old size of the bitmap. You don't have to pass the second parameter to *SetBitmapDimension*. Both functions return **true** if the operation was successful.

  The *GetBitmapDimension* and *SetBitmapDimension* functions don't actually affect the size of the bitmap in pixels. Instead they modify only the *physical* size of the bitmap, which is often used by programs when printing or displaying bitmaps. This lets you adjust the size of the bitmap depending on the size of the physical screen.

- The *GetBitmapBits* and *SetBitmapBits* functions let you query and change the bits in a bitmap. Both functions take two parameters: a *uint32* and a **void** *. The *uint32* specifies the size of the array in bytes, and the **void** * points to an array. *GetBitmapBits* fills the array with bits from the bitmap, up to the number of bytes specified by the *uint32* parameter. *SetBitmapBits* copies the array into the bitmap, copying over the number of bytes specified in the *uint32* parameter.

- You can move a bitmap to the Clipboard using the *ToClipboard* function. *ToClipboard* takes a reference to a *TClipboard* object as a parameter. Because the *ToClipboard* function actually removes the object from your application, you should usually use a *TBitmap* constructor to create a temporary object:

  ```
  TClipboard clipBoard;
  TBitmap (tmpBitmap).ToClipboard(clipBoard);
  ```

Extending TBitmap

TBitmap has three functions that have **protected** access: a constructor and two functions called *Create*.

The constructor is a default constructor. You can use it when constructing a derived class to prevent having to explicitly call the base class constructor. If you use the default constructor, you need to initialize the bitmap properly in your own constructor.

The first *Create* function takes a reference to a *TBitmap* object as a parameter. Essentially, this function copies the passed *TBitmap* object over to itself.

The second *Create* function takes references to a *TDib* object and to a *TPalette* object. *Create* creates a device context compatible with the *TPalette* and renders the DIB into a device-compatible bitmap.

TRegion class

Use the *TRegion* class to define a region in a device context. You can perform a number of operations on a device context, such as painting, filling, inverting, and so on, using the region as a stencil. You can also use the *TRegion* class to define a region for your own custom operations.

Constructing and destroying TRegion

Regions come in many shapes and sizes, from simple rectangles and rectangles with rounded corners to elaborate polygonal shapes. You can determine the shape of your region by the constructor used. You can also indirectly construct a region from a handle to a region or an existing *TRegion* object.

TRegion provides a default constructor that produces an empty rectangular region. You can use the function *SetRectRgn* to initialize an empty *TRegion* object. For example, suppose you derive a class from *TRegion*. In the constructor for your derived class, call *SetRectRgn* to initialize the region. This prevents you from having to call *TRegion*'s constructor explicitly:

```
class TMyRegion : public TRegion
{
  public:
    TMyRegion(TRect& rect);
    ⋮
};

TMyRegion::TMyRegion(TRect& rect)
{
  // Initialize the TRegion base with rect.
  SetRectRgn(rect);
}
```

You can directly create a *TRegion* from a number of different sources. To create a simple rectangular region, use the following constructor:

```
TRegion(const TRect& rect);
```

This creates a rectangular region from the logical coordinates in the *TRect* object.

To create a rectangular region with rounded corners, use the following constructor:

```
TRegion(const TRect& rect, const TSize& corner);
```

This creates a rectangular region from the logical coordinates in the *TRect* object, then rounds the corners into an ellipse. The height and width of the ellipse used is defined by the values in the *TSize* object.

To create an elliptical region, use the following constructor:

```
TRegion(const TRect& e, TEllipse);
```

This creates an elliptical region bounded by the logical coordinates contained in the *TRect* structure. *TEllipse* is an enumerated value with only one possible value, *Ellipse*. A call to this constructor looks something like this:

```
TRect rect(20, 20, 80, 60);
TRegion rgn(rect, TRegion::Ellipse);
```

To create regions with an irregular polygonal shape, use the following constructor:

```
TRegion(const TPoint* points, int count, int fillMode);
```

points is an array of *TPoint* objects. Each *TPoint* contains the logical coordinates of a vertex of the polygon. *count* indicates the number of points in the *points* array. *fillMode* indicates how the region should be filled; this can be either ALTERNATE or WINDING. There is another constructor that you can use to create regions consisting of *multiple* irregular polygonal shapes:

```
TRegion(const TPoint* points,
        const int* polyCounts,
        int count,
        int fillMode);
```

As in the other polygonal region constructor, *points* is an array of *TPoint* objects. But for this constructor, *points* contains the vertex points of a number of polygons. *polyCounts* indicates the number of points in the *points* array for each polygon. *count* indicates the total number of polygons in the region and the number of members in the *polyCount* array. *fillMode* indicates how the region should be filled; this can be either ALTERNATE or WINDING.

For example, suppose you're constructing a region that encompasses two triangular areas. Each triangle would consist of three points. Therefore *points* would have six members, three for each triangle. *polyPoints* would have two members, one for each triangle. Each member of *polyPoints* would have the value three, indicating the number of points in the *points* array that belongs to each polygon. *count* would have the value two, indicating that the region consists of two polygons.

You can create a *TRegion* from an existing HRGN:

```
TRegion(HRGN handle, TAutoDelete autoDelete = NoAutoDelete);
```

This constructor is used to obtain an ObjectWindows object as an alias to a regular Windows handle received in a message.

You can also create a new *TRegion* object from an existing *TRegion* object:

```
TRegion(const TRegion& region);
```

~TRegion deletes the region and its storage space.

Accessing TRegion

You can access and modify *TRegion* objects directly through an HRGN handle or through a number of member functions and operators. To get an HRGN from a *TRegion* object, use the HRGN operator with the *TRegion* object as the parameter. The HRGN operator is almost never explicitly invoked:

```
HRGN
TMyBitmap::GetHRgn()
{
   return *this;
}
```

This code automatically invokes the HRGN conversion operator to cast the *TRegion* object to the correct type.

Member functions

TRegion provides a number of member functions to get information from the *TRegion* object, including whether a point is contained in or touches the region:

- You can use the *SetRectRgn* function to reset the object's region to a rectangular region:

  ```
  void SetRectRgn(const TRect& rect);
  ```

  This sets the *TRegion*'s area to the logical coordinates contained in the *TRect* object passed as a parameter to the *SetRectRgn* function. The region is set to a rectangular region regardless of the shape that it previously had.

- You can use the *Contains* function to find out whether a point is contained in a region:

  ```
  bool Contains(const TPoint& point);
  ```

  point contains the coordinates of the point in question. *Contains* returns **true** if *point* is within the region and **false** if not.

- You can use the *Touches* function to find out whether any part of a rectangle is contained in a region:

  ```
  bool Touches(const TRect& rect);
  ```

  rect contains the coordinates of the rectangle in question. *Touches* returns **true** if any part of *rect* is within the region and **false** if not.

- You can use the *GetRgnBox* functions to get the coordinates of the bounding rectangle of a region:

  ```
  int GetRgnBox(TRect& box);
  TRect GetRgnBox();
  ```

The bounding rectangle is the smallest possible rectangle that encloses all of the area contained in the region. The first version of this function takes a reference to a *TRect* object as a parameter. The function places the coordinates of the bounding rectangle in the *TRect* object. The return value indicates the complexity of the region, and can be either SIMPLEREGION (region has no overlapping borders), COMPLEXREGION (region has overlapping borders), or NULLREGION (region is empty). If the function fails, the return value is ERROR.

The second version of *GetRgnBox* takes no parameters and returns a *TRect*, which contains the coordinates of the bounding rectangle. The second version of this function doesn't indicate the complexity of the region.

Operators

TRegion has a large number of operators. These operators can be used to query and modify the values of a region. They aren't necessarily restricted to working with other regions; many of them let you add and subtract rectangles and other units to and from the region.

TRegion provides two Boolean test operators, == and !=. These operators work to compare two regions. If two regions are equivalent, the == operator returns **true**, and the != operator returns **false**. If two regions aren't equivalent, the == operator returns **false**, and the != operator returns **true**. You can use these operators much as you do their equivalents for **int**s, **char**s, and so on.

For example, suppose you want to test whether two regions are identical, and, if they're not, perform an operation on them. The code would look something like this:

```
TRegion rgn1;
TRegion rgn2;

// Initialize regions...

if(rgn1 != rgn2) {
  // Perform your operations here
  ⋮
}
```

TRegion also provides a number of assignment operators that you can use to change the region:

- The = operator lets you assign one region to another. For example, the statement *rgn1 = rgn2* sets the contents of *rgn1* to the contents of *rgn2*, regardless of the contexts of *rgn1* prior to the assignment.

- The += operator lets you move a region by an offset contained in a *TSize* object. This operation is analogous to numerical addition: just add the offset to each point in the region. The region retains all of its properties, except that the coordinates defining the region are shifted by the values contained in the *cx* and *cy* members of the *TSize* object:
  - If *cx* is positive, the region is shifted *cx* pixels to the right.
  - If *cx* is negative, the region is shifted *cx* pixels to the left.

- If *cy* is positive, the region is shifted *cy* pixels down.
- If *cy* is negative, the region is shifted *cy* pixels up.

For example, suppose you want to move a region to the right 50 pixels and up 20 pixels. The code would look something like this:

```
TRegion rgn;

// Initialize region...

TSize size(50, -20);
rgn += size;

// Continue working with new region.
    ⋮
```

- The –= operator, when used with a *TSize* object, does essentially the opposite of the += operator; that is, it subtracts the offset from each point in the region. For example, suppose you have the same code as in the previous example, except that instead of using the += operator, it uses the –= operator. This would offset the region in exactly the opposite way from the += operator, 50 pixels to the left and down 20 pixels.

- The –= operator, when used with a *TRegion* object, behaves differently from when it is used with a *TSize* object. To demonstrate how the –= operator works when used with *TRegion*, consider the following code:

```
TRegion rgn1, rgn2;
rgn1 -= rgn2;
```

After execution of this code, *rgn1* contains all the area it contained originally, minus any parts of that area shared by *rgn2*. Thus any point that is contained in *rgn2* is not contained in *rgn1* after this code has executed. This is analogous to subtraction: subtract the area defined by *rgn2* from *rgn1*.

- The &= operator can be used with both *TRegion* objects and *TRect* objects (before any operations are performed, the *TRect* is converted to a *TRegion* using the constructor *TRegion::TRegion(TRect &)*). To demonstrate how the &= operator works, consider the following code:

```
TRegion rgn1, rgn2;
rgn1 &= rgn2;
```

After execution of this code, *rgn1* contains all the area it originally shared with *rgn2*; that is, areas that were common to both regions before the execution of the &= statement. This is a logical AND operation: only the areas that are part of both *rgn1* AND *rgn2* become part of the new region.

- The |= operator can be used with both *TRegion* objects and *TRect* objects (before any operations are performed, the *TRect* is converted to a *TRegion* using the constructor *TRegion::TRegion(TRect &)*). To demonstrate how the |= operator works, consider the following code:

```
TRegion rgn1, rgn2;
rgn1 |= rgn2;
```

After execution of this code, *rgn1* contains all the area it originally contained, plus all the area contained in *rgn2*; that is, it contains all of both regions. This is a logical OR operation: areas that are part of either *rgn1* OR *rgn2* become part of the new region.

- The ^= operator can be used with both *TRegion* objects and *TRect* objects (before any operations are performed, the *TRect* is converted to a *TRegion* using the constructor *TRegion::TRegion(TRect &)*). To demonstrate how the ^= operator works, consider the following code:

```
TRegion rgn1, rgn2;
rgn1 ^= rgn2;
```

After execution of this code, *rgn1* contains only that area it originally contained but did *not* share with *rgn2*, plus all the area originally contained in *rgn2* that was not shared with *rgn1*. This operator combines both areas and removes the overlapping sections. This is a logical XOR (exclusive OR) operation: areas that are part of either *rgn1* OR *rgn2* but not of both become part of the new region.

TIcon class

The *TIcon* class encapsulates an icon handle and constructors for instantiating the *TIcon* object. You can use the *TIcon* class to construct an icon from a resource or explicit info.

Constructing TIcon

You can construct a *TIcon* in a number of ways: from an existing *TIcon* object, from a resource in the current application, from a resource in another module, or explicitly from size and data information.

You can create icon objects from an existing icon encapsulated in a *TIcon* object:

```
TIcon(HINSTANCE instance, const TIcon& icon);
```

instance can be any module instance. For example, you could get the instance of a DLL and get an icon from that instance:

```
TModule iconLib("MYICONS.DLL");
TIcon icon(iconLib, "MYICON");
```

Note the implicit conversion of the *TModule iconLib* into an HINSTANCE in the call to the *TIcon* constructor.

You can create a *TIcon* object from an icon resource in any module:

```
TIcon(HINSTANCE instance, TResId resId);
```

In this case, *instance* should be the HINSTANCE of the module from which you want to get the icon, and *resId* is the resource ID of the particular icon you want to get. Passing in 0 for *instance* gives you access to built-in Windows icons.

You can also load an icon from a file:

```
TIcon(HINSTANCE instance, char far* filename, int index);
```

In this case, *instance* should be the instance of the current module, *filename* is the name of the file containing the icon, and *index* is the index of the icon to be retrieved.

You can also create a new icon:

```
TIcon(HINSTANCE instance,
      TSize& size,
      int planes,
      int bitsPixel,
      void far* andBits,
      void far* xorBits);
```

In this case, *instance* should be the instance of the current module, *size* indicates the size of the icon, *planes* indicates the number of color planes, *bitsPixel* indicates the number of bits per pixel, *andBits* points to an array containing the AND mask of the icon, and *xorBits* points to an array containing the XOR mask of the icon. The *andBits* array must specify a monochrome mask. The *xorBits* array can be a monochrome or device-dependent color bitmap.

You can also create a new *TIcon* object from an existing HICON handle:

```
TIcon(HICON handle, TAutoDelete autoDelete = NoAutoDelete);
```

This constructor is used to obtain an ObjectWindows object as an alias to a regular Windows handle received in a message.

There are two other constructors that are available only for 32-bit applications:

```
TIcon(const void* resBits, uint32 resSize);
TIcon(const ICONINFO* iconInfo);
```

The first constructor takes two parameters: *resBits* is a pointer to a buffer containing the icon data bits (usually obtained from a call to *LookupIconIdFromDirectory* or *LoadResource* functions) and *resSize* indicates the number of bits in the *resBits* buffer.

The second constructor takes a single parameter, an ICONINFO structure. The constructor creates an icon from the information in the ICONINFO structure. The *fIcon* member of the ICONINFO structure must be **true**, indicating that the ICONINFO structure contains an icon.

~TIcon deletes the icon and its storage space.

Accessing TIcon

You can access *TIcon* through an HICON. To get an HICON from a *TIcon* object, use the HICON operator with the *TIcon* object as the parameter. The HICON operator is almost never explicitly invoked:

```
HICON
TMyIcon::GetHIcon()
{
  return *this;
}
```

This code automatically invokes the HICON conversion operator to cast the *TIcon* object to the correct type.

The other access function in *TIcon*, called *GetIconInfo*, is available for 32-bit applications only. *GetIconInfo* takes as its only parameter a pointer to a ICONINFO structure. The function fills out the ICONINFO structure and returns **true** if the operation was successful. For example, suppose you create an icon object, then want to extract the icon data into an ICONINFO structure. The code would look something like this:

```
ICONINFO iconInfo;

// Load stock icon - Exclamation
TIcon icon(0, IDI_EXCLAMATION);

icon.GetIconInfo(&iconInfo);
```

TCursor class

The *TCursor* class encapsulates a cursor handle and constructors for instantiating the *TCursor* object. You can use the *TCursor* class to construct a cursor from a resource or explicit information.

Constructing TCursor

You can construct a *TCursor* in a number of ways: from an existing *TCursor* object, from a resource in the current application, from a resource in another application, or explicitly from size and data information.

You can create cursor objects from an existing cursor encapsulated in a *TCursor* object:

```
TCursor(HINSTANCE instance, const TCursor& cursor);
```

instance in this case should be the instance of the current application. *TCursor* does not encapsulate the application instance because *TCursors* know nothing about application objects. It is usually easiest to access the current application instance in a window or other interface object.

```
TCursor(HINSTANCE instance, TResId resId);

TCursor(HINSTANCE instance,
        const TPoint& hotSpot,
        TSize& size,
        void far* andBits,
        void far* xorBits);
```

You can also create a new *TCursor* object from an existing HCURSOR handle:

```
TCursor(HCURSOR handle, TAutoDelete autoDelete = NoAutoDelete);
```

This constructor is used to obtain an ObjectWindows object as an alias to a regular Windows handle received in a message.

There are two other constructors that are available only for 32-bit applications:

```
TCursor(const void* resBits, uint32 resSize);
TCursor(const ICONINFO* iconInfo);
```

The first constructor takes two parameters: *resBits* is a pointer to a buffer containing the cursor data bits (usually obtained from a call to *LookupIconIdFromDirectory* or *LoadResource* functions) and *resSize* indicates the number of bits in the *resBits* buffer.

The second constructor takes a single parameter, an ICONINFO structure. The constructor creates an icon from the information in the ICONINFO structure. The *fIcon* member of the ICONINFO structure must be **false**, indicating that the ICONINFO structure contains an cursor.

~TCursor deletes the cursor. If the deletion fails, the destructor throws an exception.

Accessing TCursor

You can access *TCursor* through an HCURSOR. To get an HCURSOR from a *TCursor* object, use the HCURSOR operator with the *TCursor* object as the parameter. The HCURSOR operator is almost never explicitly invoked:

```
HCURSOR
TMyCursor::GetHCursor()
{
  return *this;
}
```

This code automatically invokes the HCURSOR conversion operator to cast the *TCursor* object to the correct type.

The other access function in *TCursor*, called *GetIconInfo*, is available for 32-bit applications only. *GetIconInfo* takes as its only parameter a pointer to a ICONINFO structure. The function fills out the ICONINFO structure and returns **true** if the operation was successful. For example, suppose you create an cursor object, then want to extract the cursor data into an ICONINFO structure. The code would look something like this:

```
ICONINFO cursorInfo;

// Load stock cursor - slashed circle
TCursor cursor(NULL, IDC_NO);

cursor.GetIconInfo(&cursorInfo);
```

TDib class

A device-independent bitmap, or DIB, has no GDI handle like a regular bitmap, although it does have a global handle. Instead, it is just a structure containing format and palette information and a collection of bits (pixels). The *TDib* class provides a convenient way to work with DIBs like any other GDI object. The memory for the DIB is in one chunk allocated with the Windows *GlobalAlloc* functions, so that it can be passed to the Clipboard, an OLE server or client, and others outside of its instantiating application.

Constructing and destroying TDib

You can construct a *TDib* object either directly or indirectly. Using direct construction, you can specify the bitmap's width, height, and so on. Using indirect construction, you can specify an existing bitmap object, pointer to a BITMAP structure, a metafile, a *TDC* device context, and more.

Here is the constructor for directly constructing a *TDib* object:

```
TDib(int width, int height, int nColors, uint16 mode=DIB_RGB_COLORS);
```

width and *height* specify the width and height in pixels of the DIB. *nColors* specifies the number of colors actually used in the DIB. *mode* can be either DIB_RGB_COLORS or DIB_PAL_COLORS. DIB_RGB_COLORS indicates that the color table consists of literal RGB values. DIB_PAL_COLORS indicates that the color table consists of an array of 16-bit indices into the currently realized logical palette.

You can create a *TDib* object by loading it from an executable application module. This constructor takes two parameters: the first is the HINSTANCE of the module containing the bitmap and the second is the resource ID of the bitmap you want to load:

```
TDib(HINSTANCE instance, TResId resId);
```

To create a *TDib* object from the Clipboard, pass a reference to a *TClipboard* object to the constructor. The constructor gets the handle of the bitmap in the Clipboard and constructs a bitmap object from the handle.

```
TDib(const TClipboard& clipboard);
```

You can load a DIB from a file (typically a .BMP file) into a *TDib* object by specifying the name as the only parameter of the constructor:

```
TDib(const char* name);
```

You can also construct a *TDib* object given a *TBitmap* object and a *TPalette* object. If no palette is give, this constructor uses the focus window's currently realized palette.

```
TDib(const TBitmap& bitmap, const TPalette* pal = 0);
```

You can create a DIB object from an existing DIB object:

```
TDib(const TDib& dib);
```

You can also create a new *TDib* object from an existing HGLOBAL handle:

```
TDib(HGLOBAL handle, TAutoDelete autoDelete = NoAutoDelete);
```

This constructor is used to obtain an ObjectWindows object as an alias to a regular Windows handle received in a message. Because an HGLOBAL handle can point to many different kinds of objects, you must ensure that the HGLOBAL you use in this constructor is actually the handle to a device-independent bitmap. If you pass a handle to another type of object, the constructor throws an exception.

If *ShouldDelete* is **true**, ~*TDib* frees the resource and unlocks and frees the chunk of global memory as needed.

Accessing TDib

TDib provides a number of different types of functions for accessing the encapsulated DIB.

Type conversions

The type conversion functions for *TDib* let you access *TDib* in the most convenient manner for the operation you want to perform.

You can use the HANDLE conversion operator to access *TDib* through a HANDLE. To get a HANDLE from a *TDib* object, use the HANDLE operator with the *TDib* object as the parameter. The HANDLE operator is almost never explicitly invoked:

```
HANDLE
TMyDib::GetHandle()
{
   return *this;
}
```

This code automatically invokes the HANDLE conversion operator to cast the *TDib* object to the correct type.

You can also convert a *TDib* object to three other bitmap types. You can use the following operators to convert a *TDib* to any one of three types: BITMAPINFO *, BITMAPINFOHEADER *, or *TRgbQuad* *. You can use the result wherever that type is normally used:

```
operator BITMAPINFO far*();
operator BITMAPINFOHEADER far*();
operator TRgbQuad far*();
```

Accessing internal structures

The functions in this section give you access to the DIB's internal data structures. These three functions return the DIB's equivalent bitmap types as pointers to BITMAPINFO, BITMAPINFOHEADER, and *TRgbQuad* objects:

```
BITMAPINFO far* GetInfo();
BITMAPINFOHEADER far* GetInfoHeader();
TRgbQuad far* GetColors();
```

The following function returns a pointer to an array of WORDs containing the color indices for the DIB:

```
uint16 far* GetIndices();
```

This function returns a pointer to an array containing the bits that make up the actual DIB image:

```
void HUGE* GetBits();
```

Moving a DIB to the Clipboard

You can move a DIB to the Clipboard using the *ToClipboard* function. *ToClipboard* takes a reference to a *TClipboard* object as a parameter. Because the *ToClipboard* function actually removes the object from your application, you should usually use a *TDib* constructor to create a temporary object:

```
TClipboard clipBoard;
TDib(ID_BITMAP).ToClipboard(clipBoard);
```

DIB information

The *TDib* class provides a number of accessor functions that you can use to query a *TDib* object and get information about the DIB contained in the object:

- To find out whether the object is valid, call the *IsOK* function. The *IsOK* takes no parameters. It returns **true** if the object is valid and **false** if not.

- The *IsPM* function takes no parameters. This function returns **true** when the DIB is a Presentation Manager-compatible bitmap.

- The *Width* and *Height* functions return the bitmap's width and height respectively, in pixel units.

- The *Size* function returns the bitmap's width and height in pixel units, but contained in a *TSize* object.

- The *NumColors* function returns the number of colors used in the bitmap.

- *StartScan* is provided for compatibility with older code. This function always returns 0.

- *NumScans* is provided for compatibility with older code. This functions returns the height of the DIB in pixels.

- The *Usage* function indicates what mode the DIB is in. This value is either DIB_RGB_COLORS or DIB_PAL_COLORS.

- The *WriteFile* function writes the DIB object to disk. This function takes a single parameter, a **const char***. This should point to the name of the file in which you want to save the bitmap.

Working in palette or RGB mode

A DIB can hold color values in two ways. In palette mode, the DIB's color table contains indices into a palette. The color values don't themselves indicate any particular color. The indices must be cross-referenced to the corresponding palette entry in the currently realized palette. In RGB mode, each entry in the DIB's color table represents an actual RGB color value.

You can switch from RGB to palette mode using these functions:

```
bool ChangeModeToPal(const TPalette& pal);
bool ChangeModeToRGB(const TPalette& pal);
```

When you switch to palette mode using *ChangeModetoPal*, the *TPalette* **&** parameter is used as the DIB's palette. Each color used in the DIB is mapped to the palette and converted to a palette index. When you switch to RGB mode using *ChangeModetoRGB*, the *TPalette* **&** parameter is used to convert the current palette indices to their RGB equivalents contained in the palette.

If you're working in RGB mode, you can use the following functions to access and modify the DIB's color table:

- Retrieve any entry in the DIB's color table using the *GetColor* function. This function takes a single parameter, an **int** indicating the index of the color table entry. *GetColor* returns a *TColor* object.

- Change any entry in the DIB's color table using the *SetColor* function. This function takes two parameters, an **int** indicating the index of the color table entry you want to change and a *TColor* containing the value to which you want to change the entry.

- Match a *TColor* object to a color table entry by using the *FindColor* function. *FindColor* takes a single parameter, a *TColor* object. *FindColor* searches through the DIB's color table until it finds an exact match for the *TColor* object. If it fails to find a match, *FindColor* returns –1.

- Substitute one color for a color that currently exists in the DIB's color table using the *MapColor* function. This function takes three parameters, a *TColor* object containing the color to be replaced, a *TColor* object containing the new color to be placed in the color table, and a **bool** that indicates whether all occurrences of the second color should be replaced. If the third parameter is **true**, all color table entries that are equal to the first parameter are replaced by the second. If the third parameter is **false**, only the first color table entry that is equal to the first parameter is replaced. By default, the third parameter is **false**. The return value of this function indicates the total number of palette entries that were replaced.

  For example, suppose you wanted to replace all occurrences of white in your DIB with light gray. The code would look something like this:

  ```
  myDib->MapColor(TColor::LtGray, TColor::White, true);
  ```

If you're working in palette mode, you can use the following functions to access and modify the DIB's color table:

- Retrieve the palette index of any color table entry using the *GetIndex* function. This function takes a single parameter, an **int** indicating the index of the color table entry. *GetIndex* returns a *uint16* containing the palette index.

- Change any entry in the DIB's color table using the *SetIndex* function. This function takes two parameters, an **int** indicating the index of the color table entry you want to change and a *uint16* containing the palette index to which you want to change the entry.

- Match a palette index to a color table entry by using the *FindIndex* function. *FindIndex* takes a single parameter, a *uint16*. *FindIndex* searches through the DIB's color table until it finds a match for the *uint16*. If it fails to find a match, *FindIndex* returns –1.

- Substitute one color for a color that currently exists in the DIB's color table using the *MapIndex* function. This function takes three parameters, a *uint16* indicating the index to be replaced, a *uint16* indicating the new palette index to be placed in the color table, and a **bool** that indicates whether all occurrences of the second color should be replaced. If the third parameter is **true**, all color table entries that are equal to the first parameter are replaced by the second. If the third parameter is **false**, only the first color table entry that is equal to the first parameter is replaced. By default, the third parameter is **false**. The return value of this function indicates the total number of palette entries that were replaced.

Matching interface colors to system colors

DIBs are often used to enhance and decorate a user interface. To make your interface consistent with your application user's system, you should use the *MapUIColors* function, which replaces standard interface colors with the user's own system colors. Here is the syntax for *MapUIColors*:

```
void MapUIColors(uint mapColors, TColor* bkColor = 0);
```

The *mapColors* parameter should be an OR'ed combination of five flags: *TDib::MapFace*, *TDib::MapText*, *TDib::MapShadow*, *TDib::MapHighlight*, and *TDib::MapFrame*. Each of these values causes a different color substitution to take place:

This flag	Replaces...	With...
TDib::MapText	TColor::Black	COLOR_BTNTEXT
TDib::MapFace	TColor::LtGray	COLOR_BTNFACE
TDib::MapFace	TColor::Gray	COLOR_BTNSHADOW
TDib::MapFace	TColor::White	COLOR_BTNHIGHLIGHT
TDib::MapFrame	TColor::LtMagenta	COLOR_WINDOWFRAME

The *bkColor* parameter, if specified, causes the color *TColor::LtYellow* to be replaced by the color *bkColor*.

Because *MapUIColors* searches for and replaces *TColor* table entries, this function is useful only with a DIB in RGB mode. Furthermore, because it replaces particular colors, you must design your interface using the standard system colors; for example, your button text should be black (*TColor::Black*), button faces should be light gray (*TColor::LtGray*), and so on. This should be fairly simple, since these are specifically designed so that they are equivalent to the standard default colors for each interface element.

You should also call the *MapUIColors* function before you modify any of the colors modified by *MapUIColors*. If you don't do this, *MapUIColors* won't be able to find the attribute color for which it is searching, and that part of the interface won't match the system colors.

Extending TDib

TDib provides a number of **protected** functions that are accessible only from within *TDib* and *TDib*-derived classes. You can also access *TDib*'s control data:

• *Info* is a pointer to a BITMAPINFO or BITMAPCOREINFO structure, which contains the attributes, color table, and other information about the DIB.

• *Bits* is a **void** pointer that points to an area of memory containing the actual graphical data for the DIB.

• *NumClrs* is a **long** containing the actual number of colors used in the DIB; note that this isn't the number of colors *possible*, but the number actually used.

- *W* is an **int** indicating the width of the DIB in pixels.

- *H* is an **int** indicating the height of the DIB in pixels.

- *Mode* is a *uint16* indicating whether the DIB is in RGB mode (DIB_RGB_COLORS) or palette mode (DIB_PAL_COLORS).

- *IsCore* is a **bool**; it is **true** if the *Info* pointer points to a BITMAPCOREINFO structure and **false** if it doesn't.

- *IsResHandle* indicates whether the DIB was loaded as a resource and therefore whether *Handle* is a resource handle.

You can use the *InfoFromHandle* function to fill out the structure pointed to by *Info*. *InfoFromHandle* extracts information from *Handle* and fills out the attributes of the *Info* structure. *InfoFromHandle* takes no parameters and has no return value.

The *Read* function reads a Windows 3.0- or Presentation Manager-compatible DIB from a file referenced by a *TFile* object. When loading, *Read* checks the DIB's header, attributes, palette, and bitmap. Presentation Manager-compatible DIBs are converted to Windows DIBs on the fly. This function returns **true** if the DIB was read in correctly.

You can use the *LoadResource* function to load a DIB from an application or DLL module. This function takes two parameters, an HINSTANCE indicating the application or DLL module from which you want to load the DIB and a *TResId* indicating the particular resource within that module you want to retrieve. *LoadResource* returns **true** if the operation was successful.

You can use the *LoadFile* function to load a DIB from a file. This function takes one parameter, a **char *** that points to a string containing the name of the file containing the DIB. *LoadFile* returns **true** if the operation was successful.

33

Validator objects

ObjectWindows provides several ways you can associate validator objects with the edit control objects to validate the information a user types into an edit control. Using validator objects makes it easy to add data validation to existing ObjectWindows applications or to change the way a field validates its data.

This chapter discusses three topics related to data validation:

- Using the standard validator classes
- Using data validator objects
- Writing your own validator objects

At any time, you can validate the contents of any edit control by calling that object's *CanClose* member function, which in turn calls the appropriate validator object. ObjectWindows validator classes also interact at the keystroke and gain/lose focus level.

The standard validator classes

The ObjectWindows standard validator classes automate data validation. ObjectWindows defines six validator classes in validate.h:

- *TValidator*, a base class from which all other validator classes are derived.
- *TFilterValidator*, a filter validator class.
- *TRangeValidator*, a numeric-range validator class based on *TFilterValidator*.
- *TLookupValidator*, a lookup validator base class.
- *TStringLookupValidator*, a string lookup validator class based on *TLookupValidator*.
- *TPXPictureValidator*, a picture validator class that validates a string based on a given pattern or "picture."

The following sections briefly describe each of the standard validator classes.

Validator base class

The abstract class *TValidator* is the base class from which all validator classes are derived. *TValidator* is a validator for which all input is valid: member functions *IsValid* and *IsValidInput* always return **true**, and *Error* does nothing. Derived classes should override *IsValid*, *IsValidInput*, and *Error* to define which values are valid and when errors should be reported. Use *TValidator* as a starting point for your own validator classes if none of the other validator classes are appropriate starting points.

Filter validator class

TFilterValidator is a simple validator that checks input as the user enters it. The filter validator constructor takes one parameter, a set of valid characters:

```
TFilterValidator(const TCharSet& validChars);
```

TCharSet is defined in bitset.h.

TFilterValidator overrides *IsValidInput* to return **true** only if all characters in the current input string are contained in the set of characters passed to the constructor. The edit control inserts characters only if *IsValidInput* returns **true**, so there is no need to override *IsValid*: because the characters made it through the input filter, the complete string is valid by definition. Descendants of *TFilterValidator*, such as *TRangeValidator*, can combine filtering of input with other checks on the completed string.

Range validator class

TRangeValidator is a range validator derived from *TFilterValidator*. It accepts only numbers and adds range checking on the final result. The constructor takes two parameters that define the minimum and maximum valid values:

```
TRangeValidator(long min, long max);
```

The range validator constructs itself as a filter validator that accepts only the digits 0 through 9 and the plus and minus characters. The inherited *IsValidInput*, therefore, ensures that only numbers filter through. *TRangeValidator* then overrides *IsValid* to return **true** only if the entered numbers are a valid integer within the range defined in the constructor. The *Error* member function displays a message box indicating that the entered value is out of range.

Lookup validator class

TLookupValidator is an abstract class that compares entered values with a list of acceptable values to determine validity. *TLookupValidator* introduces the virtual member function *Lookup*. By default, *Lookup* returns **true**. Derived classes should override *Lookup* to compare the parameter with a list of items, returning **true** if a match is found.

TLookupValidator overrides *IsValid* to return **true** only if *Lookup* returns **true**. In derived classes you should *not* override *IsValid*; you should instead override *Lookup*. *TStringLookupValidator* class is an instance class based on *TLookupValidator*.

String lookup validator class

TStringLookupValidator is a working example of a lookup validator; it compares the string passed from the edit control with the items in a string list. If the passed-in string occurs in the list, *IsValid* returns **true**. The constructor takes only one parameter, the list of valid strings:

```
TStringLookupValidator(TSortedStringArray* strings);
```

TSortedStringArray is defined as

```
typedef TSArrayAsVector<string> TSortedStringArray;
```

To use a different string list after constructing the string lookup validator, use member function *NewStringList*, which disposes of the old list and installs the new list.

TStringLookupValidator overrides *Lookup* and *Error*. *Lookup* returns **true** if the passed-in string is in the list. *Error* displays a message box indicating that the string is not in the list.

Picture validator class

Picture validators compare the string entered by the user with a "picture" or template that describes the format of valid input. The pictures used are compatible with those used by Borland's Paradox relational database to control user input. Constructing a picture validator requires two parameters: a string holding the template image and a Boolean value indicating whether to automatically fill-in the picture with literal characters:

```
TPXPictureValidator(const char far* pic, bool autoFill=false);
```

TPXPictureValidator overrides *Error*, *IsValid*, and *IsValidInput*, and adds a new member function, *Picture*. *Error* displays a message box indicating what format the string should have. *IsValid* returns **true** only if the function *Picture* returns **true**; thus you can derive new kinds of picture validators by overriding only the *Picture* member function. *IsValidInput* checks characters as the user enters them, allowing only those characters permitted by the picture format, and optionally filling in literal characters from the picture format.

Here is an example of a picture validator that is being constructed to accept social security numbers:

```
edit->SetValidator(new TPXPictureValidator("###-##-####"));
```

Picture syntax is fully described under *TPXPictureValidator* member function *Picture* in the *ObjectWindows Reference*.

The *Picture* member function tries to format the given input string according to the picture format and returns a value indicating the degree of its success. The following code lists those return values:

```
// TPXPictureValidator result type
enum TPicResult
{
  prComplete,
```

```
    prIncomplete,
    prEmpty,
    prError,
    prSyntax,
    prAmbiguous,
    prIncompNoFill
};
```

Using data validators

To use data validator objects, you must first construct an edit control object and then construct a validator object and assign it to the edit control. From this point on, you don't need to interact with the validator object directly. The edit control knows when to call validator member functions at the appropriate times.

Constructing an edit control object

Edit controls objects are instances of the *TEdit* class. Here is an example of how to construct an edit control:

```
TEdit* edit;
edit = new TEdit(this, 101, sizeof(transfer.NameEdit));
```

For more information on *TEdit* and using edit controls, see Chapter 29.

Constructing and assigning validator objects

Because validator objects aren't interface objects, their constructors require only enough information to establish the validation criteria. For example, a numeric-range validator object requires only two parameters: the minimum and maximum values in the valid range.

Every edit control object has a data member that can point to a validator object. This pointer's declaration looks like this:

```
TValidator *Validator
```

If *Validator* doesn't point to a validator object, the edit control behaves as described in Chapter 29. You assign a validator by calling the edit control object's *SetValidator* member function. The edit control automatically checks with the validator object when processing key events and when called on to validate itself.

The following code shows the construction of a validator and its assignment to an edit control. In this case, a filter validator that allows only alphabetic characters is used.

```
edit->SetValidator(new TFilterValidator("A-Za-z. "));
```

A complete example showing the use of the standard validators can be found in OWLAPI\VALIDATE.

Overriding validator member functions

Although the standard validator objects should satisfy most of your data validation needs, you can also modify the standard validators or write your own validation objects. If you decide to do this, you should be familiar with the following list of member functions inherited from the base class *TValidator*; in addition to understanding the function of each member function, you should also know how edit controls use them and how to override them if necessary.

- *Valid*
- *IsValid*
- *IsValidInput*
- *Error*

Member function Valid

Member function *Valid* is called by the associated edit-control object to verify that the data entered is valid. Much like the *CanClose* member functions of interface objects, *Valid* is a Boolean function that returns **true** only if the string passed to it is valid data. One responsibility of an edit control's *CanClose* member function is calling the validator object's *Valid* member function, passing the edit control's current text.

When using validators with edit controls, you shouldn't need to call or override the validator's *Valid* member function; the inherited version of *Valid* will suffice. By default, *Valid* returns **true** if the member function *IsValid* returns **true**; otherwise, it calls *Error* to notify the user of the error and then returns **false**.

Member function IsValid

The virtual member function *IsValid* is called by *Valid*, which passes *IsValid* the text string to be validated. *IsValid* returns **true** if the string represents valid data. *IsValid* does the actual data validation, so if you create your own validator objects, you'll probably override *IsValid*.

Note that you don't call *IsValid* directly. Use *Valid* to call *IsValid*, because *Valid* calls *Error* to alert the user if *IsValid* returns **false**. This separates the validation role from the error-reporting role.

Member function IsValidInput

When an edit control object recognizes a keystroke event intended for it, it calls its validator's *IsValidInput* member function to ensure that the entered character is a valid entry. By default, *IsValidInput* member functions always return **true**, meaning that all keystrokes are acceptable, but some derived validators override *IsValidInput* to filter out unwanted keystrokes.

For example, range validators, which are used for numeric input, return **true** from *IsValidInput* only for numeric digits and the characters '+' and '−'.

IsValidInput takes two parameters:

```
virtual bool IsValidInput(char far* str, bool suppressFill);
```

The first parameter, *str*, points to the current input text being validated. The second parameter is a Boolean value indicating whether the validator should apply filling or padding to the input string before attempting to validate it. *TPXPictureValidator* is the only standard validator object that uses the second parameter.

Member function Error

Virtual member function *Error* alerts the user that the contents of the edit control don't pass the validation check. The standard validator objects generally present a simple message box notifying the user that the contents of the input are invalid and describing what proper input would be.

For example, the *Error* member function for a range validator object creates a message box indicating that the value in the edit control is not between the indicated minimum and maximum values.

Although most descendant validator objects override *Error*, you should never call it directly. *Valid* calls *Error* for you if *IsValid* returns **false**, which is the only time *Error* needs to be called.

Chapter

34

Visual Basic controls

ObjectWindows lets you use Visual Basic (VBX) 1.0-compatible controls in your Windows applications as easily as you use standard Windows or ObjectWindows controls.

VBX controls offer a wide range of functionality that is not provided in standard Windows controls. There are numerous public domain and commercial packages of VBX controls that can be used to provide a more polished and useful user interface.

This chapter describes how to design an application that uses VBX controls, describes the *TVbxControl* and *TVbxEventHandler* classes, explains how to receive messages from a VBX control, and shows how to get and set the properties of a control.

Using VBX controls

To use VBX controls in your ObjectWindows application, follow this process:

1 In your *OwlMain* function, call the function *VBXInit* before you call the *Run* function of your application object. Call the function *VBXTerm* after you call the *Run* function of your application object. *VBXInit* takes the application instance as a parameter. *VBXTerm* takes no parameters. Your *OwlMain* function might look something like this:

```
int
OwlMain(int argc, char* argv[])
{
  VBXInit(_hInstance);

  return TApplication("Wow!").Run();

  VBXTerm();
}
```

These functions initialize and close each instance's host environment necessary for using VBX controls.

2 Derive a class mixing your base interface class with *TVbxEventHandler*. Your base interface class is whatever class you want to display the control in. If you're using the control in a dialog box, you need to mix in *TDialog*. The code would look something like this:

```
class MyVbxDialog : public TDialog, public TVbxEventHandler
{
  public:
    MyVbxDialog(TWindow *parent, char *name)
      : TDialog(parent, name), TWindow(parent, name) {}

    DECLARE_RESPONSE_TABLE(MyVbxDialog);
};
```

3 Build a response table for the parent, including all relevant events from your control. Use the EV_VBXEVENTNAME macro to set up the response for each control event. Response tables are described in greater detail in Chapter 22.

4 Create the control's parent. You can either construct the control when you create the parent or allow the parent to construct the control itself, depending on how the control is being used. This is discussed in further detail on page 433.

VBX control classes

ObjectWindows provides two classes for use in designing an interface for VBX controls. These classes are *TVbxControl* and *TVbxEventHandler*.

TVbxControl class

TVbxControl provides the actual interface to the control by letting you:

- Construct a VBX control object

- Get and change control properties

- Find the number of control properties and convert property names to and from property indices

- Find the number of control events and convert event names to and from event indices

- Call the Visual Basic 1.0 standard control methods *AddItem*, *Move*, *Refresh*, and *RemoveItem*

- Get the handle to the control element using the *TVbxControl* member function *GetHCTL*

TVbxControl is derived from the class *TControl*, which is derived from *TWindow*. Thus, *TVbxControl* acts much the same as any other interface element based on *TWindow*.

TVbxControl constructors

TVbxControl has two constructors. The first constructor lets you dynamically construct a VBX control by specifying a VBX control file name (for example, SWITCH.VBX), control ID, control class, control title, location, and size:

```
TVbxControl(TWindow *parent,
        int id,
        const char far *FileName,
        const char far *ClassName,
        const char far *title,
        int x, int y,
        int w, int h,
        TModule *module = 0);
```

where:

- *parent* is a pointer to the control's parent.

- *id* is the control's ID, which is used when defining the parent's response table; this usually looks much like a resource ID.

- *FileName* is the name of the file that contains the VBX control, including a path name if necessary.

- *ClassName* is the class name of the control; a given VBX control file might contain a number of separate controls, each of which is identified by a unique class name (usually found in the control reference guide of third-party VBX control libraries).

- *title* is the control's title or caption.

- *x* and *y* are the coordinates within the parent object at which you want the control placed.

- *w* and *h* are the control's width and the height.

- *module* is passed to the *TControl* base constructor as the *TModule* parameter for that constructor; it defaults to 0.

The second constructor lets you set a *TVbxControl* object using a VBX control that has been defined in the application's resource file:

```
TVbxControl(TWindow *parent,
        int resId,
        TModule *module = 0);
```

where:

- *parent* is a pointer to the control's parent.

- *resId* is the resource ID of the VBX control in the resource file.

- *module* is passed to the *TControl* base constructor as the *TModule* parameter for that constructor; it defaults to 0.

Implicit and explicit construction

You can construct VBX controls either explicitly or implicitly. You explicitly construct an object when you call one of the constructors. You implicitly construct an object when you do not call one of the constructors and allow the control to be instantiated and created by its parent.

Explicit construction involves calling either constructor of a VBX control object. This is normally done in the parent's constructor so that the VBX control is constructed and ready when the parent window is created. You can also wait to construct the control until it's needed; for example, you might want to do this if you had room for only one control. In this case, you could let the user choose a menu choice or press a button. Then, depending what the user does, you would instantiate an object and display it in an existing interface element.

The following code demonstrates explicit construction using both of the *TVbxControl* constructors in the constructor of a dialog box object:

```
class TTestDialog : public TDialog, public TVbxEventHandler
{
  public:
    TTestDialog(TWindow *parent, char *name)
      : TDialog(parent, name), TWindow(parent, name)
    {
      new TVbxControl(this, IDCONTROL1);
      new TVbxControl(this, IDCONTROL2,
                      "SWITCH.VBX", "BiSwitch",
                      "&Program VBX Control",
                      16, 70, 200, 50);
    }

  DECLARE_RESPONSE_TABLE(TTestDialog);
};
```

Implicit construction takes place when you design your interface element outside of your application source code, such as in Resource Workshop. You can use Resource Workshop to add VBX controls to dialog boxes and other interface elements. Then when you instantiate the parent object, the children, such as edit boxes, list boxes, buttons, and VBX controls, are automatically created along with the parent. The following code demonstrates how the code for this might look. It's important to note, however, that what you don't see in the following code is a VBX control. Instead, the VBX control is included in the dialog resource DIALOG_1. When DIALOG_1 is loaded and created, the VBX control is automatically created.

```
class TTestDialog : public TDialog, public TVbxEventHandler
{
  public:
    TTestDialog(TWindow *parent, char *name)
      : TDialog(parent, name), TWindow(parent, name) {}
  DECLARE_RESPONSE_TABLE(TTestDialog);
};

void
TTestWindow::CmAbout()
{
  TTestDialog(this, "DIALOG_1").Execute();
}
```

TVbxEventHandler class

The *TVbxEventHandler* class is quite small and, for the most part, of little interest to most programmers. What it does is very important, though. Without the functionality contained in *TVbxEventHandler*, you could not communicate with your VBX controls. The event-handling programming model is described in greater detail in the following sections; this section explains only the part that *TVbxEventHandler* plays in the process.

TVbxEventHandler consists of a single function and a one-message response table. The function is called *EvVbxDispatch*, and it is the event-handling routine for a message called WM_VBXFIREEVENT. *EvVbxDispatch* receives the WM_VBXFIREEVENT message, converts the uncracked message to a VBXEVENT structure, and dispatches a new message, which is handled by the control's parent. Because the parent object is necessarily derived from *TVbxEventHandler*, this means that the parent calls back to itself with a different message. The new message is much easier to handle and understand. This is the message that is handled by the WM_VBXEVENTNAME macro described in the next section.

Handling VBX control messages

You must handle VBX control messages through the control's parent object. For the parent object to be able to handle these messages, it must be derived from the class *TVbxEventHandler*. To accomplish this, you can mix whatever interface object class you want to use to contain the VBX control (for example, *TDialog*, *TFrameWindow*, or classes you might have derived from ObjectWindows interface classes) with the *TVbxEventHandler* class.

Event response table

Once you've derived your new class, you need to build a response table for it. The response table for this class looks like a normal response table; you still need to handle all the regular command messages and events you normally do. The only addition is the EV_VBXEVENTNAME macro to handle the new class of messages from your VBX controls.

The EV_VBXEVENTNAME macro takes three parameters:

```
EV_VBXEVENTNAME(ID, Event, EvHandler)
```

where:

- *ID* is the control ID. You can find this ID either as the second parameter to both constructors or as the resource ID in the resource file.

- *Event* is a string identifying the event name. This is dependent on the control and can be one of the standard VBX event names or a custom event name. You can find this event name by looking in the control reference guide if the control is from a third-party VBX control library.

- *EvHandler* is the handler function for this event and control. The *EvHandler* function has the signature:

```
void EvHandler(VBXEVENT FAR *event);
```

When a message is received from a VBX control by its parent, it dispatches the message to the handler function that corresponds to the correct control and event. When it calls the function, it passes it a pointer to a VBXEVENT structure. This structure is discussed in more detail in the next section.

Interpreting a control event

Once a VBX control event has taken place and the event-handling function has been called, the function needs to deal with the VBXEVENT structure received as a parameter. This structure looks like this:

```
struct VBXEVENT
{
  HCTL hCtl;
  HWND hWnd;
  int nID;
  int iEvent;
  LPCSTR lpszEvent;
  int cParams;
  LPVOID lpParams;
};
```

where:

- *hCtl* is the handle of the sending VBX control (not a window handle).
- *hWnd* is the handle of the control window.
- *nID* is the ID of the VBX control.
- *iEvent* is the event index.
- *lpszEvent* is the event name.
- *cParams* is the number of parameters for this event.
- *lpParams* is a pointer to an array containing pointers to the parameter values for this event.

To understand this structure, you need to understand how a VBX control event works. The first three members are straightforward: they let you identify the sending control. The next two members are also fairly simple; each event that a VBX control can send has both an event index, represented here by *iEvent*, and an event name, represented here by *lpszEvent*.

The next two members, which store the parameters passed with the event, are more complex. *cParams* contains the total number of parameters available for this event. *lpParams* is an array of pointers to the event's parameters (like any other array, *lpParam* is indexed from 0 to *cParams* –1). These two members are more complicated than the previous members because there is no inherent indication of the type or meaning of each parameter. If the control is from a third-party VBX control library, you can look in the control reference guide to find this information. Otherwise, you'll need to get the information from the designer of the control (or to have designed the control yourself).

Finding event information

The standard way to interpret the information returned by an event is to refer to the documentation for the VBX control. Failing that, *TVbxControl* provides a number of methods for obtaining information about an event.

You can find the total number of events that a control can send by using the *TVbxControl* member function *GetNumEvents*. This returns an **int** that gives the total number of events. These events are indexed from 0 to the return value of *GetNumEvents* –1.

You can find the name of any event in this range by calling the *TVbxControl* member function *GetEventName*. *GetEventName* takes one parameter, an **int** index number, and returns a string containing the name of the event.

Conversely, you can find the index of an event by calling the *TVbxControl* member function *GetEventIndex*. *GetEventIndex* takes one parameter, a string containing the event name, and returns the corresponding **int** event index.

Accessing a VBX control

There are two ways you can directly access a VBX control. The first way is to get and set the properties of the control. A control has a fixed number of properties you can set to affect the look or behavior of the control. The other way is to call the control's methods. A control's methods are similar to member functions in a class and are actually accessed through member functions in the *TVbxControl* class. You can use these methods to call into the object and cause an action to take place.

VBX control properties

Every VBX control has a number of properties. Control properties affect the look and behavior of the control; for example, the colors used in various parts of the control, the size and location of the control, the control's caption, and so on. Changing these properties is usually your main way to manipulate a VBX control.

Each control's properties should be fully documented in the control reference guide of third-party VBX control libraries. If the control is not a third-party control or part of a commercial control package, then you need to consult the control's designer for any limits or special meanings to the control's properties. Many properties often function only as an index to a property. An example of this might be background patterns: 0 could mean plain, 1 could mean cross-hatched, 2 could mean black, and so on. Without the proper documentation or information, it can be quite difficult to use a control's properties.

Finding property information

The standard way to get information about a control's properties is to refer to the documentation for the VBX control. Failing that, *TVbxControl* provides a number of methods for obtaining information about a control's properties.

You can find the total number of properties for a control by calling the *TVbxControl* member function *GetNumProps*, which returns an **int** that gives the total number of properties. These properties are indexed from 0 to the return value of *GetNumProps* –1.

You can find the name of any property in this range by calling the *TVbxControl* member function *GetPropName*. *GetPropName* takes one parameter, an **int** index number, and returns a string containing the name of the property.

Conversely, you can find the index of a property by calling the *TVbxControl* member function *GetPropIndex*. *GetPropIndex* takes one parameter, a string containing the property name, and returns the corresponding **int** property index.

Getting control properties

You can get the value of a control property using either its name or its index number. Although using the index is somewhat more efficient (because there's no need to look up a string), using the property name is usually more intuitive. You can use either method, depending on your preference.

TVbxControl provides the function *GetProp* to get the properties of a control. *GetProp* is overloaded to allow getting properties using the index or name of the property. Each of these versions is further overloaded to allow getting a number of different types of properties:

```
// get properties by index
bool GetProp(int propIndex, int& value, int arrayIndex = -1);
bool GetProp(int propIndex, long& value, int arrayIndex = -1);
bool GetProp(int propIndex, HPIC& value, int arrayIndex = -1);
bool GetProp(int propIndex, float& value, int arrayIndex = -1);
bool GetProp(int propIndex, string& value, int arrayIndex = -1);

// get properties by name
bool GetProp(const char far* name, int& value, int arrayIndex = -1);
bool GetProp(const char far* name, long& value, int arrayIndex = -1);
bool GetProp(const char far* name, HPIC& value, int arrayIndex = -1);
bool GetProp(const char far* name, float& value, int arrayIndex = -1);
bool GetProp(const char far* name, string& value, int arrayIndex = -1);
```

In the versions where the first parameter is an **int**, you specify the property by passing in the property index. In the versions where the first parameter is a **char ***, you specify the property by passing in the property name.

Instead of returning the value property as the return value of the *GetProp* function, the second parameter of the function is a reference to the property's data type. Create an object of the same type as the property and pass a reference to the object in the *GetProp* function. When *GetProp* returns, the object contains the current value of the property.

The third parameter is the index of an array property, which you should supply if required by your control. You can find whether you need to supply this parameter and the required values by consulting the documentation for your VBX control. The function ignores this parameter if it is –1.

Setting control properties

As when you *get* control properties, you *set* the value of control property using either their name or their index number. Although using the index is somewhat more efficient (because there's no need to look up a string), using the property name is usually more intuitive. You can use either method, depending on your preference.

TVbxControl provides the function *SetProp* to set the properties of a control. *SetProp* is overloaded to allow setting properties using the index or name of the property. Each of these versions is further overloaded to allow setting a number of different types of properties:

```
// set properties by index
bool SetProp(int propIndex, int value, int arrayIndex = -1);
bool SetProp(int propIndex, long value, int arrayIndex = -1);
bool SetProp(int propIndex, HPIC value, int arrayIndex = -1);
bool SetProp(int propIndex, float value, int arrayIndex = -1);
bool SetProp(int propIndex, const string& value, int arrayIndex = -1);
bool SetProp(int propIndex, const char far* value, int arrayIndex = -1);


// set properties by name
bool SetProp(const char far* name, int value, int arrayIndex = -1);
bool SetProp(const char far* name, long value, int arrayIndex = -1);
bool SetProp(const char far* name, HPIC value, int arrayIndex = -1);
bool SetProp(const char far* name, float value, int arrayIndex = -1);
bool SetProp(const char far* name, const string& value, int arrayIndex = -1);
bool SetProp(const char far* name, const char far* value, int arrayIndex = -1);
```

In the versions where the first parameter is an **int**, you specify the property by passing in the property index. In the versions where the first parameter is a **char** *, you specify the property by passing in the property name.

The second parameter is the value to which the property should be set.

The third parameter is the index of an array property, which you should supply if required by your control. You can find whether you need to supply this parameter and the required values by consulting the documentation for your VBX control. The function ignores this parameter if it is –1.

Although there are *five* different data types you can pass in to *GetProp*, *SetProp* provides for *six* different data types. This is because the last two versions use both a **char** * and the ANSI *string* class to represent a string. This provides you with more flexibility when you're passing a character string into a control. In the *GetProp* version, casting is provided to allow a **char** * to function effectively as a *string* object.

VBX control methods

Methods are functions contained in each VBX control that you can use to call into the control and cause an action to take place. *TVbxControl* provides compatibility with the methods contained in Visual Basic 1.0-compatible controls:

```
Move(int x, int y, int w, int h);
Refresh();
```

```
AddItem(int index, const char far *item);
RemoveItem(int index);
```

where:

- The *Move* function moves the control to the coordinates *x, y* and resizes the control to *w* pixels wide by *h* pixels high.

- The *Refresh* function refreshes the control's display area.

- The *AddItem* function adds the item *item* to the control's list of items and gives the new item the index number *index*.

- The *RemoveItem* function removes the item with the index number *index*.

35

ObjectWindows dynamic-link libraries

A dynamic-link library (DLL) is a library of functions, data, and resources whose references are resolved at run time rather than at compile time.

Applications that use code from static-linked libraries attach copies of that code at link time. Applications that use code from DLLs share that code with all other applications using the DLL, therefore reducing application size. For example, you might want to define complex windowing behavior, shared by a group of your applications, in an ObjectWindows DLL.

This chapter describes how to write and use ObjectWindows DLLs.

Writing DLL functions

When you write DLL functions that will be called from an application, keep these things in mind:

- Calls to 16-bit DLL functions should be made far calls. Similarly, pointers that are specified as parameters and return values should be made far pointers. You need to do this because a 16-bit DLL has different code and data segments than the calling application. (This isn't necessary for 32-bit DLLs.) Use the _FAR macro to make your code portable between platforms.

- Static data defined in a 16-bit DLL is global to all calling applications because 16-bit DLLs have one data segment that all 16-bit DLL instances share. Global data set by one caller can be accessed by another. If you need data to be private for a given caller of a 16-bit DLL, you need to dynamically allocate and manage the data yourself on a per-task basis. For 32-bit DLLs, static data is private for each process.

DLL entry and exit functions

Windows requires that two functions be defined in every DLL: an entry function and an exit function. For 16-bit DLLs, the entry function is called *LibMain* and the exit function is called *WEP* (Windows Exit Procedure). *LibMain* is called by Windows for the first application that calls the DLL, and *WEP* is called by Windows for the last application that uses the DLL.

For 32-bit DLLs, *DllEntryPoint* serves as both the entry and exit functions. *DllEntryPoint* is called each time the DLL is loaded or unloaded, each time a process attaches to or detaches from the DLL, and each time a thread within a process is created or destroyed.

Windows calls the entry procedure (*LibMain* or *DllEntryPoint*) once, when the library is first loaded. The entry procedure initializes the DLL; this initialization depends almost entirely on the particular DLL's function, but might include the following tasks:

- Unlocking the data segment with UnlockData, if it has been declared as MOVEABLE
- Setting up global variables for the DLL, if it uses any

There is no need to initialize the heap because the DLL startup code (C0D*x*.OBJ) initializes the local heap automatically. The following sections describe the DLL entry and exit functions for 16- and 32-bit applications.

LibMain

The 16-bit DLL entry procedure, *LibMain*, is defined as follows:

```
int FAR PASCAL LibMain(HINSTANCE hInstance,
                       uint16 wDataSeg,
                       uint16 cbHeapSize,
                       LPSTR lpCmdLine)
```

The parameters are described as follows:

- *hInstance* is the instance handle of the DLL.

- *wDataSeg* is the value of the data segment (DS) register.

- *cbHeapSize* is the size of the local heap specified in the module definition file for the DLL.

- *lpCmdLine* is a far pointer to the command line specified when the DLL was loaded. This is almost always null, because typically DLLs are loaded automatically without parameters. It is possible, however, to supply a command line to a DLL when it is loaded explicitly.

The return value for *LibMain* is either 1 (successful initialization) or 0 (unsuccessful initialization). Windows unloads the DLL from memory if 0 is returned.

WEP

WEP is the exit procedure of a DLL. Windows calls it prior to unloading the DLL. This function isn't necessary in a DLL (because the Borland C++ run-time libraries provide a default one), but can be supplied by the DLL writer to perform any cleanup before the

DLL is unloaded from memory. Often the application has terminated by the time *WEP* is called, so valid options are limited.

Under Borland C++, *WEP* doesn't need to be exported. Here is the *WEP* prototype:

```
int FAR PASCAL WEP (int nParameter);
```

nParameter is either WEP_SYSTEMEXIT, which means Windows is shutting down, or WEP_FREE_DLL, which means just this DLL is unloading. *WEP* returns 1 to indicate success. Windows currently doesn't use this return value.

DllEntryPoint

The 32-bit DLL entry point, *DllEntryPoint*, is defined as follows:

```
bool WINAPI DllEntryPoint(HINSTANCE hInstDll, uint32 fdwReason, LPVOID lpvReserved);
```

The parameters are described as follows:

- *hInstDll* is the DLL instance handle.

- *fdwReason* is a flag that describes why the DLL is being called (either a process or thread). The flags can take the following values:
  - DLL_PROCESS_ATTACH
  - DLL_THREAD_ATTACH
  - DLL_THREAD_DETACH
  - DLL_PROCESS_DETACH

- *lpvReserved* specifies further aspects of the DLL initialization and cleanup based on the value of *fdwReason*.

Exporting DLL functions

After writing your DLL functions, you must export the functions that you want to be available to a calling application. There are two steps involved: compiling your DLL functions as exportable functions and exporting them. You can do this in the following ways:

- If you flag a function with the **_export** keyword, it's compiled as exportable and is then exported.

- If you add the **_export** keyword to a class declaration, the entire class (data and function members) is compiled as exportable and is exported.

- If you don't flag a function with **_export**, use the appropriate compiler switch or IDE setting to compile functions as exportable. Then list the function in the module definition (.DEF) file EXPORTS section.

Importing (calling) DLL functions

You call a DLL function from an application just as you would call a function defined in the application itself. However, you must import the DLL functions that your application calls.

To import a DLL function, you can

- Add an IMPORTS section to the calling application's module definition (.DEF) file and list the DLL function as an import.

- Link an import library that contains import information for the DLL function to the calling application. (Use IMPLIB to make the import library.)

- Explicitly load the DLL using *LoadLibrary* and obtain function addresses using *GetProcAddress*.

When your application executes, the files for the called DLLs must be in the current directory, on the path, or in the Windows or Windows system directory; otherwise your application won't be able to find the DLL files and won't load.

Writing shared ObjectWindows classes

A class instance in a DLL can be shared among multiple applications. For example, you can share code that defines a dialog box by defining a shared dialog class in a DLL. To share a class, you need to export the class from the DLL and import the class into your application.

Defining shared classes

To define shared classes, you need to

- Conditionally declare your class as either **_export** or **_import**.
- Pass a *TModule** parameter to the window constructors (in some situations).

Note   If you declare a shared class in an include file that is included by both the DLL and an application using the DLL, the class must be declared **_export** when compiling the DLL and **_import** when compiling the application. You can do this by defining a group of macros, one of which is conditionally set to **_export** when building the DLL and to **_import** when using the DLL. For example,

```
#if defined(BUILDEXAMPLEDLL)
  #define _EXAMPLECLASS __export
#elif defined (USEEXAMPLEDLL)
  #define _EXAMPLECLASS __import
#else
  #define _EXAMPLECLASS
#endif

class _EXAMPLECLASS TColorControl : public TControl
{
  public:
    ⋮
};
```

By defining BUILDEXAMPLEDLL (on the command line, for example) when you are building the DLL, you cause _EXAMPLECLASS to expand to **_export**. This causes the class to be exported and shared by applications using the DLL.

By defining USEEXAMPLEDLL when you're building the application that will use the DLL, you cause _EXAMPLECLASS to expand to **_import**. The application will know what type of object it will import.

The TModule object

An instance of the *TModule* class serves as the object-oriented interface for an ObjectWindows DLL. *TModule* member functions provide support for window and memory management, and process errors. See the *ObjectWindows Reference Guide* for a complete *TModule* class description.

The following code example shows the declaration and initialization of a *TModule* object. This example is conditionalized so that either 16-bit (*LibMain*) or 32-bit (*DllEntryPoint*) DLLs can use the same source file.

```
static TModule *ResMod;

#if defined(__WIN32__)
  bool WINAPI
  DllEntryPoint(HINSTANCE instance, uint32 /*flag*/, LPVOID)
#else    // !defined(__WIN32__)
  int
  FAR PASCAL
  LibMain(HINSTANCE instance,
          uint16 /*wDataSeg*/,
          uint16 /*cbHeapSize*/,
          char far* /*cmdLine*/)
#endif
  {
    // We're using the DLL and want to use the DLL's resources
    //
    if (!ResMod)
      ResMod = new TModule(0,instance);
    return true;
  }
```

Within the entry point function, the *TModule* object *ResMod* is initialized with the instance handle of the DLL. If the module isn't loaded an exception is thrown.

If your DLL requires additional initialization and cleanup, you can perform this processing in your *LibMain*, *DllEntryPoint*, or *WEP* functions. A better method, though, is to derive a *TModule* class, define data members for data global to your DLL within the class, and perform the required initialization and cleanup in its constructor and destructor.

After you've compiled and linked your DLL, use IMPLIB to generate an import library for your DLL. This import library will list all exported member functions from your shared classes as well as any ordinary functions you've exported.

Using ObjectWindows as a DLL

To enable your ObjectWindows applications to share a single copy of the ObjectWindows library, you can dynamically link them to the ObjectWindows DLL. To do this, you'll need to be sure of the following:

- When compiling, define the macro _OWLDLL on the compiler command line or in the IDE.

- Instead of specifying the static link ObjectWindows library when linking (that is, OWLWS.LIB, OWLWM.LIB, OWLWL.LIB, or OWLWF.LIB), specify the ObjectWindows DLL import library (OWLWI.LIB for 16-bit applications, or OWLWFI.LIB for 32-bit applications).

Calling an ObjectWindows DLL from a non-ObjectWindows application

When a child window is created in an ObjectWindows DLL, and the parent window is created in an ObjectWindows application, the ObjectWindows support framework for communication between the parent and child windows is in place. But you can also prepare your DLL for use by non-ObjectWindows applications.

When a child window is created in an ObjectWindows DLL and the parent window is created by a non-ObjectWindows application, the parent-child relationship must be simulated in the ObjectWindows DLL. This is done by constructing an alias window object in the ObjectWindows DLL that is associated with the parent window whose handle is specified on a DLL call.

In the following code, the exported function *CreateDLLWindow* is in an ObjectWindows DLL. The function will work for both ObjectWindows and non-ObjectWindows applications.

```
bool far _export
CreateDLLWindow(HWND parentHWnd)
{
  TWindow* parentAlias = GetWindowPtr(parentHWnd);  // check if an OWL window

  if (!parentAlias)
    parentAlias = new TWindow(parentHWnd); // if not, make an alias

  TWindow* window = new TWindow(parentAlias, "Hello from a DLL!");
  window->Attr.Style |= WS_POPUPWINDOW | WS_CAPTION | WS_THICKFRAME
                      | WS_MINIMIZEBOX | WS_MAXIMIZEBOX;
  window->Attr.X = 100; window->Attr.Y = 100;
  window->Attr.W = 300; window->Attr.H = 300;
  return window->Create();
}
```

CreateDLLWindow determines if it has been passed a non-ObjectWindows window handle by the call to *GetWindowPtr*, which returns 0 when passed a non-ObjectWindows window handle. If it is a non-ObjectWindows window handle, an alias parent *TWindow* object is constructed to serve as the parent window.

Implicit and explicit loading

Implicit loading is done when you use a .DEF or import library to link your application. The DLL is loaded by Windows when the application using the DLL is loaded.

Explicit loading is used to load DLLs at run time, and requires the use of the Windows API functions *LoadLibrary* to load the DLL and *GetProcAddress* to return DLL function addresses.

Mixing static and dynamic-linked libraries

The ObjectWindows libraries are built using the BIDS (container class) libraries, which in turn are built using the C run-time library.

If you link with the DLL version of the ObjectWindows libraries, you must link with the DLL version of the BIDS and run-time libraries. You do this by defining the _OWLDLL macro. This isn't the only combination of static and dynamic-linked libraries you can use: each line in the table below lists an allowable combination of static and dynamic-linked libraries.

Table 35.1   Allowable library combinations

Static libraries	Dynamically linked libraries
OWL, BIDS, RTL	(none)
OWL, BIDS	RTL
OWL	BIDS, RTL
(none)	OWL, BIDS, RTL

36

Turning an application into an OLE and OCX container

An OLE and OCX container is an application that can store OLE objects and OCX controls in its documents.

This chapter covers the following topics:

- Turning an application into an OLE and OCX container with ObjectWindows and Doc/View
- Turning an application into an OLE and OCX container with ObjectWindows

Turning an application into an OLE and OCX container with ObjectWindows and Doc/View

Turning a Doc/View application into an OLE container requires only a few modifications:

1 Include OWL header files.
2 Derive the application class from *TOcModule*.
3 Inherit from OLE Classes.
4 Create an application dictionary.
5 Create registration tables.
6 Create a registrar object.
7 Set up the Edit menu and the tool bar.
8 Load and save compound documents.
9 Compile and link the application.

ObjectComponents provides default behavior for all these common OLE features. Should you want to modify the default behavior, you can additionally choose to override the default event handlers for messages that ObjectComponents sends. The code examples in this section are based on the STEP14.CPP and STEP14DV.CPP sample programs in EXAMPLES/OWL/TUTORIAL. Look there for a complete working program that incorporates all the prescribed steps.

Step 1: Including OWL header files

An ObjectComponents program needs the classes, structures, macros, and symbols defined in the header files for the ObjectWindows OLE classes. The following list shows the headers needed for an OLE container that uses the Doc/View model and an MDI frame window.

```
#include <owl/oledoc.h>      // replaces DOCVIEW.H
#include <owl/oleview.h>     // replaces DOCVIEW.H
#include <owl/olemdifr.h>    // replaces MDI.H
```

An SDI application includes oleframe.h instead of olemdifr.h.

Step 2: Deriving the application class from TOcModule

The application object of an ObjectComponents program needs to derive from *TOcModule* as well as *TApplication*. *TOcModule* coordinates some basic housekeeping chores related to registration and memory management. It also connects your application to OLE. More specifically, *TOcModule* manages the connector object that implements COM interfaces on behalf of an application.

If the declaration of your application object looks like this:

```
class TMyApp : public TApplication {
  public:
    TMyApp() : TApplication(){};
    ⋮
};
```

Then change it to look like this:

```
class TMyApp : public TApplication, public TOcModule {
  public:
    TMyApp(): TApplication(::AppReg["appname"], ::Module, &::AppDictionary){};
    ⋮
};
```

The constructor for the revised *TMyApp* class takes three parameters:

- A string naming the application.

  AppReg is the application's registration table, shown later in "Creating registration tables." The expression ::AppReg["appname"] extracts a string that was registered to describe the application.

- A pointer to the application module.

  Module is a global variable of type *TModule** defined by ObjectWindows.

- The address of the application dictionary.

  AppDictionary is the application dictionary object explained in Step 4.

Step 3: Inheriting from OLE classes

ObjectWindows includes classes that let windows, documents, and views interact with the ObjectComponents classes. The ObjectWindows OLE classes include default implementations for most normal OLE operations. To adapt an existing ObjectWindows program to OLE, change its derived classes so they inherit from the OLE classes. The following table shows which OLE class replaces each of the non-OLE classes.

Non-OLE class	OLE class
TDecoratedFrame	TOleFrame
TDecoratedMDIFrame	TOleMDIFrame
TDialog	TOle Dialog
TDocument	TOle Document
TFileDocument	TOleDocument
TFrameWindow	TOleFrame
TMDIFrame	TOleMDIFrame
TView	TOleView
TWindow	TOleWindow

The *TOleFrame* and *TOleMDIFrame* classes both derive from decorated window classes. The OLE 2 user interface requires containers to handle tool bars and status bars. Even if the container has no decorations, servers might need to display their own in the container's window. The OLE window classes handle those negotiations for you.

Wherever your existing OWL program uses a non-OLE class, replace it with an OLE class, as shown here. Boldface type highlights the change.

Before

```
// pre-OLE declaration of a window class
class TMyFrame: public TFrameWindow   { /* declarations */ };
```

After

```
// new declaration of the same window class
class TMyFrame: public TOleFrame   { /* declarations */ };
```

Note If the implementation of your class makes direct calls to its base class, be sure to change the base class calls, as well. Response tables also refer to the base class and need to be updated.

Step 4: Creating an application dictionary

An *application dictionary* tracks information for the currently active process. It is particularly useful for DLLs. When several processes use a DLL concurrently, the DLL must maintain multiple copies of the global, static, and dynamic variables that represent its current state in each process. For example, the DLL version of ObjectWindows maintains a dictionary that allows it to retrieve the *TApplication* corresponding to the currently active client process. If you convert an executable server to a DLL server, your application too must maintain a dictionary of the *TApplication* objects representing each of its container clients. If your DLL uses the DLL version of ObjectWindows, then your DLL needs its own dictionary and cannot use the one in ObjectWindows.

The DEFINE_APP_DICTIONARY macro provides a simple and unified way to create the application object for any application, whether it is a container or a server, a DLL or an EXE. Insert this statement with your other static variables:

```
DEFINE_APP_DICTIONARY(AppDictionary);
```

For any application linked to the static version of the DLL, the macro simply creates a reference to the application dictionary in ObjectWindows. For DLL servers using the DLL version of ObjectWindows, however, it creates an instance of the *TAppDictionary* class.

Note Name your dictionary object *AppDictionary* to take advantage of the factory templates such as *TOleDocViewFactory* (as explained in "Step 6: Creating a registrar object").

Step 5: Creating registration tables

OLE requires programs to identify themselves by registering unique identifiers and names. OLE also needs to know what Clipboard formats a program supports. Doc/View applications also register their document file extensions and document flags. To accommodate the many new items an application might need to register, in ObjectWindows 2.5 you use macros to build structures to hold the items. Then you can pass the structure to the object that needs the information. The advantage of this method lies in the structure's flexibility. It can hold as many or as few items as you need.

Note Previous versions of ObjectWindows passed some of the same information in parameters. Old code still works unchanged, but passing information in registration structures is the recommended method for all new applications.

A Doc/View OLE container fills one registration structure with information about the application and then creates another to describe each of its Doc/View pairs. The structure with application information is passed to the TOcRegistrar constructor, as you'll see in the next section. Document registration structures are passed to the document template constructor.

Here are the commands to register a typical container:

```
BEGIN_REGISTRATION(AppReg) // information for the TOcRegistrar constructor
  REGDATA(clsid,      "{383882A1-8ABC-101B-A23B-CE4E85D07ED2}")
  REGDATA(appname,    "DrawPad Container")
END_REGISTRATION

BEGIN_REGISTRATION(DocReg)            // information for the document template
  REGDATA(progid,     "DrawPad.Document.14")
  REGDATA(description,"Drawing Pad (Step14--Container)")
  REGDATA(extension,  "p14")
  REGDATA(docfilter,  "*.p14")
  REGDOCFLAGS(dtAutoOpen | dtAutoDelete | dtUpdateDir | dtCreatePrompt |
        dtRegisterExt)
  REGFORMAT(0, ocrEmbedSource,  ocrContent,  ocrIStorage, ocrGet)
  REGFORMAT(1, ocrMetafilePict, ocrContent,  ocrMfPict|ocrStaticMed, ocrGet)
  REGFORMAT(2, ocrBitmap, ocrContent,  ocrGDI|ocrStaticMed, ocrGet)
```

```
        REGFORMAT(3, ocrDib, ocrContent,  ocrHGlobal|ocrStaticMed, ocrGet)
        REGFORMAT(4, ocrLinkSource, ocrContent,  ocrIStream, ocrGet)
    END_REGISTRATION
```

The registration macros build structures of type *TRegList*. Each entry in a registration structure contains a key, such as *clsid* or *progid,* and a value assigned to the key. Internally ObjectComponents finds the values by searching for the keys. The order in which the keys appear does not matter.

Insert the registration macros after your declaration of the application dictionary. Since the value of the *clsid* key must be a unique number identifying your application, it is recommended that you generate a new value using the GUIDGEN.EXE utility. (The *ObjectWindows Reference* entry for *clsid* explains other ways to generate an identifer.) Of course, modify the value of the *description* key to describe your container.

The example builds two structures, one named *AppReg* and one named *DocReg*. *AppReg* is an *application registration structure* and *DocReg* is a *document registration structure*. Both structures are built alike, but each contains a different set of keys and values. The keys in an application registration structure describe attributes of the application. A document registration structure describes the type of document an application can create. A document's attributes include the data formats that it can exchange with the Clipboard, its file extensions, and its document type name.

The set of keys you place in a structure depends on what OLE capabilities you intend to support. The macros in the example show the minimum amount of information a container should provide.

The following table describes all the registration keys that a container can use. It shows which are optional and which required as well as which belong in the application registration table and which in the document registration table.

Key	in AppReg?	in DocReg?	Description
appname	Optional	No	Short name for the application
clsid	Yes	Optional	Globally unique identifier (GUID); generated automatically for the *DocReg* structure
description	No	Yes	Descriptive string (up to 40 characters)
progid	No	Yes	Identifier for program or document type (unique string)
			Note: (Yes for a link source)
extension	No	Optional	Document file extension associated with server
docfilter	No	Yes	Wildcard file filter for File Open dialog box
docflags	No	Yes	Options for running the File Open dialog box
format*n*	No	Yes	A Clipboard format the container supports
directory	No	Optional	Default directory for storing document files
permid	No	Optional	Name string without version information
permname	No	Optional	Descriptive string without version information
version	Optional	No	Major and minor version numbers (defaults to "1.0")

The table shows what is required for container documents that support linking or embedding. For documents that support neither, the container needs to register only *docflags* and *docfilter*.

If your container is also a linking and embedding server or an automation server, then you should also consult the server table or the automation table in the *Borland C++ Programmer's Guide*, Chapter 38 and Chapter 39, respectively. Register all the keys that are required in any of the tables that apply to your application. For more information about registration tables, see *"The Borland C++ Programmer's Guide,"*Chapter 37. For more information about individual registration keys and the values they hold, see the *ObjectWindows Reference*.

The values assigned to keys can be translated to accommodate system language settings. for more about localization, see the *Borland C++ Programmer's Guide*, Chapters 38 and 39.

Step 6: Creating a registrar object

Every ObjectComponents application needs a registrar object to manage its registration tasks. In a linking and embedding application, the registrar is an object of type *TOcRegistrar*. At the top of your source code file, declare a global variable holding a pointer to the registrar.

```
static TPointer<TOcRegistrar> Registrar;
```

The *TPointer* template ensures that the *TOcRegistrar* instance is deleted when the program ends.

Note　Name the variable *Registrar* to take advantage of the factory callback template used in the registrar's constructor.

The next step is to modify your *OwlMain* function to allocate a new *TOcRegistrar* object and initialize the global pointer *Registrar*. The *TOcRegistrar* constructor expects three parameters: the application's registration structure, the component's factory callback, and the command-line string that invoked that application.

- The registration structure you create with the registration macros.

- The factory callback you create with a template class.

  For a linking and embedding ObjectWindows application that uses Doc/View, the template class is called *TOleDocViewFactory*. The code in the factory template assumes you have defined an application dictionary called *AppDictionary* and a *TOcRegistrar** called *Registrar*.

- The command-line string can come from the *GetCmdLine* method of *TApplication*.

```
int
OwlMain(int /*argc*/, char* /*argv*/ [])
{
  try {
    // Create Registrar object
    Registrar = new TOcRegistrar(::AppReg, TOleDocViewFactory<TMyApp>(),
                                 TApplication::GetCmdLine());
    return Registrar->Run();
  }
```

```
    catch (xmsg& x) {
      ::MessageBox(0, x.why().c_str(), "Exception", MB_OK);
    }
    return -1;
  }
```

After initializing the *Registrar* pointer, your OLE container application must invoke the *Run* method of the registrar instead of *TApplication::Run*. For OLE containers, the registrar's *Run* simply invokes the application object's *Run* to create the application's windows and process messages. However, using the registrar method makes your application OLE server-ready. The following code shows a sample *OwlMain* before and after the addition of a registrar object. Boldface type highlights the changes.

Before:
```
// Non-OLE OwlMain
int
OwlMain(int /*argc*/, char* /*argv*/[])
{
  return TMyApp().Run();
}
```

After adding the registrar object:
```
int
OwlMain(int /*argc*/, char* /*argv*/[])
{
  ::Registrar = new TOcRegistrar(::AppReg,
          TOleDocViewFactory<TMyApp>(),
          TApplication::GetCmdLine());
  return ::Registrar->Run();
}
```

The last parameter of the *TOcRegistrar* constructor is the command-line string that invokes the application. The registrar object processes the command line by searching for switches, such as -Embedding or -Automation, that OLE may have placed there. ObjectComponents takes whatever action the switches call for and then removes them. If for some reason you need to test the OLE switches, be sure to do it before constructing the registrar. If you have no use for the OLE switches, wait until after constructing the registrar before parsing the command line. For more information about command-line switches, see the *Borland C++ Programmer's Guide*, Chapter 39.

Step 7: Setting up the Edit menu and the tool bar

An OLE container places OLE commands on its Edit menu. The following table describes the standard OLE commands. It's not necessary to use all of them, but every container should support at least Insert Object, to let the user add new objects to the current document, and Edit Object, to let the user activate the currently selected object. The *TOleView* class has default implementations for all the commands. It invokes standard dialog boxes where necessary and processes the user's response. All you have to do is add the commands to the Edit menu for each view you derive from *TOleView*.

Menu command	Predefined identifier	Command description
Paste Special	CM_EDITPASTESPECIAL	Lets the user choose from available formats for pasting an object from the Clipboard.
Paste Link	CM_EDITPASTELINK	Creates a link in the current document to the object on the Clipboard.
Insert Object	CM_EDITINSERTOBJECT	Lets the user create a new object by choosing from a list of available types.
Edit Links	CM_EDITLINKS	Lets the user manually update the list of linked items in the current document.
Convert	CM_EDITCONVERT	Lets the user convert objects from one type to another.
Object	CM_EDITOBJECT	Reserves a space on the menu for the server's verbs (actions the server can take with the container's object).

If your OLE container has a tool bar, assign it the predefined identifier IDW_TOOLBAR. ObjectComponents must be able to find the container's tool bar if a server asks to display its own tool bar in the container's window. If ObjectComponents can identify the old tool bar, it temporarily replaces it with a new one taken from the server. For ObjectComponents to identify the container's tool bar, the container must use the IDW_TOOLBAR as its window ID, as shown here.

```
TControlBar *cb = new TControlBar(parent);
cb->Attr.Id = IDW_TOOLBAR;          // use this identifier
```

The *TOleFrame::EvAppBorderSpaceSet* method uses the IDW_TOOLBAR for its default implementation. A container can provide its own implementation to handle more complex situations, such as merging with multiple tool bars.

Step 8: Loading and saving compound documents

When the user pastes or drops an OLE object into a container, the object becomes data in the container's document. The container must store and load the object along with the rest of the document whenever the user chooses Save or Open from the File menu. The new *Commit* and *Open* methods of *TOleDocument* perform this chore for you. All you have to do is add calls to the base class in your own implementation of *Open* and *Commit*. The code that reads and writes your document's native data remains unchanged.

Because *TOleDocument* is derived from *TStorageDocument* rather than *TFileDocument*, it always creates compound files. *Compound files* are a feature of OLE 2 used to organize the contents of a disk file into separate compartments . You can ask to read or write from any compartment in the file without worrying about where on the disk the compartment begins or ends. OLE calls the compartments *storages*. The storages in a file can be ordered hierarchically, just like directories and subdirectories. Any storage compartment can contain other sub-storages.

Compound files are good for storing compound documents. When you call *Open* or *Commit*, ObjectComponents automatically creates storages in your file to hold whatever objects the document contains. All the document's native data is saved in the file's root storage. Your existing file data structure remains intact, isolated in a separate compartment. The following code shows how to load compound documents:

```
// document class declaration derived from TOleDocument
class _DOCVIEWCLASS TMyDocument : public TOleDocument {
  // declarations
}

// document class implementation
bool
TDrawDocument::Open(int mode, const char far* path) {
  TOleDocument::Open(mode, path); // load any embedded objects
                                  // code to load other document data
}
```

The *TOleDocument::Open* method does not actually copy the data for all the objects into memory. ObjectComponents is smart enough to load the data for particular objects only when the user activates them.

The following code shows how to save compound documents:

```
bool
TMyDocument::Commit(bool force) {
  TOleDocument::Commit(force);   // save the embedded objects
                                 // code to save other document data
  TOleDocument::CommitTransactedStorage();   // commit if in transacted mode
}
```

By default, *TOleDocument* opens compound files in transacted mode. *Transacted mode* saves changes in a temporary buffer and merges them with the file only after an explicit command. A revert command discards any uncommitted changes. *Commit* buffers a new transaction. *CommitTransactedStorage* merges all pending transactions.

The opposite of transacted mode is direct mode. *Direct mode* eliminates buffers and makes each change take effect immediately. To alter the default mode, override *TOleDocument::PreOpen*. Omit the *ofTransacted* flag to specify direct mode.

Note   In order for compound file I/O to work correctly, you need to include the *dtAutoOpen* flag when you register *docflags* in the document registration table.

Step 9: Compiling and linking the application

Containers that use ObjectComponents and ObjectWindows require the large memory model. Link them with the OLE and ObjectComponents libraries.

The integrated development environment (IDE) chooses the right build options when you ask for OLE support. To build any ObjectComponents program from the command line, create a short makefile that includes the OWLOCFMK.GEN file found in the EXAMPLES subdirectory. Here, for example, is the makefile that builds the AutoCalc sample program:

```
EXERES = MYPROGRAM
OBJEXE = winmain.obj autocalc.obj
HLP = MYPROGRAM
!include $(BCEXAMPLEDIR)\owlocfmk.gen
```

EXERES and OBJEXE hold the name of the file to build and the names of the object files to build it from. HLP is an optional online Help file. Finally, your makefile should include the OWLOCFMK.GEN file.

Name your file MAKEFILE and type this at the command-line prompt:

```
make MODEL=1
```

Make, using instructions in OWLOCFMK.GEN, builds a new makefile tailored to your project. The new makefile is called WIN16L*xx*.MAK. The final two digits of the name tell whether the makefile builds diagnostic or debugging versions of the libraries. *01* indicates a debugging version, *10* a diagnostic version, and *11* means both kinds of information are included. The same command then runs the new makefile and builds the program. If you change the command to define MODEL as *d*, the new makefile is WIN16D*xx*.MAK and it builds the program as a DLL.

For more information about how to use OWLOCFMK.GEN, read the instructions at the beginning of MAKEFILE.GEN, found in the EXAMPLES directory.

The following table shows the libraries an ObjectComponents program links with.

Large model libraries	DLL import libraries	Description
OCFWL.LIB	OCFWI.LIB	ObjectComponents
OWLWL.LIB	OWLWI.LIB	ObjectWindows
BIDSL.LIB	BIDSI.LIB	Class libraries
OLE2W16.LIB	OLE2W16.LIB	OLE system DLLs
IMPORT.LIB	IMPORT.LIB	Windows system DLLs
MATHWL.LIB		Math support
CWL.LIB	CRTLDLL.LIB	C run-time libraries

The ObjectComponents library must be linked first, before the ObjectWindows library. Also, ObjectComponents requires RTTI and exception handling. Do not use compiler command-line options that disable these features.

Turning an application into an OLE and OCX container with ObjectWindows

Turning an ObjectWindows application into an OLE container requires a few modifications.

1 Include OWL header files.

2 Create an application dictionary.

3 Derive the application class from *TOcModule*.

4 Create registration tables.

5 Create a registrar object.

6 Set up the client window.

7 Program the user interface.

8 Compile and link the application.

Code excerpts are from the OWLOCF0.CPP sample in the EXAMPLES/OWL /TUTORIAL/OLE directory. The OWLOCF0.CPP sample is based on the STEP10.CPP sample used in the ObjectWindows tutorial. It does not support OLE. OWLOCF1.CPP modifies the first program to create an OLE container.

Step 1: Including OWL header files

ObjectWindows provides OLE-related classes, structures, macros, and symbols in various header files. The following list shows the headers needed for an OLE container using an SDI frame window:

```
#include <owl/oleframe.h>
#include <owl/olewindo.h>
#include <ocf/ocstorag.h>
```

An MDI application includes olemdifr.h instead of oleframe.h.

Step 2: Creating an application dictionary

When a DLL is used by more than one application or process, it must maintain multiple copies of the global, static, and dynamic variables that represent its current state in each process. For example, the DLL version of ObjectWindows maintains a dictionary that allows it to retrieve the *TApplication* object which corresponds to the current active process. If you turn your application into a DLL server, the application must also maintain a dictionary of the *TApplication* objects created as each new client attaches to the DLL. The DEFINE_APP_DICTIONARY macro provides a simple and unified method for creating an application dictionary object. Insert the following statement with your other static-variable declarations:

```
DEFINE_APP_DICTIONARY(AppDictionary);
```

The DEFINE_APP_DICTIONARY macro correctly defines the *AppDictionary* variable regardless of how the application is built. In applications using the static version of ObjectWindows, it simply creates a reference to the existing ObjectWindows application dictionary. For DLL servers using the DLL version of ObjectWindows, however, the macro declares a instance of the *TAppDictionary* class. It is important to use the name *AppDictionary* when creating your application dictionary object. This allows you to take advantage of the factory template classes for implementing a factory callback function (see Step 5: "Creating a registrar object").

Step 3: Deriving the application object from TOcModule

ObjectWindows provides the mix-in class *TOcModule* for applications that support linking and embedding. Change your application object so it derives from both *TApplication* and *TOcModule* as shown in the following example:

```
// Non-OLE application
class TScribbleApp : public TApplication { /* declarations */ };


// New declaration of same class
class TScribbleApp : public TApplication, public TOcModule { /* declarations */ };
```

The *TOcModule* object coordinates basic housekeeping chores related to registration and memory management. It also connects your application object to OLE.

Your *TApplication*-derived class must provide a *CreateOleObject* method with the following signature:

```
TUnknown* CreateOleObject(uint32 options, TDocTemplate* tpl);
```

The method is used by the factory template class. Because containers don't create OLE objects, a container can implement *CreateOleObject* by simply returning 0. As the next section explains, servers have more work to do to implement *CreateOleObject*.

```
//
// non-OLE application class
//
class TScribbleApp : public TApplication {
  public:
    TScribbleApp() : TApplication("Scribble Pad") {}

  protected:
    InitMainWindow();

};

//
// New declaration of same class
//
class TScribbleApp : public TApplication, public TOcModule {
  public:
    TScribbleApp() : TApplication(::AppReg["description"]){}
    TUnknown* CreateOleObject(uint32, TDocTemplate*){ return 0; }

  protected:
    InitMainWindow();
```

Step 4: Creating registration tables

OLE requires programs to identify themselves by registering unique identifiers and names. ObjectWindows offers macros that let you build a structure to hold registration information. The structure can then be used when creating the application's instance of *TOcRegistrar*.

Here are the commands to create a simple container registration structure:

```
REGISTRATION_FORMAT_BUFFER(100)      // create buffer for expanding macros

BEGIN_REGISTRATION(AppReg)
  REGDATA(clsid, "{9B0BBE60-B6BD-101B-B3FF-86C8A0834EDE}")
  REGDATA(description, "Scribble Pad Container")
END_REGISTRATION
```

The first macro, REGISTRATION_FORMAT_BUFFER, sets the size of a buffer needed temporarily as the macros are expanded. The REGDATA macro places items in the registration structure, *AppReg*. Each item in *AppReg* is a smaller structure that contains a key, such as *clsid* or *progid*, and a value assigned to the key. The values you assign are case-sensitive strings. The order of keys within the registration table does not matter.

Insert the registration macros after your declaration of the application dictionary. Since the value of the *clsid* key must be a unique number identifying your application, it is recommended that you generate a new value using the GUIDGEN.EXE utility. (The *ObjectWindows Reference* entry for *clsid* explains other ways to generate an identifer.) Of course, modify the value of the *description* key to describe your container.

The *AppReg* structure built in the sample code is an *application registration structure*. A container may also build one or more *document registration structures*. Both structures are built alike, but each contains a different set of keys and values. The keys in an application registration structure describe attributes of the application. A document registration structure describes the type of document an application can create. A document's attributes include the data formats that it can exchange with the Clipboard, its file extensions, and its document type name. The OWLOCF1 sample application does not create any document registration structures.

Step 5: Creating a registrar object

Every ObjectComponents application needs to create a registrar object to manage all of its registration tasks. Insert the following line after the **#include** statements in your main .CPP file:

```
static TPointer<TOcRegistrar> Registrar;
```

The *TOcRegistrar* instance is created in your *OwlMain* function. Declaring the pointer of type *TPointer<TOcRegistrar>* instead of *TOcRegistrar** ensures that the *TOcRegistrar* instance is deleted.

Note   Name the variable *Registrar* to take advantage of the *TOleFactory* template for implementing a factory callback.

The next step is to modify your *OwlMain* function to allocate a new *TOcRegistrar* object to initialize the global pointer *Registrar*. The *TOcRegistrar* constructor requires three parameters: the application's registration structure, the component's factory callback and the command-line string that invoked that application.

- The registration structure you create with the registration macros (see the preceding section "Creating registration tables").

- The factory callback you create with an ObjectWindows factory template.

  You can write your own callback function from scratch if you prefer, but the templates are much easier to use. For a linking and embedding ObjectWindows application that doesn't use Doc/View, the template class is called *TOleFactory*. The code in the factory template assumes you have defined an application dictionary called *AppDictionary* and a *TOcRegistrar** called *Registrar*.

- The command-line string comes from the *GetCmdLine* method of *TApplication*.

Here is the code to create the registrar:

```
int OwlMain(int, char*[])
{

  // create the registrar object
  ::Registrar = new TOcRegistrar(::AppReg, TOleFactory<TScribbleApp>(),
                                 TApplication::GetCmdLine());

}
```

Factories are explained in more detail in the *ObjectWindows Reference Guide*.

After initializing the *Registrar* pointer, your OLE container application must invoke *TOcRegistrar::Run* instead of *TApplication::Run*. For OLE containers, the registrar's *Run* simply invokes the application object's *Run* to create the application's windows and process messages. In a server, however, *TOcRegistrar::Run* does more. Using the registrar's *Run* method in a container makes it easier to modify the application later if you decide to turn it into a server.

Here is the *OwlMain* from OWLOCF1, omitting for clarity the usual **try** and **catch** statements. The lines in bold are the new code.

Before:

```
// Non-OLE OwlMain
int
OwlMain(int /*argc*/, char* /*argv*/[])
{
  return TScribbleApp().Run();
}
```

After adding the registrar object:

```
int
OwlMain(int /*argc*/, char* /*argv*/[])
{
  ::Registrar = new TOcRegistrar(::AppReg, TOleFactory<TScribbleApp>(),
                                 TApplication::GetCmdLine());
  return ::Registrar->Run();
}
```

Step 6: Setting up the client window

An ObjectWindows SDI application can use a frame window that does not contain a client window. Similarly, an ObjectWindows MDI application can use MDI child windows that do not contain a client window. Omitting the client window makes it harder to convert the application from one kind of frame to another—SDI, MDI, or decorated frame. It is also awkward when building OLE 2 applications.

For example, it is easier for a container's main window to make room for a server's tool bar if the container owns a client window. To take full advantage of the ObjectWindows OLE classes, your application must use a client window. For more information about using client windows, see the ObjectWindows tutorial.

The following topics discuss setting up the Client Window:

- Inheriting from OLE Classes
- Delaying the Creation of the Client Window in SDI Applications
- Creating ObjectComponents View and Document Objects

Inheriting from OLE classes

ObjectWindows provide several classes that include default implementations for many OLE operations. To adapt an existing ObjectWindows program to OLE, change its derived classes to inherit from the OLE classes. for a list of the OLE classes and the corresponding classes they replace, see the *Borland C++ Programmer's Guide*, Chapter 37.

The *TOleFrame* and *TOleMDIFrame* classes both derive from decorated window classes. The OLE 2 user interface requires that containers be prepared to handle tool bars and status bars. Even if a container has no such decorations, servers might need to display their own in the container's window. The OLE window classes handle those negotiations for you. The following code shows how to change the declaration for a client window. Boldface type highlights the changes.

Before:

```
// Pre-OLE declaration of a client window
class TScribbleWindow : public TWindow {
    // declarations
};
DEFINE_RESPONSE_TABLE1(TScribbleWindow, TWindow);
```

After changing the declaration to derive from an OLE-enabled class:

```
// New declaration of the same window class
class TScribbleWindow : public TOleWindow {
    // declarations
};
DEFINE_RESPONSE_TABLE1(TScribbleWindow, TOleWindow);
```

Delaying the creation of the client window in SDI applications

ObjectWindows applications create their main window in the *InitMainWindow* method of the *TApplication*-derived class. Typically, SDI applications also create their initial client window in the *InitMainWindow* function. The following code shows the typical sequence:

```
void
TDrawApp::InitMainWindow()
{
  // Construct the decorated frame window
  TDecoratedFrame* frame = new TDecoratedFrame(0, "Drawing Pad",
                                           new TDrawWindow(0), true);
    // more declarations to init and set the main window
}
```

When used in the OLE frame and client classes, however, that sequence presents a timing problem for OLE. The OLE client window must be created after the OLE frame has initialized its variables pointing to ObjectComponents classes. To meet this requirement, an SDI OLE application should create only the frame window in the *InitMainWindow* function. Create the client window in the *InitInstance* method of your application class. Boldface type highlights the changes.

```
void
TDrawApp::InitMainWindow()
{
  // construct the decorated frame window
  TOleFrame* frame = new TOleFrame("Drawing Pad", 0, true);

    // more declarations to init and set the main window
}

void
TDrawApp::InitInstance()
{
  TApplication::InitInstance();

  // create and set client window
  GetMainWindow()->SetClientWindow(new TDrawWindow(0));
}
```

Creating ObjectComponents view and document objects

For every client window capable of having linked or embedded objects, you must create a *TOcDocument* object to manage the embedded OLE objects, and a *TOcView* object to manage the presentation of the OLE objects. The *CreateOcView* method from the *TOleWindow* class creates both the container document and the container view. Add a call to *CreateOcView* in the constructor of your *TOleWindow*-derived class.

```
// Pre-OLE declaration of a client window constructor
TScribbleWindow::TScribbleWindow(TWindow* parent, char far* filename)
: TWindow(parent, 0, 0)
{

}

// New declaration of client window constructor
TScribbleWindow::TScribbleWindow(TWindow* parent, char far* filename)
: TOleWindow(parent, 0)
```

```
{
    // Create TOcDocument object to hold OLE parts
    // and TOcView object to provide OLE services.
    CreateOcView(0, false, 0);
}
```

Notice that unlike the *TWindow* constructor, the *TOleWindow* constructor does not require a *title* parameter. It is unnecessary because *TOleWindow* is always the client of a frame. *TWindow*, on the other hand, can be used as a non-client window—a pop-up, for example.

Step 7: Programming the user interface

The next set of adaptations provide standard OLE user interface features such as menu merging and drag and drop. The following topics discuss programming the user interface.

Handling OLE-related messages and events

ObjectComponents notifies your application's windows of OLE-related events by sending the WM_OCEVENT message. The ObjectWindows OLE classes provide default handlers for the various WM_OCEVENT event notifications. Furthermore, the ObjectWindows classes also process a few standard Windows messages to add additional features of the standard OLE user interface. For example, if a user double-clicks within the client area of your container window, a handler in *TOleWindow* checks whether the click occurred over an embedded object and, if so, activates the object. Similarly, the *TOleWindow::EvPaint* method causes each embedded object to draw itself. The following table lists the methods implemented by the client window (*TOleWindow*) and frame window (*TOleFrame, TOleMDIFrame*) classes. If you override these handlers in your derived class you must invoke the base class version.

Method	Message	Class	Description
EvSize	WM_SIZE	Frame	Notifies embedded servers of the size change.
EvTimer	WM_TIMER	Frame	Invokes *IdleAction* so that DLL servers can carry out command enabling.
EvActivateApp	WM_ACTIVATEAPP	Frame	Notifies embedded servers about being activated.
EvLButtonDown	WM_LBUTTONDOWN	Client	Deactivates any in-place active object.
EvRButtonDown	WM_RBUTTONDOWN	Client	Displays pop-up verb menu if cursor is on an embedded object.
EvLButtonDblClk	WM_LBUTTONDBLCLK	Client	Activates any embedded object under the cursor.
EvMouseMove	WM_MOUSEMOVE	Client	Allows user to move or resize an embedded object.
EvLButtonUp	WM_LBUTTONUP	Client	Informs the selected object of position or size changes.

Method	Message	Class	Description
EvSize	WM_SIZE	Client	Informs *TOcView* object that window has changed size.
EvMdiActivate	WM_MDIACTIVATE	Client	Informs *TOcView* object that window has changed size.
EvMouseActivate	WM_MOUSEACTIVATE	Client	Forwards the message to the top-level parent window and returns the code to activate the client window.
EvSetFocus	WM_SETFOCUS	Client	Notifies any in-place server of focus change.
EvSetCursor	WM_SETCURSOR	Client	Changes cursor shape if within an embedded object.
EvDropFiles	WM_DROPFILES	Client	Embeds dropped file(s).
EvPaint	WM_PAINT	Client	Causes embedded objects to paint.
EvCommand	WM_COMMAND	Client	Processes command IDs of verbs.
EvCommandEnable	WM_COMMANDENABLE	Client	Processes command IDs of verbs.

In some cases, you might need to know what action the base class handler took before you decide what to do in your overriding handler. This is particularly true for mouse-related messages. If the base class handled a double-click action, for example, the user intended the action to activate an object and you probably don't want your code to reinterpret the double-click as a different command. The code that follows shows how to coordinate with a base class handler. These three procedures let the user draw on the surface of the client window with the mouse.

```
void
TMyClient::EvLButtonDown(uint modKeys, TPoint& pt)
{
  if (!Drawing) {
    SetCapture()
    Drawing = true;
    // additional GDI calls to display drawing
  }
}


void
TMyClient::EvMouseMove(uint modKeys, TPoint& pt)
{
  if (Drawing) {
    // additional GDI calls to display drawing
  }
}


void
TMyClient::EvLButtonUp(uint modKeys, TPoint& pt)
{
  if (Drawing) {
    Drawing = false;
    ReleaseCapture();
  }
}
```

As an OLE container, however, the client window may contain embedded objects. Mouse events performed on these objects should not result in any drawing operation. This code shows the handlers updated to allow and check for OLE-related processing. Boldface type highlights the changes.

```
void
TMyClient::EvLButtonDown(uint modKeys, TPoint& pt)
{
  TOleWindow::EvLButtonDown(modKeys, pt);

  if (!Drawing && !SelectEmbedded()) {
    SetCapture()
    Drawing = true;
    // additional GDI calls to display drawing
  }
}


void
TMyClient::EvMouseMove(uint modKeys, TPoint& pt)
{
  TOleWindow::EvMouseMove(modKeys, pt);

  if (Drawing && !SelectEmbedded()) {
    // additional GDI calls to display drawing
  }
}


void
TMyClient::EvLButtonUp(uint modKeys, TPoint& pt)
{
  if (Drawing && !SelectEmbedded()) {
    Drawing = false;
    ReleaseCapture();
  }

  TOleWindow::EvLButtonUp(modKeys, pt);
}
```

The *SelectEmbedded* method is inherited from *TOleWindow*. It returns **true** if an embedded object is currently being moved. The client window calls it to determine whether a mouse message has already been processed by the OLE base class.

Typically, your derived class must call the base class handlers before processing any event or message. The *EvLButtonUp* handler, however, calls the base class last. Doing so allows the handler to rely on *SelectEmbedded* which is likely to be reset after *TOleWindow* processes the mouse-up message.

Supporting menu merging

The menu bar of an OLE container with an active object is composed of individual pieces from the normal menus of both the container and server. The container contributes pop-up menus dealing with the application frame or with documents. The server, on the other hand, provides the Edit menu, the Help menu, and any menus that let the user manipulate the activated object.

OLE divides the top-level menus of a menu bar into six groups. Each group is a set of contiguous top-level drop-down menus. Each group is made up of zero or more pop-up menus. The menu groups are named File, Edit, Container, Object, Window, and Help. The group names are for convenience only. They suggest a common organization of related commands, but you can group the commands any way you like.

When operating on its own, a container or server provides the menus for all of the six groups. During an in-place edit session, however, the container retains control of the File, Container and Window groups while the server is responsible for the Edit, Object, and Help groups.

The *TMenuDescr* class automatically handles all menu negotiations between the server and the container. You simply identify the various menu groups within your menu resource, and ObjectWindows displays the right ones at the right times.

To indicate where groups begin and end in your menu resource, insert SEPARATOR menu items between them. Remember to mark all six groups even if some of them are empty. The *TMenuDescr* class scans for the separators when loading a menu from a resource. It removes the separators found between top-level entries and builds a structure which stores the number of pop-up menus assigned to each menu group. This information allows ObjectWindows to merge the server's menu into your container's menu bar.

The following menu resource script, taken from STEP10.RC in the ObjectWindows tutorial, illustrates defining a simple application menu before it is divided into groups.

```
COMMANDS MENU
{
  pop-up "&File"
  {
    MENUITEM "&New",      CM_FILENEW
    MENUITEM "&Open",     CM_FILEOPEN
    MENUITEM "&Save",     CM_FILESAVE
    MENUITEM "Save &As",  CM_FILESAVEAS
  }

  pop-up "&Tools"
  {
    MENUITEM "Pen &Size",  CM_PENSIZE
    MENUITEM "Pen &Color", CM_PENCOLOR
  }

  pop-up "&Help"
  {
    MENUITEM "&About",     CM_ABOUT
  }
}
```

The File menu entry belongs to the OLE File menu group. The Tools menu allows the user to edit the application's document, so it belongs to the Edit group. This application does not contain any menus belonging to the Object, Container, or Window group. And finally, the Help menu belongs to the Help group.

The following code is a modified version of the same menu resource with SEPARATOR dividers inserted to indicate where one group stops and the next begins. Boldface type highlights the changes.

```
COMMANDS MENU
{
  pop-up "&File"
  {
    MENUITEM "&New",      CM_FILENEW
    MENUITEM "&Open",     CM_FILEOPEN
    MENUITEM "&Save",     CM_FILESAVE
    MENUITEM "Save &As",  CM_FILESAVEAS
  }

  MENUITEM SEPARATOR            // end of File group, beginning of Edit group

  pop-up "&Tools"
  {
    MENUITEM "Pen &Size",  CM_PENSIZE
    MENUITEM "Pen &Color", CM_PENCOLOR
  }

  MENUITEM SEPARATOR            // end of Edit group, beginning of Container group
  MENUITEM SEPARATOR            // end of Container group, beginning of Object group
  MENUITEM SEPARATOR            // end of Object group, beginning of Window group
  MENUITEM SEPARATOR            // end of Window group, beginning of Help group

  pop-up "&Help"
  {
    MENUITEM "&About",    CM_ABOUT
  }
}
```

Insert separators in your application's menu to indicate the various menu groups. Then modify your code to use the *SetMenuDescr* method when assigning your frame window's menu. This example shows the menu assignment before and after adding menu merging. Boldface type highlights the changes.

Before:

```
// original menu assignment
void
TScribbleApp::InitMainWindow()
{
  TDecoratedFrame* frame;
    // Initialize frame and decorations etc. etc.

  // Assign frame's menu
  frame->AssignMenu("COMMANDS");
}
```

After including group indicators in the menu:

```
void
TScribbleApp::InitMainWindow()
```

```
{
    TOleFrame* frame;
       // Initialize frame and decorations etc. etc.

    // Assign frame's menu
    frame->SetMenuDescr(TMenuDescr("COMMANDS"));
}
```

Instead of using separators to show which drop-down menus belong to each group, you can use the *TMenuDescr* constructor whose parameters accept a count for each group. For more details, see the description of the *TMenuDescr* constructors in the *ObjectWindows Reference*.

Updating the Edit menu

An OLE container places OLE commands on its Edit menu. The *TOleWindow* class has default implementations for all of them. It invokes standard dialog boxes where necessary and processes the user's response. All you have to do is add the commands to the Edit menu of your frame window. It's not necessary to support all six commands, but every container should support at least CM_EDITINSERTOBJECT, to let the user add new objects to the current document, and CM_EDITOBJECT, to let the user choose verbs for the currently selected object.

ObjectWindows defines standard identifiers for the OLE Edit menu commands in owl/ oleview.rh. Update your resource file to include the header file and use the standard identifiers to put OLE commands on the Edit menu.

```
#include <owl/oleview.rh>
#include <owl/edit.rh>

COMMANDS MENU
{
    // File menu goes here

  MENUITEM SEPARATOR
  pop-up "&Edit"
  {
    MENUITEM "&Undo\aCtrl+Z",              CM_EDITUNDO
    MENUITEM Separator
    MENUITEM "&Cut\aCtrl+X",               CM_EDITCUT
    MENUITEM "C&opy\aCtrl+C",              CM_EDITCOPY
    MENUITEM "&Paste\aCtrl+V",             CM_EDITPASTE
    MENUITEM "Paste &Special...",          CM_EDITPASTESPECIAL
    MENUITEM "Paste &Link",                CM_EDITPASTELINK
    MENUITEM "&Delete\aDel",               CM_EDITDELETE
    MENUITEM SEPARATOR
    MENUITEM  "&Insert Object...",         CM_EDITINSERTOBJECT
    MENUITEM  "&Links...",                 CM_EDITLINKS
    MENUITEM  "&Object",                   CM_EDITOBJECT
    MENUITEM SEPARATOR
    MENUITEM  "&Show Objects",             CM_EDITSHOWOBJECTS
  }
    // other menus go here
}
```

Assigning a tool bar ID

If your OLE container has a tool bar, assign it the predefined identifier IDW_TOOLBAR. ObjectWindows must be able to find the container's tool bar if a server needs to display its own tool bar in the container's window. If ObjectWindows can identify the old tool bar, it temporarily replaces it with the new one taken from the server. For ObjectWindows to identify the container's tool bar, the container must use the IDW_TOOLBAR as its window ID.

```
TControlBar* cb = new TControlBar(parent);
cb->Attr.Id = IDW_TOOLBAR;
```

The *TOleFrame::EvAppBorderSpaceSet* method uses the IDW_TOOLBAR for its default implementation. A container can provide its own implementation to handle more complex situations, such as merging with multiple tool bars.

Step 8: Compiling and linking the application

ObjectWindows containers and servers must be compiled with the large memory model. They must be linked with the OLE, ObjectComponents, and ObjectWindows libraries.

For more information about compiling and linking the application, see Step 9 in the section, "Turning an application into an OLE and OCX container with ObjectWindows and Doc/View," earlier in this chapter.

37

Turning an application into an OLE server

An OLE server is an application that creates and manages data objects for other programs.

This chapter covers the following topics:

- Turning an application into an OLE server with ObjectWindows and Doc/View
- Turning an application into an OLE server with ObjectWindows
- Turning an ObjectWindows server into a DLL OLE server

Turning an application into an OLE server with ObjectWindows and Doc/View

Turning a Doc/View application into an OLE server requires only a few modifications, and many of them are the same as the changes required to create a container. If you have already modified your application according to the steps in the *Borland C++ Programmer's Guide*, Chapter 37, then much of your server work is already done.

These are the changes you will need to make to turn a Doc/View application into an OLE server:

1 Include OWL header files.

2 Create an application dictionary.

3 Derive the application class from *TOcModule*.

4 Inherit from OLE classes.

5 Build registration tables.

6 Create a registrar object.

7 Process the command line.

8 Tell clients when an object changes.

9 Load and save the server's documents.

10 Compile and link the application.

Step 1: Including OWL header files

The headers for a server are the same as the headers for a container. A server that uses the Doc/View model and an MDI frame window needs the following headers:

```
#include <owl/oledoc.h>     // replaces DOCVIEW.H
#include <owl/oleview.h>    // replaces DOCVIEW.H
#include <owl/olemdifr.h>   // replaces MDI.H
```

An SDI application includes OLEFRAME.H instead of OLEMDIFR.H.

Step 2: Creating an application dictionary

An application dictionary tracks information for the currently active process. It is particularly useful for DLLs. When several processes use a DLL concurrently, the DLL must maintain multiple copies of the global, static, and dynamic variables that represent its current state in each process. For example, the DLL version of ObjectWindows maintains a dictionary that allows it to retrieve the *TApplication* corresponding to the currently active client process. If you convert an executable server to a DLL server, it must also maintain a dictionary of the *TApplication* objects representing each of its container clients.

The DEFINE_APP_DICTIONARY macro provides a simple and unified way to create the dictionary object for any type of application, whether it is a container, a server, a DLL, or an EXE. Insert this statement with your other static variables:

```
DEFINE_APP_DICTIONARY(AppDictionary);
```

For any application linked to the static version of the DLL library, the macro simply creates a reference to the application dictionary in ObjectWindows. For DLL servers using the DLL version of ObjectWindows, however, it creates an instance of the *TAppDictionary* class.

Note Name your dictionary object *AppDictionary* to take advantage of the factory templates such as *TOleDocViewFactory* (as explained later in "Step 6: Creating a registrar object").

Step 3: Deriving the application class from TOcModule

The application object of an ObjectComponents program needs to derive from *TOcModule* as well as *TApplication*. *TOcModule* coordinates some basic housekeeping chores related to registration and memory management. It also connects your application to OLE. More specifically, *TOcModule* manages the connector object that implements COM interfaces on behalf of an application.

If the declaration of your application object looks like this:

```
class TMyApp : public TApplication {
  public:
```

```
    TMyApp() : TApplication(){};
    ⋮
};
```

Then change it to look like this:

```
class TMyApp : public TApplication, public TOcModule {
  public:
    TMyApp(): TApplication(::AppReg["description"], ::Module, &::AppDictionary){};
    ⋮
};
```

The constructor for the revised *TMyApp* class takes three parameters.

- A string naming the application

  AppReg is the application's registration table, shown later in "2. Registering a linking and embedding server." The expression *::AppReg["description"]* extracts a string that was registered to describe the application.

- A pointer to the application module

  Module is a global variable of type *TModule** defined by ObjectWindows.

- The address of the application dictionary

  AppDictionary is the application dictionary object explained in the previous section.

Step 4: Inheriting from OLE classes

A server makes the same changes to its OLE classes that a container makes. ObjectWindows wraps a great deal of power in its new window, document, and view classes. To give an ObjectWindows program OLE capabilities, change its derived classes to inherit from OLE classes.

Here are some examples:

```
// old declarations (without OLE)
class TMyDocument: public TDocument    { /* declarations */ };
class TMyView: public TView            { /* declarations */ };
class TMyFrame: public TFrameWindow    { /* declarations */ );


// new declarations (with OLE)
class TMyDocument: public TOleDocument { /* declarations */ };
class TMyView: public TOleView         { /* declarations */ };
class TMyFrame: public TOleFrame       { /* declarations */ );
```

When you change to OLE classes, be sure that those methods in your classes which refer to their direct base classes now use the OLE class names.

```
void TMyView::Paint(TDC& dc, BOOL erase, TRect& rect)
{
  TOleView::Paint(dc, erase, rect);
  // paint the view here
}
```

It is generally safer to allow the OLE classes to handle Windows events and Doc/View notifications. This is particularly true for the *Paint* method and mouse message handlers in classes derived from *TOleView*. *TOleView::Paint* knows how to paint the objects embedded in your document. (Servers are often containers as well, and a server's object might have other objects embedded in it.) Similarly, the mouse handlers of *TOleView* let the user select, move, resize, and activate an OLE object embedded or linked in your document. See the *Borland C++ Programmer's Guide*, Chapter 37, for a list of standard message handlers that provide OLE functionality.

Step 5: Building registration tables

Servers implement OLE objects that any container can use. Different servers implement different types of objects. Every type of object a server creates must have a globally unique identifier (GUID) and a unique string identifier. Every server must record this information, along with other descriptive information, in the registration database of the system where it runs. OLE reads the registry to determine which objects are available, what their capabilities are, and how to invoke the application that creates objects of each type.

ObjectComponents simplifies the task of registration. You call macros to build a table of keys with associated values. ObjectComponents receives the table and automatically performs all registration tasks.

Servers and containers use the same macros for registration, but servers must provide more information than containers. Here are the commands to build the registration tables for a typical server. This example comes from the STEP15.CPP and STEP15DV.CPP file in the EXAMPLES\OWL\TUTORIAL directory of your compiler installation.

```
REGISTRATION_FORMAT_BUFFER(100)            // allow space for expanding macros

BEGIN_REGISTRATION(AppReg)
    REGDATA(clsid,       "{5E4BD320-8ABC-101B-A23B-CE4E85D07ED2}")
    REGDATA(description,"Drawing Pad Server")
END_REGISTRATION

BEGIN_REGISTRATION(DocReg)
    REGDATA(progid,      "DrawPad.Document.15")
    REGDATA(description,"Drawing Pad (Step15--Server)")
    REGDATA(menuname,    "Drawing Pad 15")
    REGDATA(extension,   "p15")
    REGDATA(docfilter,   "*.p15")
    REGDOCFLAGS(dtAutoOpen | dtAutoDelete | dtUpdateDir | dtCreatePrompt |
            dtRegisterExt)
    REGDATA(insertable, "")
    REGDATA(verb0,       "&Edit")
    REGDATA(verb1,       "&Open")
    REGFORMAT(0, ocrEmbedSource,   ocrContent,   ocrIStorage,   ocrGet)
    REGFORMAT(1, ocrMetafilePict,  ocrContent,   ocrMfPict|ocrStaticMed, ocrGet)
    REGFORMAT(2, ocrBitmap,        ocrContent,   ocrGDI|ocrStaticMed, ocrGet)
    REGFORMAT(3, ocrDib,           ocrContent,   ocrHGlobal|ocrStaticMed, ocrGet)
    REGFORMAT(4, ocrLinkSource,    ocrContent,   ocrIStream, ocrGet)
END_REGISTRATION
```

The macros in the example build two structures. The first structure is named *AppReg* and the second is *DocReg*. ObjectComponents uses lowercase strings such as *progid* and *clsid* to name the standard keys to which you assign values. The values you assign are strings, and they are sensitive to case. The order of keys within the registration table doesn't matter. For more about the macros REGDATA, REGFORMAT, and REGDOCFLAGS, see "Understanding registration macros" on page 309. For information on the the full set of registration macros, see the *ObjectWindows Reference*.

The set of keys you place in a structure depends on what OLE capabilities you intend to support and whether the structure holds application information or document information. The macros in the example show the minimum amount of information a server with one type of document should provide.

A server registers program and class ID strings (*progid* and *clsid*) for itself and for every type of document it creates. The IDs must be absolutely unique so that OLE can distinguish one application from another. The *description* strings appear on the Insert Object dialog box where the user sees a list of objects available in the system.

The following table briefly describes all the registration keys that can be used by a server that supports linking and embedding. It shows which are optional and which required as well as which belong in the application registration table and which in the document registration table.

Key	in AppReg?	in DocReg?	Description
appname	Yes	Optional	Short name for the application
clsid	Yes	Optional	Globally unique identifier (GUID); generated automatically for the *DocReg* structure
description	Yes	Yes	Descriptive string (up to 40 characters)
progid	No	No	Identifier for program or object type (unique string)
			Note: in *DocReg* for link or embed source
menuname	No	Yes	Name of server object for container menu
extension	No	Optional	Document file extension associated with server
docfilter	No	Yes	Wildcard file filter for File Open dialog box
			Note: not in *DocReg* if *dtHidden*
docflags	No	Yes	Options for running the File Open dialog box
debugger	No	Optional	Command line for running debugger
debugprogid	No	Optional	Name of debugging version (unique string)
debugdesc	No	No	Description of debugging version
			Note: in *DocReg* if using debugprogid
insertable	No	No	Indication that object can be embedded. If omitted, the document is only a link source
			Note: in *DocReg* for embedding
verbn	No	Yes	An action the server can execute with the object
formatn	No	Yes	A Clipboard format the server can produce
aspectall	No	Optional	Options for displaying object in any aspect
aspectcontent	No	Optional	Options for displaying the object's content aspect
aspectdocprint	No	Optional	Options for displaying the object's docprint aspect
aspecticon	No	Optional	Options for displaying the object's icon aspect

Key	in AppReg?	in DocReg?	Description
aspectthumbnail	No	Optional	Options for displaying the object's thumbnail aspect
cmdline	No	Optional	Arguments to place on server's command line
path	No	Optional	Path to server file (defaults to current module path)
permid	No	Optional	Name string without version information
permname	No	Optional	Descriptive string without version information
usage	Optional	Optional	Support for concurrent clients
language	Optional	No	Language for registered strings (defaults to system's user language setting)
version	Optional	No	Major and minor version numbers (defaults to "1.0") of database

The previous table assumes that the server's documents support linking or embedding. For documents that support neither, the server needs to register only *docflags* and *docfilter*.

If the server is also a container or an automation server, then you should also consult the container table or the automation table in the *Borland C++ Programmer's Guide* in Chapters 37 and 39, respectively. Register all the keys that are required in any of the tables that apply to your application.

For more information about individual registration keys, the values they hold, and the macros used to register them, see the *ObjectWindows Reference*.

The values assigned to keys can be translated to accommodate system language settings. For more about localization, see the *Borland C++ Programmer's Guide*, Chapters 38 and 39.

Place your registration structures in the source code files where you construct document templates and implement your *TApplication*-derived class. A server always creates only one application registration table (called *AppReg* in the example). The server might create several document registration tables, however, if it creates several different kinds of documents (for example, text objects and chart objects). Each registration table needs a unique *progid* value.

After creating registration tables, you must pass them to the appropriate object constructors. The *AppReg* structure is passed to the *TOcRegistrar* constructor, as described in the section "Step 6: Creating a registrar object." Document registration tables are passed to the document template constructor.

```
DEFINE_DOC_TEMPLATE_CLASS(TMyOleDocument, TMyOleView, MyTemplate);
MyTemplate myTpl(::DocReg);
```

Some of the information in the document registration table is used only by the document template. The document filter and document flags have to do with documents, not with OLE. Previous versions of OWL passed the same information to the document template as a series of separate parameters. The old method is still supported for backward compatibility, but new programs, whether they use OLE or not, should use the registration macros to supply document template parameters.

Some of the registration macros expand the values passed to them. The REGISTRATION_FORMAT_BUFFER macro reserves memory needed temporarily for the expansion. To determine how much buffer space you need, allow 10 bytes for each REGFORMAT item plus the size of any string parameters you pass to the macros REGSTATUS, REGVERBOPT, REGICON, or REGFORMAT. For more information, see the *ObjectWindows Reference*.

Step 6: Creating a registrar object

Every ObjectComponents application needs a registrar object to manage all of its registration tasks. In a linking and embedding application, the registrar is an object of type *TOcRegistrar*. At the top of your source code file, declare a global variable holding a pointer to the registrar.

```
static TPointer<TOcRegistrar> Registrar;
```

The *TPointer* template ensures that the *TOcRegistrar* instance is deleted when the program ends.

Note   Name this variable *Registrar* to take advantage of the factory callback template used in the registrar's constructor.

The next step is to modify your *OwlMain* function to allocate a new *TOcRegistrar* object and initialize the global pointer *Registrar*. The *TOcRegistrar* constructor expects three parameters: the application's registration structure, the component's factory callback and the command-line string that invoked that application. The registration structure is created with the registration macros.

The factory callback is created with a class template. For a linking and embedding ObjectWindows application that uses Doc/View, the template is called *TOleDocViewFactory*. The third parameter, the command-line string, can be obtained from the *GetCmdLine* method of *TApplication*. The code in the factory template assumes you have defined an application dictionary called *AppDictionary* and a *TOcRegistrar** called *Registrar*.

```
int OwlMain(int, char*[])
{
  // Create Registrar object
  ::Registrar = new TOcRegistrar(::AppReg, TOleDocViewFactory<TMyApp>(),
        TApplication::GetCmdLine());
?
}
```

After initializing the *Registrar* pointer, your OLE container application must invoke the *Run* method of the registrar instead of *TApplication::Run*. *TRegistrar::Run* calls the factory callback procedure (the one the second parameter points to) and causes the application to create itself. The application enters its message loop, which is actually in the factory callback. The following code shows a sample *OwlMain* before and after adding a registrar object. Boldface type highlights changes.

Before:
```
// Non-OLE OwlMain
int
```

```
OwlMain(int /*argc*/, char* /*argv*/[])
{
  return TMyApp().Run();
}
```

After:

```
// New declaration of OwlMain
int
OwlMain(int /*argc*/, char* /*argv*/[])
{
  ::Registrar = new TOcRegistrar(::AppReg,
        TOleDocViewFactory<TMyApp>(),
        TApplication::GetCmdLine());
  return ::Registrar->Run();
}
```

The last parameter of the *TOcRegistrar* constructor is the command-line string that invoked the application.

Step 7: Processing the command line

When OLE invokes a server, it places an **-Embedding** switch on the command line to tell the application why it has been invoked. The presence of the switch indicates that the user did not launch the server directly. Usually a server responds by keeping its main window hidden. The user interacts with the server through the container. If the **-Embedding** switch is not present, the user has invoked the server as a standalone application and the server shows itself in the normal way.

When you construct a *TRegistrar* object, it parses the command line for you and searches for any OLE-related switches. It removes the switches as it processes them, so if you examine your command line after creating *TRegistrar* you will never see them.

If you want to know what switches were found, call *IsOptionSet*. For example, this line tests for the presence of a registration switch on the command line:

```
if (Registrar->IsOptionSet(amAnyRegOption))
      return 0;
```

This is a common test in *OwlMain*. If the a command line switch such as **-RegServer** was set, the application simply quits. By the time the registrar object is constructed, any registration action requested on the command line have already been performed.

The following table lists all the OLE-related command-line switches.

Switch	What the server should do	OLE places switch?
-RegServer	Register all its information and quit	No
-UnregServer	Remove all its entries from the system and quit	No
-NoRegValidate	Run without confirming entries in the system database	No

Switch	What the server should do	OLE places switch?
-Automation	Register itself as single-use (one client only)	
	Always accompanied by **-Embedding**.	Yes
-Embedding	Consider remaining hidden because it is	
	running for a client, not for itself	Yes
-Language	Set the language for registration and type libraries	No
-TypeLib	Create and register a type library	No
-Debug	Enter a debugging session	Yes

OLE places some of the switches on the program's command line. Anyone can set other flags to make ObjectComponents perform specific tasks. An install program, for example, might invoke the application it installs and pass it the **-RegServer** switch to make the server register itself. Switches can begin with either a hyphen (-) or a slash (/).

Only a few of the switches call for any action from you. If a server or an automation object sees the **-Embedding** or **-Automation** switch, it might decide to keep its main window hidden. Usually ObjectComponents makes that decision for you. You can use the **-Debug** switch as a signal to turn trace messages on and off, but responding to **-Debug** is always optional. (OLE uses **-Debug** switch only if you register the *debugprogid* key.)

ObjectComponents handles all the other switches for you. If the user calls a program with the **-UnregServer** switch, ObjectComponents examines its registration tables and erases all its entries from the registration database. If ObjectComponents finds a series of switches on the command line, it processes them all. This example makes ObjectComponents generate a type libary in the default language and then again in Belgian French.

```
myapp -TypeLib -Language=80C -TypeLib
```

The number passed to **-Language** must be hexadecimal digits. The Win32 API defines *80C* as the locale ID for the Belgian dialect of the French language. For this command line to have the desired effect, of course, *myapp* must supply Belgian French strings in its XLAT resources. For more information about localization, see the *Borland C++ Programmer's Guide*, Chapter 39.

The **-RegServer** flag optionally accepts a file name.

```
myapp -RegServer = MYAPP.REG
```

This causes ObjectComponents to create a registration data file in MYAPP.REG. The new file contains all the application's registration data. If you distribute MYAPP.REG with your program, users can merge the file directly into their own registration database (using *RegEdit*). Without a file name, **-RegServer** writes all data directly to the system's registration database. For a description of the **-TypeLib** switch, see "Creating a type library" on page 404.

Note Only EXE servers have true command lines. OLE can't pass command line switches to a DLL. ObjectComponents simulates passing a command line to a DLL server so that you can use the same code either way. The registrar object always sets the right running mode flags. For more about DLL servers, see the *Borland C++ Programmer's Guide*, Chapter 39.

Step 8: Telling clients when an object changes

Whenever the server makes any changes that alter the appearance of an object, the server must tell OLE. OLE keeps a metafile representation with every linked or embedded object so that even when the server is not active OLE can still draw the object for the container. If the object changes, OLE must update the metafile. The server notifies OLE of the change by calling *TOleView::InvalidatePart*. OLE, in turn, asks the server to paint the revised object into a new metafile. ObjectComponents handles this request by passing the metafile device context to the server's *Paint* procedure. You don't need to write extra code for updating the metafile.

A good place to call *InvalidatePart* is in the handlers for the messages that ObjectWindows sends to a view when its data changes:

```
bool TDrawView::VnRevert(bool /*clear*/) {
  Invalidate();                  // force full repaint
  InvalidatePart(invView);       // tell container about the change
  return true;
}
```

invView is an enumeration value, defined by ObjectComponents, indicating that the view is invalid and needs repainting.

Other view notification messages that signal the need for an update include EV_VN_APPEND, EV_VN_MODIFY, and EV_VN_DELETE.

Step 9: Loading and saving the server's documents

When a server gives objects to containers, the containers assume the burden of storing the objects in files and reading them back when necessary. If your server can also run independently and load and save its own documents, it too should make use of the compound file capabilities built into *TOleDocument*. For more about compound files, see the *Borland C++ Programmer's Guide*, Chapter 37.

In its *Open* method, a server calls *TOleDocument::Open*. In its *Commit* method, a server should call *TOleDocument::Commit* and *TOleDocument::CommitTransactedStorage*.

```
// document class declaration derived from TOleDocument
class _DOCVIEWCLASS TMyDocument : public TOleDocument {
  // declarations
}

// document class implementation
bool TMyDocument::Commit(bool force) {
  TOleDocument::Commit(force);   // save linked and embedded objects
```

```
     ⋮
                                    // code to save other document data
     TOleDocument::CommitTransactedStorage();    // write to file if transacted mode
     }

     bool TDrawDocument::Open(int, const char far* path) {
       TOleDocument::Open();     // load linked or embedded objects
       ⋮
                                    // code to load other document data
     }
```

Note   By default, *TOleDocument* opens compound files in transacted mode. Transacted mode saves changes in temporary storages until you call *CommitTransactedStorage*.

Step 10: Compiling and linking the application

Linking and embedding servers that use ObjectComponents and ObjectWindows require the large memory model. Link them with the OLE and ObjectComponents libraries.

The integrated development environment (IDE) chooses the right build options when you ask for OLE support. To build any ObjectComponents program from the command line, create a short makefile that includes the OWLOCFMK.GEN file found in the EXAMPLES subdirectory.

```
EXERES = MYPROGRAM
OBJEXE = winmain.obj myprogram.obj
!include $(BCEXAMPLEDIR)\ocfmake.gen
```

EXERES and OBJEXE hold the name of the file to build and the names of the object files to build it from. The last line includes the OWLOCFMK.GEN file. Name your file MAKEFILE and type this at the command-line prompt:

```
make MODEL=l
```

MAKE, using instructions in OCFMAKE.GEN, will build a new makefile tailored to your project. The new makefile is called WIN16L*xx*.MAK.

For more information, see "Building an ObjectComponents application" in Chapter 36.

Turning an application into an OLE server with ObjectWindows

Turning a non-Doc/View ObjectWindows container into an OLE server requires a few modifications. The required modifications are:

1 Include OWL header files.
2 Create an application dictionary.
3 Create registration tables.
4 Create a document list.
5 Create a registrar object.
6 Create helper objects for a document.

7 Derive the application class from *ToCModule*.

8 Compile and link the application.

The following section expands on each step required to convert your ObjectWindows container into an OLE server. Code excerpts used in the above topics are from the OWLOCF2.CPP sample in the EXAMPLES/OWL/TUTORIAL/OLE directory. OWLOCF2 converts the OWLOCF1 sample from a container to a server.

Step 1: Including OWL header files

ObjectWindows provides OLE-related classes, structures, macros, and symbols in various header files. The following list shows the headers needed for an OLE container using an SDI frame window.

```
#include <owl/oleframe.h>
#include <owl/olewindo.h>
#include <ocf/ocstorag.h>
```

An MDI application includes olemdifr.h instead of oleframe.h.

Step 2: Creating an application dictionary

An application dictionary tracks information for the currently active process. It is particularly useful for DLLs. When several processes use a DLL concurrently, the DLL must maintain multiple copies of the global, static, and dynamic variables that represent its current state in each process. For example, the DLL version of ObjectWindows maintains a dictionary that allows it to retrieve the *TApplication* corresponding to the currently active client process. If you convert an executable server to a DLL server, it must also maintain a dictionary of the *TApplication* objects representing each of its container clients.

The DEFINE_APP_DICTIONARY macro provides a simple and unified way to create the dictionary object for any type of application, whether it is a container, a server, a DLL, or an EXE. Insert this statement with your other static variables:

```
DEFINE_APP_DICTIONARY(AppDictionary);
```

For any application linked to the static version of the DLL library, the macro simply creates a reference to the application dictionary in ObjectWindows. For DLL servers using the DLL version of ObjectWindows, however, it creates an instance of the *TAppDictionary* class.

It is important to name your dictionary object *AppDictionary* to take advantage of the factory templates such as *TOleFactory* (as explained in the section "Step 5: Creating a registrar object").

Step 3: Creating registration tables

Servers implement OLE objects that any container can link or embed in their own documents. Different servers implement different types of objects. Every type of object a server can create must have a 16-byte globally unique identifier (GUID) and a unique string identifier. Every server must record this information, along with other descriptive information, in the registration database of the system where it runs. OLE reads the registry to determine what objects are available, what their capabilities are, and how to invoke the application that creates objects of each type.

A server provides registration information to ObjectComponents using macros to build registration tables: one table describing the application itself and one for each type of OLE object the server creates. Here is the application registration table from OWLOCF2.

```
REGISTRATION_FORMAT_BUFFER(100)

// application registration table
BEGIN_REGISTRATION(AppReg)
  REGDATA(clsid,       "{B6B58B70-B9C3-101B-B3FF-86C8A0834EDE}")
  REGDATA(description,"Scribble Pad Server")
END_REGISTRATION
```

The registration macros build a structure of items. Each item contains a key, such as *clsid* or *description*, and a value assigned to the key. The order in which the keys appear does not matter. In the example, *AppReg* is the name of the structure that holds the information in this table.

Servers that create several types of objects must build a document registration table for each type. (What the server creates as a document is presented through OLE as an object.) If a spreadsheet application, for example, creates spreadsheet files and graph files, and if both kinds of documents can be linked or embedded, then the application registers two document types and creates two document registration tables.

The OWLOCF2 sample program creates one type of object, a scribbling pad, so it requires one document registration table (shown here) in addition to the application registration table.

```
// document registration table
BEGIN_REGISTRATION(DocReg)
  REGDATA(progid,      "Scribble.Document.3")
  REGDATA(description,"Scribble Pad Document")
  REGDATA(debugger,    "tdw")
  REGDATA(debugprogid,"Scribble.Document.3.D")
  REGDATA(debugdesc,  "Scribble Pad Document (debug)")
  REGDATA(menuname,    "Scribble")
  REGDATA(insertable, "")
  REGDATA(extension,  DocExt)
  REGDATA(docfilter,  "*."DocExt)
  REGDOCFLAGS(dtAutoDelete | dtUpdateDir | dtCreatePrompt | dtRegisterExt)
  REGDATA(verb0,       "&Edit")
  REGDATA(verb1,       "&Open")
  REGFORMAT(0, ocrEmbedSource,  ocrContent, ocrIStorage, ocrGet)
  REGFORMAT(1, ocrMetafilePict, ocrContent, ocrMfPict,   ocrGet)
END_REGISTRATION
```

The *progid* key is an identifier for this document type. The string must be unique so that OLE can distinguish one object from another. The *insertable* key indicates that this type of document should be listed in the Insert Object dialog box. The *description, menuname,* and *verb* keys are all visible to the user during OLE operations. The *description* appears in the Insert Object dialog box where the user sees a list of objects available in the system. The *menuname* is used in the container's Edit menu when composing the string that pops up the verb menu, which is where the *verb* strings appear. The remaining registration items are used when the application opens a file or uses the Clipboard.

For a list of the keys a server should register, see the *Borland C++ Programmer's Guide*, Chapter 38. For more information about particular register keys, see the *ObjectWindows Reference*.

Place your registration structures in the source code file where you implement your *TApplication*-derived class. If you cut and paste registration tables from other programs, be sure to modify at least the *progid* and *clsid* because these must identify your application uniquely. (Use the GUIDGEN.EXE utility to generate new 16-byte *clsid* identifiers.)

Step 4: Creating a document list

The registration tables hold information about your application and its documents, but they are static. They don't do anything with that information. To register the information with the system, an application must pass the structures to an object that know how to use them. That object is the registrar, which records any necessary information in the system registration database.

In a Doc/View application, the registrar examines the list of document templates to find each document registration structure. A non-Doc/View application doesn't have document templates, so it uses *TRegLink* instead to create a linked list of all its document registration tables.

```
static TRegLink* RegLinkHead;
TRegLink scribbleLink(::DocReg, RegLinkHead);
```

RegLinkHead points to the first node of the linked list. *ScribbleLink* is a node in the linked list. The *TRegLink* constructor follows *RegLinkHead* to the end of the list and appends the new node. Each node contains a pointer to a document registration structure. In OWLOCF2, the list contains only one node because the server creates only one type of document. The node points to *DocReg*.

OWLOCF2 declares *RegLinkHead* as a static variable because it is used in several parts of the code, as the following sections explain.

Step 5: Creating a registrar object

The registrar object registers and runs the application. Its constructor receives the application registration structure and a pointer to the list of document registration structures. In a linking and embedding application, the registrar is an object of type *TOcRegistrar*. At the top of your source code file, declare a global variable holding a pointer to the registrar.

```
static TPointer<TOcRegistrar> Registrar;
```

The *TPointer* template ensures that the *TOcRegistrar* instance is deleted when the program ends.

Note   Name this variable *Registrar* to take advantage of the factory callback template used in the registrar's constructor.

Next, in *OwlMain* allocate a new *TOcRegistrar* object and initialize the global pointer *Registrar*. The *TOcRegistrar* constructor has three required parameters: the application's registration structure, the component's factory callback, and the command-line string that invoked that application.

An optional fourth parameter points to the beginning of the document registration list. In a Doc/View application, this parameter defaults to the application's list of document templates. Applications that do not use Doc/View should pass a *TRegLink** pointing to the list of document registration structures.

```
int
OwlMain(int /*argc*/, char* /*argv*/ [])
{
  try {
    // construct a registrar object to register the application
    Registrar = new TOcRegistrar(::AppReg,   // application registration structure
              TOleFactory<TScribbleApp>(), // factory callback
              TApplication::GetCmdLine(),  // app's command line
              ::RegLinkHead);                   // pointer to doc registration structures

    // did command line say to register only?
    if (Registrar->IsOptionSet(amAnyRegOption))
        return 0;
    return Registrar->Run();                    // enter message loop in factory callback
  }
  catch (xmsg& x) {
    ::MessageBox(0, x.why().c_str(), "Scribble App Exception", MB_OK);
  }
  return -1;
}
```

TOleFactory is a template that creates a class with a factory callback function. For a linking and embedding ObjectWindows application that does not use Doc/View, the template is called *TOleFactory*. The code in the factory template assumes you have defined an application dictionary called *AppDictionary* and a *TOcRegistrar** called *Registrar*.

When the registrar is created, it compares the information in the registration tables to the application's entries in the system registration database and updates the database if necessary. The *Run* method causes the registrar to call the factory callback which, among other things, enters the application's message loop.

Step 6: Creating helper objects for a document

Each new document you open needs two helper objects from ObjectComponents: *TOcDocument* and *TOcView*. Because you create a client window for each document, the window's constructor is a good place to create the helpers. The *TOleWindow::CreateOcView* function creates both at once.

In OWLOCF2, the client window is *TScribbleWindow*. Here is the declaration for the class and its constructor:

```
class TScribbleWindow : public TOleWindow {
  public:
    TScribbleWindow(TWindow* parent, TOpenSaveDialog::TData& fileData);
```

```
TScribbleWindow(TWindow* parent, TOpenSaveDialog::TData& fileData,
                TRegLink* link);
```

The second constructor is new. It is useful when ObjectComponents passes you a pointer to the registration information you provided for one of your document types and asks you to create a document of that type. Here is the implementation of the new constructor:

```
TScribbleWindow::TScribbleWindow(TWindow* parent, TOpenSaveDialog::TData& fileData,
                                 TRegLink* link)
:
  TOleWindow(parent, 0),
  FileData(fileData)
{
?
  // Create a TOcDocument object to hold the OLE parts that we create
  // and a TOcRemView to provide OLE services
  CreateOcView(link, true, 0);
}
```

The constructor receives a *TRegLink* pointer and passes it on to *CreateOcView*. The pointer points to the document registration information for the type of document being created. ObjectComponents passes the pointer to this constructor; you don't have to keep track of it yourself.

Passing **true** to *CreateOcView* causes the function to create a *TOcRemView* helper instead of a *TOcView*. The remote view object draws an OLE object within a container's window. When a server is launched to help a client with a linked or embedded object, it should create a remote view.

If your application supports more than one document type, you can choose to use a different *TOleWindow*-derived class for each one. You must then provide the additional constructor for each class. Alternatively, you can use a single *TOleWindow*-derived class that behaves differently depending on the *TRegList* pointer it receives.

Step 7: Deriving the application class from TOcModule

ObjectComponents requires that the class you derive from *TApplication* must also inherit from *TOcModule*, as described in the *Borland C++ Programmer's Guide*, Chapter 39. In addition, the application object needs to implement a *CreateOleObject* method with the following signature:

```
TUnknown* CreateOleObject(uint32 options, TRegList* link);
```

The purpose of the function is to create a server document for linking or embedding. The server must create a client window and return a pointer of type *TOcRemView**. Here is how OWLOCF2 declares this procedure:

```
class TScribbleApp : public TApplication, public TOcModule {
  public:
    TScribbleApp();
    TUnknown* CreateOleObject(uint32 options, TRegLink* link);
```

and here is how it implements the procedure:

```
TUnknown*
TScribbleApp::CreateOleObject(uint32 options, TRegLink* link)
```

```
{
  if (!link)  // factory creating an application only, no view required
    link = &scribbleLink;       // need to have a view for this app
  TOleFrame* olefr = TYPESAFE_DOWNCAST(GetMainWindow(), TOleFrame);
  CHECK(olefr);
  FileData.FileName[0] = 0;
  TScribbleWindow* client = new TScribbleWindow(olefrGetRemViewBucket(),
    FileData, link);
  client->Create();
  return client->GetOcRemView();
}
```

ObjectWindows uses the *CreateOleObject* method to inform your application when OLE needs the server to create an object. The *TRegLink** parameter indicates which object to create.

Understanding the TRegLink Document List

This topic section explains the relationship between the document registration structure, the document list, and the *CreateOleObject* method. A server builds a document registration table for each type of object that it can serve. (The variable that holds the document registration information is conventionally named *DocReg*.) the registration structure is then passed to a *TRegLink* constructor, which appends the the structure to a linked list so that all the document types can be registered.

OLE displays the *description* value for each document in the Insert Object dialog box whenever the user asks to insert an object. (OLE also displays the *description* strings for all the other available server document types.) When the user chooses to insert one of your objects into a container application, OLE launches your server and places the -Embedding switch on the command line. When the server loads, ObjectComponents calls your *CreateOleObject* method, passing the address of the registration link that was used to register the requested document type. The *TRegList* pointer lets you determine which type of object was chosen. This matters primarily for servers that register more than one document type.

The following code illustrates one possible implementation of the *CreateOleObject* method for an application that serves more than one type of object:

```
// Create a appropriate client window and return its TOcRemView pointer
TUnknown*
TServerApp::CreateOleObject(uint32 options, TRegList* link)
{
  if (link == &chartLink) {
    // Create TOleChartWindow
    // and return charWindow->GetOcRemView();
  }

  if (tpl == &worksheetLink) {
    // Create TOleWorksheetWindow
    // and return worksheetWindow->GetOcRemView();
  }

  return 0;
}
```

Step 8: Compiling and linking the application

Linking and embedding servers that use ObjectComponents and ObjectWindows must be compiled with the large memory model. They must be linked with the OLE and ObjectComponents libraries. For help building a makefile, see *Borland C++ Programmer's Guide*, Chapter 39.

Turning an ObjectWindows server into a DLL OLE server

Converting an ObjectWindows EXE server to a DLL server requires only a few modifications.

These are the tasks for building a DLL server:

1 Update your document registration table

2 Compile and link

Updating your document registration table

The document registration tables of DLL servers must contain the *serverctx* key with the string value *"Inproc"*. This allows ObjectComponents to register your application as a DLL server with OLE. EXE servers do not need to use the *serverctx* key since ObjectComponents defaults to EXE registration.

The following code illustrates the document registration structure of a DLL server. It comes from the sample Tic Tac Toe program in EXAMPLES/OWL/OCF/TTT.

```
BEGIN_REGISTRATION(DocReg)
  REGDATA(progid,      "TicTacToeDll")
  REGDATA(description,"TicTacToe DLL")
  REGDATA(serverctx, "Inproc")
  REGDATA(menuname,    "TicTacToe Game")
  REGDATA(insertable, "")
  REGDATA(extension,   "TTT")
  REGDATA(docfilter,  "*.ttt")
  REGDOCFLAGS(dtAutoDelete | dtUpdateDir | dtCreatePrompt | dtRegisterExt)
  REGDATA(verb0,       "&Play")
  REGFORMAT(0, ocrEmbedSource,  ocrContent, ocrIStorage, ocrGet)
  REGFORMAT(1, ocrMetafilePict, ocrContent, ocrMfPict,   ocrGet)
END_REGISTRATION
```

You don't need to modify your application registration structure to convert your EXE server to a DLL server. It's a good idea, however, to use different *clsid* and *progid* values, especially if you intend to switch frequently from one type to the other. You can test for the BI_APP_DLL macro to declare a registration structure that works for both DLL and EXE servers; the macro is only defined when you're building a DLL. The following code shows a sample document registration supplying two sets of *progid* and *clsid* values:

```
REGISTRATION_FORMAT_BUFFER(100)

// Application registration structure
```

```
BEGIN_REGISTRATION(AppReg)
#if defined(BI_APP_DLL)
  REGDATA(clsid,      "{029442B1-8BB5-101B-B3FF-04021C009402}")   // DLL clsid
  REGDATA(progid,     "TicTacToe.DllServer")                      // DLL progid
#else
  REGDATA(clsid,      "{029442C1-8BB5-101B-B3FF-04021C009402}")   // EXE clsid
  REGDATA(progid,     "TicTacToe.Application")                    // EXE progid
#endif
  REGDATA(description,"TicTacToe Application")                     // Description
END_REGISTRATION

// Document registration structure
BEGIN_REGISTRATION(DocReg)
#if defined(BI_APP_DLL)
  REGDATA(progid,     "TicTacToeDll")
  REGDATA(description,"TicTacToe DLL")
  REGDATA(serverctx, "Inproc")
#else
  REGDATA(progid,     "TicTacToe.Game.1")
  REGDATA(description,"TicTacToe Game")
  REGDATA(debugger,    "tdw")
  REGDATA(debugprogid,"TicTacToe.Game.1.D")
  REGDATA(debugdesc,  "TicTacToe Game (debug)")
#endif
  REGDATA(menuname,    "TicTacToe Game")
  REGDATA(insertable, "")
  REGDATA(extension,   "TTT")
  REGDATA(docfilter,  "*.ttt")
  REGDOCFLAGS(dtAutoDelete | dtUpdateDir | dtCreatePrompt | dtRegisterExt)
  REGDATA(verb0,       "&Play")
  REGFORMAT(0, ocrEmbedSource,  ocrContent, ocrIStorage, ocrGct)
  REGFORMAT(1, ocrMetafilePict, ocrContent, ocrMfPict,   ocrGet)
END_REGISTRATION
```

Notice that the debugger keys (*debugger*, *debugprogid*, and *debugdesc*) are not used when building a DLL server. They are relevant only when your server is an executable that a debugger can load.

Compiling and linking a DLL OLE server

ObjectWindows DLL servers must be compiled with the large memory model. They must be linked with the OLE, ObjectComponents, and ObjectWindows libraries.

The integrated development environment (IDE) chooses the right build options for you when you select *Dynamic Library* for Target Type and request OWL and OCF support from the list of standard libraries. You may choose to link with the static or dynamic versions of the standard libraries.

To build an ObjectWindows DLL server from the command line, create a short makefile that includes the OWLOCFMK.GEN file found in the EXAMPLES subdirectory. Here, for example, is the makefile that builds the sample program Tic Tac Toe:

```
MODELS=ld
SYSTEM = WIN16

DLLRES = ttt
OBJDLL = ttt.obj

!include $(BCEXAMPLEDIR)\owlocfmk.gen
```

DLLRES holds the base name of your resource file and the final DLL name. OBJDLL holds the names of the object files from which to build the sample. Finally, your makefile should include the OWLOCFMK.GEN file.

Name your file MAKEFILE and type this at the command-line prompt:

```
make MODEL=l
```

Make, using instructions in OWLOCFMK.GEN, builds a new makefile tailored to your project. The command also runs the new makefile to build the program. If you change the command to define MODEL as *d*, the above command will create a new makefile and then build your DLL using the DLL version of the libraries instead of the large model static libraries.

For more information about how to use OWLOCFMK.GEN, read the instructions at the beginning of MAKEFILE.GEN, found in the examples directory.

For more information, see "Building an ObjectComponents application" in Chapter 36.

38

Windows shell classes

The shell classes allow a program to navigate the Windows 95 shell hierarchical namespace. The shell namespace consists of objects such as files, directories, drives, printers, and networked computers. The root of this hierarchical namespace is the desktop.

In OWL's shell classes, every object in the shell namespace is a *TShellItem*. If an object is a folder and/or it contains sub-folders, an iterator (of type *TShellItemIterator*) can be created on it to iterate through its contents.

Before any shell navigation can take place, an initial *TShellItem* must be created. This initial *TShellItem* can be any file or directory in the file system, or any special folder such as the Desktop, the Recycle Bin, the Control Panel, or My Computer.

The general strategy for using shell classes is to:

1 Create *TShellItem* for the object (or objects) of interest.

2 Use the *TShellItem* member functions to access the object properties.

The following example shows how to display the names of the items in a folder, and its sub-folders:

1 Create an *TShellItem* for the c:\users folder.

```
TShellItem folder ("c:\\users");
```

2 Create an initialized *TShellItem* for the iterator.

```
TShellItem item;
```

3 Iterate through the folder and display the item name.

```
for (TShellItemIterator i(folder); i.valid();) {
  item = i++;
  MessageBox (0, item.GetDisplayName(), "Title", MB_OK);
  }
```

39

Windows Socket classes

The Sockets layer provides network access for application programs.

This chapter covers the following topics:

- Socket communications
- Socket modes—blocking and non-blocking
- Socket classes

Socket communications

This section discusses the two types of communication:

- Stream socket communication
- Datagram socket communication

Stream socket communication

In stream-based communication, the stream client applications request services from a server application.

The following table shows the sequence of operations for the server and the client.

Server	Client
Create a socket	
Bind an address to the socket	
Listen for service requests	
	Create a socket
Accept the connection	Connect to the server
Send and receive data	Send and receive data
Close the connection	Close the connection

Here are the steps for using a stream server, including the necessary code:

1 Create a stream socket:

```
TStreamSocket socket(TINetSocketAddress(htons(2000), INADDR_ANY);
socket.CreateSocket();
```

2 Bind the socket to a well-known name (*bind()*):

```
socket.BindSocket();
```

3 Listen for connections (*listen()*):

```
socket.Listen();
```

4 Accept a connection (*accept()*):

```
TStreamSocket client;
socket.Accept(client);
```

5 To write (*send()*):

```
socket.Write("Hello");
```

6 To read (*recv()*):

```
char buffer[80];
socket.Read(buffer, sizeof(buffer));
```

7 Close the socket (*closesocket()*):

```
socket.CloseSocket();
```

Here are the steps for using a stream client, including the necessary code:

1 Create a stream socket (*socket()*):

```
TStreamSocket socket(TINetSocketAddress());
socket.CreateSocket();
```

2 Connect to the server (*connect()*):

```
socket.Connect(TINetSocketAddress(htons(2000),
    TINetSocketAddress::ConvertAddress("soyeun@harvard.edu")));
```

3 To write (*send()*):

```
socket.Write("Hello");
```

4 To read (*recv()*):

```
char buffer[80];
socket.Read(buffer, sizeof(buffer));
```

5 Close the connection (*closesocket()*):

```
socket.CloseSocket();
```

The following sections present more detail about these steps:

- Accepting a connection
- Creating and connecting a stream server and a client
- Closing the connection

Accepting a connection

The code sample in this section, a non-blocking socket, is created on a server. This socket is bound, starts asynchronous notification, and then starts listening. Some time later, WinSock posts an accept notification, and this causes the listening socket's *DoAcceptNotification()* function to be called. At this point, the listening socket's *Accept()* function can be called to complete the acceptance.

Note that the *tempSocket* doesn't get initialized to have any address; it will get set by the *Accept()* call.

This example does not use any error checking and reporting. The next section, "Creating and connecting a stream server and a client," shows a similiar sequence of operations.

```
TStreamSocket tempListeningSocket(TINetSocketAddress(htons(47), INADDR_ANY);
TStreamSocket tempSocket;

tempListeningStreamSocket.CreateSocket();
tempListeningStreamSocket.BindSocket();
tempListeningStreamSocket.StartAcceptNotification();
tempListeningStreamSocket.Listen();
.../*Wait until tempListeningStreamSocket.DoAcceptNotification() gets called*/
tempListeningStreamSocket.Accept(tempSocket);
tempSocket.StartRegularNotification();  /*Converts socket to non-blocking*/
//  If you are now going to hand off 'tempSocket'to some other class to
//  copy it, you may want to call SetSaveSocketOnDelete() on tempSocket,
//  because tempSocket defaults to calling closesocket() when it goes out of scope.
```

Creating and connecting a stream server and a client

The following code creates a listening stream socket and waits for connections. *ShutDownApp()* is called in the event of an error.

```
define SERVICE_PORT 5001
int nError;
TStreamSocket tempListeningSocket(TINetSocketAddress(htons(SERVICE_PORT)),
                                  INADDR_ANY));

tempListeningStreamSocket.CreateSocket();
nError = tempListeningStreamSocket.BindSocket();
if(nError == SOCKET_ERROR){
   MessageBox(TSocketError(tempListeningStreamSocket.GetLastError()).
        AppendError("Error on call to BindSocket"), "Error" MB_OK);
   ShutDownApp();
}
tempListeningStreamSocket.StartAcceptNotification();
nError = tempListeningStreamSocket.Listen();
if(nError == SOCKET_ERROR){
   MessageBox(TSocketError(tempListeningStreamSocket.GetLastError()).
        AppendError("Error on call to BindSocket"), "Error" MB_OK);
   ShutDownApp();
}
for(;;){ /*Accept and service incoming connection requests indefinitely*/
   tempListeningStreamSocket.Accept(tempSocket);
   if(nError == SOCKET_ERROR){
```

```
            MessageBox(TSocketError(tempListeningStreamSocket.GetLastError()).
                AppendError("Error on call to BindSocket"), "Error" MB_OK);
            ShutDownApp();
        }
        ...do something with the socket...
        tempSocket.StartRegularNotification();  /*Converts socket to non-blocking*/
        tempSocket.CloseSocket();
    }
```

The following code creates a client stream socket that then connects to a server. There is no error checking. The code is blocking, in order to simplify reading.

```
define SZ_SERVER "131.107.1.121"

TServiceManager      myServiceManager;
TServiceEntry*       tempServiceEntry;
TStreamSocket        myStreamSocket(INetSocketAddress());
TINetSocketAddress peerAddress;

myStreamSocket.CreateSocket();
myStreamSocket.BindSocket();
myServiceManager.GetService(tempServiceEntry, "ftp");
peerAddress.SetAddress(AF_INET, tempServiceEntry.s_port,
                    TINetSocketAddress::ConvertAddress(SZ_SERVER));
myStreamSocket.Connect(peerAddress);
    ...
```

Closing the connection

The code to close a connection is identical for both client and server, whether the socket is a stream socket or datagram socket.

If you have a pointer to the socket object:

```
TSocket* socket;
```

You can close the socket connection with:

```
socket->CloseSocket().
```

Note that the destructor for the *TSocket* class will also close the socket.

Datagram socket communication

The WinSocket classes also support datagram sockets. Datagram communication does not require a connection because each datagram message contains a destination address. A datagram socket can send data to many addresses, and receive data from many sources.

Datagram communication does not use a client-server relationship. For convenience, however, these terms are used in the following table.

Server	Client
Create a socket	
Bind an address to the socket	

Server	Client
	Create a socket
Send and receive data	Send and receive data
Close the connection	Close the connection

Here are the steps for using a datagram server, including the necessary code:

1 Create the socket (*socket()*):

```
TDatagramSocket socket(TINetSocketAddress());
  socket.CreateSocket();
```

2 Bind the socket to a well-known name (*bind()*):

```
socket.BindSocket();
socket.SetPeerAddress(TINetSocketAddress(htons(2050), INADDR_BROADCAST));
```

3 To write (*sendto()*):

```
socket.Write("Hello");
```

4 To read (*recvfrom()*):

```
char buffer[80];
socket.Read(buffer, sizeof(buffer));
```

5 Close the connection (*closesocket()*):

```
socket.CloseSocket();
```

Here are the steps for using a datagram client, including the necessary code:

1 Create the socket (*socket()*):

```
TDatagramSocket socket(TINetSocketAddress());
  socket.CreateSocket();
```

2 Bind the socket to a well-known name (*bind()*):

```
socket.SetPeerAddress(TINetSocketAddress(htons(2050), INADDR_BROADCAST));
```

3 To write (*sendto()*):

```
socket.Write("Hello");
```

4 To read (*recvfrom()*):

```
char buffer[80];
socket.Read(buffer, sizeof(buffer));
```

5 Close the connection (*closesocket()*):

```
socket.CloseSocket();
```

The following sections present more detail about these steps:

- Creating a datagram socket
- Sending data from a datagram socket
- Receiving data from a datagram socket

Creating a datagram socket

In the following code, a Datagram (UDP) Socket is created with several options (including broadcasting).

```
int MySocketUsingClass::SetupASocket(u_short nPeerPortInNetworkOrder,
                                     char* szPeerIPAddressDottedDecimal)
{
    TINetSocketAddress myAddress; //(port 0, address INADDR_ANY)
    TINetSocketAddress peerAddress(nPeerPortInNetworkOrder,
                                   szPeerIPAddressDottedDecimal);
    TDatagramSocket myDatagramSocket(myAddress);

    myDatagramSocket.CreateSocket();
    myDatagramSocket.BindSocket();
    myDatagramSocket.SetBroadcastOption(TRUE); //enable broadcasting.
    myDatagramSocket.SetDebugOption(TRUE);     //record debugging information.
    myDatagramSocket.SetLingerOption(TRUE, 5); //set linger to 5 seconds.
    myDatagramSocket.SetSendBufferOption(512); //set send buffer size to 512 bytes.
    myDatagramSocket.SetPeerAddress(TINetSocketAddress(ntohs(N_PORT),
                                                       INADDR_BROADCAST);
}
```

Sending data from a datagram socket

The following code sends a C string by datagram to a given peer on a given port. Both blocking and non-blocking code is demonstrated. Note that the switch back and forth between blocking and non-blocking mode involves only a single line of code. Note also that after the last write call, the local *TDatagramSocket* object is deleted without any *closesocket()* function being called. This is because the socket cleans up after itself and calls *CloseSocket()* if it had not been called already.

```
WriteDataThreeTimes(){
    define N_PORT        501
    define SZ_PEER_ADDR  "132.162.211.199"
    char szString[]      ="Hello";

    TDatagramSocket myDatagramSocket(TINetSocketAddress(htons(N_PORT)));
    myDatagramSocket.CreateSocket();
    myDatagramSocket.BindSocket();
    myDatagramSocket.SetPeerAddress(TINetSocketAddress(ntohs(N_PORT),
                                    inet_addr(SZ_PEER_ADDR));
    myDatagramSocket.Write(szString, sizeof(szString)); //blocking write call.
    myDatagramSocket.StartRegularNotification();      //socket is now non-blocking.
    myDatagramSocket.Write(szString, sizeof(szString))  //non-blocking write call.
    myDatagramSocket.CancelNotification();              //socket is blocking again.
    myDatagramSocket.Write(szString, sizeof(szString)); //blocking write call.
} //The socket will clean up after itself; you don't have to.
```

The following code broadcasts a C string on the network, minus error-checking. Note that when you broadcast with the address "INADDR_BROADCAST", you don't need to say "htonl(INADDR_BROADCAST)" or inet_addr(INADDR_BROADCAST). This is because the definition for INADDR_BROADCAST and its related predefined addresses are already in binary network format.

```
BroadcastHelloString(){
   define N_PORT  501
   char szString[]="Hello Everybody";

   TINetSocketAddress myINetAddress     (0,              INADDR_ANY);
   TINetSocketAddress allINetAddresses(ntohs(N_PORT), INADDR_BROADCAST);

   TDatagramSocket myDatagramSocket(myINetAddress);
   myDatagramSocket.CreateSocket();
   myDatagramSocket.BindSocket();
   myDatagramSocket.SetBroadcastOption(true); //enable broadcasting
   myDatagramSocket.SetPeerAddress(allINetAddresses);
   myDatagramSocket.Write(szString, sizeof(szString)); //blocking write call.
}
```

Receiving data from a datagram socket

The following code reads data from a socket. Since this is a datagram example, we
simply read the next datagram that gets received. It is important to note that Windows
Socket classes don't consider a WSAEWOULDBLOCK return from *Recv()* as an error.
Thus, when you call *Read()* in non-blocking mode, and the *Read()* internally encounters a
WSAEWOULDBLOCK, it simply sets nBytes to zero and returns without an error. Only
real errors are returned by Windows Socket functions.

```
TDatagramSocket myDS(INetSocketAddress(nPeerPortInNetworkOrder, INADDR_ANY);
myDS.CreateSocket();
myDS.BindSocket();
myDS.StartRegularNotification(); //Turns on -non-blocking mode.
...
int            nError;
char           chBuffer[1000];
int            nBytes=1000;
SocketAddress  sAddressOfSender;

nError = myDS.Read(chBuffer, nBytes, sAddressOfSender);
if(nError == WINSOCK_ERROR){
   MessageBox(hWnd, TSocketError(nError).GetReasonString(),
                    "Sockets Error", MB_OK);
   DoLikeNovellAndBombSystemUponReceivingAnyError();
}
if(nBytes){
   ProcessTheBytes(chBuffer, nBytes);  //Some function you may have made.
}
...
```

Blocking and non-blocking modes

If a socket is in the blocking mode, the socket will not relinquish control until a socket
command has been completed. All windows applications will stop, no communications
can occur between applications, and the active window cannot be changed.

For this reason, asynchronous notification is included in order to prevent thread blocking. This is mostly useful in Windows 3.x. Nevertheless, a lot of programmers will be making even Windows NT programs with single threads, and so asynchronous read/write capabilities are still useful. In fact, even if you do use separate threads for sockets calls, you'll find that as soon as you make a blocking call on one thread, you'll have to wait until it's done to use it, or you have to create another thread. Windows non-blocking extensions are useful for all of Windows programming.

The Windows Socket classes provide support for internal notification and external notification. This provides a way for you to make calls and to be notified upon completion of the call. You don't have to respond to the WinSock asynchronous notification system yourself if you don't want to, or you can take care of all notifications yourself.

You may want to use notifications for the following classes:

TServiceManager
THostInfoManager
TSocket
TStreamSocket
TDatagramSocket

TServiceManager notifications

The *TServiceManager* manages the service database *GetXbyY()* functions. You can use it, for example, to specify a service name, such as "ftp", and retrieve the port associated with that service.

The class *TServiceManager* supports blocking and non-blocking calls, and it uses notifications to signal that a non-blocking call has completed.

You can let *TServiceManager* receive the notification itself, whereby you can call the *GetServiceRequestCompleted()* function to see if that request has completed. Otherwise, you can tell the *TServiceManager* to notify a given *TWindow* (which you supply) when the request is completed. In either case, you can call the *CancelServiceRequest()* function to cancel the pending asynchronous request.

THostInfoManager notifications

The class *THostInfoManager* has notification options that are much like the *TServiceManager* options. *THostInfoManager* manages the host entry ('hostent') database *GetXbyY()* functions. You can use it, for example, to convert a name such as "joes_computer@abc.com" to an IP address.

THostInfoManager supports blocking and non-blocking calls, and it uses notifications to signal that a non-blocking call has completed.

You can let *THostInfoManager* receive the notification itself, whereby you can call the *GetHostRequestCompleted()* function to see if that request has completed. Otherwise, you can tell *THostInfoManager* to notifiy a given *TWindow* (which you supply) when the request is completed. In either case, you can call the *CancelHostRequest()* function to cancel the pending asynchronous request.

TSocket notifications

The *TSocket* class has a couple different notification options that you can use. First, we'll give a brief description of how WinSock notification works. Then we'll talk about how it works with the Socket class and your options.

A blocking socket causes read, write, and so on, calls to sometimes block the executing thread until the call has completed, depending on whether the WinSock driver is *ready* to make the call. You cannot know for sure if any given socket read or write call will make the socket block or not.

WinSock provides a way for you to be notified by WinSock when it is ready to make a read or write call without blocking: you call the WinSock function *WSAAsyncSelect()* to tell WinSock to notify you (you supply an HWND) with FD_READ, FD_WRITE, FD_OOB, FD_ACCEPT, FD_CONNECT, and FD_CLOSE identifiers. For example, when WinSock is ready to accept read calls on the socket, it sends your HWND an FD_READ message. If you don't call *WSAAsyncSelect()*, then all socket functions you use will block.

The OWLSock *TSocket* class has both an internal notification mechanism and an external notification mechanism. In the internal mechanism, *TSocket* has an internal hidden friend window that receives all FD_XXX notifications. With the external notification mechanism, you tell the *TSocket* class that you want all FD_XXX notifications to go to the window of your choice. These two internal and external notification systems are mutually exclusive. The *TSocket* class uses internal notification by default, but you can redirect any of the notifications to a given window.

In the Windows Socket classes, the equivalent Socket functions to *WSAAsyncSelect()* are *DoAcceptNotification()* and *DoRegularNotification()*. These two functions cause a socket to be notified of FD_ACCEPT and all other FDs, respectively. Since a listening socket can do nothing else in life but listen, and a connected (read/write) socket can never be a listening socket, we have separate functions to turn on both of the notification types.

When *TSocket* gets an internal notification, it calls the appropriate *DoXNotification()* function. In the *TSocket* class, these functions are empty, while the *TStreamSocket* and *TDatagramSocket* classes do an appropriate action based on the message. You can subclass the *TSocket* class (or more likely, the *TStreamSocket* or *TDatagramSocket*) and write your own *DoXNotification()* functions to override the default behavior. For example, the *TStreamSocket::DoWriteNotification()* function tries to write any data that is in its outgoing queue. You could, for example, make a subclass called *TPOPSocket()* that sends and receives POP notifications and commands upon *DoReadNotification()* and *DoWriteNotification()* calls.

If you set *TSocket* to do external notifications, it will redirect FD_XXX notifications to the window of your choice. You can tell *TSocket* to redirect any combination of notifications to the given window by OR-ing the appropriate values together. Only the notifications that you OR together will get redirected to the window; the others go to the *DoXNotification()* functions, as usual.

You may want to redirect all notifications to a window so that you can respond to each of the notifications when they come. You could, for example, redirect only FD_ACCEPT messages to a window so that all listening sockets send FD_ACCEPT messages to the same window. You call the *SetNotificationWindow* function to set the window for the notifications to be set. These windows are set on a *TSocket* by *TSocket* basis, and you only have to set it once for a given *TSocket*. When you call *SetNotificationSet()* you tell it what notifications to redirect. There is an enumeration set (nNotifyWrite) that duplicates the FD set (FD_WRITE). You can use either set, as they are effectively equal.

Identifiers and functions for external notification:

```
//These two FD macros supplement those in winsock.h.
define FD_ALL      (FD_READ|FD_WRITE|FD_OOB|FD_ACCEPT|FD_CONNECT|FD_CLOSE)
define FD_NONE     (0)

//These enumerations duplicate those defined in 'winsock.h'
//You can OR or add these together to make a notification set.
enum NotificationSet{nNotifyNone = 0x00, nNotifyRead  = 0x01, nNotifyWrite  = 0x02,
         nNotifyOOB  = 0x04, nNotifyAccept = 0x08, nNotifyConnect = 0x10,
         nNotifyClose = 0x20, nNotifyAll  = 0x3F};

virtual void SetNotificationWindow(TWindow* windowNewNotification);
virtual void SetNotificationSet(int nNewNotificationSet);
```

TStreamSocket notifications

The *TStreamSocket* class is a subclass of the *TSocket* class, and as such it supports all the notification mechanisms that the *TSocket* class supports. Thus, you can call *StartRegularNotification()* and *SetNotificationSet()* on a *TStreamSocket* as well as on a *TSocket*.

The *TStreamSocket* class subclasses all the *DoXNotification()* functions. You can subclass *TStreamSocket* and make your own virtual *DoReadNotification()*, *DoWriteNotification()*, and so on, functions to receive these notifications in the subclass and respond to them any way you want.

TDatagramSocket notifications

The *TDatagramSocket* class, like the *TStreamSocket* class, is a subclass of the *TSocket* class, and it supports all the notification mechanisms that the *TSocket* class supports. Thus, you can call *StartRegularNotification()* and *SetNotificationSet()* on a *TDatagramSocket* as well as on a *TSocket*.

The *TDatagramSocket* class subclasses all the *DoXNotification()* functions from the *TSocket* class. You can subclass *TDatagramSocket* and make your own virtual *DoReadNotification()*, *DoWriteNotification()*, and so on, functions to receive these notifications in the subclass and respond to them any way you want.

Socket classes

The Windows Socket classes support the Transmission Control Protocol (TCP) and the User Datagram Protocol (UDP).

- The TCP protocol is used for stream socket communication.

- The UDP protocol is used for datagram socket communication.

The TCP and UDP layers support the Internet Protocol (IP) layer.

The following classes are used to create window sockets:

TDatagramSocket
THostInfoManager
TINetSocketAddress
TServiceManager
TSocket
TSocketAddress
TSocketError
TSocketManager
TStreamSocket

THostInfoManager

The *THostInfoManager* class (and its friend class *THostInfoWindow*) encapsulate the WinSock database functions *gethostbyname()*, *gethostbyaddr()*, and *gethostname()*. These blocking (*gethostby...*) and non-blocking (*gethostname*) functions return information about the host in a hostent structure.

The *THostInfoManager* supports direct equivalents to the blocking *gethostbyaddr()* and *gethostbyname()* WinSock functions. In WinSock 1.1, the *gethostbyaddr()* and *gethostbyname()* functions work only for Internet addresses. Thus, the *THostInfoManager* has the same restriction. However, the *THostInfoManager* functions accept a *TSocketAddress* as the address parameter instead of a *TINetSocketAddress*. This is to be forward-compatible with WinSock 2.0.

Let's say you have a host name, "elvis@ms.com," and you want to get its *THostInfo* (*hostent*). In WinSock, you could say:

```
tempHostent = gethostbyname("elvis@ms.com");
```

Calling the *THostInfoManager* function *GetHostInfo()* has the same effect:

```
nError = myHostInfoMgr.GetHostInfo(tempHostent, "elvis@ms.com");
```

While the above example will get you a *THostInfo* (*hostent*) structure, it doesn't give you an IP address or *TSocketAddress* directly. Most often, you'll want to use the *THostInfoManager* to convert fully qualified names such as "elvis@ms.com" to IP addresses or *TSocketAddresses*. You can use the *GetHostAddress(char* szHostAddress, const char* szHostName)* or the *GetHostAddress(SocketAddress& sAddress, const char* szHostName)* to do this. Let's say you have a host name, "elvis@ms.com," and you want to get its equivalent IP address. In WinSock, you would say:

```
char    szDottedDecimalAddress[16];
hostent* tempHostent;
in_addr tempInAddr;
char*   szAddress;
tempHostent = gethostbyname("elvis@ms.com");
tempInAddr.s_addr = *((u_long*)tempHostEntry->h_addr);
```

```
szAddress = inet_ntoa(tempInAddr);
strcpy(szDottedDecimalAddress, szAddress);
```

Calling the *HostInfoManager* function *GetHostInfo()* has the same effect, but is more concise, because it takes care of all the housekeeping:

```
char   szDottedDecimalAddress[16];
nError = myHostInfoMgr.GetHostInfo(szDottedDecimalAddress, "elvis@ms.com");
```

THostInfoManager also supports asynchronous (non-blocking) WinSock host information lookups. These correspond to the *WSAGetHostByName()* and *WSAGetHostByAddr()* functions. To use these classes in WinSock, you need to pass an HWND to these functions and wait till WinSock calls you back with an answer. In Windows Socket Class, you have two choices:

- You can give the *THostInfoManager* a *TWindow* to notify upon completion using *GetHostInfoAsync()*.

- You can let *THostInfoManager* get the notification itself, and you simply get the information from the *THostInfoManager* when the information is ready. This approach lets the *THostInfoManager* do all the work; you simply don't have to deal with HWNDs, wMsgs, wParams, and so on. This option is very similar to the Overlapped I/O concept of Windows NT: Reads and Writes don't block, but the function returns as if the data was read or sent, and a notification will be posted when the read/write actually occurs. This is very useful for times when one thread handles multiple sockets at a time.

When the asynchronous call completes, the *THostInfoManager::SetHostRequestCompleted()* function gets called, and the *HostRequestCompleted* member is set to true. You may at any time call (poll) *THostInfoManager::GetHostRequestCompleted()* to see if the last request has completed. If *GetHostRequestCompleted()* returns true, then you can examine the *THostInfoManager::HostEntry* member, or call *THostInfoManager::HostEntryToAddress()* to get an address.

The WinSock host information database functions return a pointer to a read-only hostent structure.

THostInfoManager uses a subclass of the hostent class called the *THostEntry* class. Since *THostEntry* is a subclass of hostent, it can be used anywhere that WinSock or Windows Socket Class requires a hostent.

TINetSocketAddress

The *TINetSocketAddress* class encapsulates a WinSock Internet address. This class stores a complete Internet address, which includes an address family, a port, and a 32-bit (4-byte) IP address. The Internet address-specific information is stored in the *sa_data* field of the *sockaddr*.

All addresses stored by the *TSocketAddress* class are in network byte order. While the address family field (*sa_family*) is stored in network byte order, these families are #defined in winsock.h to values which are already in network byte order. Thus, you can simply refer to them by their names (for example, AF_INET) and not have to call *htons()* on them.

The *TINetSocketAddress* class can be thought of as a C++ version of the *sockaddr_in* class. Some sockets class implementations (for example, The Distinct corp.) encapsulate only the IP address (*u_long*) in their version of an address class. However, we feel that a full Internet address encompasses both a port and the 4-byte *u_long* IP address. You can think of port and addresses in terms of the U.S. Mail system. The IP address (*u_long*) is like the address on a letter, and the port is like the name of the person that receives the letter at that address. An address on a letter received in the mail is incomplete without the name of who gets the letter. Thus, a full address includes both the address and who should receive the mail at that address. Likewise, a complete Internet address consists of both a port and an address.

There are a number of constructors for *TINetSocketAddress*. Among them are a copy constructor, an empty constructor, a constructor from a *char**, and a constructor from a port and *u_long*. These constructors set up the *sa_data* portion of the *sockaddr* structure to make it look like a properly filled-in *sockaddr_in* structure. The *TINetSocketAddress* class also has functions to get and set the addrress information, get address class information, and functions to convert between dotted-decimal and *u_long* versions of the Internet address (WinSock's *inet_ntoa()* and *inet_addr()*).

Many OWL Windows Socket functions expect a *TSocketAddress* as a parameter. You can pass an *TINetSocketAddress* or a *TSocketAddress* as the parameter.

Using TINetSocketAddress

TSocketAddress and *TINetSocketAddress* encapsulate the address objects. There are two types of addresses. The first is the generic socket address encapsulated by *TSocketAddress*. It is always stored in network-byte order. The family determines how the other bytes of the structure are used. The most common value is AF_INET.

The *TINetSocketAddress* class is derived from *TSocketAddress*. It encapsulates the Internet address. It stores a complete Internet address which includes an address family (which is AF_NET), a port, and a 32-bit (4-byte) IP address.

The class you're more likely to use is *TINetSocketAddress*. You create the address by specifying the port and an optional address on the constructor:

```
TINetSocketAddress address(80);
```

TServiceManager

The *TServiceManager* class (and its friend class *TServiceWindow*) encapsulate the WinSock database functions *getservbyname()*, *getservbyport()*, *WSAAsyncGetServByName()*, and *WSAAsyncGetServByPort()*. These blocking (*get...*) and non-blocking (*WSA...*) functions return information about the service name, port, and protocol when given only a service name or a port.

The WinSock service database functions return a pointer to a read-only servant structure.

The *TServiceManager* uses a subclass of the servant class called the *TServiceEntry* class. Since *TServiceEntry* is a subclass of servant, it can be used anywhere that WinSock or Windows Socket Class requires a servant.

The *TServiceManager* supports direct equivalents to the blocking *getservbyname()* and *getservbyport()* WinSock functions. If you wanted to find the port that the service "ftp" resides on, you could use the *TServiceManager* to give you this information. Calling the WinSock function:

```
tempServant = getservbyport("ftp");
```

will store the service name, the port, and the protocol in the servant structure. Calling the *TServiceManager* function *GetService()* has the same effect:

```
nError = GetService(tempServant, "ftp");
```

The *TServiceManager* also supports asynchronous (non-blocking) WinSock service lookups. These correspond to the *WSAGetServByName()* and *WSAGetServByPort()* functions. To use these classes in WinSock, you need to pass an HWND to these functions and wait until WinSock calls you back with an answer. In the Windows Socket Class, you have two choices:

- You can give the *TServiceManager* a *TWindow* to notify upon completion using *GetServiceAsync()*.

- You can let *TServiceManager* get the notification itself, and then get the information from the *TServiceManager* when the information is ready. This approach lets *TServiceManager* do all the work; you don't have to work with HWNDs, wMsgs, wParams, and so on. This option is very similar to the Overlapped I/O concept of Windows NT: Reads and Writes don't block, but the function returns as if the data was read or sent, and a notification will be posted when the read/write actually occurs. This is very useful for times when one thread handles multiple sockets at a time.

Using TServiceManager

The *TServiceManager* class encapsulates the service-information functions. It provides information about a service, given its name or port number and a specific protocol. The information can be retrieved in either blocking mode or non-blocking mode (see online help under blocking mode). The information is returned in the form of a *TServiceEntry* which encapsulates the WinSock servant structure.

For example, to retrieve the port number of the time service on the UDP protocol in blocking mode, you would use the following code:

```
TServiceManager manager;
int port;
manager.GetServicePort("time", port, "udp");
```

TSocket

The *TSocket* class encapsulates a WinSock SOCKET. It simplifies the use of SOCKETs while letting you fall back to WinSock API calls if desired. For example, the *TSocket* class allows you to say:

```
mySocket.SetLingerOption(true, 5);
```

Whereas in WinSock, you would have to say:

```
LINGER ling;
ling.l_onoff = 1;
ling.l_linger = 5;
setsockopt(socket, SOL_SOCKET, SO_LINGER, (LPSTR)&ling, sizeof(ling));
```

You can use a *TSocket* class anywhere you can use a SOCKET identifier, since class *TSocket* provides an automatic conversion operator from *TSocket* to SOCKET. So if you really want to use the WinSock API, you can say:

```
LINGER ling;
ling.l_onoff = 1;
ling.l_linger = 5;
TSocket myS;
setsockopt(myS, SOL_SOCKET, SO_LINGER, (LPSTR)&ling, sizeof(ling));
```

TSocket offers a number of methods for construction. These are the default constructor, a constructor from an *TSocketAddress* and protocol information, and a copy constructor. The construction from a *TSocketAddress* and protocol info is the most common form. You would say something like the following:

```
TINetSocketAddress myAddress(htons(23), INADDR_ANY);
TSocket tempStreamSocket(myAddress, AF_INET, SOCK_STREAM, IPPROTO_TCP);
```

or, equally

```
TSocket tempStreamSocket(myAddress);
```

The *TSocket* class provides socket creating, binding, and closing functions, read and write functions, socket option setting and getting functions, and more. In actuality, you will most often use the *TSocket*-derived *TStreamSocket* and *TDatagramSocket*, especially for reading and writing the socket.

The *Socket* class supports both blocking and non-blocking socket operation. By default, the *Socket* class blocks on calls to Read and Write, and so on. But, like in the WinSock API, you can turn on asynchronous notification of events like FD_READ, and so on. In the *Socket* class, you use the *StartRegularNotification()*, *StartAcceptNotification()*, and *CancelNotification()* functions. These functions cause the *Socket* functions *DoReadNotification()*, and so on, to be called when the appropriate FD_READ, and so on, messages are sent to an internal socket hidden window. You can redirect these notifications to a given window of your choice with the *Socket SetNotificationWindow()* and *SetNotificationSet()* functions. This way, you get full flexibility with *Socket* asynchronous notifications.

The *TSocket* class (and its subclasses) optionally supports read/write data queueing during asynchronous operation. This allows you to tell the socket to send a block of data with one send and have the socket save that block of data and send it automatically as soon as possible; you don't have to wait for a notification to come—the socket will take care of that for you. This queueing also applies to data receiving. You have *TSocket* bring the data in and wait until it gets to a certain size and then get what you want from the queue.

TSocketAddress

The *TSocketAddress* class stores a WinSock socket address. Note that the *TSocketAddress* class does not store Internet (IP) addresses specifically. It stores generic socket addresses. The *TINetSocketAddress* class is used to store Internet addresses.

All addresses stored by the *TSocketAddress* class are in network byte order. While the address family field (*sa_family*) is stored in network byte order, these families are #defined in winsock.h to values which are already in network byte order. Thus, you can simply refer to them by their names (for example, AF_INET) and not have to call *htons()* on them.

The *TSocketAddress* class can be thought of as a C++ version of the *sockaddr* class.

Note that the only typed data that the *sockaddr* holds is the *sa_family* field. The *sa_data* field is a raw array of bytes that can hold any address supported by WinSock. For example, the *sa_data* field can hold an Internet address in the first 6 bytes of *sa_data* and leave the other 8 bytes zeroed out. Other address formats, such as IPX/SPX addresses, can also fit within 14 bytes.

There are a number of constructors for *TSocketAddress*. Among them are a copy constructor, an empty constructor, a constructor from a *char**, and others.

Many OWLSock functions expect a *TSocketAddress* as a parameter. You can pass a *TSocketAddress* or a subclass of it as the parameter. Some functions may expect a *TINetSocketAddress* as a parameter instead of just a *TSocketAddress*.

Using TSocketAddress

TSocketAddress and *TINetSocketAddress* encapsulate the address objects. There are two types of addresses. The first is the generic socket address encapsulated by *TSocketAddress*. It is always stored in network-byte order. The family determines how the other bytes of the structure are used. The most common value is AF_INET.

The *TINetSocketAddress* class is derived from *TSocketAddress*. It encapsulates the Internet address. It stores a complete Internet address which includes an address family (which is AF_NET), a port, and a 32-bit (4-byte) IP address.

The class you're more likely to use is *TINetSocketAddress*. You create the address by specifying the port and an optional address on the constructor:

```
TINetSocketAddress address(80);
```

TSocketError

The *TSocketError* class stores an error numerical value and a string describing the error. It automatically fills in the string part of the error if you give it the numerical error value. This class can be used to help make error strings to report to the user, and to store errors for later use. Every error index defined in WinSock can be reported here.

With the *TSocketError* class you can use strings from the string table resource, or you can use static strings that are already stored directly in the source code for the class. The choice between the two is made with a compilation switch:

```
define B_USING_STRING_RESOURCES //Use the application's string
                                //table instead of static strings.
```

The advantage of static strings in the source code is that they are already done and you don't have to deal with the string table resource. The disadvantage is that static strings are harder to maintain and take up space in your program's data segment. It may be best to use static strings for pre-release work prototyping, and use string tables for the final product.

This class does not have a function here to actually print the string to the screen in, say, a *MessageBox()*. This was done to make the *TSocketError* base class more portable. You can subclass the *TSocketError* class with, for example, *WinSocketError : public TSocketError* and add one function: *ReportError()*.

Using TSocketError

TSocketError is a class provided for your convenience. It converts a WinSock error code into a string. These strings are stored in a string table resource, so you must add

```
include <owl/winsock.rc>
```

near the top of your .RC file before you can use *TSocketError*. Otherwise, the error code will convert to an empty string.

You convert an error code into a string by creating an instance of *TSocketError*:

```
THostInfoManager myHostInfoManager;
THostEntry*      tempHostEntry;
int              nError;

nError = myHostInfoManager.GetHostInfo(tempHostEntry, "j_shmoe@anywhere.com");
if (nError == SOCKET_ERROR) {
  MessageBox(TSocketError(nError).GetReasonString(), "Sockets Error");
}
```

Note that the default size of the strings cannot be greater than 128. You can increase this value by specifying the new size as an argument to the constructor.

TSocketManager

The *TSocketManager* class is a small class that can be used to do two things:

- Start up and shut down the WinSock session
- Store arrays of Sockets

You don't absolutely need the *TSocketManager* to do either of the above things, and you may never even be interested in having any class store an array of *TSockets*, but the *TSocketManager* is there to do either if you wish.

The WinSock startup function, *WSAStartup()*, returns a *WSAData* structure. *TSocketManager* uses a subclass of the *WSAData* class called the *TSocketInfo* class. Since *TSocketInfo* is a subclass of *WSAData*, it can be used anywhere that WinSock or Windows Socket Class requires a *WSAData*.

TSocketManager calls *WSAStartup()* in its constructor, and saves the result for later use. For WinSock version information, call the *TSocketManager* function *Information()*. *TSocketManager* automatically calls *WSACleanup* in its destructor.

Using TSocketManager

TSocketManager is the core of OWL's WinSock encapsulation. It initializes and deinitializes the WinSock DLL. You must create an instance of this class to work with WinSock. The lifetime of this object determines when you can communicate with WinSock.

You create an instance of *TSocketManager* by:

```
TSocketManager* manager = new TSocketManager;
```

When you're done, use:

```
delete manager;
```

Index

Symbols

MoveTo member function, TDC
396, 398
multimedia files 307
multiple printers 382

N

Name (read-only property), OLE
automation servers 158
naming
applications 194, 196
view classes 88
Windows functions, returning
11
nCmdShow data member,
TApplication 202
nCmdShow parameter 193, 202
nested classes 283
New Document (method), OLE
automation servers 158
NextGadget member function,
TGadgetWindow 373
NextProperty property 316
NO_CPP_EXCEPTIONS macro
242
NoHints enum 372
non-blocking modes, blocking,
sockets 501
nonvirtual functions 186
notification messages, views 89,
93-96
NOTIFY_SIG macro 101,
314-315
notifying gadgets window
when gadgets change size 371
NotifyViews member function,
TDocument 85, 102, 106, 113,
308-309
NumColors member function,
TDib 421
NumLock enum 377
NumScans member function,
TDib 421

O

object data members and
functions 399
object handle 390
ObjectComponents view,
creating 464
ObjectGroup enum 269
objects 48, 184
changes, client communication
482
command-enabling 229–233

exception 238–239
exceptions 240
resources and 78
retrieving 48
saving 48
view 295–296
ObjectWindows 431
DLL servers, creating 490
OLE containers, creating 458,
471
OLE servers, creating 483
ObjectWindows Help
(OWL.HLP) 477
OffsetClipRgn member
function, TDC 396
OffsetViewportOrg member
function, TDC 396
OffsetWindowOrg member
function, TDC 396
ofstream class 44
ofTransacted flags 131
OK buttons, processing 278
OLE applications 117
adding tool bars 125, 150, 152
associating objects and
processes 123
building 118, 141
changing document
registration 126
Clipboard formats 127, 148, 150
command-line options 145
connector objects 120
containers 117
converting ObjectWindows
applications 118
copying data 150
creating new views 143
current module 142
cutting data 150
dictionaries 123
document manager 302
event handling 136
frame windows 119, 124
header files 119, 140
identifiers 120
invalidating remote views 149
notifying views 149
registering 120, 122
registrar objects 121
registration tables 120, 140
remote view bucket 144
setting application connectors
125

OLE automation controllers 157
OLE automation servers
application classes, changing
157
building 157
document class 160-162
member functions,
implementing 158
methods 158
declaring 160
defining 160
exposing 163
properties 158
declaring 160
defining 160
exposing 163
OLE class factories 121
OLE classes 119, 129
deriving 123, 128, 134
inheritance 451, 463, 475
OLE container/server 165
Clipboard format, naming 170
commands, adding 171
document class,
CommitSelection function 167
document servers, changing 167
line class, 165-166
OLE message handlers 173
OpenSelection function 168
PaintLink function,
implementing 172
Select function, implementing
171
TOleLinkView class, adding
175
OLE containers
application dictionaries,
creating 459
client window, setting up 463
compiling 457, 471
creating 449
Doc/View 449, 458
ObjectWindows 458, 471
linking 457, 471
OWL header files, including 459
registrar objects, creating 461
registration tables, creating 460
user interfaces, programming
465
OLE message handlers,
enhancing 173
OLE objects
constructing 134
handling embedded 128, 132
opening 131
painting 134
reading 130
saving 131